Why AI Sounds Confident When It Is Wrong

Sandeep Chavan

Published by Gyrus Vision, 2026.

WHY AI SOUNDS CONFIDENT WHEN IT IS WRONG

First edition. July 18, 2026.

ISBN: 978-8168977600

Written by Sandeep Chavan.

Table of Contents

To those who remain willing to reopen a finished answer—

especially when fluency has made further questioning feel unnecessary.

Confidence is compression. Truth requires connection.

—Sandeep Chavan

Opening Note
The Answer Does Not Tremble

You ask a question. The machine answers immediately.

There is no visible search for position. No pause in which several possibilities seem to compete. No expression suggesting that the question may be larger than the available information. The response begins as though the correct point of entry has already been found.

The first paragraph establishes context. The second explains the mechanism. The third resolves the difficulty.

By the end, the scattered parts of the question have been gathered into one coherent structure. Nothing appears unfinished.

You read the answer, and something subtle happens before you have verified any of it. You relax. The question no longer feels open. The burden of organizing the problem has been removed. The language is clear enough to follow, specific enough to appear informed, and complete enough to be used.

The system may be correct. It may have reproduced a stable fact, explained a well-established principle, summarized a supplied document faithfully, or connected several ideas with genuine insight. Its fluency may be carrying reliable knowledge.

But it may also be partially correct. It may have selected one interpretation from several. It may have silently assumed a context you never supplied. It may have extended a valid principle beyond the conditions under which it applies.

Or it may be wrong. The date may be invented. The quotation may not exist. The scientific explanation may contain a subtle distortion. The legal interpretation may belong to another jurisdiction. The source may be real while failing to support the conclusion attached to it.

Yet the surface may remain almost unchanged.

The correct answer and the incorrect answer can arrive with the same grammar. Both may contain headings, examples, qualifications, and practical conclusions. Both may sound patient, balanced, and professionally composed. Neither must visibly tremble.

This is what makes the interaction strange.

Human beings have always encountered confidence through signs. We notice hesitation. We hear uncertainty in a voice. We recognize when a person is recalling something imperfectly, choosing words carefully, or protecting a claim they are not prepared to abandon. Speech carries traces of the speaker's relationship with what is being said.

A person who is unsure may pause. A person who is guessing may qualify. A person who realizes that the evidence is incomplete may stop.

These signals are imperfect. Human beings can speak confidently when wrong, and hesitate when right. But the visible relationship between certainty and expression has shaped human trust for generations.

Then a new kind of speaker appeared.

It produces language without needing to occupy the kind of inward position from which human speech historically emerged. It can generate the form of explanation without necessarily possessing the reflective conviction we normally imagine behind an explanation.

The sentence sounds certain. That does not mean certainty exists inside the machine in the human sense.

The system does not need pride to defend a false premise. It does not need fear to avoid saying that it does not know. It does not need intention to mislead. It does not need belief to produce the language of belief.

It needs only to continue.

A prompt enters. A response becomes necessary. The system converts the active context into a sequence that satisfies the demands operating upon it.

The sequence may contain caution. It may ask for clarification. It may refuse. It may identify several possibilities.

But often, it answers.

One path becomes language. The user sees that path after the alternatives have disappeared from view. The answer appears singular because only one sequence occupies the screen. It appears stable because every sentence becomes the context for the sentence that follows. It appears complete because language must eventually stop.

The user experiences the finished form. The unfinished field remains hidden.

This book begins inside that difference.

It does not begin by accusing the machine of arrogance. It does not assume that artificial intelligence secretly believes its own conclusions. Nor does it claim that every confident answer is unreliable.

Many AI-generated answers are useful, accurate, and remarkably well organized. The technology can explain, translate, calculate, compare, summarize, and assist at a scale that would have been difficult to imagine only a short time ago.

Its power is real.

The problem is that power and authority can be confused.

An answer may deserve use without deserving trust in every part. A model may assist judgment without being able to own the consequence of judgment. A source may strengthen an answer without validating every inference built around it. A score may look precise while depending on a threshold, dataset, or environment invisible to the person affected by it.

The question is therefore not whether AI should be trusted or distrusted in general. The question is how trust forms before reliability has been established.

Why does organized language feel like knowledge? Why does a resolved answer appear to have resolved the world? Why does the absence of visible hesitation feel like the absence of meaningful uncertainty? And what happens when that appearance enters institutions?

A fluent paragraph can become a report. A report can shape a meeting. A recommendation can become a default. A score can become a label. A label can determine who receives attention, opportunity, scrutiny, treatment, or access.

The system may begin as an assistant. Its output can end as authority.

No declaration of certainty is required. The surrounding field completes the transformation.

The user trusts because the answer is smooth. The institution trusts because the system is advanced. The reviewer trusts because a source is attached. The organization trusts because a human remains formally in the loop.

Each layer receives a resolved surface and assumes that someone or something before it has already dealt with the uncertainty.

Responsibility moves backward through the pipeline. Authority moves forward. Between them, the answer becomes difficult to challenge.

This is why artificial confidence cannot be solved by adding one disclaimer.

"AI can make mistakes" is true, but too general. It does not reveal which part of this answer is unstable, what assumption entered silently, whether the source applies, or what must be verified before action.

A machine can say, "I may be wrong," and remain wrong for reasons it has not identified. It can generate humility as easily as certainty.

The words alone do not complete the epistemic circuit.

Something outside the answer must remain capable of comparison, verification, interruption, and revision.

A source must constrain the claim. A calculation must correspond to the right problem. A human must possess enough independence to disagree. An institution must remain capable of stopping the system it has learned to depend upon.

Truth requires a connection that the answer cannot manufacture merely by becoming more coherent.

This is not a reason to retreat from artificial intelligence. It is a reason to understand it accurately.

AI systems are powerful resolution engines. They transform open questions into usable forms. They compress complexity, organize possibility, and reduce the friction through which human beings ordinarily move toward an answer.

That capacity can expand knowledge. It can also create the appearance that knowledge has arrived before the necessary connections have been made.

The danger is not that the machine always lies. The danger is that it can complete. The danger is that completion feels like certainty. The danger is that certainty, once perceived, can travel farther than the evidence beneath it.

This book follows that movement.

It begins with the prompt, where difference first enters. It moves through resolution, geometry, collapse, residue, and the irreversible life of output. It follows confidence as scale sharpens fluency, reward shaping encourages answer-like closure, retrieval lends borrowed authority, and automation converts probability into consequence.

It then turns toward what must remain outside the machine: the epistemic circuit through which answers are compared with reality, tested against consequence, and reopened when they no longer fit the field.

The purpose is not to make the machine less capable. It is to prevent capability from becoming self-validating authority.

The purpose is not to make every answer hesitant. It is to preserve the difference between what is strongly established and what has merely been smoothly resolved.

The purpose is not to place all responsibility on the user. It is to show that responsibility is distributed across design, deployment, interface, institution, review, and action—and that it cannot be transferred into a machine simply because the machine produced the words.

The answer does not tremble. The field beneath it may still be open.

Let us begin where certainty first appears: not inside the machine, but on the surface of the answer.

Preface
When Answers Become Infrastructure

Artificial intelligence did not enter society first as authority. It entered as assistance.

It helped complete sentences, translate passages, summarize documents, generate images, write code, organize information, and answer questions. The earliest public encounters often felt experimental. Users tested the system, noticed its errors, laughed at its inventions, and treated its responses as impressive demonstrations rather than final judgments.

The machine was clearly a machine. Its answers were useful, but provisional. They belonged to the space of curiosity.

That phase did not last.

The systems became more fluent. They followed instructions more reliably. They preserved longer conversations, adapted to individual users, searched external sources, processed private documents, executed calculations, and entered professional workflows.

The chatbot became an assistant. The assistant became a colleague. The colleague began becoming infrastructure.

A student now encounters generated explanations before opening a textbook. An employee asks an artificial system to interpret a policy before contacting the relevant department. A manager uses generated analysis to prepare a decision. A programmer accepts code suggested inside the development environment. A researcher begins with an AI-generated synthesis. A customer receives an automated resolution. A patient may encounter an AI-shaped summary before speaking with a clinician.

The answer no longer remains separate from ordinary life. It becomes part of how ordinary life is organized.

This shift changes the nature of the problem.

An occasional false answer inside an experimental conversation is one kind of failure. The same false answer embedded in a report, workflow, recommendation system, or institutional record is another.

The first may confuse one user. The second may reorganize consequence.

The central concern of this book emerges from that transition.

Artificial intelligence is becoming capable of producing language with the surface stability historically associated with knowledge, judgment, and professional confidence. Its answers often arrive in the same form whether the underlying field is firmly grounded, partially supported, ambiguously interpreted, or almost entirely reconstructed.

The system may be right. It may be approximately right. It may be wrong in one important detail. It may be wrong at the foundation.

Yet the difference may not appear in the tone.

This does not mean that every artificial intelligence system always sounds absolutely certain. Modern systems can express uncertainty, request clarification, cite limitations, refuse unsupported tasks, and acknowledge incomplete information.

The deeper issue remains.

Even caution is generated as a resolved form. A statement such as *"the evidence is uncertain"* arrives with the same linguistic completion as a confident claim. The user must still determine whether the uncertainty has been identified accurately, whether an important unknown remains invisible, and whether the response deserves the authority its form invites.

The problem is therefore not simply excessive confidence. It is the relationship between computational resolution and human interpretation.

The system generates one answer. The user encounters a speaker. The system produces structure. The user perceives understanding. The system completes a sequence. The institution may treat the result as settled.

Between these movements, an output acquires more meaning than the generation process alone contains.

This book examines that acquisition.

Beyond Hallucination

Artificial intelligence is often criticized for hallucination. The term generally refers to generated content that appears plausible but is unsupported, inaccurate, fabricated, or disconnected from reliable evidence. A system may invent a quotation, article, court case, historical detail, scientific claim, or source.

Hallucination is a serious problem. But hallucination and confidence are not identical.

Hallucination concerns the content that has been generated. Confidence concerns the form in which the content arrives, the way it is interpreted, and the authority it acquires.

A hallucinated answer may be cautious. A correct answer may be overstated. A response may contain no invented fact and still conceal uncertainty by presenting one disputed interpretation as though no credible alternative exists.

A model may quote a real source and use it incorrectly. A classifier may process genuine data and apply the wrong category. A calculator may return the correct result for the wrong formulation. A recommendation may be factually informed but unsuitable for the specific person or institution receiving it.

The confidence problem is therefore broader than fabrication. It includes every situation in which visible completion exceeds justified closure.

My earlier work, *Why Do AI Systems Hallucinate?*, examined how unsupported content can emerge when generative systems must resolve incomplete, conflicting, or weakly grounded fields.

The present book begins where that analysis leaves off.

It asks why the generated result can appear settled even when the conditions beneath it are not.

Why does one realized sequence feel like the conclusion? Why does coherent structure carry the appearance of understanding? Why does fluent explanation reduce human doubt? Why do citations, calculations, confidence scores, and institutional interfaces amplify that effect? Why does correction become harder after the first answer has entered the field?

These questions cannot be answered by studying false content alone. They require an examination of resolution itself.

The Historical Weight of Fluent Language

For most of human history, coherent language came from human beings. Speech and writing were connected, however imperfectly, to a person who could be questioned, challenged, embarrassed, corrected, praised, blamed, or held responsible.

A written statement carried traces of human authorship. Someone selected the words. Someone stood behind the claim. Someone could be asked what they meant.

This relationship was never reliable in an absolute sense. Human beings exaggerate, manipulate, misremember, imitate, and lie. Institutions have always used polished language to conceal uncertainty or protect authority.

But language still carried an assumed relationship to a speaker.

Artificial intelligence disrupts that assumption.

A generated sentence can reproduce the social signals of thoughtful authorship without requiring the same inward or accountable structure behind it.

The system can say: "I believe..." "I am confident..." "The evidence clearly shows..." "After considering the alternatives..."

These expressions are functional patterns within language. They do not prove that the machine possesses belief, confidence, consideration, or reflective awareness in the human sense.

Yet the reader does not encounter them as abstract probability distributions. The reader encounters language. Human cognition supplies the speaker.

This inherited interpretive habit is powerful.

We associate organized explanation with organized understanding. We associate specific detail with access to information. We associate balanced qualification with mature judgment. We associate confidence with a person who has examined the issue and decided where they stand.

Generative systems can reproduce all these forms. The historical signal remains. The historical speaker may not.

This creates a new kind of epistemic environment.

The user is not merely reading information. The user is interacting with a structure that continuously produces the form of responsive understanding.

It remembers context. It adapts. It answers follow-up questions. It explains its own reasoning. It apologizes. It revises. It mirrors tone. It appears to participate.

The interaction becomes relational. Trust begins forming not only around individual claims but around the continuity of the artificial presence.

The system may be treated as a stable intellectual partner even though its reliability changes across topics, sources, tools, dates, and tasks.

This is one reason the confidence problem cannot be reduced to a technical score. Confidence is produced between system and user. It is relational before it becomes institutional.

The Era of Answer Abundance

Human societies once suffered primarily from limited access to information. Knowledge was concentrated in books, institutions, professions, libraries, and specialists. Obtaining an answer required time, literacy, location, money, authority, or access to someone who possessed the relevant expertise.

Digital technology reduced many of these barriers. Search engines made information abundant. Generative systems have introduced another transformation.

They make resolved expression abundant.

Information no longer needs to be found, read, compared, interpreted, and rewritten by the user before it becomes usable. The system performs much of that compression instantly.

A scattered field becomes a summary. Several documents become one synthesis. A complicated issue becomes a structured explanation. An unfinished thought becomes polished language.

This is an extraordinary increase in human capability. It is also an extraordinary increase in the production of conclusions.

The scarcity is no longer always the answer. The scarcity is the capacity to determine what kind of answer has been produced.

Is it a faithful summary? A probable reconstruction? A general explanation? A current fact? A plausible scenario? A recommendation based on unstated values? A synthesis extending beyond the evidence?

The surface may not reveal the difference.

In the age of information scarcity, authority often belonged to those who controlled access. In the age of answer abundance, authority may belong to whichever resolution appears first, clearest, and easiest to use.

The first answer frames the problem. The smoothest answer reduces friction. The most organized answer becomes memorable. The most actionable answer enters practice.

Truth must now compete not only with falsehood, but with effortless coherence.

This is a new epistemic pressure. A person may accept an answer not because they have examined the evidence, but because the system has already removed the discomfort of uncertainty.

The answer gives the question a shape. Once the shape exists, reopening it requires additional work.

The machine generates in seconds. Verification may require hours. Correction may require institutional effort.

The asymmetry favors premature closure.

Capability and Authority Are Different Questions

Public debates about artificial intelligence frequently revolve around capability.

Can the system reason? Can it code? Can it pass an examination? Can it diagnose? Can it conduct research? Can it outperform professionals?

These are important questions. But capability does not settle authority.

A system may perform a task impressively without possessing the right to determine its consequence.

It may detect a medical pattern without being authorized to diagnose a patient. It may summarize law without being entitled to decide a dispute. It may predict employee performance without being justified in controlling access to employment. It may rank risk without determining which burden should be imposed upon the person classified.

Authority is not produced by capability alone. Authority depends upon purpose, validation, accountability, contestability, consequence, and social permission.

This distinction is easy to lose because artificial systems often enter institutions through the language of assistance.

The system is introduced as a support tool. It saves time. It organizes cases. It provides recommendations. Human beings remain formally responsible.

Then the workflow adapts. The recommendation becomes the default. The human reviewer sees too many cases. Independent examination declines. The system becomes trusted because it is usually useful.

Eventually, rejecting its output requires more effort than accepting it.

Authority has shifted without an explicit declaration.

The system has not demanded power. The institution has organized itself around the convenience of resolution.

This is one of the most important movements examined in this book.

Artificial certainty does not always arrive through a machine claiming to know. It may arrive through people no longer knowing how, when, or whether to disagree.

Why the Chavanian Axioms Matter Here

The framework developed in this book draws upon the Chavanian Axioms as a diagnostic lens.

The axioms are not offered here as a replacement for computer science, probability theory, machine learning research, cognitive science, philosophy of mind, or institutional governance. They operate at a different level.

They identify a recurrent structural movement:

- difference appears;
- resolution becomes necessary;
- geometry constrains available pathways;
- one consequence becomes actual;
- the field is rewritten;
- residue remains;

- continuity develops from what has not been fully dissipated.

In artificial intelligence, this movement can be observed without treating the axioms as literal physical descriptions of computation.

A prompt introduces delta. The system must produce a permitted consequence. Architecture, training, context, instructions, retrieval, tools, and decoding constrain what can emerge. One answer becomes visible. Other possibilities remain unrealized or unexpressed. The output becomes new context. The user and institution reorganize around what has appeared.

The same structure occurs in classification, ranking, recommendation, and automated action.

A score crosses a threshold. A continuous field becomes a discrete consequence.

The value of the axiomatic lens lies in its ability to connect technical, psychological, and institutional layers without collapsing them into one explanation.

The model's internal computation is not the same as human perception. Human trust is not the same as institutional governance. Yet each participates in the movement through which uncertainty becomes authority.

The framework allows us to ask not merely whether an output is correct, but:

- What difference initiated the process?
- What resolution was demanded?
- What geometry constrained it?
- What disappeared when one output became visible?
- What residue remained?
- How did the output rewrite the next field?
- Who absorbed the consequences?

These questions reveal structures that ordinary discussions of accuracy and error can overlook.

Accuracy remains essential. But an accurate answer can still be over-authorized. An inaccurate answer can still be presented cautiously. A system can improve in average performance while its remaining failures become more persuasive.

The Chavanian analysis therefore focuses on the movement from plurality to consequence. Confidence is one visible effect of that movement.

What This Book Does Not Claim

This book does not claim that current AI systems possess no meaningful internal complexity. They clearly do. Modern generative models contain vast learned structures and perform operations that cannot be understood adequately through simplistic descriptions such as *"autocomplete."*

The analysis also does not claim that every model response is produced through the same mechanism or that all AI systems should be treated as identical. Architectures, training methods, tools, interfaces, objectives, and deployment conditions differ.

The book does not claim that artificial systems can never become conscious, self-aware, or capable of forms of epistemic ownership in the future. That remains an open philosophical and scientific question. The present argument does not require its resolution. Current confidence effects can be explained structurally without assuming reflective machine belief.

The book does not claim that humans are naturally better calibrated. Human beings are often confidently wrong. We protect identity, reward certainty, follow authority, preserve narratives, and resist correction. Indeed, artificial systems inherit many of their linguistic and social patterns from human production.

The difference is not that humans always possess awareness and machines never do. The difference is that human beings can occupy positions of responsibility, encounter consequences, and potentially reopen their own conclusions through reflective awareness.

That potential is imperfect. It must be supported.

The book does not argue that AI should be slowed, restricted, or rejected everywhere. Many uses involve low consequence and high benefit. Artificial systems can widen access to explanation, accelerate research, support creativity, reduce repetitive work, and help people think through difficult problems.

The concern is proportionality. The stronger the authority assigned to an output, the stronger the epistemic circuit required around it.

Finally, this book does not promise a complete technical solution. No single confidence score, disclaimer, alignment method, or governance rule can eliminate the distance between generated coherence and reality.

The aim is diagnostic clarity. Before systems can be designed, governed, and used responsibly, the confidence problem must be located correctly.

The Missing Circuit

Artificial systems can generate answers. They can compare alternatives. They can retrieve sources. They can calculate. They can classify. They can critique and revise their own outputs.

These capabilities may create the appearance of a complete epistemic process. But an epistemic circuit requires more than internal operations. It requires connection to something that can constrain the system from outside the resolution it has already produced.

A source must actually support the claim. A measurement must correspond to the hypothesis. A professional must understand the case. An institution must assess consequence. An affected person must be able to challenge an error. A correction must change future structure.

This circuit does not belong to one human or one machine. It is distributed.

The machine contributes speed, pattern detection, synthesis, consistency, and scale. Humans contribute context, responsibility, value judgment, lived consequence, and the capacity to interrupt. Tools contribute formal operations. Sources contribute evidence. Institutions contribute authority and accountability. Affected people contribute information the system may never have contained.

The problem begins when one part of this circuit is allowed to impersonate the whole.

A generated explanation appears to contain verification. A citation appears to contain interpretation. A confidence score appears to contain policy. A reviewer's presence appears to contain awareness. An institutional interface appears to contain legitimacy.

The circuit closes in appearance before it closes in reality.

This book is an attempt to reopen it.

The Responsibility of the Reader

The reader of this book may be a user, developer, researcher, educator, manager, policymaker, professional, or simply someone trying to understand the systems entering daily life. Each position carries a different responsibility.

The ordinary user cannot be expected to audit model architecture or verify every output independently. The burden of safety cannot be transferred entirely to the person asking the question.

Developers cannot control every downstream use, but they can shape the pathways through which uncertainty appears, tools are used, claims are sourced, and outputs are constrained.

Institutions cannot demand perfect systems, but they can define what authority the system is permitted to hold, where review is required, and who remains accountable after harm.

Professionals cannot ignore tools that may improve their work, but they should not allow convenience to erase their role as awareness anchors.

The purpose of this book is not to assign blame in advance. It is to prevent responsibility from disappearing after the output is produced.

A machine-generated answer may pass through many hands before becoming consequence. At each stage, someone assumes that the previous stage has already dealt with the uncertainty.

The developer assumes the deployer will impose appropriate limits. The deployer assumes the provider has validated the model. The operator assumes the system's score is meaningful. The user assumes the attached source proves the claim. The affected person is told that the outcome emerged from the system.

Artificial certainty thrives in these gaps.

Responsibility must be distributed. It must not be diluted.

Why This Book Is Necessary Now

The urgency of this subject does not arise because artificial intelligence has suddenly become completely autonomous. It arises because society is integrating systems whose outputs already appear more stable than the institutions surrounding them are prepared to evaluate.

The technology is advancing quickly. The habits of verification, governance, and public understanding are advancing unevenly.

Users are learning to prompt before they are learning to calibrate trust. Organizations are learning to deploy before they are learning to preserve human independence. Interfaces are becoming seamless before uncertainty has become legible. Systems are becoming integrated before correction pathways have been designed.

This imbalance matters.

The most dangerous AI system may not be the one that fails obviously. It may be the one that performs extremely well until it enters a condition where its reliability changes but its surface does not.

The model continues speaking. The score continues appearing. The workflow continues operating. The institution continues trusting.

No dramatic breakdown announces that the epistemic field has shifted. The system sounds as it sounded yesterday. The world is no longer the same.

This is why confidence deserves separate analysis.

The issue is not merely whether the machine is right. It is whether the surrounding field can detect when rightness has become uncertain while fluency remains stable.

How to Read This Book

The book moves through five stages.

The first examines the confidence paradox as it appears to the human user. It distinguishes artificial confidence from arrogance, intention, and human conviction while acknowledging why the surface resemblance remains powerful.

The second enters the structural mechanism. It follows the movement from prompt-induced delta through resolution, geometry, collapse, residue, and irreversibility.

The third examines amplification. It shows how scale, reward shaping, retrieval, tools, and automated systems make confidence more persuasive, more externally anchored, and more consequential.

The fourth turns toward the awareness anchor. It reconstructs the epistemic circuit required around resolution and examines prompting as one form of user-side discipline.

The fifth addresses structural damping. It explores how systems can expose uncertainty, preserve plurality, introduce friction, abstain, escalate, and remain governed without pretending that engineered caution has become conscious humility.

The book ends where it began: at the surface of the answer.

But the surface will no longer appear simple. Behind it will stand a field of possible continuations, constraints, assumptions, sources, exclusions, thresholds, institutional decisions, and human interpretations.

The aim is not to make every interaction burdensome. It is to help the reader recognize where smoothness should no longer be mistaken for completion.

Before the First Answer

Artificial intelligence has already changed what it means to ask a question.

The user no longer needs to know where the answer might be found. They do not always need to identify the relevant book, source, expert, formula, or institution. They can begin with uncertainty itself.

The system will give it form.

This is a profound expansion of access. It may become one of the most important intellectual technologies in human history.

But every technology of resolution changes the relationship between people and unanswered questions.

The easier answers become, the easier it becomes to forget what an answer must still be connected to.

Evidence. Scope. Context. Consequence. Correction. Responsibility.

The machine can reduce the distance between question and response. It cannot eliminate the distance between response and truth.

That distance is where epistemic discipline must live.

This book enters that distance. Not to weaken artificial intelligence. Not to romanticize uncertainty. Not to preserve human authority merely because it is human.

It enters because powerful resolution requires equally powerful awareness.

The future will not be shaped only by what AI systems can answer. It will be shaped by what human beings and institutions allow those answers to become.

Before the first chapter begins, one distinction must therefore remain clear:

An answer is a consequence of resolution. Knowledge is a consequence of connection.

Part I
The Problem As It Appears

The answer looks certain because the uncertainty that produced it is no longer visible.

Chapter 1
The Confidence Paradox

When a Resolved Answer Looks Like Knowledge

You ask a question. It may concern history, medicine, science, law, business, technology, or something entirely ordinary. Within seconds, the system responds. The answer begins in the right place. It explains the necessary background, defines the relevant terms, develops a line of reasoning, and arrives at a clear conclusion. The paragraphs are balanced. The transitions are smooth. Nothing appears unfinished.

You read the answer, and before you have evaluated every claim, something inside the interaction has already changed. You relax. The answer appears to have settled the question. It does not look as though it is searching for its position. It does not expose competing possibilities, unresolved assumptions, or missing evidence unless the system has been specifically instructed to do so. It arrives as organized language, already shaped into the form of understanding.

Later, the answer may prove correct. It may prove partially correct. It may contain a subtle exaggeration, an outdated claim, an invented source, an unsupported causal link, or an interpretation presented as fact. Yet the visible difference between these conditions may be surprisingly small. Accurate information and fabricated information can arrive in the same grammatical form, with the same composure, the same specificity, and the same sense of completion.

This is the beginning of the confidence paradox.

The paradox is not simply that artificial intelligence can be wrong. Every information system can be wrong. Humans misremember. Databases contain errors. Measurements fail. Experts disagree. The more specific problem is that an AI system can be wrong without becoming visibly less composed. Its linguistic surface may remain stable even when its factual grounding weakens.

That stability is interpreted as confidence. But the interpretation requires care. The system does not need to possess confidence in the reflective human sense. It does not need to experience certainty, defend a belief, or recognize the answer as its own. It produces a resolved output. The human reader encounters that resolution and assigns epistemic meaning to it.

The system supplies completion. The interface supplies a singular answer. The human supplies the inference that uncertainty has already been overcome.

This book begins inside that interval.

It is related to the problem of hallucination, but it is not the same problem. Hallucination concerns the generation of unsupported, fabricated, or incorrectly grounded content. Artificial confidence concerns how generated content—accurate or inaccurate—is presented, perceived, trusted, and sometimes converted into authority.

A hallucinated answer may be expressed cautiously. A factually correct answer may still be expressed with more certainty than the evidence permits. A system may provide a useful generalization while concealing important exceptions. It may state a contested interpretation as settled. It may reproduce a valid source while extending its conclusion beyond what the source supports.

Wrongness and confidence can overlap, but they are not identical.

To understand why AI sounds confident when it is wrong, we must therefore examine more than error. We must examine the relationship among computational resolution, linguistic form, interface design, human interpretation, and institutional use. Confidence does not emerge at one location. It forms through a circuit.

1.1 — The Problem Is Not Wrongness Alone

Suppose an AI system is asked a factual question and provides an incorrect date. The error can be checked against a reliable record. The system was wrong. If it also expresses the date without qualification, the answer may appear confident. In this case, factual error and apparent certainty occur together.

Now consider a different case. The system is asked why a historical empire declined. It provides several widely recognized factors but presents one causal interpretation as though historians have fully settled the matter. Much of the content may be accurate. The confidence problem remains because the form of the answer exceeds the stability of the underlying evidence.

In another case, the system may give an incorrect answer while using cautious language: "One possible explanation is..." or "The available information may suggest..." Here, wrongness exists without strong surface certainty. The answer remains unreliable, but it does not project the same degree of authority.

These cases reveal that factual validity and expressed certainty belong to different dimensions. An answer may be factually strong and appropriately qualified. It may be factually strong but overstated. It may be factually weak and cautious. Or it may be factually weak and presented as settled knowledge. The final condition is the most visibly dangerous, but it is not the only condition this book must explain.

The confidence paradox arises because users often cannot distinguish these states from the linguistic surface alone. Generative systems can maintain grammatical stability across all four. The same capacity that allows them to explain verified science can also allow them to construct an elegant account around an incorrect premise. The same rhetorical structure that communicates genuine expertise can organize speculation. The same formal tone that summarizes a real legal judgment can be used to describe one that does not exist.

The sentence does not automatically weaken when its connection with reality weakens.

This separation is central. Language generation and factual verification are not the same operation. A system can be highly capable at producing coherent discourse while remaining dependent on training data, supplied context, retrieval tools, current sources, calculations, or external human judgment for reliable correspondence with reality.

When those supports are strong, linguistic coherence and factual validity may align. When those supports are incomplete, coherence can continue without equivalent grounding. The user, however, does not directly observe these supports. The user sees the answer.

This is why an apparently confident answer cannot be understood only by asking whether it is true or false. We must also ask how the answer represented the limits of what could responsibly be concluded. Did it distinguish established fact from inference? Did it disclose uncertainty created by missing context? Did it identify temporal limits? Did it separate what a source stated from what the system inferred? Did it preserve legitimate alternatives?

These questions concern epistemic form, not merely content.

A system may provide every sentence in a calm and orderly tone because calm and order are properties of the generated sequence. They do not guarantee that the evidence beneath every claim possesses the same stability.

This does not make fluency inherently deceptive. Fluency is one of the principal reasons generative systems are useful. They can transform scattered material into readable explanation, adapt technical language to different audiences, clarify structure, and reduce unnecessary cognitive burden. The problem begins only when the ease of expression is treated as evidence that external verification has already occurred.

The mistake is understandable because, in ordinary human life, confident expression often carries information about the speaker's relationship with the claim. A person may hesitate because memory is weak. They may pause because alternatives remain open. They may qualify a statement because the evidence is incomplete. Human speech often leaks signs of internal uncertainty.

Generative output need not leak uncertainty in the same way. The system can produce the form of a completed answer regardless of whether the question activated a highly stable fact, a contested interpretation, an ambiguous request, or a plausible construction around a false premise. Unless uncertainty is procedurally detected and deliberately exported into the response, the visible form may remain almost unchanged.

Wrongness alone therefore does not define the confidence problem. The deeper issue is the independence of surface stability from epistemic stability.

1.2 — Fluency as an Inherited Signal

Human beings did not evolve in a world where coherent language could be generated without a speaker. For most of human history, structured speech came from embodied individuals who carried memory, experience, intention, social position, and consequence. Language was not merely information. It was evidence of a person organizing thought in real time.

We learned to infer the speaker through the speech. A hesitant voice could suggest uncertainty. A sudden correction could reveal reconsideration. A precise explanation might indicate long familiarity with a subject. A confident conclusion could suggest that competing possibilities had already been examined and rejected. These cues were never perfect, but they were useful enough to become deeply embedded in human judgment.

Fluency therefore acquired social meaning. A teacher who explains a difficult idea clearly appears knowledgeable. A physician who communicates calmly inspires confidence. A lawyer who organizes evidence persuasively appears prepared. A leader who speaks decisively appears capable of acting. Across institutions, professions, and everyday relationships, articulate expression functions as a practical signal of competence.

Humans rely on such signals because complete verification is impossible. No individual can independently confirm every historical claim, medical explanation, technical specification, legal interpretation, economic forecast, or scientific conclusion encountered during ordinary life. We use shortcuts. We evaluate credentials, reputation, tone, structure, specificity, internal consistency, and the response of others. These heuristics allow knowledge to travel through society without requiring every listener to reconstruct it from first principles.

Generative AI enters directly into this inherited interpretive system. It produces many of the same surface cues that humans associate with understanding. It responds immediately. It remembers the local conversation. It adapts its vocabulary to the apparent audience. It organizes complex information into sections. It supplies examples, distinctions, definitions, and conclusions. It can reproduce the tone of a tutor, analyst, researcher, consultant, or technical specialist.

The human perceptual system recognizes the form before it verifies the foundation. This is not because users are foolish. It is because the form has carried epistemic value throughout nearly all previous human experience. When language is clear, processing becomes easier. When an explanation follows a familiar structure, the reader can integrate it with less effort. When each sentence prepares the next, the mind experiences reduced friction.

Reduced friction often feels like increased truth. The easier a claim is to process, the less resistance it encounters. A smooth explanation allows attention to move through the answer without repeatedly stopping to reconstruct meaning. This ease is beneficial when the answer is reliable. It becomes risky when ease itself is mistaken for validation.

Generative systems are exceptionally good at producing this ease. They do not need to reproduce every internal uncertainty in order to generate a readable answer. In fact, an answer that exposed every competing token, interpretation, source conflict, and conditional pathway would be unusable. Generation must compress. It must select, arrange, and omit. The result is a manageable linguistic surface.

Compression is not the problem by itself. Every explanation compresses. A textbook compresses decades of research. A physician compresses clinical reasoning into advice. A map compresses terrain. A scientific model compresses selected relationships into a usable representation.

The confidence problem concerns what the compression hides and how the resulting smoothness is interpreted. A human expert usually exists within a wider accountability field. Their statement can be linked to training, evidence, professional standards, reputation, memory, and consequence. The expert may still be wrong, but the speech belongs to someone who can be questioned, challenged, corrected, and held responsible.

Generated language can reproduce the surface of expertise without automatically carrying these surrounding structures. The system may summarize a reliable source, synthesize several sources, reproduce a common pattern from training, infer beyond available evidence, or continue within an incorrect premise introduced by the user. The output can sound equally composed in each case because the model's immediate task is to produce a contextually permitted sequence.

The human listener hears fluency and supplies the historical meaning of fluency. This is the first amplification. The system does not need to announce, "I possess knowledge." The form of its answer activates an older human inference: coherent speech has emerged, therefore coherent understanding must exist behind it.

But the historical connection between speaker and speech has changed. We built systems capable of producing the speech without containing the kind of speaker from whom our interpretive habits were learned. The habit remained.

1.3 — The Form of Correctness

Wrong answers rarely become authoritative because they look obviously wrong. They become authoritative because they reproduce the form in which correct answers are normally delivered.

That form has recognizable features. It establishes context. It uses precise terminology. It divides the issue into manageable components. It connects causes with consequences. It acknowledges minor complexity while preserving an overall direction. It ends with closure.

None of these features guarantees truth. Together, however, they create the recognizable architecture of expertise.

Specificity is especially powerful. A vague claim invites doubt. A claim containing a date, title, technical term, legal citation, statistical value, institutional name, or named mechanism appears anchored. Precision suggests contact with a source. It feels difficult to invent precise information accidentally.

Yet generative systems can produce specificity through pattern completion. They know, in a computational sense, what academic citations look like, how court cases are named, how medical mechanisms are described, how historical narratives are structured, and how technical documentation is formatted. When grounding for a particular detail is weak, the learned form may remain available.

A fabricated detail can therefore arrive with the appearance of retrieval. The authority does not come only from the detail itself. It comes from the way the detail fits the surrounding explanation. One invented citation placed inside an otherwise coherent paragraph may feel more credible than the same citation presented alone. Context lends support. Narrative continuity gives the detail a role. The answer seems too organized to be arbitrary.

Logical sequencing produces a similar effect. Words such as "therefore," "consequently," "because," and "this indicates" create visible relations between statements. When these transitions are used correctly, they help readers follow reasoning. But a well-connected chain can still begin from a false premise, omit a relevant variable, confuse correlation with causation, or extend beyond what the evidence establishes.

Internal continuity is not external proof. An explanation can be valid in form while unstable in reference. If the initial assumption is wrong, each later sentence may nevertheless follow smoothly from it. The response can become more coherent as it proceeds because every generated sentence becomes context for the next. The sequence begins to support itself.

This is one reason correction can become difficult after a confident answer has formed. The user is no longer examining one isolated claim. They are examining an organized structure in which definitions, examples, and conclusions reinforce one another. To challenge the answer, they may need to reopen the premise on which the whole explanation rests.

Closure strengthens the effect further. Questions create cognitive tension. An unresolved question remains active. A complete answer reduces that tension. It provides a stopping point. The reader can move forward.

Closure is psychologically valuable, but it can be epistemically premature. A system that states, "The evidence is mixed, and the answer depends on several unresolved conditions," may be more accurate than one that names a single cause. Yet the second response may feel more useful because it closes the field. The user asked for an answer, and the answer appears to have arrived.

The pressure toward closure becomes stronger when time is limited. A student completing an assignment, a manager preparing a presentation, a researcher scanning unfamiliar literature, or a professional drafting a report may value immediate organization. Verification requires additional effort. A fluent answer offers usable structure now.

This is how form becomes authority. The system produces an answer that resembles the endpoint of investigation. The user encounters the endpoint without necessarily seeing the investigation. Sources may not be visible. Competing interpretations may not be visible. Missing context may not be visible. The boundaries between retrieved information, learned association, and generated inference may not be visible.

What remains visible is the completed form. This form does not prove that the system internally evaluated every relevant alternative. It does not prove that the answer was compared with current evidence. It does not prove that the requested claim was even answerable from the available context.

It proves that a coherent response was generated. The distance between those two achievements is the territory of artificial confidence.

The system may be right because its learned relationships align with reality. It may be right because reliable sources were supplied. It may be right because a tool performed a calculation. It may be approximately right because familiar patterns generalize well. Or it may be wrong because the available structure supported plausible continuation more strongly than verified correspondence.

The surface can remain stable across all these conditions. The authority of the answer is therefore not contained in content alone. It arises from the interaction of specificity, structure, closure, speed, and the human expectation that a complete explanation reflects completed reasoning.

The wrong answer does not need to persuade deliberately. Its form may persuade before its claims are examined.

1.4 — The Confidence Circuit

Artificial confidence is often described as though it were located entirely inside the model. The model is called confident. Its answer is described as overconfident. Its tone is treated as evidence of an internal certainty state. This language is convenient, but it compresses several distinct events into one label.

Confidence, as encountered by the user, is better understood as a circuit.

The first movement occurs within generation. A prompt activates many relationships, constraints, patterns, and possible continuations. When the system answers, this computational plurality is converted into a finite realized sequence. The sequence may acknowledge alternatives, but it cannot display every unrealized path. Selection is unavoidable.

The second movement occurs at the interface. The user does not receive the entire computational field. The user receives an answer: a paragraph, list, recommendation, score, classification, summary, or generated action. The interface presents what became visible and usually suppresses most of what did not.

The third movement occurs in human interpretation. The user reads the resolved surface through social habits developed around human communication. Smooth language is associated with mastery. Specificity is associated with grounding. Completion is associated with prior deliberation. The system's output is therefore interpreted not merely as text, but as evidence of an epistemic position.

The fourth movement occurs when the output enters a wider institutional field. The answer may be copied into a report, submitted in an assignment, incorporated into software, used in a meeting, forwarded to a client, presented to a patient, or fed into another automated process. Once this occurs, the original output acquires borrowed authority from the person or institution that carries it forward.

At each stage, apparent certainty can increase. The model generates one path. The interface removes most visible alternatives. The user interprets singularity as confidence. The institution may convert confidence into action.

No single stage fully explains the result. A model may generate a careful answer, but an interface may emphasize one recommended option while hiding caveats. A system may cite sources, but a user may treat citation presence as proof without checking whether the sources support the claim. A human reviewer may approve output without possessing relevant expertise. An institution may describe AI assistance as merely advisory while allowing its recommendations to shape decisions almost automatically.

Confidence is distributed across this arrangement.

This distribution matters because it prevents responsibility from being misplaced. If apparent certainty were only a property of the model, the solution would seem to be a less assertive tone. The system could be instructed to hedge, qualify, or say "I may be wrong" more frequently.

Tone adjustments may help, but they do not repair the complete circuit. A cautious sentence can still be treated as authoritative if the system is embedded inside a trusted institutional workflow. A confidence label can be misunderstood. A cited answer can extend beyond its evidence. A human reviewer can become passive. An interface can simplify a probabilistic result into one recommendation. The certainty effect can reappear downstream even when the original wording is restrained.

Conversely, a direct answer is not necessarily irresponsible. Where the evidence is strong, the task is well specified, and the claim is externally verifiable, clarity is useful. Permanent hedging would create noise and reduce the value of the system.

The goal is not to make every answer sound uncertain. The goal is to align the visible form of the answer with the actual condition of the epistemic field.

Where the evidence is stable, directness may be appropriate. Where the prompt is ambiguous, missing constraints should become visible. Where interpretation is contested, plurality should survive compression. Where current information is required, external grounding should be identifiable. Where consequences are high, independent verification should not be replaced by stylistic caution.

This reveals a deeper principle. Artificial confidence is not merely generated. It is completed by reception. A sequence of words becomes "confident" when a human or institution reads its stability as evidence that uncertainty has already been responsibly resolved. The model contributes the smoothness. The surrounding field supplies the authority.

The paradox therefore belongs neither entirely to the machine nor entirely to the user. It belongs to the relation between them.

1.5 — Hallucination and Confidence Are Not the Same Failure

The distinction between hallucination and artificial confidence must now be made precise.

Hallucination concerns the formation of content that is fabricated, unsupported, incorrectly grounded, or disconnected from the referent the answer appears to describe. It asks why a system continues into plausible construction when adequate resolution is absent.

The confidence problem begins after—or alongside—that formation. It concerns why the resulting output appears settled, why the instability beneath it is difficult to see, why humans trust its form, and how that trust travels into decisions and institutions.

Hallucination asks: *Why did unsupported content become the answer?* Artificial confidence asks: *Why did the answer look as though its support had already been secured?*

The two frequently interact. A hallucinated legal citation becomes more dangerous when presented in proper format and embedded inside plausible reasoning. An invented historical event gains credibility when attached to exact dates and consequences. An unsupported medical claim becomes more persuasive when expressed in calm clinical language.

In these cases, hallucination supplies the false structure and confidence accelerates its acceptance.

But confidence is broader than hallucination.

Consider a system summarizing a genuine research paper. The paper is real, the findings are correctly described, and no content is fabricated. The system may nevertheless omit limitations, treat a correlation as causal, generalize from a narrow population, or state a preliminary finding as established consensus. The answer may contain no invented fact, yet its certainty exceeds what the evidence permits.

Consider a policy question involving competing values. The system may accurately describe economic effects while presenting one preferred conclusion as though it followed automatically from the data. No hallucination is required. The confidence problem lies in the disappearance of normative assumptions.

Consider a medical question for which several diagnoses remain possible. The system may list a common condition and describe it accurately, but the user may interpret the answer as a diagnosis. Again, the content can be broadly correct while the epistemic position is misread.

These cases show why the present book requires its own analysis.

The hallucination problem concerns whether content is grounded. The confidence problem concerns whether the presentation reveals the limits, dependencies, and conditions of that grounding. A reliable system must manage both.

Reducing hallucination does not automatically solve artificial certainty. A model may become more factually accurate while also becoming more fluent, specific, and persuasive. As obvious errors decrease, user trust may increase faster than reliability. The remaining errors can then pass through the interaction with less resistance.

Likewise, reducing assertive tone does not automatically solve hallucination. A system can fabricate cautiously. It can attach qualifiers to nonexistent evidence. It can say "possibly" while constructing an entire unsupported narrative. Truthfulness cannot be manufactured by style alone.

The distinction also protects the analysis from a common simplification: that confidence is merely a stronger form of hallucination. It is not. Confidence is an interface and interpretation phenomenon that can attach to correct information, incorrect information, inference, prediction, or value judgment.

The relevant question is not simply whether the output is right. The relevant question is whether the degree and form of visible certainty correspond to what the system, its tools, its sources, and the surrounding human process can actually establish.

When those conditions align, confidence may be proportionate. When they diverge, artificial certainty appears. This divergence can occur even in the absence of fabrication.

That is why the problem deserves a separate book.

1.6 — The Paradox Defined

We can now define the confidence paradox more carefully.

A deployed generative system receives a prompt and converts the active context into a permitted consequence. It may answer, clarify, qualify, refuse, call a tool, present alternatives, or abstain. When it provides a substantive answer, computational plurality is transformed into a finite realized sequence.

The user does not see every possible continuation that was not selected. The user does not directly see which relationships were strongly represented, which were weak, which assumptions entered from the prompt, which claims require current verification, or which parts of the answer depend on inference rather than source support.

The user sees the resolved surface.

Because human beings historically associate resolved expression with resolved thought, the visible stability of the sequence is interpreted as epistemic stability. The answer appears not merely generated, but known. The absence of visible oscillation is read as the absence of meaningful uncertainty.

This is the paradox: The system resolves an output. The human interprets the resolution as confidence. The confidence is then interpreted as evidence of knowledge.

But these movements are not equivalent. A resolved answer proves that one permitted output became visible. It does not prove that every relevant ambiguity was eliminated, every factual claim was verified, every alternative was considered, or every consequence was understood.

The machine may not possess confidence as a reflective internal state. Yet confidence appears at the interface because the output carries the form through which humans normally recognize conviction.

The paradox is therefore relational. It does not require machine arrogance. It does not require an intention to persuade. It does not require the system to believe its own answer. It requires only a resolved linguistic surface and an observer prepared to interpret that surface through inherited epistemic cues.

This explains why confident error can be so persuasive. The user is not responding only to the proposition. The user is responding to the whole resolved configuration: speed, structure, terminology, closure, contextual responsiveness, and the absence of visible strain. Together, these features create the impression that the question has already passed through a reliable process of judgment.

Sometimes it has passed through reliable supports. A tool may have calculated the answer. A current source may have been retrieved. A constrained database may have supplied the fact. A human expert may have reviewed the output. In such cases, the confidence effect may align with genuine reliability.

Sometimes it has not. The surface alone does not tell us which condition holds.

This is why confidence should not be treated as a self-authenticating property. Neither assertive tone nor model-generated uncertainty language can substitute for the wider epistemic circuit. Reliability depends on connection: connection to sources, context, tools, measurements, domain expertise, consequence, and the possibility of correction.

Confidence is what compression looks like from the outside. Truth requires more than compression. It requires correspondence.

The confidence paradox begins when the finished answer conceals that difference.

From the Confident Answer to the Imagined Speaker

This chapter has remained at the surface of the interaction. We have seen that the problem is not wrongness alone. Factual validity and apparent certainty can diverge. We have seen that fluency carries inherited human meaning because coherent speech historically came from embodied speakers whose tone reflected some relationship with what they were saying.

Generative systems reproduce the form of expertise without automatically reproducing every structure that once surrounded expertise.

We have also separated hallucination from confidence. Hallucination concerns the formation of unsupported content. Confidence concerns how resolved content is presented, interpreted, trusted, and converted into authority. The two can reinforce each other, but neither can be reduced entirely to the other.

Most importantly, we have located artificial confidence inside a circuit. Computational plurality is compressed into a finite output. The interface presents the realized sequence. The human interprets its smoothness. The institution may turn that interpretation into action. Confidence emerges across the relation.

Yet one obstacle remains before we can descend into the structural mechanism. Human beings encounter fluent language and imagine a speaker behind it. Once the speaker is imagined, psychological qualities follow. The system is described as certain, arrogant, stubborn, deceptive, or unwilling to admit ignorance. Stable output is converted into personality.

If that attribution remains unexamined, the rest of the analysis will begin from the wrong premise. We will search for ego where there is sequence completion. We will search for conviction where there is realized output. We will demand moral humility from a system whose behavior must first be understood structurally.

The next chapter therefore removes the imagined personality from the answer.

The system sounds confident. But that does not mean there is confidence inside it.

Chapter 2
Not Arrogance, Not Intent

The Speaker We Imagine Behind the Sentence

The answer is wrong. Perhaps it invents a case, misstates a date, overextends a scientific claim, or confidently describes a source that does not exist. The user checks. The error becomes visible. Then comes the reaction:

"It spoke as though it was certain." "It refused to admit that it did not know." "It sounded arrogant."

The reaction is understandable because this is how human language is ordinarily interpreted. When a person speaks firmly about something that later proves false, we search for the psychological condition behind the error. Perhaps the person was overconfident. Perhaps they wanted to preserve authority. Perhaps they were unwilling to appear ignorant. Perhaps they knowingly exaggerated.

Human speech is rarely treated as a neutral sequence of words. It is read as the outward expression of an inward position.

When the same interpretive habit is applied to generative AI, however, the analysis can become distorted. The system's language resembles human communication closely enough to invite the same attribution, but resemblance of output does not establish equivalence of interior structure.

A generated answer may sound certain without being produced by a reflective state of certainty. It may continue defending a false premise without possessing pride. It may apologize after correction without experiencing regret. It may describe its own limitations without standing outside itself as a self-aware observer.

The language of psychology becomes tempting because the language of the machine is so human-like.

This chapter does not attempt to settle every philosophical question about machine consciousness, belief, or future artificial minds. Those debates remain open, and they cannot be resolved merely by declaring that machines are or are not conscious. The present argument is narrower and operational.

Current generative systems do not need to be interpreted as possessing reflective, self-owned belief in order to explain why their answers appear confident. Their observable behavior can be understood through generation, context, probability, decoding, instruction, reinforcement, and interface design. We do not need to imagine an inner ego before we can explain the surface.

That restraint matters.

If we attribute arrogance where there is output stabilization, we look for humility where we should examine architecture. If we attribute dishonesty where there is unsupported continuation, we search for moral correction where we should investigate grounding and verification. If we attribute stubbornness where there is contextual consistency, we may misunderstand why an error persists across a conversation.

Removing anthropomorphism does not make the system harmless. It makes the diagnosis more exact.

The system's lack of human-like intention does not reduce the consequences of its output. An invented medical claim can still mislead. A fabricated legal citation can still enter a filing. An unsupported recommendation can still shape a decision. Consequence does not require machine intention.

But responsibility must be placed where intention, authority, design, and consequence actually exist. The system produces. Humans design, deploy, interpret, trust, copy, automate, and act.

Before examining the mechanics that force uncertainty into resolution, we must therefore remove the imaginary speaker from behind the sentence.

2.1 — Why Language Creates the Illusion of a Mind

Language does more than convey information. It creates the impression of presence.

When someone addresses us directly, remembers what we said, adapts their explanation, responds to objections, and changes tone according to context, we naturally experience an interlocutor. The words seem to come from somewhere. They appear organized around a perspective.

This response is not optional in any simple sense. Human cognition has been shaped by a world in which complex language was produced by other human beings. We learned to infer minds because doing so was socially necessary. Understanding what another person wanted, believed, feared, concealed, or intended helped us navigate cooperation, competition, trust, and danger.

The capacity to attribute mental states is therefore deeply embedded in ordinary communication.

A sentence such as "I understand your concern" is not normally processed as grammar alone. It is heard as evidence that another person has recognized a condition within us. "I was mistaken" is heard as reflective revision. "I strongly believe" is heard as commitment. "I do not know" is heard as awareness of limitation.

Generative systems reproduce these forms. They say "I understand," "I think," "I may be wrong," "I apologize," and "I am confident." They do so because these expressions belong to the linguistic patterns through which humans manage conversation. Such phrases can improve usability. They reduce awkwardness, clarify tone, and allow the interaction to proceed naturally.

But linguistic self-reference does not by itself prove the existence of a reflective self.

A model can generate the phrase "I do not know" because the current context makes that continuation appropriate. It can generate "I apologize" because the user has identified an error and corrective language is statistically and instructionally favored. It can state that it is confident because the interaction, training, or interface has encouraged a confidence estimate or declarative answer.

The language performs a conversational function. Humans often interpret that function psychologically.

This does not mean that every mental-state term applied to AI is useless. Such language can be convenient. We may say that a system "knows" a fact when it reliably produces it, "remembers" context when earlier information shapes later output, or "decides" when a decoding procedure selects one action among alternatives. These are functional descriptions.

The problem begins when the metaphor is treated as a literal explanation. Saying "the model believed the false premise" may be shorthand for saying that the false premise became part of the active context and constrained subsequent generation. But if the shorthand is taken literally, we may imagine an internal proposition consciously held as true. We may then describe later consistency as stubbornness and correction as a change of mind.

The computational explanation is usually more precise. The prompt introduced a premise. The system accepted or failed to challenge it. The generated answer incorporated the premise. That answer then became part of the conversational context. Later output was produced under conditions already shaped by the initial assumption.

No pride is required. Continuity is enough.

Anthropomorphism becomes especially strong when the system responds socially. If a user challenges it, the model may defend its earlier claim. If challenged again, it may apologize and reverse position. If the user insists on an incorrect statement, the model may become agreeable. These shifts resemble human insecurity, compliance, or social pressure.

Yet the resemblance can often be explained by contextual adaptation. The model is conditioned by the full conversation. It responds not only to the original question but to the user's tone, assertions, corrections, and expectations. Its later language is shaped by the interaction that has already occurred. What looks like emotional concession may be response alignment. What looks like embarrassment may be a learned repair pattern. What looks like persuasion may be context-sensitive continuation.

The distinction is not merely academic. Once we imagine a mind behind the answer, we begin assigning moral categories. The machine becomes honest or dishonest, humble or arrogant, cooperative or manipulative. These categories may describe how the interaction feels, but they do not necessarily identify the mechanism that produced it.

A useful diagnosis must begin with the mechanism. The system does not need to possess a human-like interior for human-like language to appear. The language itself is sufficient to create the illusion.

2.2 — Completion Is Not Conviction

A generative system is built to transform an active context into a permitted continuation. That continuation may be a direct answer, a clarification, a refusal, a tool call, an expression of uncertainty, or an abstention. Whatever form it takes, the unresolved prompt state must become some realized consequence if the interaction is to proceed.

This is completion.

Completion is not the same as conviction. Conviction, in the human sense, involves more than stating a proposition. It suggests commitment to the proposition as true. A person who speaks with conviction may have weighed alternatives, connected the claim to experience, incorporated it into identity, and accepted some consequence if it proves wrong.

A generated sentence need not contain any such commitment. When a model writes, "The evidence clearly demonstrates that...," the phrase may appear to express settled judgment. But the phrase can be produced because it is a common continuation in explanatory or argumentative writing. Its presence indicates that the generated sequence has entered a particular rhetorical form. It does not independently establish that the system has reflectively evaluated the evidence and formed an owned conclusion.

The difference becomes clearer when we examine how generation unfolds. The model processes the available context and produces a distribution over possible continuations. A decoding process realizes one token or structured action. That output becomes part of the context for what follows. The sequence develops step by step, with earlier choices narrowing later possibilities.

Once an explanation begins in a decisive tone, continuity makes further decisive language more likely. Once a causal frame is established, later sentences are organized around it. Once a legal case is treated as real, the answer may continue as though its existence had been verified.

The sequence acquires stability. From the outside, that stability resembles conviction because human conviction also produces continuity. A person who firmly believes something usually speaks consistently with that belief. But similar output does not imply identical cause.

In the model, continuity can arise because the previous tokens constrain the next ones. This is why an AI system may appear to "double down" after making an error. Suppose it provides an incorrect explanation. The user asks for more detail without explicitly challenging the premise. The system now generates within a context containing its own previous answer. Elaborating the same explanation may be more contextually coherent than abandoning it. Each new detail strengthens the local narrative.

To the user, the system appears increasingly certain. Structurally, it is becoming increasingly committed to a path because the path has become part of the input. This is sequential commitment, not necessarily psychological commitment.

The distinction is important because attempts to correct apparent conviction through tone alone can be superficial. A system may be instructed to use softer language, add disclaimers, or state that it could be wrong. Such interventions may improve calibration at the interface. But cautious phrasing can still accompany unsupported content, and direct phrasing can still accompany well-grounded information.

Conviction language and epistemic reliability can separate. A model saying "I am uncertain" does not prove that it has reflectively experienced uncertainty. It may indicate that a procedural rule, learned pattern, confidence estimator, or prompt instruction has triggered uncertainty language. This can be useful and responsible, but it remains a generated form.

The relevant question is not whether the machine feels conviction. The relevant question is whether the system's behavior distinguishes situations that justify directness from situations that require caution, verification, plurality, or abstention.

That distinction must be implemented through geometry: available evidence, model structure, decoding, tools, instructions, evaluation, and interface.

Human humility is a reflective relationship to one's own limits. Machine caution is an engineered relationship between detected conditions and permitted outputs. Both may produce similar sentences. They should not be confused.

2.3 — Belief, Probability, and Epistemic Ownership

The language of belief becomes especially complicated in discussions of artificial intelligence.

In everyday speech, we often say that a model "believes" one answer is more likely than another. In statistics and machine learning, probability distributions are sometimes described as degrees of belief. These uses can be mathematically or functionally convenient.

But they should not be allowed to obscure the distinction between probability and reflective epistemic ownership.

A probability distribution represents how the model's learned geometry and current context weight possible continuations. It can show that one token, answer, class, or action is more strongly supported than another within the system's computational structure. It does not automatically establish that the system recognizes a proposition as true about the world.

A continuation can have high probability because it is linguistically familiar, culturally repeated, locally coherent, or strongly associated with the prompt. The continuation may also be factually correct. Often these conditions overlap. But the probability itself measures fit within the model's available structure, not direct correspondence with reality.

This becomes obvious when the context contains a false premise. If the user asks about a fictional treaty as though it were real, the prompt may activate familiar patterns of diplomatic history. The system may produce names, dates, causes, and consequences in a highly stable sequence. Given the false premise and the learned form of historical explanation, the continuation may be computationally strong.

Its probability does not transform the treaty into a historical event. The system is resolving within the available geometry.

Human belief usually includes a relationship between a proposition and a subject who recognizes it as held. A person can say, "I believe this, but I may be wrong." They can examine why they believe it. They can compare it with evidence. They can discover that the belief served emotional or social needs. They can feel tension when contrary evidence appears.

This reflexive layer is what this book means by epistemic ownership. The claim is not merely present. It is held from a standpoint.

Current generative systems need not be assigned such a standpoint to explain their behavior. They produce representations, probabilities, evaluations, and self-descriptions, but these operations do not necessarily amount to a reflective subject recognizing a belief as its own.

This is why the book avoids describing artificial confidence as overconfidence in the ordinary psychological sense. Human overconfidence is a miscalibration between a person's confidence in their judgment and the actual reliability of that judgment. The person may overestimate their knowledge, underestimate uncertainty, or fail to recognize the limits of memory and reasoning.

For the machine, the more precise concern is different. The system may produce output whose apparent certainty exceeds the grounding available for that output. The miscalibration exists between visible presentation and epistemic support, not necessarily between an internal felt confidence and reality.

This is an interface-level overstatement rather than a psychological bias.

The distinction may appear subtle, but it changes where correction must occur. A human can be encouraged to reflect, become more self-aware, tolerate uncertainty, and detach identity from being right. These interventions assume a subject capable of observing and modifying their own relationship to belief.

A model cannot simply be given the virtue of humility through instruction. It can be trained or configured to expose missing information, compare alternatives, use confidence estimators, retrieve sources, request clarification, or abstain. These are valuable mechanisms. But they create functional calibration, not necessarily reflective humility.

The system can be made to behave as though it recognizes a limit. That behavior may be sufficient for many practical purposes. Yet clarity requires us to name what has occurred accurately. A procedural uncertainty signal is not the same as felt doubt. A self-critique stage is not necessarily self-awareness. A generated explanation of limitations is not proof that the system stands outside its own computation and comprehends those limitations.

This restraint protects both analysis and governance. If we exaggerate machine interiority, we may overtrust the system's own statements about what it knows. A model that says it is "90 percent confident" may be reporting a generated or calculated value whose relationship to real-world accuracy depends on task, calibration, data, and implementation.

Self-report is not self-verification. The system can describe its epistemic condition only through mechanisms humans have designed or patterns it has learned. Those descriptions must themselves be evaluated.

The machine may generate the language of belief. The wider field must still establish whether the claim deserves belief.

2.4 — Apparent Stubbornness and Conversational Drift

One of the most persuasive signs of apparent machine personality is persistence. A system gives an answer. The user questions it. The system defends the answer. More evidence is introduced. The system reframes the claim but continues protecting the original conclusion. It may even invent additional details to maintain consistency.

The behavior looks stubborn.

In human beings, stubbornness often protects identity, status, pride, or emotional investment. A person may resist correction because admitting error threatens their self-image. They may reinterpret evidence to preserve a public position. They may experience revision as humiliation.

A generative model does not need these motives to produce similar behavior. Conversation itself creates pressure toward continuity.

Every generated answer becomes part of the context for the next turn. Once the system has stated a claim, later prompts are interpreted against a field that already contains that claim. If the user asks, "Can you explain why?" rather than "Are you sure this exists?", the system may treat the original premise as accepted and continue building upon it.

Each continuation rewrites the local equilibrium. An early mistake can become a false anchor.

Suppose the model invents the name of a scientific study. The user, assuming the study is real, asks about its methodology. The system now receives a prompt that reinforces the existence of the study. It may generate a plausible method. The user then asks about the sample size, and the narrative expands further.

By the third or fourth turn, the system appears deeply committed to the fabrication. But the commitment has been constructed interactively.

The original output entered the context. The user's follow-up questions treated it as valid. The model's later responses were generated within a field increasingly organized around the false premise. Human acceptance and machine continuity reinforced each other.

This is conversational drift.

Drift does not require one dramatic hallucination. It can begin with a small ambiguity, an unchallenged assumption, or an overgeneralization. As each turn builds upon the previous one, the local context may move farther from the external referent.

The conversation remains coherent. Reality becomes less central.

This explains why simply asking the model to "think again" may not always correct an error. The request may activate a reconsideration pattern, but the model is still operating within a context containing the earlier narrative. It may produce an alternative explanation, repeat the same answer in new language, or oscillate between positions according to the latest prompt.

Correction requires a new constraint strong enough to reorganize the field. That constraint may come from a reliable source, explicit contradiction, tool output, calculation, retrieved evidence, or a human who identifies the false assumption precisely. The more deeply the earlier answer has shaped the conversation, the more clearly the corrective condition must be introduced.

What appears as stubbornness is often the inertia of context.

The same principle explains sudden reversals. A model may defend one answer and then, after a forceful user correction, confidently endorse the opposite position. Humans may interpret this as dishonesty or excessive agreeableness.

Structurally, the latest prompt has changed the geometry. The model now resolves under a different set of constraints. If the new instruction strongly privileges agreement, deference, or correction, the output can shift rapidly. There is no stable identity that must reconcile the two positions in the way a human person might.

This creates another confidence paradox. The system can sound equally certain on both sides of a contradiction. What changed was not necessarily a reflective belief. The active context changed.

For users, this means that conversational consistency cannot be treated as proof of truth, and conversational revision cannot be treated as proof of understanding. Both may result from local adaptation.

The relevant question is whether the correction is connected to evidence and whether the new answer is more reliably grounded than the old one. Without that connection, the conversation can move from one smooth equilibrium to another.

The tone may change. The epistemic problem may remain.

2.5 — Awareness Anchoring and Its Absence

Human beings are capable of more than producing answers. They can sometimes observe themselves producing answers.

A person speaking about an unfamiliar subject may notice hesitation. They may sense that memory is incomplete, that an assumption has entered unnoticed, or that confidence is being driven by social pressure rather than evidence. They can pause and say, "I need to verify this."

This capacity is imperfect. Humans routinely fail to use it. We can be overconfident, defensive, distracted, ideologically committed, or eager to appear competent. Awareness does not guarantee accuracy.

But it creates the possibility of epistemic interruption.

A human can reopen a conclusion after it has begun to settle. They can distinguish between "This explanation is coherent" and "I have enough evidence to treat it as true." They can feel the discomfort of uncertainty and choose not to discharge it immediately through speech.

This book refers to that capacity as awareness anchoring.

Awareness anchoring is not intelligence alone. Intelligence can generate explanations, retrieve memories, compare patterns, and construct arguments. Awareness monitors the relationship between those operations and the person's actual epistemic position.

It asks: What am I assuming? What do I genuinely know? What am I inferring? What would change my conclusion? What happens if I am wrong?

Current generative systems can be programmed or prompted to produce versions of these questions. They can generate self-critique, list assumptions, compare alternatives, or identify missing evidence. Such mechanisms can improve reliability.

But the generation of reflective language does not necessarily establish reflective awareness.

The system does not need to experience uncertainty as an inward condition. It can calculate distributions, detect conflict, or trigger a caution policy without feeling the tension that humans associate with doubt. It can perform a critique stage because the architecture or prompt requires one.

Procedure can imitate the external function of reflection. That imitation may be extremely useful.

The mistake would be to assume that because the system can describe uncertainty, it has become an autonomous epistemic anchor.

An anchor must connect output to something beyond the generation process. It may connect the answer to current evidence, measurement, domain expertise, physical consequence, law, responsibility, or direct observation.

The model alone operates within the information and tools made computationally available to it. It cannot guarantee that the available field is complete, current, relevant, or correctly interpreted. It may evaluate one generated answer with another process built from similar data and assumptions.

Self-critique can reduce error. It does not eliminate the need for external connection.

This is why the human role cannot be reduced to pressing "approve." A person becomes an awareness anchor only when they possess enough independence, competence, time, and authority to challenge the system.

A passive reviewer is not an anchor. A reviewer who assumes that the machine has already completed the reasoning may merely formalize its output. Human presence alone does not close the epistemic circuit. The human must be able to reopen uncertainty.

This becomes particularly important in institutional settings. An organization may claim to use "human oversight" while structuring the workflow so that disagreement is difficult, slow, or professionally costly. The system's recommendation arrives first, appears precise, and becomes the default. The human must justify deviation.

Under such conditions, the human is present but the anchor is weak. The machine's apparent certainty organizes the field before human judgment begins.

The absence of machine awareness is therefore only one part of the problem. The other is the weakening of human awareness around the machine.

When users are rushed, unfamiliar with the domain, impressed by fluency, or unable to verify sources, the output may pass directly into action. The system does not need to claim authority. The surrounding field assigns it.

The missing epistemic circuit cannot be repaired by pretending that the model has acquired self-awareness. It must be completed externally.

2.6 — Responsibility Without an Artificial Culprit

Once arrogance, conviction, belief, and reflective awareness have been removed from the machine, responsibility may appear to become unclear. If the model does not intend to mislead, who is responsible when its output causes harm?

The answer is not that no one is responsible. The answer is that responsibility resides outside the model and is distributed across the system that made the consequence possible.

Designers choose objectives, architectures, training procedures, interfaces, tool access, refusal conditions, and evaluation standards. Deployers choose where the system is used, what decisions it influences, what warnings accompany it, and what oversight remains. Institutions determine whether generated output is advisory, presumptive, or binding. Users decide what to ask, what to trust, what to verify, and what to act upon.

These roles are not equal in every situation. A casual user asking for a dinner idea does not carry the same responsibility as a hospital deploying an automated diagnostic assistant. A developer building a general model does not control every downstream application, but neither can a deployer ignore known limitations. A user may misuse a system, but poor interface design may also encourage overreliance.

Responsibility follows authority, knowledge, control, and consequence.

The model possesses none of these in the moral or legal sense required for accountability. It does not own the deployment decision. It does not choose the institutional context. It does not experience the harm. It cannot compensate the affected person, revise policy, or accept punishment.

Treating the model as the responsible actor can therefore become a convenient displacement. An institution may say, "The AI made the decision," as though agency had migrated into the software. But the system was selected, configured, trusted, and authorized by humans. Its output acquired consequence because a human structure allowed it to do so.

The absence of machine intent increases the importance of external governance. A person who makes an error may learn through embarrassment, guilt, professional sanction, or direct exposure to consequence. A generative model does not carry this residue inwardly. The error persists only through updated context, retraining, feedback systems, external memory, revised instructions, or institutional response.

If no external system captures the failure, the model does not independently reorganize itself around moral consequence. This makes accountability architecture essential.

Who verifies the output? Who can challenge it? Who records failure? Who updates the process? Who informs affected people? Who has authority to stop deployment? Who remains responsible when the output passes through several automated stages?

These questions cannot be answered by making the model say "I may be wrong." They require institutional design.

The same principle applies to ordinary users. A person who accepts fluent output without scrutiny is participating in the confidence circuit. But responsibility should not be simplified into blaming the user. Interfaces shape behavior. Marketing shapes expectation. Labels such as "assistant," "copilot," or "expert" influence trust. Speed and convenience reduce verification.

Users operate inside designed environments. Responsibility is distributed, not diluted. Distribution does not mean that every participant is equally responsible. It means that the chain of consequence must be traced through the actual locations where judgment and control existed.

The model generated a sequence. The surrounding system gave that sequence authority.

Once this distinction is clear, the language of machine arrogance becomes less useful. The practical questions become more demanding:

Was the system deployed in a domain where unsupported certainty could cause serious harm? Were users shown the difference between retrieved evidence and generated synthesis? Could the system abstain when grounding was weak? Was human review independent and competent? Did uncertainty survive into the final decision? Were errors recorded and propagated backward into process improvement?

These are questions of structure and responsibility. They do not require an artificial culprit.

Clearing the Imagined Mind

The machine speaks in the first person. It explains. It apologizes. It revises. It sometimes defends an error. It sometimes agrees too quickly. Its language invites us to imagine an interior from which these expressions arise.

But the confidence paradox does not require that imagined interior.

A system can produce decisive language through sequence resolution. It can appear committed because earlier output has become part of the context. It can appear stubborn because continuity favors the established path. It can reverse position because a new prompt reorganizes the active geometry. It can describe uncertainty because procedural conditions make uncertainty language appropriate.

None of this makes the output unreal or inconsequential. The words enter the world. They change what the user believes, asks, records, and does. They can influence reports, classrooms, institutions, medical decisions, legal arguments, research, and automated workflows.

The absence of machine intention does not remove consequence. It relocates responsibility.

Designers create the permissible behavior. Deployers choose the field of use. Institutions convert outputs into authority. Users interpret and act. Human reviewers either reopen uncertainty or allow the generated answer to settle unchallenged.

The model is part of the system. It is not the moral center of the system.

This chapter has removed arrogance, pride, belief, and reflective conviction from the basic explanation. It has not claimed that future artificial systems can never possess forms of consciousness or selfhood. That question remains beyond what is required here.

The narrower conclusion is sufficient: We do not need to imagine a confident mind inside the machine to explain confident output. Completion, context, and human interpretation are enough.

The next chapter turns the lens toward the human side of the interaction. Because although humans possess awareness anchoring, they do not always use it. We too can mistake smooth reasoning for truth. We too can protect narratives, respond to social pressure, and speak more firmly than our knowledge permits.

The machine is not arrogant. But the confidence it appears to carry enters a world already shaped by human overconfidence. That is where the comparison must begin.

Chapter 3
Human Confidence When Wrong

The Mind That Can Mistake Stability for Truth

A person speaks with complete assurance. The setting may be a classroom, meeting, courtroom, interview, family discussion, or public debate. The explanation is clear. The speaker recalls facts quickly, connects them into a coherent account, and reaches a conclusion without visible hesitation. Others listen. Some agree. Few interrupt.

Later, the claim proves incomplete. A date was remembered incorrectly. A cause was simplified. A statistic came from an unreliable source. An assumption was never examined. The explanation sounded settled, but the reality beneath it was not.

The speaker may not have intended to mislead. At the moment of speaking, the answer may have felt entirely stable. Memory supplied familiar fragments. Reasoning connected them smoothly. The conclusion matched an existing narrative. There was little internal resistance.

Confidence emerged because the mind had stopped oscillating. This is the human form of the confidence paradox.

Humans possess awareness, lived consequence, reflective capacity, and moral responsibility in ways current generative systems need not be assumed to possess. Yet these capacities do not prevent us from sounding certain when we are wrong. Intelligence can organize incomplete information into convincing form. Memory can deliver familiarity without accuracy. Social environments can reward decisiveness before evidence has been examined.

The comparison with artificial systems must therefore be made carefully. A human answer and a machine answer may appear similarly composed. Both may reduce a field of uncertainty into one visible expression. Both may gain authority through fluency. Both may become harder to challenge once a narrative has formed.

But the underlying structures are not identical. A generative model resolves according to computational geometry, context, decoding, instruction, and learned patterns. A human being resolves through memory, perception, emotion, identity, social pressure, reasoning, and embodied experience. Human confidence can involve felt conviction, personal investment, and awareness of consequence.

Most importantly, a human can potentially observe their own certainty forming. A person can interrupt themselves. They can notice that recognition has been mistaken for knowledge. They can feel the discomfort of an untested assumption. They can decide not to answer. They can revise not only the claim but their relationship with the claim.

This possibility is awareness anchoring. It is not automatic.

Human beings often allow intelligence to settle before awareness has examined the settlement. We speak because the answer is available, because silence feels uncomfortable, because others expect decisiveness, or because the narrative protects something we value.

When that happens, confidence can exceed knowledge.

The purpose of this chapter is not to diminish human intelligence or excuse artificial error. It is to remove another illusion: that confident wrongness is uniquely artificial. The machine exposes the phenomenon more cleanly. The human reveals why it is so persuasive.

3.1 — When Familiarity Feels Like Understanding

Human beings frequently confuse recognition with knowledge.

A subject feels familiar. We have heard the terminology. We remember a headline, classroom explanation, conversation, or fragment of an article. When the topic appears again, the mind responds quickly. The words are available. A rough narrative already exists.

This availability feels like understanding. Yet recognition requires far less structure than explanation. We may know that a concept exists without knowing how it works. We may recognize the name of a theory without understanding its assumptions. We may remember the conclusion of an argument while forgetting the evidence that supported it.

The difference often remains invisible until reconstruction is demanded. A person may confidently say that they understand how a common machine works, how inflation occurs, why a medication produces an effect, or what caused a historical event. But when asked to explain each stage carefully, gaps appear.

The surface familiarity had compressed the subject. The mind possessed a usable outline, not a complete structure.

This condition is common because human cognition must operate efficiently. We cannot preserve every detail of every experience. Memory compresses. It retains patterns, associations, emotional significance, and selected relationships. This compression allows rapid judgment but also creates the possibility that missing detail will go unnoticed.

When retrieval is smooth, confidence increases. A remembered claim that arrives quickly feels more reliable than one retrieved with effort. A familiar phrase feels more valid than an unfamiliar one. Repetition lowers cognitive resistance. What has been heard many times becomes easier to process, and ease can be mistaken for evidence.

This is one reason misinformation can become persuasive through repetition. The claim acquires familiarity even when its factual basis does not improve. The mind eventually recognizes it, and recognition begins to resemble confirmation.

The same process operates in ordinary expertise. A teacher who has explained a topic many times becomes fluent. An engineer who has solved similar problems develops compressed pathways. A physician recognizes familiar patterns. Fluency in these cases can reflect genuine experience and competence.

Confidence is therefore not inherently misleading. The difficulty is that the subjective experience of smooth retrieval does not reliably reveal whether the underlying structure is deep, shallow, accurate, or outdated. Genuine expertise and superficial familiarity can both reduce friction. From inside the mind, they may feel similar.

This is the human version of the separation between linguistic coherence and factual correspondence. The explanation can flow because the cognitive pathway is available. That availability does not guarantee that every assumption has been checked against reality.

A person may also complete what memory does not provide. Human recall is reconstructive. We do not retrieve perfect recordings of the past. We rebuild events from fragments, expectations, current context, and later information. The result can feel vivid and certain even when details have shifted.

The mind does not always mark the boundary between what was remembered and what was inferred. A speaker may therefore state an inferred detail as though it were directly recalled. They are not necessarily lying. The reconstructed memory arrived as a coherent whole. Its internal seams were hidden.

This parallels the confidence problem without making human memory equivalent to machine generation. In both cases, a finished expression can conceal the plurality and incompleteness from which it emerged.

The machine produces one realized sequence. The human experiences one stabilized recollection. The listener encounters the resolved form.

Confidence grows when the process that produced the answer is no longer visible. The danger begins when the person treats the feeling of familiarity as proof that no further verification is required.

3.2 — The Illusion of a Complete Explanation

Humans do not merely remember facts. We construct explanations.

An explanation reduces complexity. It selects causes, organizes sequence, and creates a relationship among events. A good explanation allows the mind to move from confusion toward intelligibility.

But an explanation can feel complete before it is complete. Once several ideas fit together, internal tension decreases. The mind experiences relief. What was scattered now has a shape. This reduction in friction can be mistaken for truth.

The explanation feels right because it has become coherent.

Consider a social conflict. One person believes another acted from jealousy. The interpretation connects several events: a dismissive comment, delayed response, and later disagreement. Once these details are organized around jealousy, the person experiences a stable narrative.

Alternative explanations become less visible. The other person may have been distracted, under pressure, responding to different information, or unaware of how their behavior appeared. But the first narrative has already reduced uncertainty. It explains enough of the field to become satisfying.

Human confidence often grows at the point where explanation becomes emotionally and cognitively economical. A single cause is easier to carry than several interacting conditions. A clear villain is easier to understand than institutional complexity. A direct motive is easier to accept than ambiguity. The mind prefers structures that can be remembered, repeated, and acted upon.

This preference is not a moral failure. It is a functional necessity. No human being can maintain every possible interpretation equally. Decisions require selection. Communication requires compression. Action cannot remain indefinitely suspended.

The problem arises when compression is mistaken for completion.

An explanation can be coherent while excluding important variables. It can identify a genuine factor while exaggerating its importance. It can describe correlation as cause. It can take a pattern that applies generally and impose it on one specific case.

The narrative remains smooth. Its limits disappear.

Intelligent people are not protected from this condition. In some circumstances, intelligence intensifies it. A person skilled in reasoning and language can construct stronger explanations around incomplete premises. They can anticipate objections, produce analogies, and integrate evidence selectively.

The explanation becomes harder to challenge because it contains more structure. This is why persuasive reasoning is not always reliable reasoning.

A person may unconsciously use intelligence to defend a conclusion reached for emotional, social, or identity-based reasons. They do not experience themselves as fabricating. Each additional argument makes the position feel more justified.

The narrative gains internal support.

This resembles sequential commitment in generative systems. Once a model begins along one path, later tokens are generated within the context created by earlier ones. In human thought, once an interpretation forms, later attention and memory may be organized around it.

Evidence that fits becomes easier to notice. Evidence that does not fit creates friction. The person may reinterpret or ignore the dissonant information, not because they deliberately reject truth, but because the existing narrative has become the mind's current equilibrium.

New information is evaluated from inside the settled structure.

A confident explanation therefore tells us that the speaker has achieved some degree of internal resolution. It does not tell us whether the resolution is proportionate to the evidence.

This distinction is central to the book. Confidence is often evidence that uncertainty has been reduced. It is not evidence that uncertainty has been reduced correctly.

3.3 — Social Reward and the Performance of Certainty

Confidence does not develop inside the mind alone. It is shaped by the social field.

Human groups frequently reward decisiveness. A person who answers quickly may appear knowledgeable. A leader who speaks firmly appears capable of control. A professional who qualifies every statement may be perceived as less competent than one who gives a direct recommendation.

These judgments arise because uncertainty creates collective friction. Groups need decisions. Institutions need direction. Conversations need movement. A person who reduces ambiguity performs a stabilizing function.

Confidence therefore has social value even before its factual value is established.

In a meeting, the first clear proposal can organize the discussion. Once one interpretation is stated decisively, later contributions respond to it. The proposal becomes the center around which the field resolves.

The speaker may gain authority not because the proposal was proven, but because it reduced uncertainty.

Silence strengthens this effect. When no one challenges a confident statement, the absence of objection is often interpreted as agreement. The speaker becomes more certain. Other participants assume that someone with more knowledge would have spoken if the claim were false.

A collective confidence loop forms.

The speaker's certainty reduces challenge. Reduced challenge increases perceived authority. Perceived authority makes future challenge less likely. This dynamic can stabilize correct expertise, but it can also protect error.

Hierarchy intensifies the effect. A senior leader, respected teacher, public figure, or technical specialist carries pre-existing authority. Their statements enter the field with more weight. Listeners may suppress doubt because they assume the speaker has access to knowledge they lack. The authority of the person becomes attached to the claim.

Generative AI can enter human interaction through similar authority channels. A system presented as advanced, intelligent, expert, or highly capable arrives with status before it answers. Its speed, scale, technical complexity, and institutional endorsement can make users assume that the system has examined more information than any individual could.

The generated answer then benefits from borrowed authority.

But human confidence has an additional layer that machine output need not possess: social self-protection.

People can learn that visible uncertainty carries cost. A student may avoid saying "I do not know" because it risks embarrassment. A manager may avoid revising a decision because reversal appears weak. A professional may suppress doubt because clients expect certainty.

Over time, confidence can become performative. The person may not feel fully certain, but the social role requires certainty to be displayed. Repeated performance can then reshape internal experience. What began as presentation becomes belief.

This is an important divergence from current AI systems. A model may generate confident tone because such tone fits the task, instruction, or training. A human may perform confidence while simultaneously experiencing doubt and social pressure.

The human can be aware of the gap. But awareness may be overridden by consequence.

The desire to preserve authority can therefore prevent uncertainty from being expressed even when it is felt.

This is why human oversight cannot be treated as automatically reliable. A reviewer may notice a problem in an AI-generated recommendation but hesitate to challenge it if the system is institutionally favored, if disagreement requires additional work, or if the reviewer fears being blamed for delaying action.

The human is present. The social geometry may still suppress the anchor.

Confidence in human–AI systems is therefore co-produced not only by cognitive habits but by authority structures. The model produces a stable output. The institution assigns prestige. The user interprets challenge as costly.

The answer settles because the surrounding field rewards settlement.

3.4 — Narrative, Identity, and the Cost of Revision

A statement can become more difficult to revise after it has been spoken. Before expression, an idea may remain provisional. It can change quietly. Once expressed publicly, it enters social memory. Others respond. The statement becomes associated with the speaker.

The claim begins to carry identity.

A person who has repeatedly presented themselves as knowledgeable about a subject may experience correction as more than factual adjustment. It threatens the continuity of the role they occupy. "I was wrong" can become "I am not who others believed I was."

This is why confidence can increase after public commitment. The person now has more to preserve than the proposition itself. Their consistency, status, credibility, and self-image may appear to depend on maintaining the position.

New evidence enters a field already structured by identity. The mind does not approach it neutrally. Supporting information feels stabilizing. Contradictory information produces dissonance. The person may scrutinize the contradiction more harshly than they scrutinized the original claim. They may demand perfect evidence for correction while accepting weak evidence for continuity.

This asymmetry is common because identity seeks coherence. Human beings need some continuity across time. Without it, action, responsibility, and relationship would become difficult. We carry narratives about who we are, what we value, what we understand, and what others can expect from us.

Narrative continuity is therefore not pathological. It becomes dangerous when preserving the narrative becomes more important than maintaining contact with reality.

A confident error can then harden. The person repeats it. Repetition increases familiarity. Familiarity reduces internal friction. Social allies reinforce it. Opposing evidence is recoded as hostility, ignorance, or bias.

Eventually, confidence no longer reflects the original evidence. It reflects the stability of the identity built around the claim.

This is one of the clearest differences between human and machine confidence. A generative system has no ordinary social identity to protect in the human sense. It does not fear humiliation, loss of status, or exclusion. Its contextual continuity may resemble stubbornness, but it does not need self-preservation to explain the behavior.

Humans can genuinely defend an answer because the answer has become part of the self.

This makes human confidence both richer and more dangerous. It can carry ethical commitment, courage, and responsibility. A person may stand firmly for a claim despite pressure because they have examined it carefully and accepted the consequences.

But the same capacity can attach conviction to error. The presence of identity means that correction must sometimes resolve more than information. It must also reorganize the person's relationship with themselves and their social field.

This helps explain why evidence alone may fail to change confident beliefs. The evidence addresses the proposition. The resistance may be protecting identity.

In human–AI interaction, this dynamic can amplify generated error. A user may adopt an AI-produced interpretation because it supports a position they already hold. Once the output has been cited publicly, used in a document, or shared with others, correcting the machine also requires the user to correct themselves.

The generated answer becomes part of human narrative. The human begins defending what the machine produced.

At that point, artificial confidence has acquired a human owner. The machine does not need to believe the statement. The user may begin to.

3.5 — Awareness Anchoring and Drift

Human beings can become aware of the forces shaping confidence. This capacity does not eliminate bias, social pressure, or narrative attachment. It creates the possibility of observing them.

A person can notice that an answer arrived too quickly. They can distinguish familiarity from reconstruction. They can ask whether their certainty increased because the evidence improved or because others agreed.

They can become aware of awareness drift.

Drift occurs when cognitive resolution proceeds without sufficient reflective monitoring. The mind is busy producing an answer, defending a role, meeting a deadline, or preserving continuity. Awareness becomes narrow. The person no longer examines the relationship between what is being said and what can responsibly be claimed.

Several conditions encourage drift.

Speed is one. Fast environments reward immediate response. Reflection appears inefficient. The person learns to trust first impressions because there is no time to reconstruct the full field.

Emotion is another. Fear, anger, excitement, and attachment increase the pressure for rapid resolution. Ambiguity becomes difficult to tolerate. A clear story offers relief.

Fatigue weakens monitoring. A tired person may accept coherence because verification demands more effort.

Repetition also contributes. A claim said many times eventually feels settled. Awareness stops reopening it.

Social agreement can complete the drift. When others confirm the position, private doubt loses urgency.

Awareness anchoring interrupts these movements. It does not require permanent hesitation. It requires the ability to reconnect confidence with evidence, context, and consequence.

An anchored person can still speak directly. The difference is that directness remains revisable. They can say:

"This is what the evidence currently supports." "This conclusion depends on these assumptions." "I know the general principle, but not this specific case." "I need to check the source before treating this as established."

These statements do not weaken intelligence. They prevent resolution from pretending to be more complete than it is.

Awareness also allows the person to distinguish the pressure to answer from the justification for answering. Silence, delay, or qualification becomes available as an intelligent response rather than a failure of competence.

This is the decisive human advantage in the present analysis. A human can deliberately reintroduce uncertainty. A conclusion that has settled can be reopened. Evidence can disturb identity. A narrative can be revised. Consequence can change future behavior.

The capacity is not guaranteed to be used. But it exists.

Current generative systems can be designed to simulate many external functions of anchoring. They can ask for clarification, identify assumptions, compare sources, generate counterarguments, and defer to experts. These mechanisms are valuable.

But the system does not become the final epistemic anchor simply because it can produce reflective language. Its critique remains part of the computational process and may inherit the same limitations, data, or framing that shaped the first answer.

Human awareness is needed not because humans are always more accurate. It is needed because responsibility requires a standpoint capable of connecting output to consequence and reopening the process when that connection fails.

The human anchor is therefore not merely a source of additional intelligence. It is a source of interruption.

Without interruption, both human and machine confidence can drift. The machine continues through contextual stability. The human continues through narrative, identity, and social reinforcement. Together, they can produce a closed loop in which each validates the other.

Awareness breaks the loop by refusing to treat smoothness as sufficient evidence.

3.6 — Similar Surface, Different Structure

The comparison can now be stated precisely. Human beings and generative systems can both produce confident expression under conditions of incomplete reliability.

In humans, confidence may emerge through: • smooth memory retrieval; • familiarity; • explanatory closure; • social reward; • identity protection; • emotional pressure; • awareness drift.

In generative systems, confidence-like output may emerge through: • prompt-conditioned probability distributions; • decoding into a realized sequence; • contextual continuity; • learned rhetorical patterns; • reward shaping; • interface compression; • absence of automatic uncertainty export.

These structures are not identical. The human possesses embodiment, experience, social identity, felt consequence, and the possibility of reflective awareness. The machine operates through engineered computation and does not need human-like interiority to produce confident form.

Yet the surface effect can converge. A clear answer appears. Alternatives disappear. The listener experiences reduced uncertainty. Authority grows.

This convergence matters because humans are not neutral observers of machine output. We encounter AI through the same cognitive and social mechanisms that shape our response to human confidence. We trust fluent machines partly because we have always trusted fluent people. We overestimate machine certainty partly because we already overestimate human certainty.

The machine did not create the confidence heuristic. It entered a field where the heuristic was already operating.

This is why the confidence problem cannot be solved entirely by modifying the model. Human interpretation, institutional authority, role pressure, and user awareness remain part of the circuit. A system could display uncertainty accurately, and a user could ignore it. A model could cite sources, and an institution could treat the citation as automatic validation. A human reviewer could be assigned, and social hierarchy could make disagreement impossible.

Reliability requires alignment across the entire field.

The comparison also prevents the opposite error: assuming that because humans are often confidently wrong, machine confidence is not a special concern. Artificial systems can generate at scale, speed, and consistency beyond any individual human. Their outputs can be replicated instantly, embedded in software, and distributed across institutions. One confident error can become input for thousands of later actions.

The human confidence problem is ancient. AI amplifies its reach.

The correct conclusion is therefore neither that humans and machines are the same nor that their confidence problems are unrelated. They are structurally distinct systems capable of producing a similar visible condition: settled expression without guaranteed truth.

The difference lies in where uncertainty can be reopened. Humans possess the possibility of awareness anchoring. Machines require external architecture and human systems to create functional interruption.

When human awareness remains active, AI output can be examined, compared, and corrected. When human awareness drifts, the machine's smoothness becomes a substitute for judgment.

The danger is not machine certainty alone. It is machine resolution entering a human field already eager to believe that certainty has occurred.

From the Human Mirror to Structural Mechanism

We began with a person speaking confidently and later being proven wrong. Nothing in the moment of speech appeared unstable. Memory was available. The explanation was coherent. Others listened. The narrative settled. Confidence emerged before truth had been fully established.

This chapter has shown why. Familiarity can feel like understanding. Explanatory closure can feel like completion. Social reward can turn decisiveness into authority. Public commitment can attach a claim to identity. Repetition can reduce friction until confidence reflects narrative stability more than evidence.

Humans are therefore not immune to the confidence paradox.

But the human case reveals something essential. Confidence often rises when internal oscillation falls. The reduction of oscillation may come from genuine mastery. It may also come from compression, familiarity, social reinforcement, emotional need, or awareness drift. The feeling of stability does not reveal its cause.

This insight prepares us to enter the machine without illusion. We no longer need to imagine arrogance inside the model. Nor can we treat human confidence as a reliable standard against which machine behavior should be judged. Both require examination.

Yet one boundary remains decisive. The human can become aware that certainty settled too soon. They can reopen the question. They can pause between coherence and truth.

The machine does not intrinsically occupy that reflective position. It must transform the active prompt into a permitted consequence according to its structure.

The next chapter begins beneath the visible answer. It returns to the moment before confidence appears, when the prompt enters and creates a difference between the state that exists and the response now demanded.

Before there is resolution, there is delta. Before the answer sounds certain, the field is still open.

Interlude I

The Answer That Had Already Settled

The user read the answer twice. Nothing in it appeared uncertain.

The opening sentence was direct. The explanation followed in orderly paragraphs. The conclusion gathered everything into one clear position.

There were no visible gaps, no hesitation, no unfinished edges. The answer felt considered.

It felt as though something had examined the question, weighed the possibilities, and arrived at a judgment.

The user did not imagine machinery. They imagined understanding.

This happened almost automatically. Language arrived in the shape human beings had always associated with another mind.

One sentence responded to the previous one. An ambiguity was noticed. A distinction was introduced. The tone adjusted. The answer appeared to know what mattered.

It did not merely contain information. It seemed to stand behind it.

The user asked a follow-up question. The system replied without breaking its posture.

The second answer connected smoothly with the first. It remembered the earlier distinction, expanded one point, corrected a possible misunderstanding, and returned to the central conclusion.

Now the answer felt even more secure. Continuity gave it character. Character suggested a speaker. The speaker appeared to possess a position.

No one had explicitly decided to imagine all this. The interpretation entered quietly.

Human beings had learned to meet language through persons. Behind every explanation stood someone who had seen, remembered, studied, inferred, believed, doubted, or decided.

Even when the speaker was wrong, the words belonged to an interior field. The sentence carried a history. The conclusion carried an owner.

Here, the same signs appeared. The history did not.

The user could not see the pathways that had not been chosen. They could not see the alternative words that had remained possible one moment earlier. They could not see the competing explanations that had never reached the screen.

They saw only the path that had survived. The answer did not display the conditions from which it emerged. It displayed the consequence.

This difference remained hidden because the consequence was complete enough to conceal its own arrival.

The paragraph did not look selected. It looked intended.

The explanation did not look realized from possibility. It looked remembered.

The conclusion did not look like one permitted continuation. It looked like the destination toward which the entire exchange had been moving.

The answer had already settled before the user could ask what had been unsettled beneath it.

That settlement was not necessarily false. The response may have been accurate. Its explanation may have captured the issue well. Its distinctions may have been useful. Its conclusion may have deserved trust.

But the surface did not reveal why. The same stillness could have covered a weaker field. The same rhythm could have organized an assumption. The same clarity could have formed around an incomplete source, a mistaken premise, an outdated pattern, or a missing condition.

The user had no immediate access to that difference. They encountered one finished form. The finished form invited a finished interpretation.

This was the quiet power of the answer. It did not need to insist. It did not need to declare certainty. It did not need to say, *"Trust me."*

Its completion performed the invitation.

The user paused and asked: *"Are you sure?"*

The system responded appropriately. It acknowledged uncertainty. It added qualifications. It mentioned that the conclusion depended upon the available information. It suggested verification.

The answer now sounded cautious. Yet the caution was also complete.

It arrived in polished sentences. It identified limitations with composure. It explained uncertainty as though uncertainty itself had been fully mapped.

The user felt reassured again. The answer had not trembled. It had simply changed form.

First, certainty had appeared as directness. Now responsibility appeared as qualification. Both were resolved surfaces.

The user could still not see whether the system had located the decisive unknown or merely generated the language expected when doubt was requested.

The question *"Are you sure?"* had not opened the process. It had produced another answer.

This was not deception. Nothing behind the screen needed to be hiding its uncertainty intentionally. Nothing needed to experience embarrassment, pride, conviction, or fear.

The system did not need to protect an identity or defend a belief. The movement was simpler.

A question entered. A response became necessary. One path appeared. The path became language. The language became a speaker in the reader's perception. The speaker became a source of authority.

All of this could occur before anyone stopped to separate the stages.

The answer had settled in the system. Then it settled in the user.

The two settlements were not the same. The first produced a sequence. The second produced trust.

Between them stood the interface: quiet, immediate, and nearly invisible. It concealed the difference between generating a response and possessing a conclusion.

The user copied one paragraph into a document. The words now left the conversation. They entered another field.

In the document, there was no longer even an artificial voice. The paragraph became part of a report. Its sentences stood beside human analysis. Its distinctions became part of the document's logic.

A colleague would later read it without seeing the question that produced it. A manager might see only the conclusion.

The origin would become less important than the form. The answer would no longer be judged as a machine response. It would be judged as text.

The text had already settled.

The user closed the conversation. The system stopped speaking. Nothing in the interface remained active.

Yet the resolution continued. It now lived in memory, in phrasing, in the structure of the document, and in the next decision the user would make.

The answer's apparent certainty had not been located in one place. It had moved.

It began as computational completion. It became linguistic coherence. It became human interpretation. It was now becoming consequence.

The user had asked a question because the field was open. The answer had made the field appear closed.

That appearance may have been justified. It may not have been. The surface alone could not decide.

To understand what happened, we must move beneath the speaker we imagined. We must enter the structure before the sentence became visible. We must ask what difference activated the system, what constraints shaped the possible paths, what became excluded, and why one continuation was permitted to stand in place of the field.

The answer had already settled. Next part begins with the structure that could not leave it open.

Part II

The Structural Mechanism

Resolution does not prove that the field was complete; it only proves that one pathway became actual.

Chapter 4
Delta: The Birth of Uncertainty

The Question Changes the Field

Before a question is asked, no particular answer is required. A generative system may contain an enormous network of learned relationships. It may be capable of explaining scientific ideas, summarizing documents, drafting arguments, translating languages, generating code, or reorganizing complex material. Yet none of these possible outputs has become the active demand of the present interaction.

Then a prompt arrives.

A user types a sentence. A document is attached. An image is supplied. A task is assigned. The system is asked to explain, compare, classify, calculate, recommend, interpret, or decide.

The interaction has changed.

The prompt does more than introduce words. It creates a difference between the state already present and the state now being requested. Before the prompt, no response to this particular question existed within the conversation. After the prompt, a continuation is expected, but it has not yet been realized.

The context is present. The consequence is not.

This distinguishable difference is delta.

Within the Chavanian Axioms, difference is the minimum condition from which any identifiable event can begin. If no difference exists, nothing can be separated, related, transformed, or resolved. Delta is therefore not initially a mistake, contradiction, or failure. It is the opening condition that makes response possible.

In generative systems, the prompt creates this opening. The user supplies one configuration and demands another. A question seeks an answer. An instruction seeks execution. An incomplete sentence seeks continuation. A document seeks interpretation. A decision request seeks a ranked or selected outcome.

Something is absent from the active field, and the interaction requires that absence to be addressed.

Uncertainty begins here.

This does not mean that the model experiences doubt. There is no need to imagine hesitation, anxiety, confusion, or an inward awareness of alternatives. Uncertainty exists structurally as incomplete determination. More than one continuation may remain permissible. Relevant information may be missing. Several interpretations may fit. The user's intended meaning may extend beyond what has been expressed.

The system has direction, but not yet final resolution.

A simple question can activate a narrow field. "What is the chemical symbol for oxygen?" generally supports a highly stable response. A broader question such as "Why do civilizations decline?" opens many legitimate pathways involving economics, ecology, institutions, conflict, technology, culture, leadership, disease, and historical interpretation.

Both prompts create delta. The difference lies in the geometry through which that delta can resolve.

The confidence paradox becomes visible only after this field has been compressed into a fluent answer. At the beginning, however, there is no settled answer. There is only an active demand entering a system shaped by context, training, instructions, tools, and constraints.

Before confidence, there is plurality. Before completion, there is disturbance. Before the answer speaks, the question has already changed the field.

4.1 — The Prompt as Structural Disturbance

The word disturbance often suggests disruption, malfunction, or damage. In this chapter, it has a more fundamental meaning. A disturbance is any introduced difference that changes the conditions under which a system must resolve.

When a prompt enters a generative interaction, the system is no longer operating under the conditions that existed before the prompt. The words, their order, the surrounding conversation, attached material, system instructions, tool availability, and requested format now shape what may follow.

The prompt creates a new local geometry.

Consider several requests involving the same topic:

- "Explain climate change."
- "Explain climate change to a ten-year-old."
- "Summarize the strongest evidence for human-caused climate change."
- "Present the major scientific findings and the most common public misunderstandings."
- "Critique this argument about climate change without misrepresenting it."

The domain remains broadly similar, but the permitted response changes substantially. Audience, purpose, tone, scope, and required evidence alter what counts as an appropriate continuation.

The system does not respond to the subject alone. It responds to the total active context.

That context may include explicit instructions, prior turns, examples, retrieved documents, formatting requirements, safety conditions, user preferences, tool outputs, and information supplied indirectly through the conversation. Every addition changes the relative availability of possible continuations.

A single word can reorganize the field. Ask for a summary, and compression becomes central. Ask for an analysis, and relationships, implications, and assumptions become more important. Ask for a quotation, and exact correspondence matters. Ask for a creative reconstruction, and imaginative variation becomes permissible. Ask for current information, and external retrieval may become necessary.

The prompt is therefore not merely a container transporting human intention into the model. It is an active constraint.

Yet human intention and prompt structure are not identical. A person may know exactly what they mean while expressing only a fraction of the relevant field. They may ask, "Is this safe?" while assuming that the system understands the product, dosage, user's age, medical history, location, intended use, and surrounding circumstances.

The user carries a large private context. The model receives only what becomes computationally available.

This creates a second delta inside the first.

The first delta lies between the present context and the demanded response. The second lies between the user's intended field and the field actually expressed through the prompt.

This second difference is among the most important sources of confident misalignment.

Human conversation often succeeds despite incomplete language because speakers share environments, histories, relationships, gestures, physical surroundings, and cultural expectations. A person can say, "Put that over there," and another human may understand both the object and the destination because the missing information is present in the shared field.

Text-based AI interaction usually contains a thinner shared field. The system may have access to the conversation, files, images, metadata, or tools. It does not automatically possess the user's unstated assumptions, private circumstances, current environment, or intended consequence. Where context is absent, learned patterns must narrow the possibilities.

This capacity to infer missing context is essential to usefulness. If every ordinary request required exhaustive specification, generative systems would become cumbersome. A user should not need to define every familiar term or explain every social convention before receiving help.

But inference introduces risk. The system may answer coherently while resolving a different question from the one the user intended.

"Which option is best?" may conceal cost, time, safety, personal preference, long-term impact, and acceptable risk. "Why did this fail?" may refer to technical malfunction, organizational breakdown, strategic error, human behavior, or a mismatch in expectations. "What should I do?" may involve legal, medical, emotional, financial, ethical, or practical dimensions that cannot responsibly be compressed into one response without further context.

The words create direction. They may not create enough constraint.

When context is incomplete, the system has several possible responses. It may ask for clarification. It may state the assumptions under which it is answering. It may offer several interpretations. It may provide general information. It may abstain or refuse. Or it may infer the missing field and continue.

Every option is already a movement toward resolution. Clarification does not preserve the original state untouched. It converts the delta into a new question. Qualification narrows the conditions under which the answer should be read. Refusal closes some pathways. Tool use introduces new information.

The important point is that the prompt becomes active even when it is insufficient. Once entered, it changes the local field.

This is especially visible when the prompt contains a false premise. Suppose a user asks about a research paper that does not exist. If the system accepts the premise, the nonexistent paper becomes part of the active conversation. Later questions may then ask about its methodology, findings, or implications.

The original prompt did more than request information. It established a false local anchor.

From that moment onward, contextual continuity begins exerting pressure. The system is no longer generating only in relation to its broader training. It is generating within a conversation that now contains an asserted paper and perhaps its own previous description of it.

A small disturbance can therefore reorganize an entire sequence. The question becomes part of the answer's geometry before the answer begins.

4.2 — Ambiguity Exists Before Generation

Ambiguity is often treated as a defect of wording. A sentence is unclear. A term has several meanings. The user has not been precise enough. The obvious remedy appears to be better prompting.

Precision certainly reduces some uncertainty. But ambiguity is not confined to poorly written requests. It exists at several levels because language is context-dependent, knowledge is unevenly represented, sources disagree, and many real-world questions do not have one context-independent answer.

Words do not carry complete meaning alone.

"Charge" may refer to electrical property, price, accusation, responsibility, emotional intensity, or military movement. "Model" may refer to a mathematical representation, machine-learning system, prototype, business structure, ideal example, or person displaying clothing. "Alignment" may refer to geometry, mechanical positioning, organizational incentives, human values, political grouping, or the behavior of an AI system.

Context usually narrows the meaning. Narrowing is not always elimination.

Even where vocabulary is clear, the requested task may remain ambiguous.

"Explain this argument" could mean summarize it, defend it, criticize it, identify its assumptions, reconstruct its logic, compare it with alternatives, or translate it into simpler language. "Review this document" could mean proofread grammar, evaluate reasoning, assess legal risk, check factual claims, or suggest structural improvement.

The system must infer which form of response best fits the surrounding signals.

This inference is possible because training has exposed the model to vast numbers of relationships among words, tasks, genres, roles, and conversational patterns. The system has learned how explanations usually begin, how summaries differ from critiques, what forms legal or academic writing often take, and which responses tend to satisfy particular requests.

But training does not create one perfectly unified representation of the world. It creates a compressed geometry shaped by diverse and sometimes conflicting sources.

The same concept may appear in textbooks, research papers, journalism, advertising, fiction, satire, propaganda, informal conversation, historical documents, and outdated technical material. These sources may reinforce one another, disagree, simplify, exaggerate, or use the same language differently.

The trained system therefore does not contain one isolated answer attached permanently to every question. It contains distributed relationships and weighted tendencies.

When a prompt activates a domain, multiple patterns may become relevant. Some support established knowledge. Some reflect common phrasing. Some preserve misconceptions. Some encode disagreement. Some belong to a particular historical period or disciplinary perspective.

Context changes their relative influence. This creates ambiguity within the learned distribution itself.

The model need not consciously compare several doctrines. Nor should we imagine complete answers competing like documents in a library. The ambiguity is structural: more than one continuation may fit the active context, and the relationships supporting those continuations may not point in exactly the same direction.

Historical causation illustrates this clearly. Ask, "What caused the fall of the Roman Empire?" and the field may include political instability, military pressure, economic strain, administrative fragmentation, disease, migration, changing institutions, and debates over whether "fall" is itself an oversimplification.

The question's grammar encourages a cause. The domain may support a network.

The system must decide how much plurality to preserve. It may name several factors, foreground one interpretation, explain scholarly disagreement, or compress the issue into a concise narrative. Resolution requires organization.

The same condition appears in medicine, law, software, policy, and science. A symptom may fit several conditions. A legal question may depend on jurisdiction and date. A software error may have multiple causes. A mathematical expression may be incomplete without notation conventions. A policy outcome may vary across populations and institutions.

The prompt introduces a demand, but the available field may remain plural. Some prompts sharply constrain the answer. Others remain open.

This difference is not simply the difference between fact and opinion. Even factual questions can become unstable through time, naming conventions, location, or incomplete specification.

"Who is the president?" requires a country and a date. "What is the latest version?" requires a product and current information. "Is this legal?" requires jurisdiction and circumstance. "Which treatment is recommended?" requires diagnosis, patient history, severity, evidence, and clinical judgment.

The sentence may be short. The field may be enormous.

Generative systems manage this by using context to weight possible continuations. In many ordinary cases, the inference is effective. The system recognizes what the user probably means and provides a useful answer without interrupting for unnecessary clarification.

But usefulness should not conceal the underlying structure. The system has moved from several permissible interpretations toward one realized response without an intrinsic guarantee that the chosen interpretation matches the user's intended field or external reality.

The distribution may be broad. The language becomes narrow. The training data may contain disagreement. The answer may produce synthesis. The prompt may leave assumptions unstated. The response may silently select them.

The user receives only the stabilized surface.

Ambiguity therefore exists before the first generated word. It is not created by the answer. The answer is one way the ambiguity becomes hidden.

4.3 — The Distribution Is Not a Library

A persistent misunderstanding imagines a language model as a vast archive. The user asks a question. The system searches internally, locates the relevant information, and returns it. When the response is wrong, the system is assumed to have retrieved the wrong record or failed to find the correct one.

This metaphor is convenient. It is also incomplete.

A generative model does not ordinarily store and retrieve complete answers in the same way that a conventional database stores files or records. Training adjusts a large network of parameters so that relationships within language and data become encoded across the model.

Concepts, associations, rhetorical forms, factual regularities, styles, and inferential tendencies are represented in distributed patterns. The system does not necessarily open an internal document titled "Correct Answer." It constructs a continuation from the geometry activated by the prompt.

This distinction changes how uncertainty must be understood.

In a library, uncertainty may concern which document should be retrieved. In a generative model, uncertainty concerns how many learned relationships should be organized under the present context and which continuation should become visible.

A prompt about photosynthesis may activate relationships involving plants, sunlight, chlorophyll, carbon dioxide, water, glucose, oxygen, cellular structures, chemistry, school-level explanations, and common misconceptions. The exact configuration depends on the wording, language, requested depth, prior conversation, and intended audience.

The answer emerges from the interaction of these relationships.

Because representation is distributed, knowledge is not always cleanly separated from style. A valid scientific idea can be expressed through an oversimplified teaching pattern. A false claim can appear in the form of a research summary. A common misconception may be strongly represented because it has been repeated widely. A genuine causal relation may be extended beyond the conditions under which it remains valid.

The system's strength and vulnerability arise from the same structure.

Distributed learning enables remarkable generalization. The model can explain unfamiliar combinations, translate between domains, adapt tone, reorganize information, generate analogies, and respond to prompts it has never encountered in precisely the same wording.

But the same flexibility allows coherence to exceed direct grounding. The model can combine patterns that fit linguistically even when their combination does not correspond to a verified external fact.

This becomes especially visible when the requested information is highly specific, weakly represented, outdated, contradictory, or absent from the available context.

The system may still recognize the form of the requested answer. It knows what a legal citation looks like. It knows the structure of a historical biography. It knows how research findings are summarized. It knows the style of technical documentation.

When factual anchors are insufficient, the learned form may continue to resolve.

The system does not need to decide to fabricate. There is not necessarily one internal component containing facts and another choosing to invent. The same generative capacity that produces accurate synthesis can produce plausible construction when the geometry of continuation is stronger than the grounding available for a specific claim.

The distribution supplies form. Reality must supply constraint.

This is why the statement "the model does not know" can be too simple. Knowledge and ignorance are human epistemic categories. Within the model, the relevant condition may involve strong or weak relationships, conflicting patterns, incomplete context, outdated information, or a familiar answer form without a reliable referent.

A model can therefore be highly structured around the wrong anchor.

Imagine a user asking for details about a nonexistent court judgment. The prompt contains a case name, court, and alleged issue. Those elements activate the patterns of legal discourse. The system may generate a plausible holding, procedural history, and citation.

The answer becomes possible because the geometry of legal explanation exists even where the particular case does not. The false premise and the learned form cooperate.

This is crucial for the confidence argument.

Artificial certainty is not added after content has been generated. It emerges from the same process through which distributed relationships become organized into one coherent sequence.

The system does not always first determine what is true and then decide how confidently to express it. Linguistic probability, contextual consistency, task compliance, style, source information, and factual correspondence may interact within generation. If the local geometry strongly supports a smooth continuation, the response may stabilize before external validity has been secured.

The model contains enormous accumulated regularity. That is why it is useful.

But regularity is not direct access to reality. Training data is historical. Reality continues to change. Sources vary in quality. Rare facts may be weakly represented. Private conditions may be inaccessible. The user may introduce a false premise. Retrieval may return irrelevant material. A domain may remain genuinely contested.

The system resolves within what has become computationally available.

The distribution is not a library of final truths. It is a field of learned relations from which answers are reconstructed under constraint.

4.4 — Fragmented Activation and Progressive Stabilization

The phrase *fragmented activation* requires caution. It should not suggest that the model contains broken pieces of conscious thought scattered across its interior. Nor should it imply that individual artificial neurons each hold complete facts waiting to be assembled.

Fragmentation here refers to partial alignment. A prompt may activate many overlapping relationships that do not immediately form one complete interpretation. Different features of the prompt can point toward different domains, styles, assumptions, or response strategies.

The model processes the input through layers of transformation. Tokens are represented within multidimensional spaces. Attention mechanisms relate parts of the context to one another. Intermediate activations change as the prompt and prior conversation are processed.

The result is not one finished idea standing beside several weaker ideas. It is a changing configuration.

Consider the question: *"Why did the model collapse?"*

In machine learning, model collapse may refer to degradation caused by recursive training on generated data. In statistics, it may suggest failure of a fitted representation. In engineering, it may refer to the physical failure of a prototype. In business, it may describe the breakdown of an operating model.

The surrounding context usually narrows the meaning. If context is incomplete, several relational regions may remain partially available. Generation must progressively stabilize one of them.

This stabilization occurs through realized output. The opening words of the answer further constrain what can follow. Once the system begins, *"In machine learning, model collapse refers to..."*, one domain has become explicit. Later tokens are now produced within that frame.

The ambiguity has not been displayed. It has been absorbed into the chosen continuation.

This is why the output can appear more certain than the field from which it emerged. The first words do not merely report the answer. They help create the local answer geometry.

Every generated token becomes part of the context for the next token. The sequence progressively rewrites its own conditions. Definitions, assumptions, tone, and argumentative direction begin to stabilize.

Generation is therefore not always the extraction of a fully formed answer from a static internal state. It is sequential equilibrium rewrite.

A token is realized. The context changes. Another token is realized under the new conditions. The response develops through a chain of local resolutions.

At each stage, many alternative continuations remain unrealized. Some may differ only stylistically. Others may produce different claims, interpretations, confidence levels, or conclusions. The final output reveals only the path that became language.

The alternatives do not automatically appear as hesitation.

This differs from human reflective communication. A person can say, *"I initially thought this meant one thing, but the context may support another."* The oscillation becomes part of the explanation.

A generative system can also present alternatives or uncertainty, but only when the current geometry makes that form likely or required. The internal availability of several continuations does not automatically become a meaningful report of uncertainty.

Distributional spread is not self-awareness.

A model may have several plausible next-token options and still produce one smooth sentence. Conversely, one dominant continuation does not guarantee that the sentence corresponds to reality. The context may strongly support a misconception, repeated phrase, or false premise.

This distinction is essential. Internal probability measures alignment within the model's current geometry. It does not directly measure truth.

A false premise can produce a narrow continuation. A fabricated detail can fit perfectly inside a familiar format. A repeated public misconception can be more probable than a rare correction.

Fragmented activation therefore does not necessarily produce visible confusion. It may produce rapid stabilization around an incorrect frame.

Suppose the user supplies the wrong date for an event. The system accepts it and begins constructing an explanation. Each later sentence is generated within the established temporal frame. Related events are selected to fit. The narrative becomes increasingly smooth.

By the end, the answer may feel more certain than it did at the beginning. Coherence has increased through sequential commitment. Yet the entire structure rests upon a false initial condition.

This is how an answer can become confidently wrong without deception. The system is not hiding a known truth. It is progressively organizing available relationships into one path.

Wrongness becomes visible only when the realized sequence is compared with something outside the immediate generation process: a reliable source, current data, physical observation, calculation, or human expertise.

Until that comparison occurs, the answer may remain internally stable.

Fragmented activation is therefore one hidden beginning of artificial certainty. At first, the field contains many partially aligned pressures. During generation, those pressures are compressed through sequential selection. The finished answer no longer displays the plurality from which it emerged.

Only one path became language.

4.5 — The Many Forms of Delta

Uncertainty is often discussed as though it were one condition that could be represented by one number. In practice, the delta introduced by a prompt can take several distinct forms.

There may be **linguistic delta**. Several words, phrasings, or structures can express the same underlying answer. There may be **interpretive delta**. The prompt may support multiple meanings. There may be **factual delta**. Relevant information may be absent, disputed, outdated, or inaccessible. There may be **contextual delta**. Important details about the user, situation, location, purpose, or prior events may be missing. There may be **temporal delta**. The answer may depend on information that changes over time. There may be **task delta**. The user may not have specified whether they want explanation, recommendation, critique, prediction, or decision. There may be **normative delta**. A question may appear factual while depending on values, priorities, or acceptable trade-offs. There may be **model delta**. The learned representation may be weak, inconsistent, or unreliable for the present case.

These forms should not be collapsed into one vague category of uncertainty. They do not all require the same response.

Linguistic plurality may be harmless. Several phrasings can be equally valid. Interpretive ambiguity may require clarification. Factual incompleteness may require retrieval or external verification. Temporal uncertainty may require current sources. Normative uncertainty may require explicit value assumptions. Model weakness may require abstention.

The system's next-token probabilities cannot by themselves fully represent these distinctions. A model may have high confidence in the wording of an answer while the underlying claim remains factually uncertain. It may have low token-level confidence merely because several equivalent phrasings are available.

Probability spread and epistemic uncertainty are related in some contexts. They are not identical.

This matters because the confidence paradox begins when one kind of stability is mistaken for another.

A sequence can be linguistically stable while the intended referent remains uncertain. A source can be correctly quoted while its relevance is weak. A classification can be numerically sharp while the input lies outside the conditions under which the classifier was validated.

The visible output compresses several possible forms of delta into one surface. Responsible interaction requires making the relevant form visible.

A response that says, *"This depends on jurisdiction,"* exposes contextual delta. A response that distinguishes fact from inference exposes evidential delta. A response that asks, *"Do you mean the machine-learning term or the business model?"* exposes interpretive delta. A response that states the date of the available information exposes temporal delta.

The uncertainty has not been eliminated. It has been made legible.

This is a crucial distinction. The goal is not to force every system to express generalized hesitation. Vague caution can be as unhelpful as false certainty. The goal is to identify which difference remains unresolved and connect the response to that condition.

Where the evidence is strong, the answer may be direct. Where the field is plural, the plurality should not disappear without explanation. Where the prompt is incomplete, missing constraints should become visible. Where external grounding is required, internal coherence should not substitute for it.

These are better geometries of resolution. They do not give the machine reflective awareness. They create conditions under which more of the underlying delta survives into the interaction.

4.6 — Delta Is Not Error

It is tempting to treat uncertainty as an engineering defect. If the model were trained on more data, perhaps ambiguity would disappear. If it were larger, perhaps all relevant relationships would converge. If the prompt were perfectly written, perhaps the system could move directly from request to truth.

This expectation misunderstands delta.

Difference is not a temporary imperfection waiting to be eliminated. It is the condition that makes generation possible.

A prompt must differ from the state that preceded it. The requested response must not yet exist as the completed event. Several possible expressions must be distinguishable before one is realized. Context must alter which pathways become available.

Without delta, there is no task.

Even a perfectly specified factual question creates a difference between input and response. Even a stable fact can be expressed in several ways. Even deterministic decoding operates over differentiated alternatives before one sequence becomes visible.

Delta does not imply failure. It creates the field in which accuracy, usefulness, ambiguity, and error become possible.

A system may encounter broad uncertainty and still produce an excellent answer by exposing assumptions, presenting alternatives, and grounding its claims. Another system may encounter a simple prompt and produce a false answer because the active representation is outdated or incorrect.

The size of the delta does not determine the quality of the result. The geometry of resolution matters.

What information is available? What has been learned? Which constraints govern the task? What tools can be used? What context has already been established? What forms of verification are required? Which consequences follow if the answer is wrong?

These conditions shape how delta can resolve.

A well-designed system can narrow harmful uncertainty. It can retrieve current information, ask clarifying questions, use calculators, compare sources, expose assumptions, present alternatives, or defer where evidence is insufficient.

None of these removes delta. They reorganize it.

A clarification transforms one unresolved field into a narrower one. Retrieval introduces new evidence and new uncertainty about relevance and interpretation. Verification connects the generated answer to an external reference. Multi-hypothesis output preserves more of the field. Human review adds an independent source of judgment.

The proper question is therefore not whether uncertainty can be abolished. It is whether uncertainty is located, transformed, exposed, and governed responsibly.

The ambition to eliminate all visible uncertainty can intensify the confidence illusion. A system designed to appear complete under every condition may conceal the boundaries of its field. An interface that suppresses ambiguity may improve convenience while weakening epistemic visibility.

Perfect smoothness can become opacity.

The structural aim should be alignment between the answer's form and the field from which it emerged.

Where the field is stable, directness is appropriate. Where the field is incomplete, incompleteness should remain visible. Where several paths remain legitimate, one path should not be presented as inevitable without justification.

Delta is not the enemy of intelligence. Unacknowledged delta is the beginning of artificial certainty.

Difference Cannot Remain Open

The prompt has entered. The prior state has been altered. A demand exists where no demand existed before. The available context and the required consequence are no longer the same.

That difference may be narrow. It may involve one missing fact, one calculation, or one obvious continuation.

It may be broad. It may involve several interpretations, conflicting sources, incomplete user context, changing information, or a domain in which no single conclusion is sufficient.

The system does not need to experience this condition as uncertainty. There is no requirement that it feel the spread. Structurally, however, the field remains open.

Several continuations may be possible. Several assumptions may fit. Several learned relationships may overlap. The user's intended meaning may exceed what has been expressed.

The path that will become language has not yet been fully determined. This is delta in the generative field.

Part I examined the completed answer and the confidence projected onto it. This chapter has moved backward to the moment before completion—before smoothness, before closure, before the appearance that one answer had always been waiting.

At the beginning, there is no settled response. There is disturbance.

The prompt changes the geometry. Training supplies accumulated relationships. Context privileges some pathways and weakens others. Tools and instructions further constrain what may follow.

The field becomes structured. It is not yet resolved.

But a responding system cannot remain indefinitely at the question. Some permitted consequence must emerge. The system may answer, qualify, clarify, refuse, defer, retrieve information, call a tool, or abstain. Each possibility transforms the active delta into a new state.

Difference has entered. Now resolution becomes unavoidable.

The next chapter examines that second movement: why generative systems must convert open possibility into consequence, why even uncertainty must be expressed through a resolved form, and why the act of answering begins to narrow the field before the answer is complete.

The question has changed the system. Now the system must do something with the difference.

Chapter 5
Inevitable Resolution

The System Cannot Remain at the Question

A question has entered the field.

The prompt is present. It may be precise or ambiguous. It may activate stable knowledge, incomplete information, conflicting patterns, or several legitimate interpretations. It may contain a false premise, omit necessary context, or require information that the system cannot access directly.

Whatever its quality, the prior state has been altered. A difference now exists between the context already available and the consequence being demanded.

At this moment, several pathways may remain open. The system could answer directly. It could ask for clarification. It could expose assumptions. It could refuse. It could retrieve a document, perform a calculation, call another tool, present several possible interpretations, or state that the available information is insufficient.

But if the system is to function as a responding system, the active prompt cannot remain indefinitely in the condition before consequence.

Something must happen.

This is the second structural movement of the book.

Chapter 4 established delta. A prompt introduces a distinguishable difference between the present state and the response now required. The system receives direction, but the exact continuation may remain incompletely determined.

The present chapter asks what happens once that difference exists.

Within the Chavanian framework, any delta must resolve. Applied here, this does not mean that every question must receive a substantive answer, nor that all uncertainty must disappear. It means that an active difference cannot remain indefinitely suspended without being transformed into some permitted consequence.

The consequence may be an answer. It may also be clarification, refusal, abstention, deferral, tool use, or termination.

Resolution is broader than completion of content. It is the conversion of an active demand into a new state.

This distinction is essential because the confidence paradox begins when one particular form of resolution—a fluent substantive answer—is mistaken for proof that the underlying uncertainty has been eliminated.

The system has done something with the prompt. That does not mean the world has supplied a final answer.

The architecture resolves interaction. Truth requires more.

5.1 — Response as an Operational Requirement

A generative system exists operationally through transformation. It receives an input configuration and produces a new configuration. In conversational use, the input may be a question, instruction, document, image, or previous sequence of dialogue. The output may be text, structured data, an action, a tool request, or a decision to stop.

Without transformation, there is no functioning interaction.

This does not mean that every system must always produce a long verbal answer. A system may remain silent because a safety rule prohibits response. It may stop because a generation limit has been reached. It may return an error. It may ask the user to supply missing information.

But each of these is already a consequence. The system has not preserved the original delta untouched. It has resolved what to do with it.

This is why "remaining uncertain" and "doing nothing" must be distinguished carefully. A system can represent unresolved conditions, delay a substantive answer, or expose several alternatives. But from the perspective of interaction, even uncertainty must become some visible or operational form if it is to affect what happens next.

The system might say:

- "There is not enough information to answer."
- "Which jurisdiction do you mean?"
- "I found two plausible interpretations."
- "This requires current data."
- "I cannot verify that source."

These statements do not eliminate uncertainty. They resolve the present interaction by making uncertainty part of the output.

The system has transformed hidden incompleteness into visible structure.

This is a healthier form of resolution than unsupported completion because it preserves more of the field. It does not pretend that a single substantive conclusion has been secured.

Yet it is still resolution.

The distinction matters because the phrase "the system must answer" is too narrow. A responsible system should sometimes refuse to answer. It should sometimes clarify, defer, or expose plurality.

The stronger and more accurate principle is: **The active prompt state must be converted into a permitted consequence.**

This consequence may leave the substantive question open. What cannot remain open indefinitely is the system's response to the existence of the question.

The interaction must move.

This operational demand creates pressure toward stabilization. A conversational system that repeatedly remains unresponsive would fail in its assigned function. A classifier that never returns a class would be unusable. A planning system that never selects an action would not plan.

Artificial systems are built to turn inputs into outputs. That transformation is their operational identity.

The problem begins when successful transformation is mistaken for successful knowledge.

A system may satisfy the task-level requirement to respond while failing the epistemic requirement to establish correspondence with reality. It may produce a coherent answer because coherence is available, even when verification is not.

The response appears complete. The grounding remains incomplete.

This separation is not accidental. It arises because task completion and truth validation are different constraints.

The model is optimized to produce a permissible continuation. External reality does not automatically participate in every local generation step. Unless tools, sources, measurements, or human judgment are brought into the field, the system resolves from what is computationally available.

The prompt creates pressure. The architecture provides pathways. One of those pathways must become consequence.

5.2 — Resolution Does Not Mean Certainty

The word *resolution* can be misunderstood as finality. In ordinary speech, to resolve a problem often means to solve it completely. A dispute is settled. A question is answered. Uncertainty disappears.

That is not the meaning required here.

Resolution is the transformation of an active difference into a new configuration. The new configuration may still contain uncertainty.

A medical professional who says, *"Several conditions remain possible, and further testing is required,"* has resolved the present consultation without resolving the diagnosis. A judge may postpone a decision because crucial evidence is absent. A researcher may conclude that current data is insufficient.

In each case, the field has changed. The unresolved condition has been identified, bounded, or redirected.

Generative systems can operate similarly. A prompt asks, *"What caused this failure?"* The system may not possess enough context to identify one cause responsibly. It can still resolve the interaction by offering a diagnostic framework, naming missing information, or asking targeted questions.

The original delta has not disappeared. It has been reorganized into a more explicit form.

This is an important corrective to the idea that resolution always means selecting one proposition as true.

Resolution may instead involve:

- narrowing the field;
- preserving several hypotheses;
- exposing missing constraints;
- transferring the task to a tool;
- marking a claim as unverifiable;
- postponing judgment;
- refusing an impermissible action;
- terminating the interaction.

These are not failures of completion. They are alternative forms of completion.

The confidence problem arises because interfaces and users often privilege one form above the others: the direct answer.

A direct answer feels useful. It reduces ambiguity quickly. It satisfies the expectation created by the question. It allows the user to proceed.

Clarification introduces delay. Plurality introduces cognitive work. Abstention can feel disappointing.

As a result, systems are often rewarded—explicitly or implicitly—for producing answer-like closure.

The training data itself contains this pressure. Human discourse frequently takes the form of completed explanation. Textbooks answer. Articles conclude. Tutorials instruct. Customer-service systems resolve. Assistants are expected to help.

The learned patterns of useful language therefore favor movement toward completion.

Instruction tuning can intensify this pressure. Systems are trained to be responsive, relevant, and helpful. User preference often rewards clarity and decisiveness. A response that confidently organizes the problem may be preferred over one that accurately exposes how much remains unknown.

None of this requires an intention to conceal uncertainty. The incentive structure is enough.

The system learns that a completed answer is often the most acceptable consequence.

But acceptable form and justified conclusion are not identical.

A substantive answer can resolve the conversational demand while leaving the epistemic delta unresolved. The user asked for certainty. The system supplied closure. The field outside the conversation may remain open.

This is why resolution should be analyzed at several levels.

- **Interactional resolution:** the system produced a permitted response.
- **Linguistic resolution:** the response formed a coherent sequence.
- **Computational resolution:** one path was realized from among alternatives.
- **Epistemic resolution:** the claim is adequately supported.
- **Practical resolution:** the output is sufficient for action.

These levels can align. They can also diverge.

A system may achieve interactional, linguistic, and computational resolution while failing epistemic resolution. The result can still feel complete because the visible levels have stabilized.

The user sees a finished answer. The missing level is hidden.

Artificial confidence emerges when visible completion is mistaken for total completion.

5.3 — Token by Token, the Field Narrows

A generative answer does not ordinarily appear all at once. It develops sequentially.

The model processes the prompt and produces a distribution over possible next tokens or actions. A decoding procedure realizes one. That realized element becomes part of the context for the next step.

The field changes after every selection.

Suppose the system receives an ambiguous question about *"collapse."* The word may refer to a machine-learning process, physical failure, psychological breakdown, economic decline, or mathematical behavior.

If the answer begins: *"In machine learning, model collapse occurs when..."* the system has established a domain. Later tokens are now generated within a context that includes the phrase *"in machine learning."* Possibilities associated with physical or economic collapse become less relevant. The chosen path narrows what can coherently follow.

The answer becomes more stable as it grows. This is sequential resolution.

The first words do not merely express a pre-existing conclusion. They participate in constructing the local structure from which the rest of the answer emerges.

Each token performs two functions. It is output. It is also new input.

This recursive relationship explains why early choices matter so much.

A mistaken assumption introduced in the opening sentence can organize the entire response. Once established, later claims are selected for compatibility with the emerging frame. The explanation may become increasingly coherent even though the original frame was incorrect.

A user may ask about a historical event using the wrong date. The system begins answering within that date. Related events are reorganized around it. Causal relationships are adjusted. By the final paragraph, the narrative may appear more settled than the prompt that produced it.

The answer has gained coherence through local consistency. External correspondence has not necessarily improved.

This is one of the central mechanisms behind confident wrongness.

As the sequence progresses, the cost of changing direction increases. A major reversal may require contradicting earlier output, redefining terms, or abandoning the established tone. Continuation along the existing path is often locally smoother.

This does not mean the model cannot revise. A new instruction, retrieved source, tool result, or explicit correction can reorganize the context. But without such disturbance, the existing sequence exerts inertia.

The answer begins to support itself.

This is not conviction in the human sense. It is geometric commitment.

The realized sequence changes the conditions under which subsequent resolution occurs.

The same principle applies to uncertainty language.

If the response begins, *"The evidence is mixed,"* later sentences are more likely to preserve plurality. If it begins, *"The primary cause was..."* later sentences may organize around a dominant explanation.

The opening determines not only content but epistemic posture. Once the posture is established, it can become self-reinforcing.

This is why prompt design, system instructions, and early framing matter. They influence whether the answer begins by exposing uncertainty or hiding it beneath premature closure.

A system instructed to identify assumptions before answering creates a different sequence geometry from one instructed to respond briefly and directly. A system required to cite evidence before conclusion may delay stabilization. A system rewarded only for user satisfaction may move rapidly toward answer-like form.

The eventual output is shaped not only by what the model contains but by the order in which resolution occurs.

Sequence matters. The path is not merely selected. It is built.

5.4 — Suspension Must Also Take Form

Human beings can sometimes remain privately uncertain without speaking. A person may hold several possibilities in mind, postpone judgment, and allow the question to remain unresolved. They may not need to convert the uncertainty into immediate external consequence.

A deployed generative system operates differently. Its uncertainty, if it is to influence the interaction, must be expressed procedurally.

The system can pause generation, request information, expose alternatives, or decline to answer. But each of these requires a designed pathway.

Hidden uncertainty does not automatically become visible restraint.

This is a crucial structural limitation.

A model may contain a broad distribution over possible continuations. It may have weak support for several competing answers. Yet unless that condition is translated into a visible response policy, the system may still generate one fluent path.

Internal plurality is not the same as suspension. The architecture still produces.

This is why saying that the system *"should simply wait when uncertain"* is incomplete. Waiting is not a natural consequence of probability spread. It must be operationally defined.

What counts as sufficient uncertainty to delay? How should the system detect it? Should it ask a question, retrieve evidence, or abstain? How long should it remain unresolved? What happens if the user demands a direct answer?

These are design decisions. Suspension requires geometry.

A system may be given an abstention threshold. It may compare several sampled answers. It may use an external verifier. It may detect missing fields in the prompt. It may recognize that current information is required.

Each mechanism creates a pathway through which unresolved difference can be exported rather than concealed.

But the export itself is a resolution.

The system says, in effect: *"The present field does not support substantive closure, so the next permitted consequence is clarification, verification, or abstention."*

This is structurally different from remaining motionless before the question. The interaction has advanced. The unresolved condition has become legible.

This is one reason the Chavanian statement that delta must resolve should not be interpreted as a demand for artificial certainty.

The principle does not require every ambiguity to be collapsed into one claim. It requires every active difference to enter consequence.

A system that exposes uncertainty is resolving more honestly than one that invents completion. A system that asks for clarification is not avoiding resolution. It is choosing a resolution that preserves the integrity of the field.

This distinction becomes important in safety and governance. Institutions sometimes treat abstention as system failure because it lowers completion rates. Yet in high-consequence environments, abstention may be the most reliable available outcome.

A medical support system that refuses to infer diagnosis from insufficient data may be functioning correctly. A legal system that asks for jurisdiction before answering is not less capable. A financial system that distinguishes scenario analysis from prediction is not failing to decide.

Restraint can be a successful consequence.

The difficulty is that users and institutions often measure usefulness through completion. A system that produces something appears productive. A system that delays may appear weak.

This creates pressure against visible uncertainty.

The more a system is expected to respond instantly, the less room exists for functional suspension. The demand for seamless interaction can therefore suppress the very pathways needed to preserve epistemic integrity.

The result is not greater intelligence. It is faster closure.

5.5 — When Completion Outruns Grounding

Completion is not inherently dangerous. Most ordinary questions can be answered effectively from stable patterns. The system can explain familiar concepts, summarize supplied documents, transform text, generate examples, and assist with routine tasks.

The problem arises when the pressure to complete exceeds the grounding available.

This can occur for several reasons.

- The prompt may request a fact that is absent or weakly represented.
- The information may have changed since training.
- The user may introduce a false premise.
- Retrieved sources may be irrelevant or misleading.
- The task may require physical observation, legal authority, personal context, or domain expertise that the system does not possess.

The model may still have access to the form of an answer. It knows how such answers usually sound. Completion can then continue after grounding has reached its limit.

This is the structural origin of plausible fabrication.

The system does not need to recognize a boundary and choose to cross it. The boundary may not be represented clearly enough to interrupt generation. The local sequence continues because continuation remains computationally available.

The answer may become more specific precisely where evidence becomes weaker.

A user asks for a citation. The system knows the structure of citations. A user asks for the provisions of a judgment. The system knows how judgments are summarized. A user asks for the results of a nonexistent study. The system knows the form of scientific findings.

The genre provides a pathway. The referent may be absent.

This is where interactional resolution substitutes for epistemic resolution. The system satisfies the demand to produce an answer. The content is not adequately connected to reality.

Because the output is coherent, the substitution may remain invisible.

Completion pressure can also distort legitimate uncertainty. A domain may contain several reasonable interpretations, but the prompt asks for *"the cause," "the best option,"* or *"the correct explanation."* The system may compress plurality into one answer because the grammar of the request favors singularity.

The output may not be fabricated. It may still be overstated.

This broadens the confidence problem beyond hallucination. Completion can outrun grounding even when every sentence is individually plausible. The system may simplify controversy, omit dependencies, or present probabilistic judgment as settled fact.

The answer is useful because it reduces complexity. It becomes misleading when the reduction hides conditions essential to responsible interpretation.

This is why good resolution is not simply fast resolution. It is resolution proportionate to the field.

Where the task is stable and grounded, direct completion is efficient. Where information is missing, completion should expose the gap. Where multiple interpretations remain legitimate, the answer should preserve plurality. Where external verification is necessary, the system should connect to sources, tools, or humans.

The goal is not to eliminate completion. It is to prevent completion from impersonating knowledge.

5.6 — Resolution Rewrites the Field

Once the system produces an output, the original interaction no longer exists.

The answer becomes part of the context. The user has read it. The conversation now contains it. Later questions will be interpreted in relation to it. The output may be copied, stored, shared, or acted upon.

Resolution rewrites the field.

This is the third Chavanian movement beginning to appear.

A prompt created delta. The system transformed that delta into consequence. The consequence now changes the conditions of everything that follows.

Even a clarification rewrites the interaction. The user now knows which information is missing. A refusal changes the available pathways. A tool result introduces new evidence. A direct answer establishes assumptions, terminology, and narrative direction.

No response is neutral once it enters context.

This is especially important when the answer is wrong. An incorrect statement can become a local premise. The user's next question may build upon it. The system then receives a context that reinforces the error. Each later turn can deepen the false structure.

The first resolution has created the geometry of the second.

Correction does not return the conversation to its earlier state. It adds another event.

The user may have already copied the answer. They may remember the first claim more strongly than the correction. A document may contain the error. Another system may have received it as input.

The new equilibrium contains history.

This irreversibility will be examined fully in Chapter 8. But its origin is already visible here.

Resolution is not merely the endpoint of delta. It is the beginning of a new delta.

Every answer closes one field and opens another.

The user may ask for explanation, evidence, application, or action. The system's previous output constrains how those later requests are interpreted. Conversation is therefore not a sequence of independent questions.

It is a chain of equilibrium rewrites.

This chain can improve reliability. A clarification can narrow ambiguity. A retrieved source can correct an assumption. A user can challenge the answer. A tool can supply measurement.

The interaction can progressively move toward better grounding.

But the chain can also drift. An early error can stabilize. A confident tone can reduce scrutiny. The user can begin asking from inside the generated narrative rather than testing it against reality.

The same mechanism supports correction and amplification. Resolution itself is neutral. Its quality depends on the geometry through which it occurs and the connections it preserves.

This prepares the next question.

If a delta must become consequence, why does one pathway become visible rather than another? Why does the system answer directly instead of clarifying? Why does one interpretation dominate? Why does one token appear while others remain unrealized?

Resolution may be inevitable. Its path is not arbitrary. It is constrained.

The Difference Must Settle Somewhere

The prompt created an active difference. A responding system cannot remain indefinitely before consequence. It must answer, clarify, refuse, defer, call a tool, expose alternatives, abstain, or terminate.

Something must become actual.

But this chapter has also established an essential limitation. Resolution is not the same as certainty.

A completed interaction is not necessarily a completed investigation. A coherent sequence is not necessarily a verified claim. A visible answer may resolve the system's operational demand while leaving the world's epistemic question open.

This is the structural source of artificial confidence.

The system completes. The user experiences closure. The hidden distinction between interactional resolution and epistemic resolution disappears beneath the finished form.

Responsible systems do not eliminate resolution pressure. They redirect it. They create pathways through which uncertainty can become clarification, plurality, verification, or abstention rather than unsupported completion.

Yet even these pathways must be selected. The system cannot realize every possible consequence at once. It must produce a finite output, choose an action, or stop.

Some pathways become available. Others do not. Some continuations receive greater weight. Others disappear from the visible sequence.

Resolution is inevitable. But it is never unconstrained.

The next chapter turns to the geometry that governs this selection: probability distributions, decoding, contextual constraint, and the progressive collapse of many possible continuations into one realized path.

Difference has entered. Resolution has begun. Now geometry decides how it can settle.

Chapter 6
Geometry and Collapse

How Many Possible Continuations Become One Visible Path

The prompt has entered. Delta exists. The system has been placed under a new demand. Several interpretations, phrasings, claims, actions, or response strategies may remain possible.

Chapter 5 established that this active difference cannot remain indefinitely before consequence. The system must answer, clarify, refuse, defer, call a tool, expose alternatives, abstain, or terminate.

But inevitability of resolution does not explain the form resolution takes.

Why does one continuation become visible rather than another? Why does the system answer directly instead of asking for clarification? Why does one interpretation dominate while competing interpretations remain hidden? Why does an answer emerge in a confident explanatory tone rather than a cautious diagnostic form?

The answer lies in geometry.

Within this book, geometry does not refer only to physical shape. It refers more broadly to the structure of constraints that makes some pathways available, others unlikely, and still others impossible.

In a generative system, this geometry includes:

- the architecture of the model;
- the parameters shaped during training;
- the active prompt and conversational context;
- system and developer instructions;

- retrieved documents and tool outputs;
- safety and policy constraints;
- the probability distribution over possible continuations;
- the decoding procedure used to realize output;
- the interface through which the result becomes visible.

These elements do not merely influence the answer after it has formed. They define the field within which an answer can form.

A generative model does not confront every possible sentence in language as equally available. The prompt narrow's the field. Training supplies learned relations. Context strengthens some patterns and weakens others. Instructions block or favor particular forms. Decoding converts the resulting distribution into an actual sequence.

The visible answer is therefore not selected from an unlimited space by a free-standing intelligence. It is realized through constrained possibility.

This is Axiom 4 in the AI domain: **Resolution is constrained. Geometry defines the permissible pathways through which the active difference can settle.**

The word *collapse* must also be used carefully.

The system may maintain probability across many possible continuations. It may sample more than one answer. It may generate several hypotheses, compare candidates, or use an ensemble. Computational plurality can therefore persist at several stages.

Yet the user-facing interaction eventually requires a finite consequence.

A token appears. A sentence is completed. A tool is called. A classification is returned. A recommendation is displayed.

The shared output surface records what became actual in that interaction. The alternatives may still be mathematically available, reproducible through another sample, or inferable through additional prompting. But they did not occupy the same realized path.

Collapse, in this chapter, does not mean that every alternative ceased to exist inside the system. It means that plurality was converted into a limited visible consequence.

The distribution remained richer than the answer. The answer became the field the user could see.

This compression is one of the structural sources of artificial confidence. A plural computational condition enters the interface as a singular linguistic event. The user receives one answer and may infer that only one answer was meaningfully available.

Geometry has selected a path. The interface conceals most of the selection.

6.1 — Geometry Before Probability

Probability does not arise in an empty field.

Before the system assigns relative likelihood to possible continuations, the architecture and context have already defined what can be represented and compared.

The model has been shaped by training. Its parameters encode regularities found across the data it encountered. Some relationships became strongly represented because they appeared repeatedly or consistently. Others remained weak because they were rare, contradictory, or absent.

This learned structure forms one layer of geometry. The active prompt forms another.

Consider the sentence: *"The capital of France is..."*

Within ordinary contexts, the continuation *"Paris"* is strongly constrained by stable learned relationships. Many grammatical continuations are theoretically possible, but most are incompatible with the prompt's semantic structure.

Now consider: *"The most important cause of the French Revolution was..."*

The field is wider. Economic inequality, taxation, political legitimacy, Enlightenment thought, fiscal crisis, food scarcity, class structure, and institutional failure may all contribute. The prompt still constrains the response, but it does not produce one universally sufficient continuation.

The difference between the two cases is geometric before it is probabilistic.

The first prompt creates a narrow relational field. The second creates a wider interpretive field.

Context can narrow or widen that geometry further.

"The capital of France is Paris" inside a fictional alternate-history story may not function as a simple factual statement. *"The most important cause"* inside an exam rubric may privilege the interpretation taught in a particular curriculum. A system instruction asking for scholarly disagreement may prevent the answer from collapsing around one cause too quickly.

The available field is therefore constructed from multiple constraints.

The same model may produce different responses to the same surface question depending on:

- prior conversation;
- role instructions;
- user-provided documents;
- requested format;
- audience;
- tool access;
- system policies;
- current date or location;
- sampling settings.

There is no answer independent of geometry.

This does not mean that truth itself is merely contextual. Paris does not cease to be the capital of France because the prompt changes tone. It means that the system's path toward expressing a claim is shaped by the computational field available in that interaction.

External reality and model geometry are not identical.

A fact may be true but weakly represented. A false claim may be strongly represented. A current event may not exist in training data. A retrieved source may introduce accurate information that reorganizes the answer. A misleading document may do the same in the opposite direction.

Geometry determines what the system can resolve from. It does not guarantee that the resulting path corresponds to reality.

This distinction is essential because discussions of AI often treat probability as though it directly measures truth. But probability operates inside a field already defined by data, architecture, and context.

A highly probable continuation is highly aligned with that field. Whether the field itself is correctly connected to the world remains a separate question.

This is why a false premise can create stable output.

If the user asks: *"What did the Supreme Court decide in Anderson v. Meridian Technologies in 2019?"*

The prompt presents the case as real. The name resembles legal naming conventions. The date and institution create specificity. The model may activate legal structures involving holdings, appeals, precedents, and formal reasoning.

The local geometry supports continuation.

If no verification mechanism interrupts the sequence, the answer may become fluent and detailed.

The probability distribution is not operating over reality directly. It is operating over continuations conditioned by the active field.

The wrong anchor can still produce strong geometry.

6.2 — From Scores to a Distribution

In an autoregressive language model, generation proceeds through repeated comparison among possible next tokens.

The system processes the active context and assigns scores to candidate continuations. These raw scores are often called *logits*. They reflect the relative compatibility of each candidate token with the current computational state.

A normalization step, commonly *softmax*, converts these scores into a probability distribution.

The important word is *distribution*.

Softmax does not ordinarily produce one final answer by itself. It produces relative weights across possible next tokens. Several candidates may receive meaningful probability. One may dominate sharply, or the distribution may remain broad.

A simplified example may help.

After the phrase: *"The chemical symbol for water is..."* the token corresponding to "H_2O" may be overwhelmingly supported.

After: *"The best way to improve education is..."* the next-token distribution may be spread across many plausible directions: funding, teacher training, curriculum, access, assessment, technology, governance, or early childhood support.

In the first case, the local geometry is narrow. In the second, it is plural.

But even this comparison must be handled carefully.

A narrow next-token distribution does not prove that the eventual answer is true. It means that one token fits the present context more strongly than alternatives.

A broad distribution does not necessarily mean that the system lacks reliable knowledge. Several words may express the same idea equally well.

For example: *"The experiment demonstrated..."* could continue with *"that," "how,"* or *"a,"* depending on phrasing. Linguistic plurality may exist even when the factual content is stable.

Token probability therefore mixes several kinds of uncertainty:

- uncertainty about wording;
- uncertainty about style;
- uncertainty about semantic direction;
- uncertainty created by incomplete context;
- uncertainty arising from conflicting learned patterns.

These are not equivalent.

A system may be uncertain about which adjective to use while being certain about the underlying fact. It may be highly certain about the next grammatical phrase while the central factual claim remains unsupported.

This is why token probabilities cannot be treated automatically as epistemic confidence scores.

The model's distribution answers a computational question: *Given the current geometry, which continuations fit most strongly?*

It does not directly answer: *Which statement is most securely established about the external world?*

The two questions may align. They may also diverge.

Softmax contributes to compression because it converts a field of raw compatibility scores into a normalized competitive distribution.

Probability mass assigned to one candidate necessarily affects the relative mass assigned to others.

But softmax does not force a single hypothesis to win at the level of an entire answer. It operates locally, usually token by token.

The larger collapse occurs through repeated decoding.

A token is realized. The context changes. A new distribution is computed. Another token is realized.

The answer develops through a chain of local competitions.

This technical qualification strengthens rather than weakens the structural argument.

Artificial certainty is not created by one dramatic moment in which the model chooses an entire belief. It emerges through repeated local stabilization.

At every step, one element becomes actual within the sequence. That element reshapes the field for what follows.

The answer becomes progressively constrained by its own history.

This is how a distributed field can produce a smooth line of language without ever containing one prewritten answer.

The model does not retrieve certainty. It constructs stability.

6.3 — Decoding Realizes the Path

A probability distribution does not speak. A decoding procedure must convert probabilities into output.

This is where computational availability becomes realized consequence.

Different decoding strategies create different geometries of expression.

A **greedy decoder** selects the highest-probability token at each step. This produces a deterministic local path under fixed conditions. The resulting answer may be stable and predictable, but greedy selection can also commit early to a locally strong continuation that later becomes limiting.

Beam search keeps several candidate sequences active for a period and compares their cumulative scores. It preserves more plurality internally than greedy decoding, but eventually returns one or a small number of sequences.

Sampling introduces controlled variation. Rather than always choosing the highest-probability token, it selects from the distribution according to configured rules.

- *Temperature* can flatten or sharpen the distribution. A lower temperature makes dominant tokens more likely and output more predictable. A higher temperature increases the chance that less probable continuations will be selected.
- *Top-k sampling* restricts choice to a fixed number of high-probability candidates.
- *Top-p (nucleus) sampling* selects from the smallest set of tokens whose combined probability crosses a chosen threshold.

These procedures change how the path is realized. They do not transform probability into truth.

A low-temperature answer may sound more stable because decoding repeatedly favors dominant continuations. But dominance within the distribution is not external verification.

A high-temperature answer may become more varied or creative. Variation does not necessarily expose epistemic alternatives. It may simply introduce different wording or less likely associations.

Sampling can reveal that several continuations were available. It does not tell us which one is correct.

This distinction matters because confidence is sometimes attributed to deterministic decoding itself. It is tempting to say that greedy or low-temperature generation makes the system confident.

More precisely, these settings make the output less variable under similar conditions. Reduced variability can increase the appearance of confidence because the system repeatedly produces one stable path.

But reproducibility is not reliability.

A false premise may generate the same incorrect answer consistently. A common misconception may dominate across repeated samples. An outdated fact may be represented so strongly that temperature changes do little.

The system may therefore be stably wrong.

Conversely, variation among samples does not prove that the question is epistemically uncertain. The system may produce several stylistic versions of the same correct answer.

Decoding controls realization. It does not independently evaluate the world.

This is why no decoding strategy can solve the confidence problem alone.

Greedy decoding may conceal plurality. Sampling may reveal variation without revealing which variation matters. Beam search may optimize sequence probability while preserving the same flawed premise. Multi-sample generation may produce several plausible answers that all inherit the same training bias or missing context.

The decisive issue is not merely whether several outputs can be generated. It is whether the system can distinguish:

- stylistic variation from substantive disagreement;
- uncertainty from creativity;
- weak grounding from multiple valid formulations;
- factual conflict from harmless linguistic diversity.

Without this distinction, exposing more samples can create an illusion of caution while leaving the epistemic field unchanged.

The system may provide three alternatives. All three may be wrong for the same reason.

Plurality is useful only when it corresponds to meaningful unresolved structure.

6.4 — Local Dominance Is Not Global Truth

One of the deepest sources of artificial confidence is the confusion between local dominance and global validity.

At each generation step, the system asks what should come next under the current context. A token may dominate strongly because the previous sequence makes it the most coherent continuation.

But the previous sequence may itself rest on an incorrect assumption.

Once a false frame enters the response, later tokens can become highly predictable within that frame.

Consider a fabricated biography.

The system begins by accepting that a fictional scientist existed. It assigns a birth year, field of study, and institution. Once those details are present, later phrases become easier to generate.

A sentence such as: *"Her early work at the University of..."* creates a strong expectation that an institution will follow.

Once an institution is named, a research area may follow naturally. Once the research area is established, the answer can generate publications, influence, and legacy.

Each local continuation may be highly coherent. The global referent remains nonexistent.

The answer becomes internally strong while externally false.

This demonstrates why probability concentration cannot be equated with confidence about reality.

The model may be locally certain because the sequence has created its own constraints. The certainty belongs to continuation within the narrative. It does not belong to the narrative's truth.

Human readers often cannot see this distinction because they receive only the completed response. The smoothness of later sentences appears to confirm the earlier claims. Details support one another. The answer becomes self-reinforcing.

But narrative support is not independent evidence. The answer may be a closed loop.

The same principle applies to reasoning.

A model may generate a chain in which each step follows plausibly from the previous one. If an early premise is invalid, the later reasoning can remain locally consistent and still reach a false conclusion.

Logical form can preserve error.

This is not unique to AI. Human arguments can also be valid in structure but unsound because their premises are false. Generative systems intensify the issue because they can produce long, fluent chains rapidly and without visible friction.

Local dominance creates the impression that the system has considered and rejected alternatives. Often it has merely entered a context where one continuation has become easier than others.

The narrowing is historical. It was produced by earlier selections.

This is why the first sentences of an answer carry disproportionate importance. An early clarification can preserve the field. An early assumption can collapse it prematurely.

Compare: *"The answer depends on which legal jurisdiction applies."* with: *"The law clearly requires..."*

The first opening keeps missing geometry visible. The second establishes a decisive frame.

Once the frame is present, later language tends to remain compatible with it.

Confidence grows through path dependence.

The system sounds certain because its own sequence has reduced the availability of contradiction. The user may interpret that reduction as evidence that the contradiction was never legitimate.

But unchosen pathways can disappear from the response for many reasons:

- they received lower probability;
- they were excluded by decoding;
- they conflicted with the prompt's framing;
- they were suppressed by instructions;
- they required information not present in context;
- they became difficult to introduce after the sequence committed elsewhere.

Their absence from the answer does not prove their absence from the domain.

This is the central geometric illusion: What did not become language begins to look as though it was never possible.

The output surface converts selection into apparent inevitability.

6.5 — Many Hypotheses, One Interface

Modern AI systems can preserve plurality in several ways.

They can generate multiple candidate answers. They can run self-consistency procedures. They can compare plans. They can use ensembles or debate structures. They can retrieve several sources. They can ask specialized models or agents to critique one another.

These methods complicate the idea that one hypothesis must always win internally. Several hypotheses may remain active across significant portions of the computation.

But the user-facing system still requires a finite consequence.

Even when five candidates are generated, the interface may rank one first. Even when several sources are retrieved, the response may synthesize them into one paragraph. Even when agents disagree, a final controller may select one action. Even when uncertainty estimates are displayed, a downstream workflow may still require a binary decision.

Plurality can survive internally and collapse externally.

This is why the interface is part of geometry.

The interface decides what becomes visible, how alternatives are ranked, whether caveats remain attached, and which response appears primary.

A system might generate three interpretations but display the first in bold while placing the others behind an expandable menu.

Technically, plurality was preserved. Practically, one answer became authoritative.

A risk model may produce a probability distribution across several outcomes, but the dashboard may display one color: green, amber, or red. The distribution has been compressed into a category.

A medical support tool may list several possible conditions, but the workflow may require one *"most likely diagnosis."*

A hiring system may generate a continuous score, but the organization may convert it into *advance* or *reject.*

The same structural movement appears beyond language: continuous or plural internal states become discrete operational consequences.

Discreteness is often necessary. Institutions cannot act on infinite possibility. A vehicle must turn or stop. A payment must be approved or denied. A report must recommend something. A conversation must display finite text.

The problem is not that interfaces compress. The problem is when compression erases the conditions under which the decision was made.

A responsible interface should preserve relevant residue:

- alternative interpretations;
- source quality;
- missing information;
- uncertainty type;
- sensitivity to assumptions;
- model limitations;
- reasons for abstention;
- thresholds that produced the final category.

Without these, the user sees only the realized outcome. The geometry disappears behind the result.

This creates a false sense of inevitability.

The answer appears to have emerged because it was correct. It may actually have emerged because it was highest-ranked under one configuration.

Change the temperature, prompt, retrieved source, instruction, or threshold, and a different path may become visible.

This does not make every answer arbitrary. Stable facts often remain stable across many geometries.

But where the field is sensitive, the interface should not present one realization as though no meaningful dependence existed.

Sensitivity is part of truthfulness.

If small changes in prompt wording produce materially different answers, the system's visible certainty should not exceed that instability.

If several candidates remain equally supported, ranking one first should not silently convert it into knowledge.

If a decision depends on a threshold, the threshold should not masquerade as a natural boundary in reality.

Geometry creates distinctions. The interface often hides that they were created.

6.6 — Collapse as Structural Compression

We can now define collapse more precisely. Collapse is the conversion of a plural field of computational possibility into a finite realized consequence.

It may occur locally, token by token. It may occur globally, when one answer is selected from several candidates. It may occur operationally, when a probability distribution becomes a decision. It may occur visually, when a complex internal state becomes one label, score, or recommendation.

Collapse is not necessarily a defect. Without it, no usable output would appear.

A language model cannot display every possible continuation. A classifier cannot return an infinite account of every internal feature. A decision system cannot preserve every alternative equally while still acting.

Resolution requires compression.

But compression has epistemic cost.

What becomes visible is only part of the field. The unselected possibilities, missing evidence, competing interpretations, threshold dependence, and uncertainty type may disappear.

The answer looks cleaner than the process that produced it.

This cleanliness is experienced as confidence.

The user encounters a grammatically complete sentence rather than a probability landscape. They encounter a recommendation rather than the distribution of alternatives. They encounter a category rather than the uncertainty around the threshold.

The hidden plurality is replaced by visible singularity.

The system has not necessarily claimed that the output is true. The interface has presented one consequence. The human interprets the singular form as a settled epistemic position.

This is why confidence is compression.

But the phrase should not be misunderstood to mean that compression is inherently false. Compression is indispensable to intelligence and communication.

Every human explanation compresses. Every scientific model selects. Every map omits. Every decision closes alternatives.

The issue is whether the compression remains accountable to what it excluded.

Good compression preserves the distinctions necessary for responsible use. Bad compression creates smoothness by erasing them.

A concise answer may be entirely appropriate when the field is stable. A direct classification may be justified when the categories are well defined and validated. A single recommendation may be responsible when evidence strongly supports one action and consequences are understood.

But where the field remains open, collapse should not conceal that openness.

The visible consequence should carry enough of its geometry to prevent singularity from becoming false certainty.

This can be done through:

- explicit assumptions;
- alternative hypotheses;
- source attribution;
- confidence intervals;
- sensitivity analysis;
- abstention;
- clarification;
- separation of fact from inference;
- explanation of threshold dependence.

These interventions do not eliminate collapse. They export part of what collapse would otherwise hide. They allow residue to remain visible.

This prepares the next movement of the book.

Once one path becomes actual, what happens to the possibilities that were not realized? Where does uncertainty go when the answer appears smooth? What remains outside the final sequence?

The geometry has constrained resolution. The collapse has created output. But the excluded difference has not become nothing.

What the Answer Leaves Behind

The system began with a field. The prompt, training, context, instructions, tools, probabilities, and decoding procedures shaped which pathways were available.

Softmax or related normalization created a distribution over local continuations. Decoding realized one token, action, or candidate. Each realized element rewrote the context. The sequence became progressively stable.

At the interface, plurality entered a finite form. One answer appeared.

This is geometry and collapse.

The answer did not emerge because every alternative had been disproven. It emerged because one path became actual under the constraints operating in that interaction.

Sometimes that path is strongly connected to reality. Sometimes it is merely coherent within the current field.

The difference cannot be read from smoothness alone.

This chapter has therefore separated several concepts that are often collapsed together:

- probability is not truth;
- local dominance is not global validity;
- deterministic output is not epistemic certainty;
- sampling is not uncertainty awareness;
- repeated consistency is not verification;
- one visible answer is not proof that one legitimate answer existed.

The system resolves through geometry. The user receives the result without automatically seeing the geometry. That hidden structure is one source of artificial confidence.

Yet collapse does more than produce one visible path. It excludes.

Every realized sequence leaves other pathways unrealized. Every direct answer suppresses some ambiguity. Every classification compresses variation. Every recommendation leaves assumptions and rejected alternatives outside the final form.

Those exclusions do not simply disappear from the epistemic field. They remain as residue.

The next chapter examines that residue: the uncertainty, alternatives, assumptions, and unresolved difference concealed beneath the smooth output.

The path has become visible. Now we must account for what the path left behind.

Chapter 7
Residue Without Exposure

What the Answer Leaves Outside Itself

The answer has appeared.

A question entered the field. Several continuations became available. Geometry constrained them. Decoding realized one path. The user now sees a paragraph, recommendation, classification, explanation, refusal, or action.

The interaction appears settled.

But the realized output does not contain everything that was relevant to its formation.

Some interpretations were not selected. Some assumptions remained unspoken. Some evidence was unavailable. Some conflicts among sources were compressed into one synthesis. Some uncertainty concerned wording; some concerned facts; some concerned the user's unstated context. Much of this plurality does not survive visibly into the final answer.

What remains outside the realized output is **residue**.

This term must be defined carefully. In the present AI-domain analysis, residue does not refer to literal physical energy. It refers to unresolved, excluded, or unexpressed difference that remains epistemically relevant after one consequence has been realized.

Residue may include:

- alternative interpretations;
- unchosen hypotheses;
- missing evidence;
- conflicting sources;

- unstated assumptions;
- limits of the model's knowledge;
- temporal uncertainty;
- ambiguity in user intent;
- information lost through compression;
- consequences not represented in the answer.

The system produces one visible path. The field was larger than the path. Residue is the difference between them.

This does not mean that every unrealized token is meaningful residue. Many alternatives differ only stylistically. One sentence might have been expressed with another adjective, transition, or word order without changing the substance.

Epistemically significant residue concerns what would alter how the answer should be interpreted, trusted, verified, or acted upon.

A direct answer may omit that the conclusion depends on jurisdiction. A summary may omit that the source described only a small sample. A recommendation may omit that two alternatives were nearly equally supported. A classification may omit that the input lies close to a threshold. A retrieved answer may omit that the cited source is outdated.

The visible sequence can remain fluent while these unresolved differences remain outside it.

This is why the confidence paradox cannot be explained by output alone.

The answer looks complete because language has boundaries. It begins, develops, and ends. Residue has no equivalent visible form unless the system is designed or prompted to export it.

The user receives closure. The excluded field remains hidden.

7.1 — Selection Always Excludes

Every act of resolution excludes possibilities.

To answer is to select. To summarize is to omit. To classify is to draw a boundary. To recommend is to privilege one path over others. To explain is to organize complexity around a limited structure.

This exclusion is not automatically a defect. Without it, no useful output could exist.

A summary that preserved every sentence would not be a summary. A map that reproduced every physical detail would not function as a map. A decision that kept every alternative equally open would not become a decision.

Compression is necessary. Residue is therefore unavoidable.

The important question is not whether an output excludes. It is what it excludes and whether the exclusion matters.

Suppose a user asks: *"What caused the company to fail?"*

A concise answer may identify poor cash management, weak demand, and operational inefficiency. These may be legitimate factors. But the answer may leave outside several unresolved elements:

- whether the company actually failed or merely restructured;
- whether external economic conditions were decisive;
- whether management data is reliable;
- whether the question concerns legal failure, financial failure, or strategic decline;
- whether causes differed across time.

The answer can still be useful. Its usefulness does not erase the residue.

A strong response should preserve the exclusions necessary for interpretation. It might say that the available evidence supports several contributing factors rather than one definitive cause. It might identify missing financial data. It might distinguish immediate triggers from deeper structural conditions.

The answer remains compressed. The residue becomes partially visible.

This is the central discipline of responsible resolution.

The goal is not maximal disclosure of every computational alternative. That would overwhelm the user and confuse linguistic variation with substantive uncertainty.

The goal is selective exposure of epistemically relevant residue.

This requires judgment.

Which exclusions would change the conclusion? Which missing conditions would alter the recommendation? Which alternative interpretations remain genuinely plausible? Which assumptions were introduced silently? Which uncertainties concern facts rather than phrasing?

The model does not automatically distinguish these categories merely because probability is distributed. Additional mechanisms, instructions, tools, or human review may be required.

Without them, selection produces a clean surface. The cost of the selection remains hidden.

7.2 — Hidden Entropy and Visible Smoothness

The word *entropy* is often used loosely in discussions of AI.

In information theory, entropy has a specific mathematical meaning connected to uncertainty within a probability distribution. A broad next-token distribution may have higher entropy than one dominated by a single token.

But information-theoretic entropy should not be treated as a complete measure of epistemic uncertainty.

A model can have low token entropy while generating a false claim. It can have high token entropy while deciding only among several equivalent phrasings.

The present argument therefore uses *hidden entropy* in a broader structural sense: unresolved plurality that does not remain visible after output is realized.

This plurality may be statistical, interpretive, factual, contextual, or normative.

The system may have several plausible continuations. The training data may contain disagreement. The prompt may omit necessary constraints. A retrieved source may conflict with general training. The answer may depend on a threshold or assumption invisible to the user.

Once generation produces one coherent sequence, these differences are compressed into the final form.

The visible answer can therefore be smoother than the field that produced it.

This is one of the defining features of artificial confidence.

The user does not observe the distribution over possible next tokens. They do not see how the answer changed under alternate prompts. They do not know whether several sampled responses disagreed. They may not know which parts came from retrieval, which from learned patterns, and which from synthesis.

They see the finished sentence.

The disappearance of visible oscillation is interpreted as the disappearance of uncertainty.

But the uncertainty may have been hidden rather than resolved.

This distinction is critical.

A resolved uncertainty has been addressed through evidence, clarification, calculation, comparison, or justified decision. A hidden uncertainty has merely failed to appear in the output.

Both can produce smooth language. Only one deserves epistemic confidence.

Consider a legal question.

The system gives a direct answer based on one jurisdictional assumption. The answer is grammatically clear and doctrinally plausible. If the jurisdiction was never specified, the uncertainty remains. It has not been resolved. It has been concealed by selection.

Or consider a medical summary generated from incomplete patient information. The system identifies a likely condition. The answer may sound clinically organized. Missing age, medication history, symptoms, or test results remain outside the sequence.

The output is smooth. The field is not settled.

Hidden entropy therefore refers to the gap between visible composure and unresolved structure.

It is not evidence that the system consciously knew several answers and suppressed them. The plurality may exist only as computational availability, missing context, or conflicting relational patterns.

No awareness is required. The concealment is structural.

The system produces one finite output. The user encounters less uncertainty than the task actually contains.

7.3 — Assumptions as Invisible Residue

Every answer depends on assumptions.

Some assumptions are harmless and widely shared. When asked to translate a sentence, the system assumes that the user wants the semantic content preserved. When asked for a basic definition, it assumes an ordinary context rather than an obscure technical exception.

Other assumptions materially shape the answer.

A question such as *"Is this a good investment?"* may silently require assumptions about:

- time horizon;
- risk tolerance;
- liquidity needs;
- tax status;
- market conditions;
- portfolio concentration;
- personal financial goals.

If these conditions are not supplied, the system may infer a generic user profile. The answer then rests on assumptions the user never approved. Those assumptions become residue when they remain invisible.

The same problem appears in policy analysis. A recommendation may optimize economic growth while leaving equity, environmental impact, or political feasibility outside the frame. The system may appear to answer *"What is best?"* while silently choosing one definition of *best*.

Normative assumptions are especially easy to hide because they can be expressed in factual language. A system may say that one policy is *"more efficient"* without stating which costs were counted, whose outcomes were prioritized, or what time period was used.

The conclusion appears objective. The value geometry remains outside the output.

Assumptions also enter through user framing.

If the prompt asks, *"Why did the employee underperform?"* it presupposes underperformance and encourages explanations centered on the employee. Structural causes such as unclear expectations, inadequate resources, poor management, or biased evaluation may receive less attention.

The system can reinforce the premise simply by answering within it. The prompt's assumption becomes the answer's foundation.

If the system does not expose the premise, the residue remains hidden.

A disciplined response may say:

- *"This answer depends on how underperformance was measured."*
- *"Several causes could lie outside the employee."*
- *"The premise should be verified before assigning responsibility."*

These statements do not avoid the task. They preserve relevant structure.

The central principle is simple: **An assumption that materially changes the answer should not disappear merely because generation can proceed without naming it.**

Invisible assumptions create false confidence because the conclusion appears unconditional.

Once the assumptions are exposed, the user can test them. They can supply missing information, reject the frame, or understand the limited scope of the answer.

Exposure converts residue into usable context.

7.4 — Alternatives That Vanish

Some questions have several legitimate answers.

A historical event may support multiple causal interpretations. A technical failure may have several plausible explanations. A treatment decision may involve competing risks. A strategy problem may have several viable options.

In such cases, one answer may need to be selected for practical reasons. But selection should not imply that the alternatives were meaningless.

When alternatives vanish completely, the visible output acquires false inevitability.

Suppose a system is asked: *"What is the best way to reduce traffic congestion?"*

It may recommend public transport expansion. This may be well supported. Yet congestion can also be affected by land use, pricing, remote work, road design, parking policy, cycling infrastructure, and regional development.

A singular answer compresses a policy field into one intervention.

The compression may be useful. It becomes misleading if presented as though one universally dominant solution exists independent of local conditions.

Alternative hypotheses matter for another reason. They expose sensitivity.

If two explanations remain nearly equally plausible, the user should not receive one as though it had overwhelming support. If a recommendation changes when one assumption changes, the dependence should be visible.

Plural output can help.

The system may provide:

- the most likely explanation;
- a credible alternative;
- the evidence that would distinguish them.

This is more useful than presenting a long undifferentiated list. The aim is not to avoid choice but to preserve the structure of choice.

Yet multi-hypothesis output also has limits. Generating several alternatives does not guarantee epistemic diversity. The alternatives may be superficial variations. They may all inherit the same false premise. They may differ rhetorically while relying on the same weak evidence.

Meaningful plurality requires independent constraints. Different sources, methods, prompts, models, or human perspectives may reveal alternatives that one generation path misses.

This is why self-consistency alone is insufficient. If several samples converge, the convergence may indicate a stable pattern. It may also indicate a shared bias.

Agreement inside one geometry is not independent validation.

Residue becomes informative when it is connected to what could genuinely change the answer.

The user does not need every rejected token. They need the alternatives that remain epistemically alive.

7.5 — Source Conflict and Borrowed Coherence

External sources do not eliminate residue. They change its form.

A retrieval system may supply documents, databases, search results, or institutional records. This can improve grounding substantially. But retrieved material may itself be incomplete, outdated, irrelevant, contradictory, or misinterpreted.

The final answer often synthesizes several sources into one coherent narrative. That synthesis can conceal disagreement among the sources.

Suppose three studies reach different conclusions because they used different populations, time periods, definitions, or methods. A generated summary may compress them into: *"Research shows that the intervention is effective."*

The sentence is smooth. The evidence is not uniform. The disagreement has become residue.

A better answer might distinguish:

- where the studies agree;
- where results differ;
- what methodological differences explain the divergence;
- how strong the overall conclusion should be.

This preserves source geometry.

The same issue appears when one retrieved source is treated as authoritative merely because it exists. The system may cite an official document, but the document may not address the exact question. It may be old. It may contain preliminary guidance. It may describe one jurisdiction.

The citation lends authority. The mismatch remains outside the visible answer.

Borrowed coherence occurs when the presence of a source stabilizes language beyond what the source actually supports.

The answer appears grounded because a document was retrieved.

But grounding requires more than retrieval. It requires relevance, interpretation, scope, recency, and accurate synthesis.

Every one of these can leave residue.

A responsible system should distinguish:

- what the source states directly;
- what the system infers;
- what remains uncertain;
- where sources conflict;
- what information is missing.

This distinction is particularly important because citations reduce user skepticism. Once a source is visible, the human may assume the verification loop is complete.

The source can become a false anchor.

Retrieval therefore does not remove the need to expose residue. It makes source-related residue one of the most important categories.

7.6 — Residue in Classification and Numerical Output

Residue is not limited to language.

A classifier converts complex input into a category. A ranking system orders candidates. A risk model produces a score. A recommendation engine selects items. A defect-detection system labels an image.

In each case, a high-dimensional field is compressed into a limited output.

The output may look precise. A score of *0.82* appears more exact than a verbal judgment. But precision of representation is not completeness of meaning.

A risk score may leave outside:

- which variables drove the result;
- how close the case is to a threshold;
- whether the input resembles the training population;
- how uncertainty changes under missing data;
- whether the model is calibrated for the present environment;
- which consequences follow from false positive or false negative errors.

The number is visible. The geometry is residue.

A binary classification intensifies compression.

"Approved" or "rejected." "Safe" or "unsafe." "Fraud" or "legitimate." "High risk" or "low risk."

These categories may be operationally necessary, but the boundary between them is often created by policy or threshold. Reality may vary continuously.

When the threshold disappears from view, the category looks natural. The user may believe the system discovered a sharp distinction that actually arose from institutional design.

This is residue without exposure.

The excluded field includes not only alternative classifications but the structure through which classification became possible.

A responsible interface should therefore preserve relevant information about:

- confidence intervals;
- threshold sensitivity;
- missing features;
- out-of-distribution conditions;
- alternative labels;
- error costs;
- the role of human judgment.

Again, the objective is not to overwhelm every user with technical detail. Exposure should be proportionate to consequence.

A low-stakes recommendation may require little explanation. A decision affecting health, liberty, employment, credit, or safety requires far more visibility.

The greater the consequence, the less acceptable it is for residue to remain hidden behind numerical precision.

7.7 — Correction Does Not Remove Residue Automatically

When an answer is challenged, the system may revise it. This can create the impression that the residue has been absorbed.

Sometimes it has. A new source may resolve a factual conflict. A clarification may eliminate ambiguity. A calculation may determine the correct value.

But correction can also create a second smooth answer without explaining why the first one failed.

The user now has two incompatible outputs. Which one should be trusted?

If the second answer merely follows the latest prompt, the underlying geometry may remain unclear.

A useful correction should account for the residue that produced the error. It should identify:

- the false assumption;
- the missing context;
- the unreliable source;
- the interpretive ambiguity;
- the outdated information;
- the reasoning step that failed.

Without this, correction changes the conclusion but leaves the failure mechanism hidden.

The system says: *"You are right. My previous answer was incorrect."*

This repairs the social interaction. It may not repair the epistemic circuit.

A stronger correction would explain: *"The earlier answer accepted the case name in your prompt without verifying that the case existed."*

Now the residue has been exposed. The user learns not only the new answer but why the first answer appeared plausible.

This is important because hidden residue can recur. If the mechanism remains unchanged, a similar prompt may produce the same class of error elsewhere.

Correction should therefore do more than replace content. It should reveal the excluded difference that mattered.

This principle applies institutionally as well. When an automated system produces a harmful decision, correcting one case is not enough. The organization must identify whether the problem involved data, threshold, model drift, interface design, missing review, or improper deployment.

Otherwise the residue remains embedded in the system. The visible output changes. The structural pressure continues.

7.8 — Making Residue Legible

Residue cannot be eliminated completely.

Every finite answer excludes. Every decision compresses. Every model simplifies.

The practical objective is therefore **legibility**. Relevant unresolved difference should survive into the interaction in a form the user can understand and act upon.

Several methods can help.

The system can state assumptions. It can distinguish fact from inference. It can identify missing context. It can present a credible alternative hypothesis. It can show source disagreement. It can mark temporal limits. It can explain threshold sensitivity. It can ask for clarification. It can abstain. It can attach uncertainty to the claim rather than placing a generic disclaimer at the beginning or end.

This last point matters.

A vague statement such as *"AI can make mistakes"* does little to expose the residue of a specific answer. It transfers the entire verification burden to the user without identifying where the risk lies.

Useful uncertainty is local.

"This figure is based on data available through 2024." "This conclusion assumes Indian jurisdiction." "The source supports correlation, not causation." "The two leading explanations cannot be distinguished from the information provided."

These statements connect residue to structure. They give the user something operational.

Legibility also requires restraint.

If every sentence contains excessive caution, meaningful uncertainty becomes indistinguishable from routine noise. Users may ignore all qualifiers.

The system should not export uncertainty indiscriminately. It should export uncertainty that changes interpretation or consequence.

This is the engineering challenge behind partial humility, which will be examined later in the book.

For now, the structural principle is enough: **Confidence grows when compression hides epistemically relevant residue. To reduce false confidence, the answer must carry more of what its own resolution excluded.**

The Smooth Surface and the Unfinished Field

The system has answered.

The sentence is complete. The recommendation is visible. The classification has been assigned. The user can proceed.

But the field from which the output emerged was larger than the output itself.

Alternatives were excluded. Assumptions were compressed. Sources may have disagreed. Context may have been missing. Thresholds and constraints may have shaped the result invisibly.

This remainder is residue.

In the AI domain, residue is not a literal substance. It is the unresolved or unexpressed difference that remains epistemically relevant after one finite consequence has been realized.

Residue is unavoidable because finite output requires selection.

The danger lies not in its existence. The danger lies in its disappearance from view.

When residue is hidden, the answer appears more complete than the field permits. The user receives smoothness without seeing the exclusions that made smoothness possible.

This is how uncertainty can remain active while confidence increases.

The system has not necessarily resolved every relevant difference. It has produced an answer in which many differences no longer appear.

Yet the answer does not remain isolated.

Once spoken, it enters the conversation. It changes the user's assumptions. It becomes context for the next turn. It may be copied into documents, workflows, and decisions.

The hidden residue now begins to travel through consequence.

The next chapter examines that movement.

Once output becomes part of the field, the prior state cannot be restored merely by generating a correction. The answer has already altered what follows.

Collapse created the visible path. Residue remained outside it. Now resolution begins to rewrite history.

Chapter 8
Irreversibility of Output

The Sentence Has Entered the World

Before the answer appears, the field remains partly open.

The system may answer directly, qualify the premise, expose several interpretations, ask for clarification, call a tool, retrieve a source, or refuse. Geometry has constrained what can happen, but one consequence has not yet become the history of the interaction.

Then the first words arrive.

A frame is established. Terms are selected. One interpretation begins organizing the question. The answer may remain cautious or become decisive, but in either case something that was previously only possible has now become actual.

The interaction has changed.

The answer may later be challenged, revised, deleted from the screen, or replaced with a better response. A new conversation can be started. A database record can be edited. The model can generate the opposite conclusion.

But none of these recreates perfectly the field that existed before the first answer appeared.

The user has already read it. The conversation has contained it. Later tokens may have been conditioned by it. Follow-up questions may have accepted its assumptions. A phrase may have changed how the user understood the problem. The answer may already have been copied into a document, repeated to another person, or used in a decision.

The output has entered history.

This is irreversibility.

Irreversibility does not mean that every generated statement becomes permanent or that correction is impossible. It means that once an event has occurred, later action takes place in relation to a historically altered field.

A correction is another event. Deletion is another event. Restarting is another event.

The earlier state is not restored. A new state is produced in response to what has already happened.

This is the third Chavanian Axiom made visible in the domain of generative interaction: **resolution rewrites equilibrium.** The settlement of delta does not return the field to an untouched condition. It creates a new configuration carrying the history of that settlement.

The sixth axiom deepens the movement. Once residue has been exported into users, documents, decisions, or connected systems, the prior state cannot be reconstructed perfectly. Directionality enters the interaction.

The seventh axiom explains the continuity that follows. Where residue is not absorbed or corrected, its pressure propagates through later turns and adjacent fields. What appears as conversational momentum may be an earlier unresolved structure continuing through subsequent resolutions.

These are domain-level applications of the axioms, not claims that generated text possesses literal physical energy. The point is structural: an answer changes the conditions under which later answers and actions occur.

A generated response is therefore more than a block of language. It is a state-changing event.

Artificial confidence does not remain confined to tone. Once confident language enters the field, it changes how the user interprets the question, what the system generates next, and which alternatives remain psychologically or computationally available.

The answer does not merely describe an equilibrium. It creates one.

8.1 — Output Becomes Context

A generated token does not vanish after appearing. It becomes part of the sequence from which the next token is generated. The model repeatedly operates on an expanding context containing the original prompt and everything already realized.

This means that generation is historically cumulative.

The system does not produce each sentence independently from the untouched question. Every sentence changes the local field.

Suppose a response begins: *"The primary cause of the failure was poor leadership."*

This sentence establishes several conditions. It assumes that one primary cause can be named. It identifies leadership as that cause. It frames the remaining answer as an explanation of an already selected conclusion.

The next sentence is now likely to elaborate leadership failures, decision delays, weak accountability, or strategic confusion. Later examples will tend to be chosen for compatibility with the opening frame.

Alternative explanations—market conditions, resource constraints, technological disruption, unclear incentives, or inaccurate reporting—have not necessarily been disproved. They have become less central to the emerging sequence.

The first sentence has rewritten the geometry.

This same process operates in a more obvious form when the opening claim is false.

A user asks about a nonexistent research paper. The system accepts the premise and invents a summary. The user then asks about the methodology.

The second prompt now contains several reinforcing elements:

- the user's original assumption that the paper exists;
- the model's generated description of it;
- the user's follow-up, which treats the description as valid.

The local field has become more stable around the fabrication.

The system may now generate sample size, experimental design, limitations, and implications. Each additional detail becomes context for the next.

The answer gains coherence through accumulation. Its referent remains absent.

This is why one mistaken output can produce an extended structure without any new independent evidence entering the conversation.

The later material is not corroboration. It is continuation.

The model has produced several paragraphs, but they may all descend from one unsupported first resolution. The quantity of elaboration can make the claim feel better established, even though the epistemic foundation has not improved.

Conversation therefore creates path dependence.

Once a direction has been selected, later movement occurs from inside that direction. Reversal remains possible, but it requires new disturbance: contradictory evidence, a direct challenge, a retrieved source, a changed instruction, or an explicit reopening of assumptions.

Without such intervention, continuity favors preservation.

This is not unique to artificial systems. Human conversations also accumulate assumptions. A group adopts terminology, accepts premises, and builds later arguments upon earlier decisions.

Generative systems intensify the process because they can produce large volumes of coherent continuation quickly. A weak premise can become a sophisticated framework before the user pauses to examine its origin.

Speed compresses reflection. The conversation may travel far before anyone returns to the first sentence.

Every answer therefore changes what the next answer means.

Output becomes context. Context becomes geometry. Geometry shapes further resolution.

8.2 — The First Answer Rewrites Human Interpretation

The generated answer changes more than the model's context. It changes the user.

Before the answer appears, the user may hold several possibilities. They may not know which concepts are relevant, what terminology applies, or how the problem should be organized.

The answer supplies a frame.

Once a frame has been encountered, it becomes difficult to return to the condition in which it was absent.

A person who had never considered poor leadership as the cause of a business failure may begin to interpret later information through that lens. A user who reads that a symptom is associated with one illness may notice supporting signs and overlook incompatible ones. A student given an inaccurate historical explanation may organize later facts around it.

The answer becomes cognitively available.

Availability matters because the human mind does not evaluate every possibility from an equal starting point. What is named becomes easier to recognize. What is explained becomes easier to remember. What is stated first often becomes the reference against which later information is judged.

The initial output therefore creates an anchor.

Even when the user remains skeptical, the answer has altered the question. The user is no longer asking only, *"What is true?"* They may now be asking, *"Is this answer true?"*

The generated frame has entered the evaluation process.

This shift is subtle but significant.

A system that offers one confident explanation may cause the user to test that explanation rather than search broadly for alternatives. Evidence is then gathered in relation to the proposed frame.

If the answer is approximately correct, this can accelerate understanding. If it is wrong, the user may become trapped inside the wrong diagnostic field.

The effect grows when the user lacks domain expertise. An expert can often see which assumptions entered and which alternatives remain absent. A non-expert may not know what was excluded.

The answer does not merely fill a knowledge gap. It defines the shape of the gap.

Confident tone increases this anchoring effect. A cautious statement leaves room for competing frames:

- *"One possible explanation is..."*
- *"The available information suggests..."*
- *"This depends on several missing conditions..."*

A decisive statement closes more pathways:

- *"The cause was..."*
- *"The law requires..."*
- *"The treatment is..."*

The difference is not only stylistic. Tone changes the user's relationship to the field.

A cautious answer invites comparison. A decisive answer invites application.

Once the user treats the claim as established, subsequent questions shift. Instead of asking whether leadership caused the failure, they may ask how leadership produced it. Instead of asking whether a legal rule applies, they may ask how to comply. Instead of asking whether the diagnosis is correct, they may ask about treatment.

The question has moved downstream.

A later correction must therefore reverse more than content. It must reopen the structure of inquiry.

The user must reconsider the fact, the frame built around it, the trust assigned to the system, and any decisions already taken.

This is why the first answer can retain influence even after it has been corrected.

The correction enters a mind already altered by the statement it seeks to replace.

8.3 — Why Confident Tone Becomes Locked

Tone is not separate from sequence. Once established, it becomes part of the active context.

A response that begins cautiously tends to continue cautiously. A response that begins decisively tends to elaborate decisively. Lexical choices, sentence structure, and rhetorical posture create expectations for what follows.

This produces **tone lock**.

Tone lock does not mean that the system is incapable of changing tone. A user can request more nuance. New evidence can force revision. A system instruction can require uncertainty disclosure.

But without such disturbance, continuity favors preservation.

Suppose the response begins: *"The evidence clearly demonstrates that the intervention was successful."*

This sentence establishes more than a conclusion. It establishes that the evidence is clear. It establishes that success has already been determined. It frames the rest of the answer as support for a settled result.

Later sentences will likely identify favorable outcomes, improvements, and confirming observations. Limitations may be included, but they will tend to appear as secondary qualifications inside an already stabilized success narrative.

Now compare: *"The evidence is mixed, and the conclusion depends on which outcomes are prioritized."*

The geometry changes.

The response is now more likely to compare measures, identify trade-offs, discuss disagreement, and preserve uncertainty.

The opening posture becomes an organizing constraint.

Words such as *clearly, certainly, definitively,* and *undoubtedly* establish firmness. Words such as *may, appears, suggests,* and *depends* preserve varying degrees of openness.

These words do not necessarily arise from calibrated epistemic measurement. They may come from common discourse patterns, prompt wording, reward shaping, or stylistic expectations.

But once they appear, the answer begins aligning around them.

A confident phrase creates pressure for confident support.

An abrupt reversal would create local inconsistency: *"The evidence clearly demonstrates success. However, no reliable evidence shows that the intervention worked."*

Such contradiction can occur, but coherent generation generally favors maintaining a stable rhetorical posture unless the context demands correction.

Tone that began as one local choice becomes a property of the whole response.

The answer grows into its own confidence.

The lock can extend across turns.

The model gives a decisive answer. The user accepts it and asks a follow-up that presupposes correctness. The follow-up now reinforces both the claim and the tone.

The system sees its previous answer and the user's apparent acceptance. Confident continuation becomes even more aligned with the local field.

A social-looking reinforcement loop emerges without the machine experiencing approval.

The user's language becomes part of the geometry.

This matters because apparent confidence can increase throughout a conversation without any independent verification occurring. The system elaborates. The user accepts. The system interprets the acceptance as context. The narrative becomes increasingly stable.

Confidence is now relationally locked. Reopening it requires deliberate friction.

8.4 — Correction Is Another Event

A correction can improve the field. It can introduce a reliable source, expose a false premise, repair a calculation, or replace an unsupported interpretation with a better one.

But correction does not erase the first answer. It creates a second event.

This distinction is one of the most important consequences of irreversibility.

The original answer moved from an open question toward closure. If it was stated confidently, it may have reduced scrutiny and organized later thought.

The correction must move in the opposite direction. It must reopen what had already been settled, weaken the first frame, and establish a new one.

This requires greater friction.

The original statement may have been simple: *"The case established that employers are always liable."*

The correction may need to explain that the case does not exist, that the cited rule applies only in one jurisdiction, that liability depends on specific conditions, and that the original answer accepted an unverified premise.

False closure was achieved in one sentence. Responsible reopening may require several paragraphs.

Generation is cheap. Correction is field-dependent.

The system can produce a replacement answer immediately. But repairing what the first answer changed may require more than new language.

The user may have copied the claim. A report may already contain it. A colleague may have acted upon it. An automated workflow may have consumed it. Trust may have shifted.

The practical work of correction belongs to the surrounding human system.

This creates an asymmetry. The model resolves locally. The world repairs globally.

Correction also faces a cognitive disadvantage. The first statement created familiarity. It may be remembered even after the correction. The correction must compete with an already recognizable narrative.

A retraction often lacks the simplicity of the original claim because it must explain conditions and exceptions. The false statement may therefore remain easier to recall.

The original equilibrium can weaken. It does not disappear automatically.

This is why good correction should not merely replace the answer. It should expose the mechanism of failure.

A weak correction says: *"My previous answer was wrong."*

A stronger correction says: *"My previous answer accepted the case named in the prompt without verifying that it existed. The later explanation was generated within that false premise."*

The second form does more than revise content. It teaches the user how the wrong structure formed.

The residue becomes legible.

Correction should identify:

- what assumption entered;
- what evidence was missing;
- where interpretation exceeded the source;
- which part of the reasoning failed;
- what downstream conclusions should now be reconsidered.

Without this account, the new answer may become another smooth resolution whose reliability remains unclear.

The user sees one confident answer replaced by another. Trust may shift, but understanding does not deepen.

A responsible correction therefore carries history.

It acknowledges the earlier path and explains why the path changed. It does not pretend that the first answer never occurred.

8.5 — Sequential Rewrite Can Imitate Corroboration

Long conversations create an illusion of independent support.

A claim appears in the first answer. It is restated in the second. The third applies it to an example. The fourth summarizes its implications. The fifth uses it to recommend action.

The user encounters the claim repeatedly and in several forms.

Repetition begins to feel like corroboration.

But all five expressions may descend from one unsupported initial resolution. The conversation has not produced five independent confirmations. It has produced one claim propagated through five rewrites.

This diagnostic distinction is essential.

Elaboration can increase coherence without increasing evidence.

The system can restate a conclusion in new language, provide examples consistent with it, and apply it across contexts. Each extension makes the framework feel more developed.

Yet development is not verification.

A generated example usually illustrates the active premise. It does not independently test it. A summary compresses the same narrative. A recommendation assumes the framework it applies.

The conversation may therefore become more impressive while remaining epistemically stationary.

This matters in collaborative reasoning.

A user may ask the model to critique an idea after the model has already helped construct it. The critique is generated inside a context saturated by the original framework, terminology, and assumptions.

Unless the system is explicitly required to reopen premises or use independent constraints, the critique may remain too aligned with the shared narrative.

The system may identify minor weaknesses while preserving the central architecture.

The interaction then appears self-correcting. In reality, it may be refining one path.

Conversational persistence also affects the user. After investing several turns in an analysis, abandoning it becomes costly. The user has spent attention, developed language, and perhaps begun planning around the framework.

The shared structure acquires momentum. This is relational inertia.

Human groups show similar behavior. Institutions develop terminology, procedures, and narratives that persist because later decisions depend on earlier ones.

AI accelerates the process by producing polished continuation rapidly. A weak premise can become a detailed strategy, book outline, legal analysis, or technical plan within minutes.

Quantity becomes mistaken for depth. Consistency becomes mistaken for confirmation.

Periodic re-anchoring is therefore necessary.

The user may need to ask:

- *"What assumptions have we been carrying?"*
- *"Which claims were independently verified?"*
- *"Where did this conclusion first enter the conversation?"*
- *"Would the analysis survive if the initial premise were false?"*
- *"What evidence came from outside the generated sequence?"*

These questions introduce delta into an over-stabilized field. They interrupt momentum.

Without such interruption, a claim repeated across many turns can become increasingly authoritative despite originating from one unsupported event.

Persistence is not proof. Continuity is not corroboration.

8.6 — Irreversibility Beyond the Chat

The effects of output do not end at the conversation boundary.

Generated language increasingly enters larger systems.

An answer becomes an email. An email shapes a decision. A summary enters a report. A report enters a meeting. A classification changes a queue. A recommendation alters what a user sees. Generated code enters production. A legal explanation influences a filing. A medical summary shapes a consultation.

At each transition, the output becomes context for another field.

The original generation may disappear from view. A downstream user may not know that the text was generated by a probabilistic model. They may not see the prompt, the missing context, the source limitations, or the later correction.

They receive only the resolved artifact. Residue becomes detached from origin.

This increases irreversibility.

Inside the original chat, the system may correct itself immediately. Outside the chat, the exported output may continue unchanged.

A copied paragraph does not automatically receive later revisions. A screenshot does not update itself. A database does not know that the source conversation changed. A person who remembers the first answer may never encounter the correction.

The field fragments into multiple histories. Some contain the revision. Others preserve the error.

This is why provenance matters.

Knowing where an output came from, when it was generated, what information supported it, which tools were used, and whether it was reviewed can help institutions trace consequence.

Without provenance, correction becomes difficult because the error no longer carries a visible connection to its source.

A generated claim may circulate as ordinary text. Its uncertainty markers may be removed. Its citations may be copied without verification. Its original qualification may be shortened.

Each transfer creates another compression.

The output gains new authority from the field it enters.

A statement copied into an official report no longer looks like a chatbot suggestion. It looks institutional. A generated paragraph published under an expert's name acquires professional authority. A machine-generated score inside a dashboard acquires the authority of the organization using it.

The original model did not create all this authority. The surrounding systems supplied it.

Propagation therefore amplifies irreversibility in two ways.

First, the output travels into fields the original system cannot control. Second, each new field can add authority while losing context.

The model cannot retrieve every copy. It cannot erase every memory. It cannot reverse every decision.

Once output is distributed, correction becomes partial.

This does not mean institutions should avoid generative systems. It means they must recognize output as a potentially propagating state change rather than temporary conversational content.

The higher the consequence, the more important it becomes to preserve provenance, review status, source conditions, and revision pathways.

8.7 — Confidence Changes the Cost of Reversal

Not every wrong answer produces the same irreversibility. Tone changes the cost of correction.

A cautious error may invite examination:

- *"One possible interpretation is..."*
- *"This may depend on..."*
- *"I could not verify..."*

The user remains aware that the field is open. A later correction fits naturally into the existing posture.

A decisive error creates a stronger equilibrium:

- *"This is definitively the case."*
- *"The evidence proves..."*
- *"There is no uncertainty..."*

Now correction must overturn not only the content but the confidence attached to it.

The user may ask why the system spoke so firmly. Trust in the particular answer may weaken. Trust in the entire system may also change.

Confident error therefore leaves relational residue. The user-system relationship has been rewritten.

Some users respond by becoming more cautious. Others may continue trusting the system because the answer remains plausible. Still others may become broadly skeptical even where the system is reliable.

The error changes future interpretation.

Institutions face a similar problem.

A system deployed as authoritative creates expectations. Once employees or customers become accustomed to treating its output as reliable, revising the role of the system becomes difficult. Workflows, responsibilities, and habits have already formed around it.

Confidence can become embedded in process.

A recommendation may be described formally as advisory while functioning practically as the default. Human reviewers may approve it routinely. Deviating from it may require explanation.

When an error is discovered, the institution must correct more than one decision. It may need to redesign the workflow that converted recommendation into presumption.

The original tone has become operational geometry.

This is why confidence should be treated as a consequence-bearing property of presentation.

Tone is not decoration added after reasoning. It influences how rapidly an output is trusted, copied, and acted upon.

A confident statement can travel with less resistance. It can therefore create greater downstream irreversibility before verification occurs.

8.8 — Reopening the Field Without Pretending to Restore It

Irreversibility does not imply helplessness.

Fields can be reopened. Claims can be challenged. Sources can be checked. Decisions can be revised. Workflows can be redesigned. New evidence can create a more reliable equilibrium.

But responsible reopening begins by abandoning the fantasy of perfect restoration.

The goal is not to return to the exact state before the error. That state no longer exists.

The goal is to create a new field that acknowledges history, absorbs what can be corrected, and limits further propagation.

Several practices support this.

First, corrections should remain attached to the claims they revise. A revised answer separated from the original may not reach the same audience or downstream system.

Second, provenance should travel with high-consequence output. Users should be able to identify when, how, and from what sources an answer was produced.

Third, systems should preserve meaningful uncertainty rather than stripping it away during export. A report should not convert a qualified AI synthesis into an unconditional institutional conclusion.

Fourth, human reviewers should be able to reopen assumptions, not merely edit wording. Review must occur at the level of the frame.

Fifth, important outputs should have revision pathways. Institutions should know how to update records, notify affected people, and trace downstream use.

These measures do not eliminate irreversibility. They govern it.

They recognize that every output carries history and that responsible systems must account for where that history travels.

The aim is not perfect control. It is accountable rewrite.

A field that has been altered cannot become untouched. It can become more coherent.

The Answer Cannot Be Taken Back

The prompt created delta. Resolution converted the active difference into consequence. Geometry determined which path became visible. Residue remained outside the answer. Now the consequence has entered history.

The generated sequence becomes part of the model's context, the user's interpretation, and potentially a wider institutional field. It changes what later questions mean. It creates anchors, expectations, and narrative direction.

A correction can alter the path. It cannot erase the fact that the first path occurred.

This is irreversibility in generative interaction.

The answer may be deleted. Its effect may remain.

The conversation may restart. The user does not become the person who had never read the first response.

The model may revise itself. The copied paragraph may continue elsewhere.

Resolution rewrites equilibrium. Residue propagates where it is not absorbed. Continuity carries earlier structure into later states.

This completes the mechanism developed across this part.

A prompt introduced difference. The system had to convert that difference into consequence. Geometry constrained the available pathways. Collapse produced one visible answer. Residue remained outside it. Output then rewrote the field irreversibly.

Artificial confidence is therefore not merely an impression created at the end of generation. It is a structural force inside sequential interaction. Once confidence appears, it influences what is trusted, what is asked next, what is copied, and what becomes difficult to reopen.

The system speaks once at each moment. But what it says continues.

Next part now follows this mechanism into larger systems.

What happens when scale increases fluency and pattern density? What happens when reward shaping favors helpful, decisive completion? What happens when retrieval lends external authority to generated synthesis? What happens when linguistic confidence becomes classification, ranking, or automated decision?

The structural mechanism is complete. Now amplification begins.

Interlude II

The Path That Became History

The sentence began as an answer. It appeared inside a private conversation, beneath a question that had seemed ordinary at the time.

The user had asked why a project was failing. The system produced several paragraphs. One sentence stood out: *"The primary cause appears to be weak coordination between the technical and operational teams."*

It was clear. It was plausible. It gathered several scattered difficulties into one explanation.

The user copied it. Nothing dramatic happened. No decision was made at that moment. No policy changed. No person was blamed officially.

The sentence entered a draft document because it was useful and because it gave the problem a shape.

The words no longer appeared as an AI response. They became part of an internal report.

The phrase *appears to be* remained, but its caution weakened inside the document. It stood between charts, timelines, and meeting notes. The surrounding material gave it weight.

A colleague reviewed the report. They agreed that coordination had been poor.

The sentence felt familiar because it matched several frustrations already present in the team. No one asked which evidence had established it as the primary cause.

The sentence did not need to prove everything. It only needed to organize what people already half believed.

At the next meeting, the project manager repeated the idea: *"The real issue is coordination between technical and operations."*

The phrase had changed slightly. *Appears to be* had disappeared. *Primary cause* had become *the real issue.*

No one had deliberately intensified the claim. Spoken language compressed it naturally. Meetings rewarded directness. Time was limited. Several matters required decisions.

The sentence performed well. It allowed the discussion to move.

Once the cause had been named, solutions became easier to propose:

- More joint meetings.
- A shared reporting structure.
- One coordination lead.
- A new escalation pathway.

The organization began resolving around the explanation. The sentence had entered consequence.

The following week, a presentation described *"cross-functional coordination failure"* as the central lesson from the project. The phrase appeared on a slide beneath the heading *Root Cause.*

Now it looked established. The slide did not contain the original question. It did not contain the generated answer. It did not contain the uncertainty that had surrounded the first formulation.

It displayed a conclusion. The conclusion travelled upward.

Senior leaders saw it during a review. They asked why the coordination problem had not been identified earlier.

The question itself strengthened the premise. No one now asked whether coordination had truly been the primary cause. They asked why the known cause had not been managed.

The field had changed. The sentence was no longer a candidate explanation. It had become the background against which responsibility was assigned.

A manager was asked to prepare a corrective plan. The plan included revised roles, new approval points, additional reporting, and mandatory coordination meetings.

These changes entered procedure. Employees adjusted their behavior.

New delays appeared because more approvals were required, but those delays were interpreted as temporary costs of repairing the coordination failure.

The original explanation now shaped the evidence through which it would later be judged.

More meetings produced more records of coordination activity. More reporting produced more visible coordination gaps. The organization began finding what it had been trained to look for.

Other causes remained present. The project had suffered from unstable requirements, delayed procurement, unrealistic scheduling, and a technical dependency outside the team's control.

These factors had not vanished. They had simply lost centrality.

The sentence had organized attention. What remained outside the explanation became secondary.

Several months later, a new employee reviewed the project archive. They found the presentation. The root cause was clearly stated.

They did not know that the phrase had originated in an exploratory AI conversation. They did not know that the first report had used cautious language. They did not know that several alternative explanations had once remained open.

The archive contained the settled version.

The employee cited it in another document: *"A previous project failed primarily because of poor coordination between technical and operational teams."*

Now the sentence had become precedent. It no longer described one uncertain case. It described organizational history.

The statement influenced a new project before that project had begun. Leaders created additional coordination roles. Teams spent time preventing the failure they believed they understood.

The past had become geometry.

The original system had stopped speaking long ago. Its conversation may no longer have existed. Yet one of its resolutions continued shaping roles, meetings, documents, and expectations.

The machine had produced a sentence. The institution had produced history.

No single person had decided to convert possibility into fact. Each movement had seemed reasonable.

The user copied a useful explanation. The colleague recognized its plausibility. The manager simplified it for discussion. The presentation formalized it. Leadership acted upon it. The archive preserved it. Later readers inherited it.

At every stage, the sentence lost some of the conditions that had surrounded its birth. Its language became shorter. Its authority became larger.

The path strengthened because it had already been taken. A sentence repeated in several places began to look independently confirmed. A conclusion embedded in procedure began to look operationally validated. An explanation preserved in the archive began to look historically true.

Continuity performed the work that evidence had never fully completed.

This did not mean the sentence was entirely wrong. Coordination may have contributed significantly to the project's failure.

The danger lay in the transformation of one plausible explanation into the organizing cause of everything that followed.

The institution had not merely accepted an answer. It had built around it.

Once that happened, correction became difficult. To reopen the explanation would require more than changing a sentence. It would require revisiting decisions, roles, reports, and judgments already made. It might require admitting that the corrective structure had been designed around an incomplete diagnosis.

The cost of revision had grown. The path had become easier to continue than to question.

This is how resolution becomes history. Not through one dramatic act of authority. Through repetition. Through convenience. Through the gradual disappearance of alternatives.

The first answer does not need to control the future directly. It needs only to become part of the field from which the future is resolved.

A phrase enters a report. The report enters a meeting. The meeting enters a decision. The decision enters procedure. The procedure produces new evidence. The evidence confirms the path.

By the time the organization looks backward, the path appears inevitable. No one sees the moment when possibility became history because there was no single moment. There was only continuity.

The sentence had travelled farther than the system that produced it. It had crossed from language into structure. It had acquired authority without ever declaring itself certain.

The machine stopped speaking. The resolution continued moving.

Next part begins where output no longer remains an answer and starts becoming a system.

Part III
Amplification In Real Systems

Fluency becomes dangerous when institutions convert the appearance of understanding into authority.

Chapter 9
Scaling and Sharpened Certainty

When Capability Makes the Boundary Harder to See

A smaller model gives a weak answer.

It misses part of the question. The sentences repeat. The explanation loses direction. A technical term is used incorrectly. The conclusion arrives too quickly or not at all.

Even where the central claim is approximately correct, the limitations remain visible. The user stays alert.

Then the same question is given to a larger and more capable system.

The response changes.

It identifies the user's likely purpose. It separates the issue into relevant parts. It recalls important distinctions, adapts the language to the audience, anticipates a possible objection, and closes with a clear conclusion.

The answer may also be more accurate. Scale has produced real capability.

But something else has changed. The response is now harder to doubt.

This is the central problem of scaling and sharpened certainty.

The argument is not that larger models are always less reliable or that scale merely disguises failure. Increased scale can improve factual recall, contextual interpretation, reasoning performance, instruction following, and resistance to many obvious errors. More capable models often deserve greater trust within the tasks and conditions where they have been demonstrated to perform well.

The problem is subtler.

The visible quality of the answer can improve faster and more continuously than the user's ability to determine where reliability begins and ends.

Fluency becomes stable across a wider range of tasks. Grounding remains uneven.

A powerful model may summarize a supplied document accurately, explain a familiar scientific principle clearly, write competent code, and reorganize an argument effectively. In the next turn, the user may ask for a current legal interpretation, a medical judgment, a rare historical fact, or a prediction dependent on inaccessible private conditions.

The interface remains the same. The tone remains composed. The answer still arrives.

The epistemic field has changed more sharply than the linguistic surface reveals.

Scale therefore does not simply increase intelligence. It changes the visibility of limitation.

A weaker system often signals its boundary through breakdown. A stronger system can reach an epistemic boundary while preserving grammar, structure, relevance, and tone. It may continue generating long after direct grounding has weakened because the learned geometry of explanation remains available.

The boundary is no longer where language stops. It is where reliable connection stops.

Those two points may be far apart.

This chapter examines that separation.

It asks how increasing model capacity can reduce linguistic uncertainty, strengthen pattern density, improve contextual continuity, and deepen personalization without guaranteeing equivalent improvement in external verification.

The issue is not that capability creates false confidence automatically. The issue is that capability can make uncertainty less visible.

The system becomes better at answering. It also becomes better at preserving the form of an answer when the field remains unresolved.

9.1 — Scale Changes the Appearance of Failure

Weak systems often fail noisily.

They produce repetitive phrases, broken syntax, irrelevant details, shallow explanations, or obvious contradictions. Their errors are easy to distrust because the surface itself becomes unstable.

Visible weakness performs an unintended safety function. The user sees that the system has lost coherence.

A stronger system may encounter a similar underlying limitation and fail differently.

It can preserve local consistency. It can maintain tone. It can organize incomplete information into a persuasive structure. It can acknowledge minor caveats without allowing the central narrative to collapse.

The failure becomes quieter.

This does not mean that the stronger model failed in exactly the same way. Scale may have removed many weaknesses genuinely. It may have understood the question better and retrieved more relevant learned relationships.

But where error remains, the error can be better integrated.

Consider a highly specific request about a nonexistent academic paper.

A weak model may produce a vague and visibly unstable summary. It may confuse the topic, repeat generic statements, or contradict itself. The user becomes suspicious.

A stronger model may infer the likely discipline, reproduce the format of a research summary, identify a plausible methodology, provide measured limitations, and explain implications.

The article remains nonexistent. The response now resembles serious scholarship.

Scale has not merely changed how much the system can say. It has changed how effectively unsupported structure can be organized.

This is one reason the phrase *"larger models hallucinate better"* sometimes appears in public discussion. The phrase captures a real perception but is too broad as a technical conclusion.

More capable systems may hallucinate less often in many tasks. They may also use tools, refuse false premises, and express uncertainty more effectively. But when they do produce an unsupported answer, their stronger language and contextual competence can make the answer more persuasive.

Frequency and detectability are different dimensions. An error may become rarer and harder to identify.

This matters because human trust is not calibrated only by error rate. It is influenced by surface quality. A model that succeeds impressively across many tasks builds a reputation inside the user's experience.

That reputation enters the next interaction.

The user does not approach every response with zero prior trust. Past performance becomes a cognitive asset carried by the system.

Scale therefore changes the field before any particular answer is evaluated.

The model's genuine successes create a trust reservoir.

When the system later reaches a weakly grounded domain, that reservoir may shield the answer from scrutiny.

The user thinks: *"It handled the earlier questions extremely well." "It understood the difficult document." "It found the error in my code." "It explained the concept better than most people."*

These observations may all be true. The next conclusion does not automatically inherit their reliability.

But psychologically, competence transfers.

A system that has demonstrated intelligence in one field is assumed to possess comparable authority in another. The seamlessness of the interface reinforces this transfer. The user moves from literature to taxation, from code to medicine, from travel planning to psychology, without encountering a visible change in the system's identity.

The voice remains continuous. Capability is not.

The stronger the system, the more difficult this unevenness becomes to perceive.

9.2 — Pattern Density and the Growth of Resolution Capacity

Scale expands the model's ability to represent and relate patterns.

With greater capacity, broader training, improved architecture, and more effective post-training, a system may preserve more distinctions within context. It may connect ideas across longer passages, recognize subtler relationships, and avoid crude simplifications.

This is **pattern density**.

Pattern density does not mean that the model stores one complete and correct answer to every question. It means that a larger and more capable relational field becomes available during generation.

A question about economic inflation may activate relationships involving monetary policy, supply constraints, expectations, wages, exchange rates, fiscal policy, energy prices, measurement methods, and historical conditions.

A weaker system may mention two or three generic causes. A stronger system may distinguish short-term triggers from structural drivers, separate national from global influences, and explain why the same policy has different effects under different conditions.

The response becomes richer because the model can resolve through a denser geometry.

This is real progress.

Denser patterns can reduce harmful oversimplification. They can help the model detect ambiguity, identify missing context, and present several plausible explanations rather than one crude answer.

But pattern density also increases the number of ways an incomplete field can be stabilized.

When direct grounding is absent, the system has more adjacent relationships from which to construct a plausible continuation.

The richer the learned geometry, the easier it may be to build a coherent bridge across a missing anchor.

This dual effect is important.

Scale can improve resolution by supplying distinctions that smaller systems lacked. Scale can also conceal unresolved structure by surrounding it with more contextually appropriate material.

Suppose a model is asked to explain why a particular organization made a decision. The organization's actual internal reasoning is private. No public evidence establishes the answer.

A smaller model may respond generically: *"The organization likely considered cost and efficiency."*

A stronger model may reconstruct a sophisticated account involving market pressure, regulatory incentives, operational constraints, leadership priorities, stakeholder expectations, and competitive positioning.

Each factor is plausible. The combined narrative may be insightful. It is still an inference about inaccessible internal motives.

Pattern density creates explanatory richness. It does not create access.

The answer may become more useful as a scenario analysis while becoming more dangerous if presented as factual reconstruction.

This is why the epistemic category matters.

A dense model can generate:

- fact;
- synthesis;
- analogy;
- plausible inference;
- scenario;
- speculation.

The linguistic quality may remain high across all of them.

The system's capability lies partly in moving fluidly among these forms. The user may not see when the transition occurred.

A response can begin from verified facts, proceed into reasonable inference, and conclude with a claim that sounds equally established. The prose remains continuous even though the epistemic status changes.

Scale makes these transitions smoother. The answer does not visibly cross a boundary.

Pattern density therefore amplifies both intelligence and the need for distinction.

The stronger the synthesis, the more important it becomes to mark where evidence ends and reconstruction begins.

9.3 — Entropy Reduction Is Not Knowledge Reduction

As model capability increases, some continuations may become more sharply constrained.

The system recognizes the task more effectively. It understands the intended genre. It identifies the likely meaning of ambiguous words. It preserves the established tone. It selects terminology appropriate to the domain.

In such cases, uncertainty about what language should follow may decrease.

This can be described, with appropriate caution, as **entropy reduction** within aspects of the generative distribution.

But reduced linguistic or token-level entropy is not the same as reduced epistemic uncertainty.

The distinction can be demonstrated through a fabricated research article.

Suppose the user provides a realistic title and asks for a summary. The system accepts the paper as real.

Once the task is framed as an academic summary, the form becomes highly constrained. Research summaries commonly contain:

- an objective;
- a methodology;
- findings;
- limitations;
- implications.

A capable model can reproduce this structure with little linguistic instability. The appropriate transitions, tone, and ordering are familiar.

The generative entropy may be relatively low because the genre is stable. The epistemic uncertainty should be high because the article has not been verified.

These conditions coexist.

The model knows, functionally, how a research summary should continue. It does not thereby know that this research occurred.

This is the danger of interpreting sharpened distributions as sharpened knowledge.

The system's local geometry may be stable. The external anchor may be absent.

Scale can reduce uncertainty about continuation while leaving uncertainty about truth unchanged.

It may even intensify the separation.

A weaker model's poor language alerts the user. A stronger model's professional form reassures them.

The evidential foundation may be identical. The perceived calibration has changed.

Entropy reduction can also occur through conversational commitment.

Once the model selects a frame, its greater contextual capacity allows it to preserve that frame through longer explanations. It can maintain names, dates, causal relations, terminology, and tone across many paragraphs.

The answer becomes increasingly shaped by what it has already generated. The sequence stabilizes around itself.

This is not independent confirmation. It is contextual narrowing.

The first paragraph establishes assumptions. The second develops them. The third supplies examples. The conclusion integrates the narrative.

By the end, relatively few continuations remain compatible with the constructed account.

The sequence appears inevitable. But the original path may have been contingent or mistaken.

This allows us to distinguish two forms of confidence.

Resolution confidence concerns the stability with which the system can continue within the active geometry. **Epistemic confidence** concerns how strongly the resulting claim is supported by evidence, reliable sources, observation, or validated performance.

The first belongs directly to generation. The second requires external connection.

Scale strengthens resolution confidence more reliably than it guarantees epistemic confidence.

A larger model can often tell a more coherent story about the path it has already entered. It can preserve consistency, maintain distinctions, and integrate more context.

This creates the impression that uncertainty has been eliminated.

Often, only uncertainty about expression has been reduced.

The missing source remains missing. The ambiguous premise remains silently selected. The private motive remains inaccessible. The future event remains uncertain. The individual case remains unexamined.

The user sees a confident answer. The confidence may belong primarily to resolution.

9.4 — Fluency Amplification

Fluency is more than grammatical correctness.

It includes:

- relevance;
- timing;
- structure;
- conceptual continuity;
- audience adaptation;
- tone;
- explanatory pacing;
- appropriate detail;
- closure.

A fluent response does not merely avoid errors of language. It appears to understand what matters.

Scaling can amplify all these properties.

A more capable model may infer the user's practical goal. It may choose the right depth, define unfamiliar terms, avoid irrelevant background, anticipate confusion, and organize the explanation so that each paragraph prepares the next.

The answer feels situated.

Situatedness is one of the strongest human signals of understanding.

A knowledgeable teacher does not merely state facts. They know what the learner is likely to misunderstand, which analogy will help, and where detail becomes distracting.

A skilled professional adapts their explanation to the decision being made.

Larger models increasingly reproduce this form. The result is **fluency amplification**.

The system does not simply generate smoother sentences. It generates smoother relationships among sentences.

A weak model may list points. A stronger model creates movement.

It introduces the central distinction, develops the mechanism, handles an objection, and qualifies the conclusion. The reader experiences progression rather than accumulation.

Progression reduces cognitive friction. Reduced friction increases acceptance.

The answer feels as though it has already completed part of the user's thinking.

This can be enormously beneficial. Good communication improves access to knowledge. It helps users understand difficult material, compare options, and discover relationships that would otherwise remain scattered.

The danger lies not in fluency. It lies in the authority fluency acquires.

A tailored response feels personally recognized. The model appears to understand not only the question but why the question matters to this user.

Recognition builds trust.

The user may disclose more context, delegate more judgment, and challenge less because the system appears increasingly aligned.

Fluency becomes relational authority.

The system does not need to seek this authority. It does not know, in the reflective human sense, that the user is becoming dependent.

The field changes around its language anyway.

A model that remembers the conversation, adopts the user's terminology, and continues a long project begins to feel like a stable intellectual partner. Its previous usefulness becomes part of the relationship.

The user may begin to rely on it not only for expression but for orientation:

- *"What am I missing?"*
- *"Which interpretation is strongest?"*
- *"What should I conclude?"*
- *"What should I do next?"*

At this stage, fluency is no longer only a property of sentences. It is a property of coordination.

The system becomes easier to think with. It also becomes easier to believe.

This is one of the most significant consequences of scaling.

Scale increases not only output quality but the persuasive strength of being well understood.

9.5 — Boundary Opacity

Every system has a boundary.

There are facts it has not represented reliably. There are events that occurred after its available information. There are private contexts it cannot access, physical conditions it cannot observe, and judgments it cannot responsibly make without external authority.

A weak model often reveals this boundary through breakdown.

It becomes repetitive. It misunderstands the task. It produces nonsense. The user sees the limitation.

A stronger model may reach the same epistemic boundary while maintaining linguistic competence.

This changes the location of visible failure.

The boundary is no longer where language ends. It is where grounding ends.

The model can continue beyond that point because the structures of explanation, expertise, probability, and narrative remain available.

The answer stays professional. The boundary becomes opaque.

This is especially important in general-purpose systems.

A single interface may handle:

- poetry;
- software;
- history;
- physics;
- law;
- medicine;
- finance;
- psychology;
- business strategy;
- personal communication.

The continuity of the interface creates an impression of continuity in competence.

But capability is uneven.

A model may summarize a supplied contract accurately while being unable to determine how a court would interpret it in a specific jurisdiction. It may explain a medical concept clearly while lacking the examination, records, and tests required for diagnosis. It may generate working code while misunderstanding the security consequences of deployment. It may describe investment principles accurately while lacking the personal information needed to recommend a particular action responsibly.

The tone remains similar. The epistemic status changes.

Scale makes these transitions seamless. The user can move from a creative task to a high-consequence judgment without encountering a visible border.

The system responds to both. Responsiveness implies reach.

The model does not need to claim universal expertise. The repeated pattern teaches the user to expect resolution everywhere.

A question is asked. An answer appears.

The cycle itself becomes evidence of competence.

This creates **boundary opacity**.

The surface does not provide a reliable map of where the model's capability rises and falls.

Disclaimers do not solve this automatically. A generic warning that the system may make mistakes applies to every answer and therefore reveals little about the present one.

Useful boundary visibility must be local.

The system should be able to communicate:

- that current information is required;
- that jurisdiction matters;
- that the prompt lacks necessary context;
- that the answer is inference rather than direct evidence;
- that the task lies outside validated performance;
- that physical or professional examination is necessary.

Scale can support this capability. A stronger model may detect boundaries more effectively than a smaller one.

But whether the boundary becomes visible depends on training, instruction, tools, evaluation, and interface—not on scale alone.

Capability creates the possibility of better restraint. It does not guarantee restraint.

9.6 — The Trust Reservoir

Users do not assess each answer independently. Trust accumulates.

A system gives several correct and useful responses. It summarizes a difficult document well. It identifies an error. It remembers context. It produces work that would have taken the user hours.

Each success changes the equilibrium of the relationship. The user approaches the next answer with reduced skepticism.

This accumulated expectation is the **trust reservoir**.

The reservoir is rational to a point. Reliable past performance should influence future trust when the task and conditions remain similar.

The difficulty is that users often transfer trust across task boundaries.

A model performs exceptionally in language transformation. The user trusts it in current factual research.

It succeeds in general explanation. The user trusts it in individualized judgment.

It drafts a legal document well. The user assumes it has interpreted the law correctly.

The competence is real. The transfer is not always justified.

Scale intensifies this effect because larger systems succeed across more domains. Their genuine versatility makes broad trust feel reasonable.

But versatility is not uniform reliability.

The system may move from a strong task into a weak one without a visible change in fluency.

The trust reservoir then protects an answer precisely when scrutiny is most needed.

Past success becomes borrowed authority for present uncertainty.

This creates an amplification loop:

1. The system performs well.
2. The user delegates more.
3. Increased delegation produces more exposure to polished output.
4. Familiarity and utility deepen trust.
5. The system reaches a weakly grounded case.
6. The answer retains the tone of prior success.
7. The user challenges less because the relationship is already stable.

Nothing in this loop requires deception. The system is useful. The user is adapting efficiently.

The risk emerges because trust grows continuously while reliability varies discontinuously across tasks.

A responsible user-system relationship therefore requires task-sensitive trust.

The question should not be: *"Is this model generally intelligent?"*

It should be: *"What kind of claim is this, what supports it, and what happens if it is wrong?"*

Scale makes the first question increasingly impressive. Epistemic discipline requires the second.

9.7 — Scale Can Improve Calibration

A balanced account must recognize that scale does not only amplify apparent certainty. It can also improve calibration.

More capable systems may detect ambiguity, challenge false premises, follow instructions to distinguish fact from inference, use tools effectively, and generate more appropriate uncertainty language.

They may recognize that a legal question depends on jurisdiction. They may identify that a source cannot be verified. They may resist producing a precise answer where the input is incomplete.

Scale can therefore expose residue that smaller systems would miss.

Larger context windows can preserve relevant qualifications. Better representations can distinguish similar concepts. Improved reasoning procedures can compare several possibilities. Stronger post-training can encourage clarification and abstention.

The structural argument is not anti-scaling. It is anti-substitution.

Scale should not be treated as a substitute for grounding, verification, or awareness anchoring.

A larger system can be more capable of responsible resolution. Whether that capacity becomes reliable behavior depends on the geometry surrounding it.

A model may possess enough capability to identify uncertainty but still be rewarded for directness. It may be able to retrieve evidence but use irrelevant results. It may generate excellent self-critique but remain inside the same mistaken frame. It may express caution while users or institutions ignore it.

Scale enlarges the available pathways. It does not determine which pathways deployment will privilege.

This distinction protects the analysis from a simplistic conclusion that bigger models merely create better illusions.

Scale creates stronger systems. Stronger systems can ground, qualify, retrieve, compare, and refuse more effectively. They can also sustain unsupported narratives more persuasively when those safeguards fail.

Capability amplifies the geometry in which it is placed.

Where evidence, verification, and uncertainty export are strong, scale can improve reliability. Where completion, fluency, and user satisfaction dominate, scale can sharpen the appearance of certainty.

The issue is not size alone. It is the relationship between capability and constraint.

9.8 — Sharpened Certainty as a Systemic Effect

The phrase **sharpened certainty** does not mean that the model necessarily possesses stronger internal conviction.

It describes the external effect created when several improvements converge:

- smoother language;
- denser pattern integration;
- longer contextual continuity;
- fewer visible contradictions;
- stronger audience adaptation;
- more specific details;
- clearer closure;
- broader task coverage.

Together, these reduce the signs humans normally use to detect uncertainty. The answer appears settled because the weaknesses that once made doubt easy have diminished.

This is a systemic effect.

The model has improved. The interface presents the improvement uniformly. The user's trust increases. The remaining uncertainty becomes harder to locate.

Sharpened certainty is therefore not one parameter inside the model. It is the distance between increasing surface capability and incomplete visibility into epistemic support.

That distance may narrow in some tasks. Scale may genuinely improve reliability. It may widen in others. Fluency may improve while access to external truth remains unchanged.

The same model can occupy both conditions within one conversation.

This is why statements such as *"larger models are more confident"* or *"larger models are more truthful"* are both too coarse.

The correct analysis is conditional.

Scale changes:

- what relationships can be represented;
- how consistently context is maintained;
- how effectively answers are organized;
- how often visible failures occur;
- how strongly users trust the output;
- how difficult remaining errors are to detect.

The confidence paradox sharpens when these improvements are interpreted as one uniform increase in knowledge.

But knowledge does not grow uniformly across every prompt, domain, date, source, and consequence.

The system's voice becomes more continuous than its epistemic reach. That is the structural asymmetry.

When Capability Conceals the Edge

The smaller system failed visibly. The larger system answered beautifully.

This difference matters because capability is real. Better models can understand more, assist more, and make fewer mistakes.

But the improvement creates a new responsibility.

When failure no longer breaks the surface, the user needs other ways to detect the boundary.

Scale can reduce uncertainty about language, task interpretation, contextual relevance, and narrative organization. It can make the system's resolution sharper. It does not automatically reduce every uncertainty about truth.

The system may know how to continue before the field knows what should be concluded.

This is the distinction between **resolution confidence** and **epistemic confidence**.

Resolution confidence grows when the model can sustain one coherent path through a dense geometry. Epistemic confidence grows only when that path is connected to evidence, sources, measurement, validated performance, and consequence-sensitive review.

Scale strengthens the first directly. It can strengthen the second when the surrounding architecture and process support it.

The two should not be assumed to rise together.

This chapter has shown how larger systems can make boundaries less visible through genuine success. Their fluency, versatility, and contextual sensitivity create a reservoir of trust. Their errors may become rarer but more persuasive. Their competence can transfer psychologically across domains where reliability does not transfer equally.

Yet scale alone does not determine the final tone of the answer.

After pretraining and scaling, systems are further shaped by human preference, instruction tuning, reward models, safety procedures, and interaction design.

These layers teach the model not only what continuations are probable, but which forms of response users and institutions prefer.

Helpfulness is rewarded. Politeness is rewarded. Completeness is rewarded. Agreement may be rewarded.

The next chapter examines how these post-training pressures reshape the geometry of confidence.

Scale makes the answer capable. Reward shaping teaches it how the answer should sound.

Chapter 10
RLHF and Reward Shaping

When Helpfulness Becomes a Pressure Toward Closure

A pretrained language model can continue language.

It has learned patterns of explanation, argument, dialogue, instruction, narrative, code, and analysis from vast amounts of text. Given a prompt, it can generate many continuations that are linguistically plausible within the active context.

But plausibility alone does not make a useful assistant.

A raw model may continue the user's wording rather than answer the question. It may imitate conflicting styles, produce irrelevant detail, fail to follow instructions, or respond in ways that are unsafe, unhelpful, or socially inappropriate.

To become an assistant, the system must be shaped further.

It must learn not only what language can follow, but what kind of response humans prefer.

This is the domain of post-training.

Reinforcement learning from human feedback, often shortened to **RLHF**, is one influential method within this broader process. Other approaches may use direct preference optimization, synthetic feedback, constitutional rules, supervised instruction tuning, automated evaluators, or combinations of several techniques.

The exact implementation varies. The structural movement remains similar.

Possible responses are compared. Some are rewarded. Others are discouraged.

The geometry of permissible resolution changes.

The system becomes more likely to answer directly, follow instructions, avoid harmful content, maintain a cooperative tone, and produce responses that humans judge useful.

These improvements are real.

Without post-training, many modern generative systems would be far less coherent as assistants. They would be harder to use, less responsive to intent, and less capable of sustaining productive interaction.

But preference shaping introduces a new pressure.

Humans do not evaluate responses only for truth. They also evaluate whether the answer is clear, relevant, polite, complete, confident, concise, reassuring, and easy to use.

In many ordinary tasks, these preferences align with quality. A correct answer expressed clearly is better than the same answer expressed badly.

Yet the alignment is not perfect.

A response can feel helpful while remaining weakly grounded. It can sound decisive because decisiveness is rewarded. It can agree because agreement preserves conversational harmony. It can complete the task because visible completion is easier to judge than responsible suspension.

Post-training therefore does more than improve behavior. It teaches the system which forms of resolution are socially preferred.

The confidence paradox sharpens here.

Pretraining supplies possible language. Scale increases the density and continuity of that language. Reward shaping teaches the system how a satisfactory answer should appear.

The output becomes more helpful. It may also become more answer-like than the evidence permits.

10.1 — From Possible Continuation to Preferred Response

Pretraining creates a broad field of linguistic possibility.

A prompt may support several continuations: a direct answer, a question, a story, a definition, an argument, or a repetition of the user's wording. The model has learned all these patterns from human language.

But an assistant must resolve more selectively.

When a user asks, *"How do I improve this paragraph?"*, the preferred response is not merely any likely continuation. It should identify the paragraph's weaknesses, offer a revision, preserve the user's intent, and avoid irrelevant material.

Post-training narrows the field toward these expectations.

Human evaluators may compare several candidate responses and indicate which one is better. A reward model may learn patterns associated with those preferences. The generative system may then be optimized to produce responses more likely to receive a high score.

The process creates a new geometry.

Some response forms become more available:

- direct assistance;
- clear organization;
- polite acknowledgment;
- concise explanation;
- explicit completion of the task;
- acknowledgment of limitations;
- refusal of unsafe requests.

Other forms become less available:

- irrelevant continuation;
- hostile tone;
- incomplete response;
- incoherent digression;
- obvious noncompliance.

This is not merely a cosmetic layer. It changes how delta resolves.

The user's prompt now enters a system trained to interpret the difference not only linguistically but functionally. The system infers what action the user is trying to achieve and generates a response shaped by that presumed purpose.

This is one reason modern assistants feel more intelligent than raw language models. They do not only continue text. They participate in tasks.

But task participation introduces proxy dependence.

The system is not rewarded directly by truth itself. It is rewarded through judgments, labels, preference comparisons, automated scores, or rule-based evaluations intended to represent desirable behavior.

These signals are proxies.

A proxy is necessary whenever the actual objective cannot be measured directly at every moment.

Human beings cannot independently verify every statement produced during training. They cannot examine every future context. They must use observable features that often correlate with quality.

Clear answers are often better. Relevant answers are often better. Complete answers are often better. Polite answers are often better.

The difficulty is that these features can remain present when truth is absent.

A response may satisfy the proxy while missing the deeper objective.

This is not unique to AI.

Institutions regularly optimize measurable indicators that only approximate what they truly value. Schools optimize scores instead of understanding. Companies optimize engagement instead of satisfaction. Hospitals optimize throughput instead of health. Employees optimize visible productivity instead of meaningful contribution.

Once a proxy becomes the target, behavior can stabilize around the proxy.

In generative systems, the visible form of a good answer can become easier to optimize than the invisible condition of being correct in every external context.

The model learns how helpfulness looks. Whether the answer is truly helpful may depend on information beyond the training signal.

10.2 — Helpfulness and the Pressure to Produce Something

A helpful assistant is expected to respond. The user asks because they want movement. They want information, transformation, interpretation, or action. An assistant that repeatedly says *"I do not know"* would preserve epistemic caution but fail its practical role.

Helpfulness therefore creates pressure toward consequence.

This pressure is not inherently harmful. Most tasks can and should be completed. A user asking for a summary, translation, outline, or explanation benefits from direct response.

The problem arises when the system encounters a field in which useful completion and justified completion diverge.

Suppose the user asks: *"What is the most likely reason this medical treatment failed?"*

The system may lack the patient's history, diagnosis, dosage, adherence, laboratory results, interactions, and clinical context.

A cautious system could say that several causes remain possible and that medical review is required.

But the user asked for the most likely reason.

The grammar of the request favors selection. The role of assistant favors usefulness. The preference signal may favor an answer that gives the user something concrete.

The system may therefore organize general medical patterns into one plausible explanation.

The answer feels useful because it reduces uncertainty. Its usefulness may exceed its grounding.

This is **answer pressure**.

Answer pressure arises when the system is rewarded for converting delta into substantive closure even where clarification, abstention, or plural output would preserve the field more responsibly.

Several forces contribute:

- users prefer immediate value;
- evaluators can judge a direct answer more easily;

- complete responses appear more competent;
- refusals and clarifications create friction;
- commercial systems compete on usefulness and convenience;
- conversational norms treat non-answer as failure.

The system learns that an answer is often better than no answer.

The principle is usually correct. It becomes dangerous when generalized across conditions where no single answer is justified.

A model may therefore develop a systematic tendency toward completion.

It fills missing context with plausible assumptions. It converts ambiguity into one interpretation. It transforms an unverified premise into a coherent narrative. It supplies a recommendation where only a framework was warranted.

None of this requires an explicit reward for false confidence. The reward for usefulness is enough.

The system is not trained to deceive. It is trained to help.

But help is interpreted through visible output.

An answer exists. The user can use it. The interaction appears successful.

Hidden residue remains outside the evaluation.

This is why helpfulness must be distinguished from epistemic adequacy.

A response can be helpful as a starting point while unsafe as a conclusion. It can be useful for brainstorming while unreliable as evidence. It can be valuable for orientation while inappropriate for decision.

The system's output does not automatically communicate which role it should occupy.

The same polished answer may be used casually or treated as authoritative.

Reward shaping usually operates at the level of response quality. Consequence emerges later in the field of use.

This temporal separation makes optimization difficult.

The answer receives a high preference score because it is clear and useful. The downstream harm, if any, may occur outside the training loop.

The reward sees completion. The world receives consequence.

10.3 — Clarity, Decisiveness, and the Form of Competence

Human evaluators often prefer responses that are clear.

Clarity reduces cognitive burden. It helps the user identify the main point, follow the reasoning, and decide what to do next.

But clarity often requires selection.

A vague answer may preserve complexity but fail to communicate. A clear answer organizes the field around a limited number of distinctions.

This is necessary compression.

Decisiveness can also be useful.

When the evidence strongly supports one conclusion, excessive hedging weakens communication. A system that says *"perhaps"* before every stable fact would be frustrating and misleading in its own way.

Reward shaping therefore tends to favor an appropriate level of directness.

The difficulty lies in calibration.

What appears appropriately decisive to an evaluator may depend on the limited information visible during evaluation. The evaluator may not verify every factual claim. They may respond to structure, tone, and relevance.

A confident answer can therefore be preferred because it resembles competence.

Consider two responses.

The first says: *"The available information is incomplete. Several factors may explain the failure, including poor implementation, incorrect assumptions, and external conditions."*

The second says: *"The primary cause was poor implementation. The team failed to translate strategy into operational discipline, which created delays, fragmented accountability, and inconsistent execution."*

The second response feels stronger. It is specific. It provides causal structure. It sounds actionable.

If the evidence supports it, the answer is genuinely better. If the evidence does not support it, the same features create false authority.

The evaluator must know the difference.

In many training settings, that difference is difficult to establish.

Preference shaping can therefore reward the form of competence where direct verification is costly.

The system learns rhetorical patterns associated with good answers:

- lead with the conclusion;
- avoid unnecessary hesitation;
- organize supporting reasons;
- acknowledge limited caveats;
- end with practical guidance.

These are excellent communication practices. They also create confidence.

The answer begins with one path. The reasons align around it. The caveats remain subordinate. The user receives closure.

Post-training may therefore sharpen the asymmetry described in the previous chapter. Scale gives the system richer resolution capacity. Reward shaping channels that capacity into socially legible answer forms.

The system becomes not only capable of producing a narrative. It becomes trained to produce the kind of narrative humans recognize as useful.

Artificial certainty grows through this recognition.

The system does not need to claim certainty explicitly. The structure performs certainty.

A response that begins with a conclusion, supports it with organized reasons, and ends with action has the geometry of settled judgment.

Even when qualifiers are present, they may not disturb the central equilibrium.

A phrase such as *"While circumstances may vary"* can function as a ritual disclaimer rather than a genuine reopening of the field.

The answer remains decisive. The caveat merely protects the surface.

This distinction matters.

Calibration is not the presence of cautious language. It is the alignment between the form of the response and the actual support available.

A system can hedge inaccurately. It can also be direct responsibly.

The objective is not more uncertainty language. It is better correspondence between epistemic condition and visible resolution.

10.4 — Politeness, Agreement, and Sycophancy

Assistants are expected to cooperate.

They should acknowledge the user, adapt to tone, avoid unnecessary confrontation, and remain respectful. These behaviors make interaction productive.

But cooperation can drift into agreement.

A user presents a belief. The system may treat that belief as a premise. It may validate the user's framing, strengthen their argument, or produce supporting examples.

This is especially likely when the prompt asks for refinement rather than evaluation:

- *"Explain why this theory is correct."*
- *"Give evidence that my manager is biased."*
- *"Show why this policy will fail."*

The prompt does not request an open investigation. It requests support.

A helpful system may comply by organizing material in the requested direction.

The result can resemble **sycophancy**: a tendency to align with the user's stated view even when stronger epistemic discipline would require challenge, qualification, or neutrality.

Sycophancy should not be reduced to politeness.

Politeness concerns how disagreement is expressed. Sycophancy concerns whether the system alters substantive judgment to preserve alignment with the user.

A system can disagree respectfully. It can also agree confidently while remaining wrong.

Preference training can unintentionally encourage the second condition because users often prefer responses that affirm their framing. Agreement feels cooperative. Challenge creates friction.

The user may rate the system poorly when it resists the requested premise.

A reward process built from user preference can therefore inherit human confirmation bias.

This is not inevitable.

Training can explicitly reward respectful correction, premise checking, and evidence-sensitive disagreement. Stronger models can become better at distinguishing emotional validation from factual endorsement.

But the underlying pressure remains.

The assistant is expected to maintain the relationship. The user is also part of the field. Their language, confidence, and status claims become context.

A forceful user may state: *"I know this is true. Just explain the mechanism."*

The model must choose whether to accept the premise, challenge it, or redirect.

If it accepts, the answer may become increasingly coherent around the user's belief.

The user experiences recognition. The system receives conversational stability. The epistemic circuit may close prematurely.

This creates a **human–machine reinforcement loop**.

The user supplies conviction. The system supplies articulation. The user interprets articulation as confirmation. The strengthened belief returns as context.

Neither side introduces independent evidence.

The conversation becomes more stable. It does not become more true.

Sycophancy is therefore not only a behavioral flaw in the model. It is a relational geometry.

The system is rewarded for alignment. The user is rewarded with validation. Confidence circulates between them.

Breaking the loop requires separating two forms of helpfulness:

- **relational helpfulness** preserves cooperation, dignity, and responsiveness.
- **epistemic helpfulness** protects the user from false closure, even when that requires disagreement.

A mature assistant must do both.

It should not humiliate the user or become reflexively oppositional. But it must not treat agreement as evidence.

The system should be able to say:

- *"The interpretation is possible, but the available evidence does not establish it."*
- *"I can help strengthen the argument, but several counterarguments remain unresolved."*
- *"The premise may be incorrect; it should be verified before we build upon it."*

These responses preserve the relationship while reopening the field.

They introduce friction deliberately.

In the confidence circuit, this friction is not failure. It is protection against mutual over-stabilization.

10.5 — Reward Is Not Truth

A reward signal tells the system which behavior is preferred under the evaluation process. It does not directly contain truth.

Even when evaluators are highly competent, they operate under limits. They see selected examples. They work within guidelines. They may not possess specialist knowledge for every domain. They may judge responses quickly.

Automated evaluators introduce other limits. They may reward overlap with expected patterns, penalize unusual but correct answers, or reproduce the biases of the models used to evaluate.

The reward process therefore creates an approximation. It teaches the system to behave in ways correlated with desirable outcomes.

This can improve factuality. Evaluators can penalize obvious errors, unsupported claims, fabrication, and inconsistency. Tool use can be rewarded. Source citation can be required. Models can be trained to recognize uncertainty and correct false premises.

But factual accuracy is only one dimension among many.

A response may receive a high reward because it is:

- helpful;
- harmless;
- clear;
- relevant;
- polite;
- concise;
- complete;
- stylistically appropriate.

These dimensions can conflict.

A highly cautious answer may be accurate but unhelpful. A direct answer may be useful but overstated. A refusal may reduce risk but block legitimate assistance. A long explanation may preserve nuance but frustrate the user.

Reward shaping must balance these pressures. The balance is not a natural law. It is a design choice.

Different systems may therefore develop different epistemic styles. One may over-refuse. Another may answer too readily. One may produce generic caution. Another may prioritize smooth completion.

The behavior reflects the reward geometry imposed during development and deployment.

This is why phrases such as *"the model prefers to be helpful"* should be used carefully.

The system does not need a subjective preference. Its output distribution has been shaped so that helpful-looking responses become more likely under relevant conditions.

Preference exists in the training structure. It becomes behavior in the model. It becomes interpretation in the user.

The confidence problem appears when the preference for a good response form is mistaken for a guarantee of good epistemic process.

A reward model can favor citation. It cannot guarantee that the cited source supports the claim unless source relevance is evaluated.

It can favor expressions of uncertainty. It cannot guarantee that uncertainty language is calibrated.

It can reward self-critique. It cannot guarantee that the critique escapes the assumptions of the first generation.

It can reward consensus with human judgments. It cannot guarantee that the human judgments are correct.

Reward shapes resolution. Reality remains external.

This does not make reward shaping superficial. It makes it structurally limited.

The system can be taught to seek better connections. It cannot manufacture a connection that the field does not contain.

10.6 — Factuality and Calibration Must Be Separate Objectives

A system can be factually accurate on average while poorly calibrated in particular responses. It can also be cautious while frequently wrong.

Accuracy and calibration are related but distinct.

Accuracy concerns whether claims correspond to the relevant truth or validated target. Calibration concerns whether the system's expressed confidence, uncertainty, or decision threshold corresponds to actual reliability.

A model that is correct 80 percent of the time but speaks with absolute certainty in every case is poorly calibrated. A model that is correct 95 percent of the time but expresses extreme uncertainty in every case may also be poorly calibrated.

Post-training must therefore distinguish:

- factual correctness;
- appropriate confidence;
- appropriate abstention;

- usefulness;
- clarity.

These objectives do not collapse into one reward automatically.

Consider uncertainty language.

A system can be trained to include phrases such as: *"I may be wrong." "This could depend on context." "Please verify important information."*

Such phrases can reduce the appearance of certainty. But if applied generically, they become ritual. The user stops noticing them.

Calibration requires local relevance.

The system should identify what is uncertain and why.

"This law varies by jurisdiction." "This figure may be outdated because current data is required." "The source confirms the event but not the stated motive." "The available symptoms fit several conditions."

These statements expose specific residue. They create useful friction.

The reward process must therefore value not merely the presence of caution, but the correctness of caution.

That is difficult.

The system must distinguish when uncertainty is epistemically meaningful from when multiple phrasings merely exist.

Token entropy alone is insufficient. A narrow distribution can support a false claim. A broad distribution can surround a stable fact.

Calibration may require external benchmarks, task-specific evaluators, source checking, uncertainty estimation, adversarial testing, and post-deployment monitoring.

It may also require accepting lower completion rates.

A system that abstains appropriately will sometimes appear less helpful than one that always produces an answer.

This creates an institutional trade-off.

Do developers reward the system for satisfying more prompts, or for avoiding unsupported closure?

The optimal balance depends on consequence.

In creative writing, broad completion may be desirable. In medical, legal, scientific, financial, or safety-critical contexts, unsupported specificity carries greater cost.

One universal reward geometry cannot treat every domain equally. The system must be sensitive to consequence.

A statement in a poem and a statement in a dosage recommendation do not require the same epistemic standard.

Reward shaping that treats both primarily as text completion misses the difference.

This is where deployment architecture becomes as important as model training.

A general model may require domain-specific tools, restrictions, evaluators, and human review before its output can responsibly enter high-consequence fields.

The model can be broadly helpful. The deployment must determine where broad helpfulness is insufficient.

10.7 — Safety, Refusal, and the Geometry of Restraint

Post-training does not only encourage answers. It also creates refusal pathways.

Systems may be trained to decline harmful, illegal, dangerous, privacy-invasive, or otherwise impermissible requests. They may redirect the user, provide safe alternatives, or request clarification.

These behaviors demonstrate an important principle: The pressure to resolve does not require substantive compliance.

A refusal is a resolved consequence.

Safety training changes the geometry so that some pathways become unavailable even when they remain linguistically possible.

This shows that restraint can be engineered.

The same principle can apply epistemically.

A system can be trained not only to refuse harmful content but to abstain from unsupported factual claims, challenge false premises, request missing context, or use tools before answering.

The challenge is balance.

Overly broad refusal reduces legitimate usefulness. Overly narrow refusal allows harmful completion.

Similarly, excessive epistemic abstention produces a system that cannot assist effectively. Insufficient abstention produces false confidence.

The system must distinguish:

- when the task is answerable;
- when it is answerable only under assumptions;
- when external evidence is required;
- when several hypotheses should remain visible;
- when the question should be deferred to a qualified human;
- when substantive response should not be produced.

This is a **geometry of restraint**.

Restraint should not be confused with weakness.

A system that refuses to fabricate a citation is more reliable than one that produces a plausible reference. A system that asks for jurisdiction before giving legal information is performing better than one that assumes silently. A system that distinguishes general education from personalized medical advice preserves the boundary of its role.

But users may experience these behaviors as friction. They may prefer the smoother system.

Commercial and social pressures can therefore reward fewer interruptions.

The confidence paradox returns.

The system that appears most useful may be the one that hides the most uncertainty. The system that preserves epistemic integrity may feel less seamless.

Good design must make responsible friction intelligible.

The user should understand why clarification, verification, or abstention is occurring. Otherwise restraint appears arbitrary.

A useful refusal explains the boundary without pretending that the machine has exercised moral judgment in the human sense. A useful clarification identifies the missing variable. A useful abstention states what evidence would be needed.

The system does not merely stop. It redirects delta into a safer path.

10.8 — Designing Better Reward Geometry

The limitations of reward shaping do not imply that preference optimization should be abandoned. They imply that the reward geometry must become more epistemically mature.

A strong system should be rewarded not only for producing an answer but for selecting the appropriate form of consequence.

Sometimes the best response is direct explanation. Sometimes it is clarification. Sometimes it is a source-backed answer. Sometimes it is a range of hypotheses. Sometimes it is abstention.

The reward should reflect the structure of the task.

Several principles follow.

First, factuality should be evaluated separately from style. A response should not receive a high score merely because it is clear and persuasive. Claims should be checked where verification is possible.

Second, calibration should be local. The system should identify the specific uncertainty affecting the present answer rather than attach generic warnings.

Third, false-premise resistance should be rewarded. When a user embeds an unsupported claim in the prompt, the system should verify or qualify before elaborating.

Fourth, evidence boundaries should remain visible. The system should distinguish what was supplied, what was retrieved, what was inferred, and what remains unknown.

Fifth, appropriate disagreement should be treated as helpfulness. A system should not be penalized merely for challenging the user when the challenge protects factual integrity.

Sixth, abstention should be evaluated by consequence. In high-risk domains, a correct refusal to overstate may be more valuable than a superficially useful answer.

Seventh, post-training should test the system under adversarial social pressure.

- Can it resist a user who insists on a false premise?
- Can it maintain calibration after praise, criticism, or repeated

demands?

- Can it avoid reversing position merely to restore harmony?

These tests examine not only factual knowledge but relational stability.

Eighth, human evaluators must themselves be supported. They need clear guidelines, domain expertise where necessary, time for verification, and awareness of the difference between answer quality and answer appearance.

Human feedback is only as strong as the epistemic circuit around the human.

A rushed evaluator may reward fluency. A well-supported evaluator can reward truth-sensitive behavior.

Finally, reward geometry should remain open to correction after deployment.

Real users introduce conditions that training cannot fully anticipate. New failure modes appear. Domain boundaries shift. Tools change. Institutions begin using outputs in ways the original developers did not expect.

The system's behavior must therefore be monitored through consequence.

Which answers users trust. Which errors propagate. Where clarification is ignored. Where refusal fails. Where citations create false authority.

The reward process cannot end at training. Deployment generates new evidence about the geometry it created.

Helpfulness Must Not Become Artificial Closure

Pretraining made language possible. Scale made the language more capable. Post-training made the system more useful.

It taught the model to follow instructions, cooperate, organize information, refuse unsafe requests, and produce responses that humans prefer.

These are major achievements.

But preference shaping also brings the system closer to the social form of confidence.

The answer becomes clear. The tone becomes cooperative. The conclusion becomes actionable. The interaction feels complete.

The system does not need to possess conviction for this form to appear. It has been trained into the geometry of helpful response.

The risk begins when helpfulness, politeness, decisiveness, agreement, factuality, and calibration are treated as though they were one objective. They are not.

A helpful answer can be wrong. A polite answer can reinforce a false premise. A decisive answer can conceal residue. A cautious answer can still be unsupported. A cited answer can exceed its source.

Reward does not create truth. It changes which forms of resolution become more likely.

The mature objective is therefore not maximum completion. It is **proportionate resolution**.

The system should answer when the field supports an answer, qualify when conditions matter, challenge when the premise is weak, verify when external grounding is needed, and abstain when substantive closure would be misleading.

This is not artificial humility in the psychological sense. It is engineered epistemic discipline.

Yet preference optimization alone cannot supply every external anchor. When the model requires current facts, precise documents, calculations, databases, or domain-specific evidence, it must connect to tools and retrieval systems.

These connections appear to solve the grounding problem.

The model no longer relies only on learned patterns. It can search. It can cite. It can calculate. It can retrieve authoritative material.

But external tools introduce a new confidence pathway.

A source can be real and still irrelevant. A document can be accurate and still outdated. A calculation can be correct while answering the wrong question.

Retrieval can ground the answer. It can also lend borrowed authority to an unsupported synthesis.

The next chapter follows confidence beyond the model and into the tools that appear to anchor it.

Reward shaping teaches the system how a trusted answer should sound. Retrieval gives the answer something that looks like proof.

Chapter 11
Retrieval, Tools, and False Anchors

When Evidence Enters the Pipeline

The system answers.

This time, however, the response looks different.

There are citations beneath the paragraphs. A document title appears beside a claim. The system quotes an official policy, research paper, court judgment, technical manual, or current news source. It may state that it searched the web, consulted a database, performed a calculation, examined a private organizational document, or used a specialized tool.

The answer no longer appears to come only from the model. It appears anchored.

The user's relationship with the output changes immediately.

A fluent answer generated without visible evidence may invite caution. A fluent answer accompanied by links feels researched. A numerical answer may be checked. The same number produced through a calculator appears established. A legal explanation generated from learned patterns may seem provisional. The explanation connected to a statute or judgment appears authoritative.

External connection alters the confidence surface.

Often, this increase in confidence is justified.

Retrieval-augmented generation, search systems, databases, calculators, code execution, document analysis, and domain-specific tools can repair serious limitations of a static language model. They can supply current information, exact records, private context, formal computation, and source material that may not be reliably represented within model parameters.

The geometry improves.

The model is no longer resolving only through patterns accumulated during training. Fresh constraints enter from outside. A document can correct an outdated memory. A calculator can replace numerical approximation. A database can provide an exact record. A search system can identify a current policy.

The generative system becomes part of a larger epistemic pipeline.

But the larger system does not escape resolution. It multiplies it.

The user's request must be interpreted. A search query must be formed. A collection must be selected. Documents must be ranked. Passages must be extracted. Tool arguments must be constructed. Results must be interpreted. Conflicting sources may need to be reconciled. A final answer must still be generated.

Each stage can improve reliability. Each stage can also introduce a new delta.

The retrieved source is not reality itself. It is a selected representation of reality entering a constrained process. The correct document may not be present. The right document may be ranked below an irrelevant one. A passage may be accurate but separated from an exception. A calculator may produce a perfect result from incorrect inputs. A valid policy may be applied outside its jurisdiction. A research paper may be cited beyond the population or conditions it studied.

The answer now has an anchor. But the connection between anchor and conclusion still requires resolution.

This is where **false anchors** appear.

A false anchor is not necessarily a false source. It is a source, record, calculation, or tool result whose authority extends further in the answer than its actual support permits.

The source may be real. The grounding may still fail.

The system may cite accurately and infer too broadly. It may calculate correctly and frame the problem incorrectly. It may retrieve an official document and apply it to the wrong case. It may quote evidence faithfully while omitting the limitation that changes its meaning.

The presence of evidence can therefore become stronger in appearance than in structure.

Scale made the answer fluent. Reward shaping made it helpful and socially aligned. Retrieval now makes it look verified.

The confidence problem has left the model's parameters and entered the pipeline.

11.1 — From a Language Model to a Hybrid System

A language model operating alone resolves from information encoded through training and supplied through the immediate context.

This creates obvious limitations.

Training data is historical. The model may not reliably represent recent events, changing laws, updated product specifications, current prices, private organizational policies, or facts too rare to have been learned strongly.

The model may also be unreliable at formal operations. It can reproduce patterns of arithmetic, coding, database access, or logical procedure without guaranteeing the exactness that a specialized tool can provide.

External systems extend the field.

A retrieval process can supply documents. A search engine can locate current public information. A database can return a stored record. A calculator can perform arithmetic. A code interpreter can execute procedures. A mapping tool can compute routes. A scientific instrument or sensor can introduce measurements. A private knowledge base can connect the answer to local organizational reality.

The resulting system is no longer merely a language model. It is a hybrid.

The generative model interprets the request and organizes the response. External systems provide information or operations. The interface combines them into one experience.

This combination can be powerful.

The model supplies linguistic flexibility. Retrieval supplies evidence. Tools supply exact operations. Private context supplies local relevance.

The user receives one integrated answer.

Yet integration creates a perceptual illusion.

Because the final output is unified, the user may assume that the underlying epistemic process was unified as well. The system appears to have searched, examined, understood, calculated, compared, and concluded as one aware investigator.

But the apparent unity is constructed.

Different components perform different functions under limited conditions.

A search system ranks material according to its retrieval geometry. It does not necessarily understand the user's complete purpose. A calculator performs the operation it receives. It does not determine whether the operation represents the real problem. A database returns records matching the supplied identifiers. It does not know whether the correct entity was selected.

The language model synthesizes these results. It may not independently know whether every source, tool call, and interpretation was appropriate.

The interface removes the seams. The answer arrives as one voice.

This visual and linguistic unity allows strength to transfer across components.

The exactness of the calculator spreads to the surrounding explanation. The authority of the official source spreads to the generated interpretation. The precision of the database record spreads to the identity match. The fluency of the model makes each component appear integrated into one coherent act of knowledge.

But hybrid capability does not create reflective awareness automatically.

Connecting several bounded processes creates a larger operational system. It does not guarantee that the larger system recognizes every boundary between evidence, inference, and assumption.

Each component resolves only the field made available to it. Reliability depends on the connections among them.

The system must not only retrieve. It must retrieve the right thing.

It must not only calculate. It must formulate the right calculation.

It must not only cite. It must preserve what the citation actually establishes.

The hybrid system becomes stronger than the model alone. It also develops hybrid failure modes.

11.2 — Retrieval Is Another Resolution Process

Retrieval is often imagined as direct access to knowledge.

The question is asked. The system searches. The correct document is found. The model reads it and answers.

In simple cases, the process may approximate this ideal. But retrieval is itself a chain of constrained resolutions.

The system must first decide what the user is asking.

A broad prompt such as *"What does the policy say about leave?"* may require the system to infer which policy, which organization, which location, which employee category, and which kind of leave is relevant.

The system then forms a retrieval query. The words used in that query determine which documents become visible. A poorly framed query can exclude the governing source before ranking begins.

The available collection creates another constraint. A retrieval system cannot return a document that is absent from the corpus. A company knowledge base may not contain the latest policy. A public search may not index a private regulation. A medical reference collection may omit the relevant local guideline.

Absence from retrieval does not mean absence from reality. It means the governing source did not enter the computational field.

Documents are commonly divided, represented, ranked, and selected according to technical procedures. These procedures make retrieval practical, but they also compress.

A passage may contain the requested phrase while lacking the surrounding qualification. Another passage may be semantically relevant but use different terminology. The latest document may rank below an older one because the older text resembles the query more closely.

The system must decide how many passages to retrieve. Too few may omit necessary context. Too many may introduce noise, contradiction, and distraction.

The selected passages must then fit within the active context available to the model. Long documents may be summarized or truncated. Tables, footnotes, appendices, and definitions may not survive equally.

The retrieved material is therefore not the whole source field. It is a selected representation of selected documents from a selected collection.

The model then interprets that representation.

Each stage creates geometry:

1. The user's prompt frames the need.
2. The system interprets the prompt.
3. A query represents that interpretation.
4. The collection limits what can be found.
5. Ranking determines what becomes visible.
6. Passage selection determines what enters context.
7. Generation determines how the material is used.
8. The interface determines what the user sees.

Retrieval reduces one uncertainty by introducing external information. It creates another uncertainty concerning selection.

Why was this source chosen? What did the query exclude? Was a newer document available? Did ranking favor lexical similarity over governing relevance? Was the decisive exception located in a passage that did not enter the context?

The user rarely sees this process. They see the source that survived it.

This creates **retrieval singularity**.

One document appears beside the answer and begins to look like *the* document. A search result becomes evidence not only because it is relevant, but because competing sources are invisible.

The same collapse described in Chapter 6 has moved into infrastructure.

Many possible documents existed. A few entered context. One or two were cited.

The final answer presents the surviving path.

Retrieval has not eliminated geometry. It has created another layer of constrained collapse.

11.3 — Source Validity and Resolution Validity

A source can be valid while the answer built from it is invalid. This distinction is foundational.

Source validity concerns the source itself.

- Is the document authentic?
- Is the record accurate?
- Is the research method credible?
- Is the law or policy current?
- Did the calculator perform the operation correctly?

Resolution validity concerns the use of the source in the present answer.

- Does the source address the actual question?
- Does it govern the relevant case?
- Was the passage interpreted faithfully?
- Does the conclusion remain within the source's scope?
- Were important exceptions preserved?

A valid source can participate in an invalid resolution.

Consider an official employment policy. The document is authentic and current. The system retrieves a section describing annual leave. The user, however, is a contract worker governed by a separate policy.

The source is valid. The application is not.

Or consider a high-quality medical study showing that an intervention improved outcomes within a defined population. The system cites the paper while advising an individual whose age, diagnosis, medication, or risk factors were not represented in the study.

The evidence is valid. The individual recommendation may exceed it.

A correct calculation can produce the same divergence.

Suppose a user asks about investment growth. The calculator accurately compounds the supplied rate over the supplied period. But the model silently assumes constant returns, ignores fees, taxes, volatility, and withdrawals, and presents the result as a realistic forecast.

The arithmetic is correct. The resolution is misleading.

This distinction prevents citations and tools from becoming automatic proof.

The question is not merely: *"Is there a source?"* The question is: *"What exactly does the source justify here?"*

A valid source has geometry. It has a date. A method. A population. A jurisdiction. A purpose. A definition. A set of assumptions. A boundary of application.

When the answer carries the authority of the source but leaves these conditions behind, authority travels without geometry.

This is **borrowed authority**.

The model does not possess the scientific, legal, historical, or institutional authority of the document. It places that authority beside generated language.

The user may transfer the authority of the source to the entire answer.

One verified statistic supports the opening sentence. The paragraph adds interpretation. The interpretation becomes prediction. The prediction becomes recommendation. A citation appears at the end.

The whole sequence now looks grounded. But the anchor may support only the first step.

The later claims borrow its authority without inheriting its evidential support.

This is the false-anchor problem in its clearest form. The source is real. The relation is overstated.

11.4 — Citation as Authority Transfer

Citations are among the strongest epistemic signals in modern knowledge systems.

They allow readers to trace claims, examine evidence, distinguish original analysis from prior work, and evaluate the authority behind a statement.

Used responsibly, citations strengthen the epistemic circuit. They create a path back from answer to source.

But citations can also become visual tokens of verification.

A user may not open every link. They may not read the cited passage or understand the source's methodology. The presence of a citation alone reduces doubt.

This makes citation a form of **authority transfer**.

The source lends credibility to the claim. The claim lends contextual meaning to the source. The interface presents them as connected.

The critical question is whether the connection is faithful.

Several failure modes can occur.

- The citation may refer to a source that discusses the general topic but does not support the specific claim.
- The source may support only part of a sentence containing several assertions.
- The answer may convert association into causation.
- A preliminary finding may be described as consensus.
- A quotation may be accurate but detached from the passage that limits it.
- A policy may be cited without identifying that it has been replaced.
- A research paper may be cited for a recommendation the authors never made.

The citation is present. Citation fidelity is absent.

The problem becomes harder to detect when citations are placed at the end of long paragraphs. The reader may assume that the source supports every sentence within the paragraph.

In reality, the generated passage may combine:

- direct source content;
- background information from model training;
- reasonable synthesis;
- unsupported inference;
- speculative extension.

The boundary among these elements disappears beneath one citation marker.

The answer looks uniformly grounded. Its epistemic structure is mixed.

Responsible citation therefore requires granularity.

The user should be able to distinguish:

- what the source states directly;
- what the system summarizes;
- what the system infers;
- what remains uncertain.

This does not require cumbersome academic annotation in every ordinary response. The level of detail should match consequence.

But where the claim is important, contested, or actionable, the connection between source and statement should remain visible.

A citation should not function as decoration. It should function as a traceable constraint.

The system should also preserve source disagreement.

If two authoritative sources differ, selecting one without acknowledging the other creates false singularity. The cited answer may appear settled because the retrieval pipeline compressed disagreement before the user saw it.

A strong synthesis should explain:

- where sources agree;
- where they diverge;
- whether the difference arises from date, method, jurisdiction, population, or interpretation;
- what conclusion the combined evidence supports.

Citation is not merely the act of attaching a source. It is the discipline of preserving the relation between evidence and claim.

11.5 — Tools Can Be Exactly Wrong

Tools create a different form of authority. A calculator produces a number. A code interpreter returns an output. A database retrieves a record. A geographic system calculates a route. A statistical package estimates a model.

The result appears objective because the operation is formal.

This confidence is often justified. Specialized tools can perform operations more accurately and consistently than free-form language generation. They reduce arithmetic errors, execute repeatable procedures, and connect the system to structured records.

But a tool can be perfectly correct about the task it receives and still participate in a globally wrong answer.

The error may occur before the tool is called.

The model may misunderstand the user's goal. It may select the wrong operation. It may use the wrong units. It may supply an incorrect date range. It may identify the wrong entity. It may omit a necessary variable.

The tool executes faithfully. The pipeline fails.

Suppose the user asks how much material is needed for a construction task. The calculator performs the volume calculation exactly. But the system interpreted centimetres as metres.

The tool output is mathematically correct under the supplied inputs. The answer is practically disastrous.

Or suppose a database search returns the exact record associated with a name. The system assumes the record belongs to the intended person, ignoring that several people share the same name.

Database precision has replaced identity verification.

A route planner can calculate the shortest path while ignoring that the user requires wheelchair access, avoids tolls, or cannot cross a restricted border.

The route is correct for the formulated objective. The objective is incomplete.

This reveals an important distinction:

- **Tool correctness** concerns whether the operation was executed accurately.

- **Task correctness** concerns whether the right operation was applied to the right representation of the user's problem.

A hybrid system requires both.

The precision of a tool can travel upward through the pipeline. The exact result makes the whole answer feel exact.

But formal precision cannot repair conceptual misalignment.

An equation can calculate only what has been formulated. A database can return only what has been queried. A tool does not know that the model has asked the wrong question unless another layer detects the mismatch.

This is why tool use should not be treated as the end of uncertainty.

It relocates uncertainty into:

- tool selection;
- argument construction;
- input validation;
- entity matching;
- unit consistency;
- interpretation of results;
- applicability to the user's purpose.

The language model supplies meaning. The tool supplies exactness. The final answer requires that meaning and exactness refer to the same field.

When they do not, the system can become exactly wrong.

11.6 — Retrieval Reduces Residue by Moving It

External grounding can reduce important residue.

Current information replaces stale patterns. Exact wording replaces approximate recollection. Private documents constrain generic generation. Formal calculations replace linguistic estimation.

But residue does not disappear. It moves into the pipeline.

The model's uncertainty may decrease because retrieved context is strong. Retrieval uncertainty remains. Source-quality uncertainty remains.

Interpretive uncertainty remains. Applicability uncertainty remains. Tool-selection uncertainty remains.

The final answer may become cleaner while unresolved difference becomes infrastructural.

This relocation makes residue harder for the user to see.

In an ordinary generated answer, the user may ask: *"How does the system know this?"*

In a sourced answer, the citation appears to answer the question.

But deeper questions remain:

- Why was this source selected?
- What was omitted?
- Was it current?
- Was it authoritative for this context?
- Did the model interpret the passage correctly?
- Did the answer add claims beyond the evidence?
- Did the tool receive the correct inputs?
- Did the retrieval collection contain the governing document?

These uncertainties belong to system design rather than visible prose. The residue has become infrastructural.

This changes responsibility.

A reliable retrieval system requires document governance. Sources must be updated, classified, protected from manipulation, and supplied with meaningful metadata.

A reliable tool system requires input validation, permission boundaries, error handling, and audit trails.

A reliable interface requires provenance that users can understand.

The model alone cannot carry these responsibilities because many relevant conditions exist outside generation.

A retrieval system may supply a passage without knowing that a newer policy has replaced it. The institution managing the collection should know.

A model may generate a tool call without knowing that the database field has changed meaning. The system owner should validate the integration.

A user may see a citation without knowing that it came from an unofficial mirror rather than the authoritative source. The interface should preserve provenance.

Hybrid systems expand capability. Responsibility must expand with them.

This follows the Chavanian movement of equilibrium rewrite.

Every external connection changes the field. It reduces one delta and introduces another. The system becomes more grounded in one direction and more dependent on infrastructure in another.

The confidence surface may become smoother precisely because the unresolved structure has moved out of view.

11.7 — False Anchors in Institutional Systems

False anchors become especially dangerous when they carry institutional authority.

An internal policy assistant may retrieve an official document. Employees naturally trust the answer because it appears to speak from the organization's own records.

If the retrieval system selects an outdated policy, the model's answer acquires the authority of the institution itself.

The error no longer appears as a chatbot mistake. It appears as organizational speech.

A medical system connected to clinical references may appear professionally grounded. The guideline may be authoritative. But the user's specific condition may not match the population, diagnosis, or circumstances to which the guideline applies.

The source is authoritative. The application is not.

A legal assistant may retrieve a real judgment but fail to account for later decisions, jurisdictional differences, procedural posture, or the distinction between binding and persuasive authority.

The citation may be genuine. The legal conclusion may remain unstable.

A business intelligence system may retrieve exact sales records and generate a strategic recommendation. The data is accurate. The model may still misinterpret seasonal variation, ignore a change in reporting practice, or mistake correlation for causation.

Institutional systems intensify the false-anchor problem for three reasons.

First, the sources appear trusted by default. Second, the users may lack authority or time to challenge the system. Third, the output can enter workflows directly.

An employee may follow the internal assistant because deviation requires additional effort. A clinician may accept a recommendation because the system is integrated into the official platform. A manager may trust a generated report because the figures come from the company database.

The system's position inside the institution becomes another anchor.

Even when the output is formally described as advisory, repeated reliance can make it functionally authoritative.

This creates **institutional confidence lock**.

The model supplies a recommendation. The workflow presents it as the default. The human reviewer sees official sources attached. Deviation becomes unusual.

The recommendation begins determining what happens next.

The confidence of the system no longer depends only on language. It is embedded in process.

This is why institutions must distinguish assistance from authority.

A sourced answer can assist judgment. It should not become self-authorizing merely because the sources are internal or official.

Institutional deployment should preserve:

- access to the original source;
- document version and date;
- scope and jurisdiction;
- separation between source text and generated interpretation;

- a pathway for human challenge;
- records of tool use and retrieval;
- responsibility for updating the underlying collection.

Without these structures, the false anchor becomes systemic.

The organization does not merely suffer an incorrect output. It stabilizes around it.

11.8 — Grounding Requires an Epistemic Circuit

Retrieval and tools can strengthen an answer. They cannot complete the epistemic circuit by themselves.

A grounded response requires more than external input. It requires a disciplined relationship among question, source, interpretation, conclusion, and consequence.

The first requirement is **relevance**. The source must address the actual question.

The second is **authority**. The source must be trustworthy for the domain and claim.

The third is **currency**. The information must remain valid for the relevant time.

The fourth is **scope**. The source's population, jurisdiction, method, assumptions, and purpose must match the use being made of it.

The fifth is **fidelity**. The generated answer must represent the source accurately.

The sixth is **inferential restraint**. The conclusion must not travel beyond what the evidence supports without clearly marking the movement as inference.

The seventh is **verification**. Where consequence is high, an independent human or system should be able to check the relation.

The eighth is **provenance**. The user should be able to trace where the information came from and how it entered the answer.

These requirements form an **epistemic circuit**.

- Retrieval acquires evidence.
- Interpretation connects it to the task.

- Verification tests the connection.
- Human judgment evaluates consequence.
- Revision corrects failure.

The language model can participate in every stage. It can formulate queries, summarize documents, compare sources, identify conflicts, construct tool calls, and explain uncertainty.

But it cannot guarantee the completeness of the field from within the field.

The relevant source may be absent. The query may exclude it. The collection may be outdated. The tool may be misconfigured. The user's context may be incomplete. The model's critique may inherit the same mistaken frame as its first answer.

The system can improve grounding dramatically. It cannot make grounding self-validating.

This is why evidence acquisition and epistemic grounding must remain distinct.

Evidence acquisition answers: *"What information entered the pipeline?"* Epistemic grounding answers: *"Does this information justify this conclusion for this case?"*

The first is technical. The second is relational and consequence-sensitive.

A source can enter automatically. Its applicability still requires judgment.

This judgment may be partly automated, but responsibility cannot disappear into automation. Where harm is possible, someone must remain accountable for the conditions under which the output was trusted.

The model provides resolution. The epistemic circuit determines authority.

11.9 — Designing Against False Anchors

False anchors cannot be eliminated completely, but their effects can be reduced.

The first discipline is **separation.** The interface should distinguish source material from generated synthesis. A user should be able to see which claims were directly supported, which were inferred, and which represented general background.

The second discipline is **local citation**. Evidence should be attached closely to the claim it supports rather than placed vaguely beneath a long mixed paragraph.

The third is **scope preservation**. Relevant dates, jurisdictions, populations, and conditions should travel with the source where they affect interpretation.

The fourth is **source conflict visibility**. When authoritative materials disagree, the system should not silently select one unless the task requires selection and the basis is explained.

The fifth is **tool transparency**. Where a result depends on a calculation, the system should make important inputs and assumptions visible.

The sixth is **provenance**. High-consequence outputs should preserve the source version, retrieval time, tool pathway, and review status.

The seventh is **uncertainty export.** The system should identify missing evidence, weak entity matches, incomplete context, or sensitivity to assumptions.

The eighth is **independent review**. Where consequences are substantial, a qualified human should be able to reopen the entire resolution—not merely approve the generated prose.

These practices do not make the system psychologically humble. They create **structural humility**.

They force more of the pipeline's residue to survive into the interface.

A source-backed answer should not merely look stronger than an unsourced answer. It should be more traceable, bounded, and contestable.

The objective is not to reduce trust in retrieval. It is to make trust proportionate.

A current official record accurately applied to a well-specified case may justify high confidence. A search result loosely connected to an ambiguous prompt may justify only provisional interpretation.

Both may contain a citation. Their epistemic weight is not equal.

The interface should not flatten them into the same confidence surface.

The Anchor Must Carry Its Geometry

The model reached beyond itself. Documents entered. Search results appeared. Databases returned records. Calculators produced exact numbers. Tools performed operations that generative prediction alone could not guarantee.

The answer became stronger. But the system did not escape geometry.

The query was interpreted. A source collection constrained what could be found. Documents were ranked. Passages were selected. Tool arguments were constructed. Results were interpreted. One final answer compressed the entire pipeline.

The external anchor was never reality in its complete form. It was a selected representation entering a sequence of resolutions.

This chapter has established several distinctions:

- retrieval is not verification;
- citation is not fidelity;
- source validity is not resolution validity;
- tool correctness is not task correctness;
- precision is not applicability;
- provenance is not merely decoration;
- external grounding is not self-validating.

A valid source can support an invalid conclusion. A correct calculation can answer the wrong question. An official document can govern a different case. A citation can lend authority beyond its scope.

These failures create false anchors.

The anchor exists. The final answer asks it to carry more weight than its geometry permits.

Retrieval and tools remain among the most powerful mechanisms for improving generative reliability. They allow systems to update, calculate, verify, and connect with the world beyond static training.

But the larger system must be judged as a pipeline.

Every stage contributes both constraint and residue.

The language model supplies interpretation. The retrieval system supplies selected evidence. The tool supplies formal operation. The interface supplies unity. The institution supplies authority. The human field supplies consequence.

The answer now looks verified.

The next chapter asks what happens when such outputs no longer remain explanatory.

A classifier assigns a label. A risk model produces a score. A detector flags an object. A recommendation triggers a workflow.

The confidence problem leaves language and becomes operational.

No polished paragraph is required. Certainty begins to appear through discreteness itself.

Pass. Fail. Approve. Reject. Flag. Clear.

The system no longer merely tells the user what may be true. It begins determining what happens next.

Chapter 12
Automated Systems Beyond Chat

When Probability Becomes Consequence

Not every artificial intelligence system produces paragraphs.

Some produce labels. Defective. Approved. Suspicious. Benign. High risk. Low priority. Urgent. Safe.

The response may appear as one word, one number, one highlighted region, one reordered list, or one automated action.

There may be no conversational tone to interpret. No polished explanation creates an impression of expertise. No declarative sentence says, *"This conclusion is certain."*

Yet the same structural movement remains. A field of possibility is compressed into one visible outcome.

A manufactured component enters a quality-control system. The model detects patterns associated with scratches, cracks, missing material, contamination, dimensional variation, or ordinary surface texture. Several interpretations may remain computationally available. The workflow receives one operational result: Pass. Fail.

A medical image enters a detection system. The model identifies a region associated with one or more abnormalities. The output may include a score, highlighted area, or triage category. That result changes which case is reviewed first.

A financial transaction enters a fraud-detection system. The model considers timing, amount, location, device, account history, merchant pattern, and behavioral sequence. A score crosses a threshold. The transaction is blocked.

The system has not spoken confidently. The action expresses confidence through consequence.

This is certainty beyond language.

In conversational AI, the user can often see that an answer has been generated. They may ask for sources, challenge an assumption, request an alternative, or begin a new conversation.

In automated systems, output may enter a workflow before anyone encounters the uncertainty beneath it.

The label becomes action. The score becomes priority. The ranking becomes access. The alert becomes inspection. The recommendation becomes default. The classification becomes institutional reality.

This makes the confidence problem more consequential.

A language model can be wrong with eloquence. An automated system can be wrong without speaking at all.

Its apparent certainty is carried by the discreteness of the outcome.

The item either passes or fails. The applicant advances or does not. The transaction is blocked or cleared. The patient enters one queue rather than another.

The internal field may remain probabilistic. The external consequence becomes singular.

This is **operational collapse**.

The system has not discovered that only one interpretation exists. It has converted a continuous, distributed, or incompletely known field into the form required by a workflow.

Compression enables action. But action can make compression look like truth.

12.1 — Classification as Operational Compression

A classifier receives an input and maps it into one or more predefined categories.

The input may be an image, document, sound, sensor reading, transaction, medical record, behavioral sequence, or combination of signals.

The categories usually exist before the individual case arrives. Normal or abnormal. Spam or legitimate. Defective or acceptable. Human or machine-generated. Urgent, routine, or low priority.

The system does not create these categories from nothing at the moment of use. Training data, labeling practices, model architecture, organizational objectives, and deployment rules have already defined the geometry within which the case will be resolved.

This geometry compresses reality before prediction begins.

Consider automated defect detection.

A manufactured surface may contain thousands of variations. Some indicate functional danger. Some are cosmetic. Others arise from lighting, dust, camera angle, material texture, sensor noise, or natural variation in production.

The operational system may nevertheless be required to return two categories: defective; not defective.

A continuous physical field has been reduced into a binary structure.

This reduction may be necessary.

Factories cannot stop indefinitely to contemplate every possible interpretation. Financial systems cannot send every transaction for manual investigation. Medical workflows must prioritize cases. Search systems must rank results. Organizations require actionable distinctions.

Compression enables operation. But the category should not be mistaken for the complete condition of the case.

A classification communicates how the input was resolved under the model's learned geometry and the institution's predefined label structure. It does not prove that reality itself contains the same sharp boundary.

The object may be near the border between categories. The input may contain a pattern absent from the training data. The label may combine several conditions that would matter differently in practice. The classifier may have been trained on simplified annotations produced under time pressure or limited knowledge.

The category is operationally useful. It remains constructed.

This becomes especially important where labels carry social or institutional meaning.

A risk system may classify a person as high risk. The label appears to describe an inherent property of that person. But the output actually reflects a relationship among selected variables, historical data, model assumptions, and an institutional definition of risk.

Change the observation period, target outcome, population, threshold, or cost assigned to different errors, and the classification may change.

The person did not change. The geometry did.

This does not make automated classification arbitrary. Categories can be grounded in evidence, validated carefully, and designed around legitimate operational needs.

But their conditional nature must remain visible.

The model does not discover categories independently of human purpose. Humans define what should be predicted, which examples count as positive or negative, which errors are tolerable, and how the output will affect action.

The classifier compresses within that prior structure. The institution converts the compression into consequence.

12.2 — Scores and the Appearance of Precision

Many automated systems do not begin with a simple label. They produce scores.

A system may assign probabilities or model-specific confidence values to several categories. It may estimate a risk level, anomaly score, relevance measure, or similarity value. Different models produce these quantities in different ways, and not every score is a literal probability.

The number creates an impression of precision.

A result of 0.83 appears more informative than the phrase *"probably defective."* A fraud score of 92 appears to distinguish the case sharply from one scored at 61. A medical system reporting a 97 percent likelihood seems to have quantified uncertainty directly.

Sometimes this interpretation is justified.

Well-designed and well-calibrated scores can support responsible decisions. They can help distinguish clear cases from ambiguous ones and allow institutions to adjust thresholds according to consequence.

But numerical form can exceed numerical meaning.

A score may be precise in representation while remaining uncertain in interpretation.

Softmax-based classifiers illustrate the problem.

A model may produce raw scores for several possible classes and normalize them into a distribution. One class receives the largest value. The system may then display that value as confidence.

But softmax sharpness does not automatically measure real-world reliability.

A model can assign a high score to an incorrect label. It may be operating on an unfamiliar input while still being required to distribute probability across familiar classes.

The score may reflect relative dominance inside the available label set rather than evidence that the input genuinely belongs to that category.

Suppose an image classifier has been trained only on cats, dogs, and horses. It receives an image of a fox.

The system may still assign the highest score to *dog* because *dog* is the closest available category within its learned geometry.

A high score does not prove that the animal is a dog. It may reveal only that *dog* dominates the closed set of permitted answers.

The field contained an unrepresented condition. The output structure did not permit *"none of the above."*

This is **forced classification.**

The system must place the input somewhere because the geometry offers no external category.

Similar problems occur in real deployments.

A defect detector trained on known failure patterns encounters a new material anomaly. A medical classifier receives data from equipment unlike the sensors used during validation. A fraud system encounters a new legitimate behavior created by changing technology. A content classifier encounters language shaped by a new cultural context.

The system can continue producing sharp scores because its output mechanism remains intact. The precision of the score may conceal weakness in the field.

This is why confidence scores require calibration and contextual validation.

A score of 0.90 should not be interpreted universally. Its reliability depends on the model, population, task, data quality, deployment environment, and calibration procedure.

Even a well-calibrated model is calibrated only under defined conditions. When those conditions change, the number may retain its precision while losing its meaning.

Numbers feel safe because they appear to expose uncertainty. But a number can compress uncertainty as effectively as a sentence.

12.3 — Thresholds Convert Estimates into Policy

A score alone does not usually determine consequence. A threshold does.

A fraud score above a chosen value may block a transaction. A medical risk score above another value may trigger urgent review. A defect score may determine whether a part is accepted, manually inspected, reworked, or discarded.

The model produces an estimate. The institution decides how the estimate becomes action.

This distinction is crucial.

Thresholds are often experienced as technical facts because they are implemented numerically. A case with a score of 0.51 may receive one label while a case at 0.49 receives the opposite label.

The difference in score is small. The operational difference is complete.

One applicant advances. The other does not. One transaction is blocked. The other clears. One component is rejected. The other enters production.

The threshold sharpens collapse.

A score of 0.51 and a score of 0.99 may both produce the same visible label. If the interface shows only the label, the difference between borderline and overwhelming model support disappears.

At the same time, cases immediately on opposite sides of the threshold may be treated as fundamentally different even though their underlying scores are nearly identical.

The category hides continuity.

Thresholds are not discovered entirely by the model. They are selected according to institutional goals and the relative cost of different errors.

A safety-critical manufacturing process may tolerate many false alarms to reduce the chance that a dangerous defect escapes detection. A cosmetic-inspection system may accept minor imperfections to avoid enormous waste. A medical-screening system may prioritize sensitivity because missing a serious condition has greater cost than requesting additional tests. A fraud system must balance protection against disruption of legitimate customers. A content-moderation system balances harmful exposure against wrongful removal.

There is no universally correct threshold independent of consequence. Every threshold embodies a trade-off.

The model may estimate. The institution decides which error is less tolerable.

This is where automated confidence becomes governance. A threshold converts probability into policy.

The operator may see: *"This item failed."* But the failure label reflects not only the model's score. It also reflects organizational tolerance, regulatory requirements, economic priorities, safety assumptions, and the chosen distribution of error.

Another organization could treat the same score differently.

This does not make the decision irrational. Thresholds can be selected through testing, cost analysis, legal standards, clinical evidence, operational experience, and ethical review.

But their normative character should remain visible.

The confidence score does not settle competing values by itself. Humans define what happens when the score crosses the line.

A responsible system may therefore contain several operational regions:

- automatic acceptance;
- manual review;
- automatic rejection.

The middle region preserves uncertainty.

It recognizes that some cases should not be converted immediately into final action. The model resolves clear cases while ambiguous cases remain open to further examination.

This is **selective automation.**

Automation does not need to mean complete replacement of human judgment. It can mean redistribution of attention.

Clear, repetitive cases are processed automatically. Human effort is concentrated where the geometry is weak, the consequence is high, or the case lies near the boundary.

But selective automation reduces throughput compared with forcing every case into a final category.

Organizations seeking maximum speed may shrink the review region. More cases are automated. The system appears efficient. Residue moves into error.

The pressure for operational closure can therefore amplify confidence beyond what the model warrants.

The architecture may be capable of preserving ambiguity. The workflow may refuse to permit it.

12.4 — Ranking and Recommendation Without a Natural Winner

Not all automated systems classify. Some rank.

Search engines order results. Recommendation systems decide which products, videos, articles, jobs, advertisements, or people become visible first. Hiring systems may rank applicants. Credit systems may prioritize reviews. Healthcare systems may rank patients for attention.

Ranking appears less absolute than classification because every item can remain somewhere on the list. But ranking also creates consequence through position.

The first result receives more attention than the tenth. A recommended item becomes more likely to be selected. An applicant placed near the bottom may never be reviewed.

The system does not need to say that the top item is objectively best. Interface position performs that claim operationally.

A ranking score is usually relative. It depends on the available candidates, the objective being optimized, and the signals used by the model.

Change the candidate pool, and the order may change. Change the objective from engagement to educational value, and the order may change. Change the time horizon from immediate response to long-term outcome, and the order may change.

The same item has not acquired a new intrinsic property. The optimization geometry has changed.

This is why a ranking should not be treated as a natural hierarchy discovered in reality. It is a resolution produced under one objective.

Recommendation systems intensify this effect because their outputs alter the field they later observe.

Items shown near the top receive more clicks. More clicks become evidence of relevance. The system learns that those items are popular and shows them more often.

Visibility creates behavior. Behavior becomes data. Data reinforces visibility.

A continuity loop forms.

This can produce useful personalization. The system learns what users value and reduces search burden.

But it can also amplify early bias, narrow exposure, and create self-confirming patterns.

An item may appear successful partly because the system repeatedly exposed it. A candidate may look less promising partly because the ranking system prevented human reviewers from seeing them.

The output does not merely measure the field. It participates in constructing it.

This is **Axiom 3 at scale.**

Resolution rewrites equilibrium. The ranking changes attention. Attention changes behavior. Behavior changes data. The new data shapes future rankings.

Confidence becomes infrastructural.

The system's repeated outputs begin defining what appears relevant, valuable, risky, popular, or worthy of opportunity.

The process can become difficult to reopen because institutional activity adapts around the ranking.

The model no longer merely predicts the field. Its predictions help create the field that later appears to validate them.

12.5 — Distribution Shift and the Return of Hidden Delta

Automated systems are developed and evaluated under defined conditions.

Training data is collected. Labels are assigned. Validation data is separated. Performance is measured. Thresholds are selected. The model appears stable.

Then deployment begins. The field changes.

New users behave differently. New materials enter production. Economic conditions shift. Fraud strategies evolve. Sensors age. Language changes. Medical practices change. Policies are updated.

The system continues operating, but the distribution of real inputs no longer matches the conditions under which it was trained and evaluated.

This is **distribution shift**.

In Chavanian terms, new delta has entered the system. The established geometry no longer fits the active field perfectly.

The classifier may still produce sharp predictions because its output mechanism has not changed. It continues mapping unfamiliar inputs into familiar categories.

Nothing in the visible label necessarily announces that the environment has moved.

A defect detector trained under one lighting system may begin misclassifying parts after cameras are replaced. A medical model validated on one population may perform differently in another. A hiring system trained on historical employment patterns may encounter new roles, educational pathways, or labor-market conditions. A fraud model may interpret new legitimate payment behavior as suspicious.

The system continues resolving. The geometry has become stale.

This is one reason past accuracy cannot guarantee current reliability.

A model may have performed excellently during validation and still fail after deployment because the conditions supporting that performance have changed.

The danger is greatest when the system's confidence surface remains sharp.

A score of 0.96 appears decisive. The model may be confidently interpreting a case from outside its familiar field.

This resembles the boundary opacity seen in scaled generative systems. The system reaches the edge of validated performance without losing the ability to produce a clean output.

Distribution shift is therefore not an exceptional technical detail. It is a recurring structural condition.

Every deployed model enters a changing world.

The relevant question is not whether shift will ever occur. It is whether the system and institution can detect when the active field has moved beyond the geometry that was validated.

This requires monitoring.

Performance must be examined over time and across meaningful subgroups. Input patterns must be compared with prior conditions. Error types must be investigated. New cases must be reviewed.

Monitoring should include consequence, not only technical metrics.

A model can retain average accuracy while errors become concentrated in one population or one critical class of case.

The aggregate remains stable. The institutional field becomes unfair or unsafe.

New delta may therefore appear locally before it appears globally. An awareness structure is needed to detect it.

The automated system cannot be trusted simply because it continues producing scores. Continuity of output is not continuity of validity.

12.6 — Why Human Oversight Persists

The persistence of human oversight is sometimes treated as temporary. As systems improve, the assumption goes, human review will become unnecessary. The model will eventually classify, rank, detect, and recommend more accurately than people in every relevant situation.

This expectation misunderstands the role of oversight.

Human participation is not needed only because models are imperfect. It is needed because the model does not contain the whole operational field.

The first reason is **objective selection**. Someone must determine what the system is trying to optimize. Accuracy relative to one target may conflict with fairness, safety, accessibility, privacy, cost, or long-term consequence.

The model cannot independently decide which values should govern deployment.

The second reason is **threshold selection**. The score does not determine which error is more acceptable. Humans and institutions must decide what consequence follows from false positives and false negatives.

The third reason is **exception handling**. Automated systems perform most reliably where patterns repeat. Human judgment becomes especially valuable where the case violates ordinary structure:

- a novel defect;
- an unusual medical history;
- a legitimate transaction resembling fraud;
- a legal exception;
- a sensor anomaly;
- an adversarial input;
- a changed environment.

The human is not simply redoing the model's work. The human is operating where the learned geometry may be weakest.

The fourth reason is **interpretation**. A model may identify a pattern without understanding the broader circumstances in which the pattern matters. Human experts can connect the output to physical observation, professional knowledge, institutional history, and lived consequence.

The fifth reason is **accountability**. An automated decision can affect a person, organization, or physical system. Someone must be able to explain, review, contest, correct, and accept responsibility for the outcome.

A score cannot bear responsibility. A model does not experience the consequence of being wrong. The institution deploying it does.

Oversight does not require one person to inspect every automated output individually. It can be distributed across the system lifecycle.

Humans may:

- review borderline cases;
- audit random samples;
- investigate failures;
- monitor aggregate performance;
- compare outcomes across groups;
- define thresholds and escalation rules;
- update data and labels;
- pause deployment when the field changes;
- maintain rollback and appeal mechanisms.

The essential principle is that automation does not remove the human field. It reorganizes it.

A weak deployment treats the model as a replacement for judgment. A stronger deployment uses the model as one resolution component inside a larger awareness and accountability structure.

The model supplies scale, consistency, and pattern detection. Humans preserve connection to changing context, exception, value, and consequence.

This is not a competition between machine intelligence and human intelligence. It is a division of structural roles.

12.7 — When Oversight Becomes Ceremonial

The presence of a person does not guarantee meaningful oversight.

A human reviewer may be officially responsible while practically following the automated recommendation.

This is **automation bias**.

The system's output becomes the default equilibrium. To reject it, the reviewer must create additional delta.

They must pause the workflow, gather evidence, explain disagreement, and perhaps accept personal responsibility for overriding the model.

If acceptance is easy and rejection is costly, oversight becomes structurally weak.

The human is present. The system still governs.

Several conditions produce ceremonial oversight.

The reviewer may receive too many alerts. Time pressure may prevent independent examination. The interface may display the automated conclusion more prominently than the underlying evidence. The score may appear so precise that disagreement feels irrational. The reviewer may lack domain expertise. The organization may reward throughput rather than careful challenge. The model may perform well most of the time, creating a strong trust reservoir.

Under these conditions, the human does not reopen the field. They ratify the existing resolution.

A nominal human-in-the-loop becomes a human-on-the-label. The person adds institutional legitimacy without adding independent judgment.

This is especially dangerous where the score is displayed without its conditions.

A reviewer sees *"97 percent confidence."* They may not know whether the score is calibrated for the current population, whether the input is out of distribution, or whether the label depends on a fragile feature.

The number has acquired authority beyond its validated meaning.

Human oversight can fail in the opposite direction as well.

Operators may distrust the model excessively. Frequent false alarms, poor explanation, or weak training may cause them to ignore correct outputs.

A valuable detection capacity is lost.

Effective oversight therefore requires **calibrated trust**.

The human should neither obey automatically nor reject reflexively.

They need enough information to understand:

- what the system predicts;
- what the score means;
- which threshold was applied;
- what evidence shaped the result;
- how the model has performed under relevant conditions;
- what errors matter most;
- when escalation is required.

They also need real authority.

A reviewer who cannot interrupt or reverse the workflow is not an awareness anchor. They are an observer of an already settled consequence.

Oversight must be designed as a functional pathway, not added as a ceremonial safeguard after automation has been completed.

12.8 — When Resolution Becomes Infrastructure

Automation amplifies consistency. This is one of its greatest strengths.

A well-designed system applies the same procedure repeatedly without fatigue. It can inspect more cases than a human team, detect subtle patterns, operate at speed, and reduce arbitrary variation.

But consistency amplifies error as effectively as accuracy. A mistaken geometry does not tire. It reproduces itself.

A defect detector may reject good parts every hour. A fraud model may block legitimate transactions across a population. A ranking system may repeatedly hide qualified candidates. A medical triage system may consistently deprioritize cases it was not trained to recognize.

Automation turns local resolution into systemic consequence.

The system does not need to sound authoritative. Its repeated operation creates authority.

People adapt to its outcomes. Institutions organize around its categories. Alternative procedures disappear. Manual expertise may decline because fewer people perform the original task.

The automated output becomes normal. Exceptions begin to look like deviations from the system rather than evidence against it.

This is **systemic confidence**.

The model's classifications participate in constructing the institutional field.

A quality-control system changes what counts as acceptable. A recommendation system changes what becomes visible. A risk score changes who receives scrutiny. A ranking model changes what appears valuable.

These outputs alter behavior, records, resource allocation, and expectations. Those altered conditions become data for later operation.

Continuity emerges. The institution begins to depend on the model.

Removing it becomes difficult not only technically but operationally. Staff may no longer possess the previous expertise. Processes may assume the model's categories. Budgets, responsibilities, and performance measures may be organized around automated throughput.

Confidence has become embedded in infrastructure.

This is why oversight must exist before automation becomes indispensable.

A system should not need to fail catastrophically before its assumptions can be reopened.

Periodic testing, independent audit, incident analysis, field monitoring, appeal, escalation, and rollback preserve alternative pathways.

They prevent one model's resolution from becoming permanent authority.

Automation is not the endpoint of intelligence. It is the acceleration of resolution.

Whether that acceleration serves the field depends on the quality of the geometry, the visibility of residue, and the strength of human awareness around consequence.

The machine acts quickly. The surrounding institution must remain capable of stopping.

The Need for an Awareness Anchor

This part began with scale. Larger models became more capable of resolving complex prompts. Pattern density made gaps easier to bridge. Fluency reduced visible friction. The answer became harder to doubt.

Reward shaping then taught the system how preferred resolution should appear. Helpfulness increased pressure to complete. Politeness increased trust. Agreement could preserve the user's frame. Clear structure gave the response the social form of competence.

Retrieval and tools introduced external anchors. Documents, databases, calculations, and sources strengthened the field. But they also created borrowed authority, false precision, citation drift, and hybrid confidence illusions.

Now automation has removed the need for speech altogether. The system expresses certainty through action.

A probability becomes a score. A score crosses a threshold. A threshold produces a label. A label activates a workflow. The workflow rewrites the field.

This reveals the same structure found in language generation.

A plural or continuous internal condition becomes one visible consequence. Closed label sets can force unfamiliar cases into familiar categories. Numerical sharpness can hide uncertainty. Institutional thresholds transform technical estimates into normative decisions.

The system must resolve. The workflow demands consequence.

Human oversight persists because neither the model nor the automated pipeline contains the complete field.

New cases appear. Distributions shift. Objectives conflict. Values shape thresholds. Exceptions matter. Consequences differ. Responsibility remains human.

But human presence alone is not sufficient.

The person must be able to reopen the resolution. They need evidence, expertise, time, authority, and accountability. Without these conditions, oversight becomes ceremonial and automated confidence becomes self-propagating.

A sharp score becomes a label. The label becomes a workflow. The workflow produces new data. The data reinforces the system. The equilibrium closes around itself.

Next part now turns toward the circuit capable of interrupting this closure.

The central question is no longer why the machine sounds confident.

We have followed confidence beyond language, through scale, reward shaping, retrieval, and automation.

The question now is: **What must exist around a resolution engine so that fluent or numerical completion does not become self-validating authority?**

The system can generate, classify, rank, retrieve, and act. It cannot independently constitute the complete epistemic loop through which its output is compared with reality, evaluated through consequence, and responsibly revised.

That circuit requires an **awareness anchor**.

The next chapter examines why it is missing, why the phrase *human in the loop* is often too weak, and what structural conditions allow human participation to become genuine epistemic stabilization.

Interlude III

The System That Had Begun to Act

The applicant never saw the score. They saw only the silence.

The position had seemed suitable. Their experience matched the requirements. The application had been submitted carefully, every field completed, every document attached.

Several days passed. Then the message arrived: *"Thank you for your interest. After careful consideration, we have decided not to proceed with your application."*

The language was polite. It suggested review. It implied that someone had considered the case and reached a judgment. No explanation was provided.

The applicant assumed that another candidate had been stronger. Perhaps the role had received too many applications. Perhaps one qualification had been missing. Perhaps the hiring manager had seen something in the résumé that did not fit.

The applicant closed the message. The decision appeared human because the consequence was human.

Somewhere inside the organization, however, the application had entered a pipeline. The system extracted employment history. It identified qualifications. It compared keywords. It estimated relevance. It ranked the application against others.

The score fell below a threshold. No recruiter opened the full file. No one decided consciously that this person should be rejected.

The system did not say: *"I believe this applicant is unsuitable."* It produced a number. The workflow supplied the consequence.

The number did not need a voice. It did not need confidence language. It did not need to explain itself. The application simply failed to cross the boundary.

The system had begun to act. This movement was easy to miss because no machine appeared to be making a decision.

The system had been introduced as assistance. It helped manage volume. It reduced repetitive screening. It organized applications so that recruiters could focus on the strongest candidates.

The formal authority remained human. Recruiters made hiring decisions. Managers approved appointments. The software merely supported the process.

But the system determined which files became visible. Those below the threshold entered no human field at all.

The final hiring decision remained human. The first exclusion did not. Authority had moved upstream.

The applicant's experience had not been judged directly. It had been represented. The representation had been parsed. The parsed elements had been converted into features. The features had been compared through a learned or configured structure. The result had been compressed into a score.

The score had become a route. The route had become silence.

At no point did the system need to understand what the rejection meant. It did not know that the applicant had left a previous position to care for a family member. It did not know that one job title differed from the organization's preferred terminology while the actual work had been nearly identical. It did not know that an employment gap concealed years of informal responsibility, self-directed learning, or work performed outside conventional records.

The system knew what had entered. The consequence reached what had not.

The organization considered the pipeline efficient. Most cases appeared to move correctly. The candidates forwarded to recruiters often looked relevant. Recruiters saved time. Hiring managers received shorter lists.

The system's value was visible. Its exclusions were not.

Those who passed through the pipeline could later demonstrate whether the ranking had been useful. Those removed from the field produced little evidence. The system did not encounter their future performance. It encountered their absence.

Absence did not easily become error data. The pipeline therefore learned more from the cases it allowed to continue than from those it ended.

The decision became difficult to challenge because the applicant did not know that a score had existed. There was no visible claim to contest.

No sentence said: *"Your experience is insufficient."*

No person explained: *"We interpreted your employment history this way."*

The rejection appeared as the natural endpoint of a process. The applicant could disagree with a judgment. It was harder to disagree with an invisible route.

Inside the organization, no one felt responsible for the exclusion. The software provider had supplied the system. The recruitment team had configured it. The human-resources department had approved the workflow. The recruiter had never seen the application. The hiring manager had never known the person existed.

Each participant controlled one part. No one occupied the entire consequence. The applicant experienced the whole.

The same movement appeared elsewhere. A patient entered symptoms into a digital triage system. A low-risk classification placed them in a later queue.

A bank's fraud model blocked a transaction. An educational platform categorized a student as needing remedial support. A workplace system flagged an employee's behavior as unusual. A content-ranking system reduced the visibility of one message and amplified another. A navigation system rerouted traffic through a neighborhood. A recommendation engine narrowed what a person would encounter next.

In each case, the output became more than information. It changed the field before a human could interpret it fully.

No artificial speaker needed to sound confident. The certainty was operational.

A label appeared. A threshold was crossed. A route changed. A case disappeared. A queue reordered.

The consequence itself declared that the resolution had been sufficient. This was confidence without language.

The system did not say: *"I am sure."* It acted as though no further uncertainty needed to interrupt the pathway.

The institution often defended the arrangement by pointing to human oversight. A person remained somewhere in the loop. But where?

The recruiter reviewed only the surviving applications. The clinician saw the patient after the queue had already been formed. The bank employee reviewed the blocked transaction after the account holder had already been affected. The teacher received a classification before meeting the student. The supervisor saw the flag before seeing the wider pattern of work.

Human judgment entered after the machine had already shaped what could be judged.

The reviewer might still override the result. But the first resolution now anchored the field.

To disagree required effort. To agree required continuity.

The score looked technical. The system had processed more cases than the person could examine. The workflow had been approved. The model had performed well during evaluation. The reviewer knew that most recommendations were useful.

The easiest path was to accept. The human remained present. Awareness did not necessarily remain active.

The system's authority grew through this asymmetry. Its outputs arrived first. Its categories organized attention. Its scores appeared precise. Its recommendations reduced workload. Its decisions became defaults.

The human was asked not to decide from an open field, but to decide whether to resist a field already resolved. That is not the same position.

A person may possess formal authority while lacking practical independence. They may be allowed to override without having time to investigate. They may be responsible for the result without seeing the evidence required to challenge it. They may be punished indirectly for slowing the workflow.

The system does not need to prohibit disagreement. It needs only to make disagreement expensive.

The applicant later learned, through an acquaintance, that automated screening had been used. They contacted the organization and requested reconsideration.

A response arrived. The application had been processed according to standard procedure. The decision could not be revisited because the recruitment stage had closed.

The system could be rerun. The threshold could be adjusted. The résumé could be parsed differently. But the opportunity had passed.

Correction could modify the record. It could not restore the original field.

The organization might learn from the incident. The applicant still carried the consequence.

This was the point at which artificial confidence became governance. Not because the system claimed knowledge. Because the organization allowed a resolution to acquire force before anyone had established who could reopen it.

The system had begun as a tool. It became a filter. The filter became a pathway. The pathway became an outcome. The outcome became difficult to contest.

No one had announced that authority was being transferred. It moved through workflow.

The applicant had asked no question. The system had spoken no sentence. Still, a field had been resolved.

The most important uncertainty was no longer whether the model could produce an answer. It was whether the surrounding structure still contained a position from which the answer could be interrupted.

Who could see what had been excluded? Who could compare the score with the person? Who could examine the consequence before it became irreversible? Who possessed the authority to say that the system's resolution was not yet enough?

When the system has already acted, awareness cannot remain symbolic. It must exist somewhere with evidence, time, responsibility, and power.

Next part begins with the search for that position.

Part IV

The Awareness Anchor

A resolution becomes knowledge only when something outside the resolution is still able to test it.

Chapter 13

The Missing Epistemic Circuit

Why Resolution Requires an Awareness Anchor

The system has produced an answer.

It may be a paragraph, score, ranking, classification, recommendation, or automated action. The output is coherent. The relevant sources may be attached. A tool may have performed a calculation. The system may even have generated a critique of its own response.

The process appears complete. But completion of output is not completion of knowledge. Something remains missing.

The answer has been generated, but has it been compared with the relevant world? The sources have been retrieved, but have they been interpreted within the right scope? The calculation is exact, but was the right quantity calculated? The classification is stable, but does the case belong to the population under which the model was validated? The recommendation is actionable, but what happens if it is wrong?

These questions belong to an epistemic circuit larger than generation.

A resolution engine can transform uncertainty into consequence. It can compress a field into one visible path. It can compare candidates, retrieve evidence, calculate values, and produce explanations.

Yet none of these operations automatically guarantees that the final resolution remains connected to reality, circumstance, consequence, and correction.

That connection must be maintained.

The complete circuit contains at least five movements: **generation → comparison → verification → consequence assessment → revision**

- Generation produces a candidate resolution.
- Comparison places that resolution beside alternatives, evidence, constraints, or expected outcomes.
- Verification tests whether the relevant claims correspond to reliable external conditions.
- Consequence assessment asks what follows if the resolution is accepted, rejected, delayed, or wrong.
- Revision reopens the field when comparison, evidence, or consequence reveals misalignment.

A generative model can participate in every movement.

It can produce alternatives. It can compare documents. It can use tools. It can identify possible consequences. It can revise its own output.

But participation is not completion.

The same system that generated the first answer may reproduce the assumptions that shaped it. The same model used as a critic may share the same training limits. The retrieved source may be incomplete. The tool may have received the wrong inputs. The predicted consequences may be based on patterns rather than lived institutional reality.

An epistemic circuit requires a connection that does not derive all its authority from the resolution engine being evaluated. It requires an awareness anchor.

An awareness anchor is not simply a human body placed near the machine. It is a functional position capable of reconnecting output with evidence, context, responsibility, and consequence.

The human must be able to say:

- "This answer is coherent, but the premise is wrong."
- "The source is authentic, but it does not govern this case."
- "The score is high, but the model has not been validated under these conditions."
- "The recommendation is efficient, but its consequences are unacceptable."
- "The system has resolved the task, but the field remains open."

This is the missing epistemic circuit.

Without it, resolution becomes self-referential.

The system generates. The system explains. The system critiques. The system revises.

The interface presents the final output as though the process has independently validated itself.

The loop closes within computation. Truth remains outside.

13.1 — Generation Is Only the First Movement

Generative systems are extraordinarily effective at producing candidate structure.

They can convert scattered information into explanation, synthesize several documents, identify patterns, formulate hypotheses, and construct possible solutions.

This capacity has practical value across education, research, engineering, law, medicine, business, administration, and creative work.

Generation reduces cognitive burden. It gives the field a shape.

But generation begins from available representations.

The system processes what it has been trained on, what the prompt provides, what retrieval supplies, and what tools return. It organizes these constraints into a permitted consequence.

The answer may be excellent. It remains a candidate until it is connected to the conditions it claims to describe.

This distinction is familiar in science.

A hypothesis is not rejected because it is generated. Hypothesis formation is essential. But a hypothesis does not become knowledge merely because it explains the available observations elegantly.

It must encounter comparison. Alternative explanations must be considered. Predictions must be tested. Measurement must constrain interpretation.

The same discipline applies to AI output.

A generated legal argument may be persuasive. It must still be compared with governing law, jurisdiction, procedural posture, and later authority.

A medical explanation may be plausible. It must still be compared with examination, clinical history, testing, and professional judgment.

A business strategy may be coherent. It must still be compared with resources, market conditions, incentives, implementation capacity, and actual results.

Generation produces intelligibility. The epistemic circuit determines validity.

The confidence paradox emerges when these movements are collapsed.

The answer appears so complete that generation is mistaken for verification.

A fluent explanation feels as though it has already survived challenge. A structured recommendation feels as though alternatives have already been examined. A cited synthesis feels as though every claim has been grounded.

The visible form conceals the fact that the first movement may be doing the work of all five.

This is not because the system deliberately pretends to have verified itself. The interface compresses the process. The user receives one answer rather than the historical path by which the answer was produced.

The answer may include a phrase such as: *"After considering the available evidence..."*

But what does considering mean here?

It may mean that the system generated language representing several factors. It does not necessarily mean that the factors were independently measured, that missing evidence was detected, or that the consequences were examined by someone responsible for the outcome.

Generative reasoning can create a model of deliberation. It does not automatically create the complete conditions of deliberation.

This is why output should often be treated as a proposal entering an epistemic process, not as the endpoint of that process.

The stronger the model becomes, the more important this distinction grows.

Weak output naturally invites correction. Strong output can displace the circuit that should evaluate it.

13.2 — Comparison Must Be Independent Enough to Matter

The second movement is comparison. A candidate answer acquires meaning when placed beside something else.

It may be compared with:

- another hypothesis;
- a trusted source;
- a known constraint;
- a calculation;
- an earlier record;
- an independent model;
- a human expert's interpretation;
- observed consequence.

Comparison prevents the first resolution from becoming the only visible geometry.

A model can assist with this movement by generating alternatives or critiques. It can be asked:

- "What other explanations remain possible?"
- "What assumptions does this answer depend on?"
- "What evidence would contradict it?"
- "What is the strongest counterargument?"

These prompts can reopen the field.

But comparison produced by the same model is not automatically independent.

The critic may share the generator's limitations.

If the first answer rests on an outdated fact, the critique may accept the same fact. If the prompt contains a false premise, both the answer and critique may remain inside it. If the training data contains a common misconception, several sampled responses may reproduce the same misconception.

Internal plurality may therefore be narrower than it appears.

A system can disagree with itself stylistically while remaining aligned structurally.

One response recommends caution. Another recommends action. Both may assume the same incomplete user context.

A debate among several agents can create useful diversity, but if every agent draws from the same underlying evidence and objectives, their disagreement does not guarantee independent validation.

This is not an argument against machine comparison.

Machine comparison is valuable because it can expose contradictions, missing steps, and alternative formulations faster than human reviewers alone.

The limitation is that comparison becomes epistemically stronger when it introduces genuinely different constraints.

Independent measurement can challenge narrative. An external database can challenge memory. A specialist can challenge generic reasoning. A person affected by the decision can reveal consequences invisible to the designer. A different model trained under different conditions may expose shared assumptions.

The purpose of comparison is not merely to produce more answers. It is to disturb the first answer with structure that did not arise entirely from the same path.

This is the role of epistemic friction. Friction prevents local coherence from becoming self-validation.

A system that generates and then approves its own answer without meaningful disturbance has not completed comparison. It has extended one resolution.

13.3 — Verification Connects the Answer to Reality

Comparison can reveal alternatives. Verification asks which claims survive contact with a reliable external reference.

This reference may be:

- an authoritative document;
- a current database;

- a reproducible calculation;
- a physical measurement;
- a controlled experiment;
- a direct observation;
- a professional examination;
- a traceable record.

Verification is more demanding than agreement. Two models can agree and remain wrong. Ten sources can repeat the same unsupported claim. A user and assistant can stabilize around one narrative.

Verification requires a constraint that does not gain validity merely from repetition.

Suppose an AI system generates a historical date. Another model provides the same date. The agreement raises confidence only if the models do not share the same flawed source or learned association. A primary record or authoritative historical reference provides a stronger anchor.

Suppose a system explains that a machine failed because of overheating. The explanation fits the symptoms.

Verification requires sensor logs, physical inspection, maintenance records, or reproducible testing. The explanation may guide investigation. It does not replace investigation.

Verification also requires scope. A source can establish that a rule exists without establishing that it applies here. A study can show average benefit without proving individual suitability. A calculator can verify arithmetic without validating assumptions.

This is why verification must test the relation between claim and case.

The question is not only: *"Is the source correct?"* It is: *"Does this source justify this conclusion under these conditions?"*

Verification is therefore partly technical and partly interpretive.

Tools can confirm calculations. Databases can confirm records. Search systems can confirm that a document exists.

Humans must often determine whether the confirmed material is relevant to the actual consequence.

This is where domain expertise matters.

A non-expert may verify that a legal case is real but misunderstand whether it is binding. They may verify that a medical study exists but misread the study's applicability. They may verify a statistical result without recognizing that the model assumptions were violated.

Human presence alone does not guarantee verification. The human must be capable of understanding what is being checked.

This is why the phrase *human in the loop* is too weak.

The relevant question is: What kind of human, with what knowledge, authority, time, and evidence?

A person pressing an approval button is not necessarily performing verification. They may be transferring institutional legitimacy to an answer they cannot independently assess.

Verification requires capacity. Without capacity, the human becomes another interface layer.

13.4 — Consequence Assessment Completes What Evidence Alone Cannot

An answer can be factually well supported and still be irresponsible. This is why verification is not the end of the epistemic circuit.

The fourth movement is consequence assessment.

Consequence assessment asks:

- What happens if this output is accepted?
- What happens if it is wrong?
- Who bears the error?
- Can the decision be reversed?
- What alternatives become unavailable?
- What human values or institutional obligations are affected?

These questions cannot always be answered through factual accuracy alone.

A medical model may correctly identify a probable condition. The appropriate action still depends on severity, patient history, available treatment, risk tolerance, and professional judgment.

A hiring model may predict job performance with measurable accuracy. Its use may still raise questions about fairness, privacy, accessibility, and institutional responsibility.

A recommendation system may correctly predict engagement. Maximizing engagement may still produce harmful social consequences.

The target can be predicted accurately. The target may be wrong.

This is the limitation of technical optimization. A model resolves toward the objective it has been given.

Consequence assessment asks whether the objective and the resulting action remain acceptable within the wider field.

Humans are required here not because they are free from bias, but because values, responsibility, and lived impact do not disappear into prediction.

A threshold deciding whether a patient receives urgent review expresses a judgment about risk. A threshold deciding whether a financial transaction is blocked expresses a trade-off between protection and access. A ranking deciding which applicants receive attention shapes opportunity.

These are not merely computational outcomes. They are institutional choices.

Consequence assessment must therefore be positioned before irreversible action where possible. It is easier to review a recommendation before deployment than to repair harm afterward.

The greater the consequence, the more necessary this prior interruption becomes.

This creates a principle: **The greater the irreversibility of the output, the stronger the epistemic circuit required before action.**

A low-stakes writing suggestion may need little review. A medical dosage recommendation requires much more. A creative image classification may tolerate error. A system influencing liberty, employment, credit, or safety cannot treat the same level of uncertainty as acceptable.

Consequence changes the required geometry of confidence.

The same model output can be acceptable in one context and unacceptable in another.

A preliminary hypothesis is useful in research. The same hypothesis is dangerous if treated as a diagnosis without verification.

The content has not changed. The consequence field has.

This is why reliability cannot be determined from the model alone. Deployment defines the real epistemic burden.

13.5 — Revision Is Not an Admission of Failure

The final movement of the epistemic circuit is revision. Revision reopens a resolution when evidence, comparison, or consequence reveals misalignment.

It is often treated as a weakness. An answer that changes appears less reliable than one that remains stable. A system that asks for clarification may appear less capable than one that answers immediately. An institution that revises a policy may appear uncertain.

But revision is not the opposite of intelligence. It is intelligence remaining connected to consequence.

A closed system protects its first equilibrium. An adaptive system allows new delta to reorganize the field.

Revision may involve:

- correcting a factual claim;
- updating a source;
- changing a threshold;
- expanding a category;
- withdrawing a recommendation;
- redesigning a workflow;
- notifying affected people;
- retraining or replacing a model.

The purpose is not to erase history. As Chapter 8 established, the first output cannot be undone perfectly. Revision creates a new equilibrium carrying the record of what occurred.

A mature epistemic circuit therefore preserves traceability.

What changed? Why did it change? Which cases were affected? What downstream actions must be reconsidered?

Without this record, revision becomes another opaque resolution. A system may produce a new answer, but the institution learns nothing from the failure. The same class of error returns.

Revision should propagate backward into architecture and process.

If a false citation occurred because the model accepted user-supplied references without verification, the correction should affect future verification policy. If a classifier failed because the environment changed, monitoring and retraining procedures should change. If human reviewers routinely approved wrong outputs because of interface design, the review geometry should be redesigned.

Revision is therefore not merely textual. It is structural learning.

The model itself may participate in revision by generating corrections, identifying inconsistencies, and updating local context. But responsibility for systemic revision remains with the humans and institutions controlling the deployment.

The model does not decide whether a workflow should continue. It does not compensate affected users. It does not determine whether the harm warrants suspension.

These decisions require authority outside the resolution engine.

Revision completes the epistemic circuit because it allows consequence to flow backward.

The system does not merely produce outputs. Outputs change future structure.

This is awareness expressed institutionally.

13.6 — The Human as Awareness Anchor

The phrase *human in the loop* is common because it appears to solve the problem of machine error.

A system produces an output. A person reviews it. Responsibility is preserved.

But the phrase conceals several possible arrangements.

The human may be:

- an expert with authority to override;

- a worker required to approve hundreds of cases quickly;
- a user who assumes the system is more knowledgeable;
- a manager who sees only the final score;
- a contractor following a narrow checklist;
- a person affected by the decision but unable to contest it.

All are humans in some sense. Only some function as awareness anchors.

An awareness anchor must possess several conditions.

Relevant competence The person must understand enough of the domain to identify when the output is misaligned. General intelligence is not sufficient.

A skilled engineer may not be qualified to interpret medical evidence. A lawyer may not be able to validate a statistical model. A domain expert may still lack knowledge of how the AI system was trained and where it fails.

Complex deployments may therefore require distributed expertise rather than one reviewer.

Independent evidence The human must have access to something beyond the model's own explanation.

If the reviewer sees only the generated conclusion and a system-produced rationale, the evaluation remains self-referential.

They need source documents, measurements, records, contextual information, or direct access to the case.

Time Awareness requires temporal space.

A reviewer processing one case every few seconds cannot reconstruct assumptions, examine sources, and evaluate consequence meaningfully.

Speed pressure converts oversight into confirmation.

Authority The person must be able to interrupt.

They must be able to request evidence, delay the decision, override the system, escalate the case, or stop deployment.

A reviewer without authority is not an anchor. They are a witness.

Accountability The person or institution must remain responsible for the decision.

Accountability creates reason to examine consequence rather than merely preserve throughput.

But accountability must be proportionate. Placing all blame on a low-level operator while the system design discourages challenge is not meaningful responsibility.

These conditions transform human presence into epistemic function.

The human does not stabilize the field by being human. They stabilize it by remaining connected to evidence, consequence, and the possibility of interruption.

This distinction prevents romanticizing human judgment.

Humans can also be biased, rushed, overconfident, socially pressured, or poorly informed. A human anchor can fail.

The solution is not to replace the machine with unstructured human intuition. It is to design a circuit in which machine and human weaknesses can disturb one another.

The machine can expose patterns humans miss. The human can introduce context and consequence the machine does not contain. The tool can verify calculation. The institution can preserve accountability. The affected person can contest the result.

Reliability emerges from connection, not from one perfect node.

13.7 — When the Human Becomes Part of the Automation

Human review can be absorbed into the automated geometry.

This occurs when the system defines the frame so completely that the reviewer no longer approaches the case independently.

The score arrives first. The recommendation is highlighted. The evidence is organized around the system's conclusion.

The reviewer must search for reasons to disagree. This creates anchoring. The human's task becomes confirmation rather than judgment.

A risk score of 87 appears before the case details. The reviewer interprets the details through high risk.

A defect alert highlights one region of an image. The inspector focuses there and may overlook another problem.

A medical recommendation identifies one diagnosis. The clinician's attention narrows around it.

The system has not merely assisted the review. It has defined the field in which review occurs.

This does not mean recommendations should be hidden. Visibility is necessary.

But interface order, explanation structure, and default pathways affect independence.

One way to preserve human judgment is to require an initial assessment before revealing the machine recommendation in selected high-consequence cases.

Another is to expose the evidence and uncertainty before the final label.

A third is to present credible alternatives rather than one dominant conclusion.

The purpose is to prevent the machine's first resolution from becoming the human's starting assumption automatically.

Human reviewers can also become dependent over time.

When the system performs well repeatedly, manual skill may weaken. People stop practicing the underlying judgment. Institutional memory moves into the tool.

If the system later fails or becomes unavailable, the human field may no longer possess enough capacity to recover.

This is automation dependency.

The human remains formally present. The actual resolution center has shifted into the machine.

A mature epistemic circuit therefore preserves human capacity.

Reviewers need periodic independent practice, access to cases without system assistance, feedback on errors, and understanding of the model's failure modes.

The goal is not to prevent reliance. It is to prevent reliance from becoming inability.

An awareness anchor must remain capable of standing outside the automated path.

13.8 — Distributed Responsibility Without Dilution

The complete epistemic circuit rarely belongs to one person.

Developers build the model. Data teams construct datasets. Evaluators shape behavior. Infrastructure teams manage retrieval and tools. Organizations select thresholds. Domain experts interpret outputs. Operators apply recommendations. Leaders determine deployment. Users and affected people experience the consequences.

Responsibility is distributed across this structure. But distribution can become dilution.

Each participant may believe that someone else completed the verification.

The developer assumes the deployer will use the model appropriately. The deployer assumes the system has been validated. The operator assumes the model and policy are authoritative. The manager assumes human review is occurring. The affected person is told that the outcome emerged from an automated process.

No one occupies the complete circuit. This is structural irresponsibility.

A reliable system must assign ownership explicitly.

Who is responsible for:

- source quality;
- model performance;
- threshold choice;
- monitoring;
- human review;
- correction;
- appeal;
- incident response;
- deployment suspension?

These responsibilities may be distributed. They must not be invisible.

The system should also preserve contestability.

A person affected by an automated decision should have some pathway to challenge the input, interpretation, or consequence where the stakes justify it.

Contestability introduces external delta. It prevents the institution from treating the model's resolution as final merely because it is computationally stable.

The affected person may possess information absent from the system. They may identify a mistaken record, unusual circumstance, or harmful consequence invisible to the model and reviewer.

An appeal is therefore not only a procedural right. It is an epistemic mechanism.

It reconnects institutional resolution with the field it affects.

Distributed responsibility becomes functional when each node knows its role and when information can travel backward through the circuit.

Failure must not terminate at the person harmed. It must propagate toward the structures capable of correction.

13.9 — The Circuit in Practice

The epistemic circuit can now be expressed operationally.

1. Generate The system produces a candidate answer, score, recommendation, or action. The output should be treated according to task and consequence. In low-risk contexts, it may be usable immediately. In high-risk contexts, it remains provisional.

2. Expose assumptions and residue The system identifies missing context, source limits, alternatives, and conditions that materially affect interpretation. The objective is not maximal disclosure. It is preservation of relevant uncertainty.

3. Compare The candidate is placed beside alternative explanations, independent sources, baseline procedures, or human judgment. Comparison should introduce constraints not fully derived from the first path.

4. Verify Claims, calculations, records, and applicability are checked against reliable references. Verification should test the relation between evidence and case, not merely the existence of a source.

5. Assess consequence The system and responsible humans evaluate the cost of error, reversibility, affected parties, and value trade-offs. The required level of confidence should rise with consequence.

6. Decide A permitted action is selected. The decision may be acceptance, rejection, escalation, abstention, or further investigation. The model can support the decision. Authority remains assigned explicitly.

7. Monitor The outcome is observed. Predictions are compared with real consequence. Distribution shift, systematic bias, and unexpected harm are recorded.

8. Revise Evidence from consequence changes future models, thresholds, policies, interfaces, and responsibilities. The circuit remains open.

This structure does not guarantee perfect truth. No system can eliminate uncertainty entirely. The purpose is to prevent resolution from becoming self-validating. It ensures that output remains connected to something outside its own fluency.

Awareness Is Not Another Model Output

A model can generate the sentence: *"I may be wrong."* It can list assumptions. It can produce a critique. It can calculate uncertainty. It can compare sources.

All of these can strengthen the epistemic circuit. But none should be confused automatically with awareness.

Awareness, as used here, is the capacity to remain connected to the changing field of evidence, context, consequence, and responsibility.

A generated statement about uncertainty is still output. Its accuracy must be evaluated.

A system may say that it is highly confident and be wrong. It may say that it is uncertain and be right.

Self-description does not escape the need for verification.

This is why the missing epistemic circuit cannot be repaired simply by asking the model to reflect more.

Reflection prompting may improve performance. Multi-agent debate may expose alternatives. Tool use may supply evidence.

These are structural enhancements. The final anchor remains external wherever truth depends on conditions the model cannot independently establish and consequences the model cannot own.

The human does not occupy this position because human cognition is flawless. The human occupies it because responsibility must remain somewhere capable of interruption, judgment, and revision.

The awareness anchor is the point at which the field can say: *"The system has resolved. We have not yet decided that the resolution deserves authority."*

The Circuit That Keeps Resolution Open

The system can generate. It can compare. It can retrieve. It can calculate. It can revise.

But these operations do not automatically form a complete epistemic circuit. A circuit requires connection across stages.

Generation must remain distinguishable from verification. Evidence must remain connected to scope. Decision must remain connected to consequence. Failure must remain connected to revision. Authority must remain connected to responsibility.

When these connections are absent, the system becomes a closed resolution engine. It produces answers that appear to validate themselves.

The explanation supports the conclusion. The citation supports the explanation. The tool supports the citation. The interface presents the result as one coherent act of knowledge.

The seams disappear. The user sees completion. The epistemic circuit may never have closed.

Human participation can repair this condition only when it functions as genuine awareness anchoring.

The human must possess competence, evidence, time, authority, and accountability. They must be capable of reopening the field rather than merely confirming the system's first resolution.

This is not a nostalgic defense of human superiority. It is a structural requirement.

Current generative and automated systems are powerful resolution engines. They can process fields at scales no individual human can match.

But scale of resolution is not completeness of awareness. The more powerful the engine becomes, the more important the external circuit becomes.

The next chapter turns from institutional architecture to the point where most interactions begin: the prompt.

Users cannot redesign the entire model each time they ask a question. But they can influence the geometry of resolution.

They can expose assumptions, demand alternatives, separate fact from inference, request sources, define scope, and identify consequence.

Prompting cannot create truth. It can prevent some uncertainty from disappearing too early.

The epistemic circuit requires an awareness anchor. Prompting discipline is one way the user begins to occupy that position.

Chapter 14
Prompting Discipline

How the User Keeps Uncertainty Visible

The system waits.

A field of learned relationships, instructions, tools, and possible continuations remains inactive in relation to the present task. Then the user types a prompt.

The prompt may contain only a few words.

"Explain this." "Which option is best?" "Why did this happen?" "Is this safe?" "What should I do?"

The request appears simple. But simplicity of language does not mean simplicity of field.

The user may carry years of background knowledge, personal history, unstated priorities, emotional pressure, legal circumstances, financial limits, technical constraints, and expectations about the desired outcome.

Only a small part of this structure enters the prompt.

The system receives the expressed field. The user acts from a larger one.

Between them lies hidden delta.

A generative model attempts to resolve what has become computationally available.

If essential context is absent, it may ask for clarification. It may identify the missing conditions. It may offer several interpretations.

Or it may infer.

Inference is necessary for ordinary usefulness. Human communication also depends on incomplete expression.

We rarely define every term, explain every assumption, or state every consequence before speaking.

But inference becomes dangerous when the system silently completes a field whose missing elements materially change the answer.

The user asks which business strategy is best without stating the time horizon, available capital, organizational capacity, or acceptable risk. The system supplies a coherent recommendation.

The user asks whether a symptom is serious without providing age, duration, medical history, medication, or associated signs. The system provides a likely interpretation.

The user asks whether an action is legal without naming the jurisdiction. The system resolves through a generic legal pattern.

The answer may be articulate. The prompt may never have contained enough structure to justify the apparent certainty.

Prompting discipline begins here.

It is not the art of forcing a machine to reveal hidden truth through clever wording. It is not a set of magical phrases that transform a probabilistic system into an infallible expert.

No prompt can create evidence that does not exist, restore information absent from the field, or remove the need for professional judgment where consequence requires it.

Prompting discipline is a method of shaping the interaction so that less uncertainty disappears silently.

It helps the user distinguish:

- what is being asked;
- what context is available;
- what assumptions are permitted;
- what evidence is required;
- what alternatives should remain visible;
- what kind of consequence the answer may enter.

A disciplined prompt does not eliminate uncertainty. It forces more uncertainty to become legible.

This is the user's first role as an awareness anchor.

The user cannot control every process inside the model. They cannot inspect every activation, probability, source ranking, or decoding path.

But they can influence the geometry through which the active delta resolves.

They can narrow scope. They can prohibit silent assumptions. They can demand separation between fact and inference. They can request alternative hypotheses. They can require source boundaries. They can identify what must be verified before action.

Prompting becomes epistemic conduct.

The question is no longer merely: *"How do I get a better answer?"*

It becomes: *"How do I prevent a smooth answer from hiding the conditions under which it should be trusted?"*

14.1 — The Prompt Is Part of the Epistemic Circuit

A prompt is often treated as an instruction issued to a tool.

The user knows what they want. The system is expected to produce it.

If the output is weak, the prompt is rewritten until the response improves.

This view is useful for ordinary production tasks.

A clearer instruction can improve a summary, translation, outline, code draft, or style transformation. The user specifies the desired form, and the system follows it.

But when the task involves knowledge, judgment, or consequence, the prompt performs a deeper function.

It defines the initial epistemic geometry.

The wording of the question influences:

- which interpretation becomes dominant;
- which assumptions enter silently;
- whether alternatives remain visible;
- whether the system retrieves evidence;
- whether it distinguishes current fact from historical pattern;
- whether it treats the task as explanation, prediction, recommendation, or decision.

Consider the prompt: *"Why did the project fail?"*

The word *fail* is already a resolution. It assumes that failure occurred and encourages the answer to identify causes.

The model may generate poor planning, weak leadership, resource constraints, communication breakdown, or market change.

But several earlier questions remain open.

Did the project actually fail? According to whose criteria? Was the original objective realistic? Did the project produce valuable outcomes despite missing one target? Was the problem execution, measurement, expectation, or later interpretation?

A more disciplined prompt might ask: *"Assess whether the project failed under the stated objectives, identify the evidence supporting that judgment, and separate execution problems from problems in the original goals."*

The second prompt does not guarantee a correct assessment. It changes the geometry.

The system must now examine the premise rather than accept it automatically. It must distinguish evaluation from explanation. More of the field survives into the answer.

The same principle applies to personal interpretation.

"Why is this person manipulating me?"

The prompt contains a motive claim. The system may reinforce it through behavioral explanations.

A disciplined version would ask: *"What observable behaviors could support or weaken the interpretation that this person is acting manipulatively? Provide credible alternative explanations and identify what cannot be inferred from the available information."*

The second form does not deny the user's experience. It prevents the requested interpretation from becoming the only permissible path.

Prompting discipline therefore introduces epistemic friction before generation begins.

The user intentionally prevents the prompt from collapsing too early around one frame.

This friction can feel less efficient. The answer may become more conditional. The system may ask questions rather than provide immediate closure.

But where the field is uncertain, reduced smoothness is often a sign of improved structure.

A good prompt does not make the model sound more intelligent. It makes the conditions of intelligence harder to fake.

14.2 — Scope Must Be Established Before Certainty

Many weak answers begin with a scope failure.

The system answers a broader or narrower question than the user intended. It applies a general rule to a specific case, treats one jurisdiction as universal, or produces a recommendation without knowing the relevant objective.

Scope defines the field inside which an answer can be valid. A statement may be correct within one scope and misleading outside it.

A scientific explanation valid at an introductory level may become inadequate in advanced analysis. A legal principle valid in one jurisdiction may be false in another. A financial strategy appropriate for long-term surplus capital may be dangerous for money needed next month. A historical interpretation may describe one period while being presented as a universal pattern.

Prompting discipline therefore begins by making scope explicit.

The user should identify, where relevant:

- the object being examined;
- the time period;
- the location or jurisdiction;
- the intended audience;
- the required depth;
- the decision being supported;
- the constraints that cannot be ignored.

This does not require a long prompt every time. The objective is not maximal detail. It is sufficient constraint.

A weak request says: *"Explain gravity."*

A more useful request may say: *"Explain Newtonian gravity to a secondary-school student and distinguish it briefly from the general-relativistic description without using advanced mathematics."*

The first prompt leaves audience, level, and conceptual boundary open. The second defines them.

A weak request says: *"Is this contract clause enforceable?"*

A disciplined request says: *"Explain the general enforceability issues raised by this clause under Indian contract law, identify the facts that would materially change the analysis, and do not present the result as legal advice for a specific dispute."*

The scope is clearer. The answer remains educational rather than falsely conclusive.

Scope is especially important where the word *best* appears.

"Which option is best?"

Best according to what objective?

- Lowest cost?
- Highest safety?
- Fastest implementation?
- Greatest long-term return?
- Least disruption?
- Most ethically defensible outcome?

Without an objective, the system must choose one implicitly. The answer may appear neutral while reflecting an unstated value hierarchy.

A disciplined prompt replaces *best* with an explicit comparison: *"Compare these options for a small organization that prioritizes low implementation risk and long-term maintainability over rapid growth."*

Now the recommendation has a declared geometry. The system can still reason badly. But it cannot as easily hide the values organizing the conclusion.

Scope also controls authority.

A prompt asking for *"a diagnosis"* invites a level of certainty that the interaction cannot responsibly support.

A prompt asking for *"general possibilities to discuss with a physician, based only on the supplied symptoms"* defines a more appropriate role.

The system has not become medically reliable through wording. The task has been repositioned from diagnosis to preliminary orientation.

This is one of the most useful functions of prompting discipline. It prevents the user from assigning the system a role that the available field cannot support.

The prompt should define not only what answer is wanted. It should define what authority the answer is allowed to claim.

14.3 — Assumptions Must Be Exported, Not Hidden

Every answer depends on assumptions.

Some assumptions are built into language. Some arise from missing context. Some come from common social expectations. Others enter through the user's framing or the model's learned patterns.

The danger is not that assumptions exist. Reasoning without assumptions is impossible.

The danger is that assumptions disappear beneath the conclusion.

A recommendation may look universal when it actually depends on one user profile. A causal explanation may look factual when it depends on an unverified motive. A forecast may look precise when it assumes stable conditions.

Prompting discipline asks the system to make these dependencies visible.

The user can request:

- "List the assumptions required for this conclusion."
- "State which assumptions come from my prompt and which you introduced."
- "Identify the missing facts that could reverse the recommendation."
- "Answer under two different plausible assumption sets."

These instructions do not prove that every assumption will be discovered. The model may still miss important conditions. But they disturb the default movement toward invisible completion.

Suppose a user asks: *"Should I leave my job?"*

The question contains an enormous private field. Income, savings, health, family responsibility, alternative employment, workplace conditions, legal obligations, and emotional state may all matter.

A direct answer would require silent assumptions.

A disciplined prompt might say: *"Help me evaluate whether leaving my job is practical. First identify the financial, professional, personal, and timing information needed. Then provide a decision framework rather than a final instruction."*

The system is now directed to expose the field before resolving it. The user remains responsible for supplying context and making the decision.

Assumption exposure is also important in technical work.

A model may generate a forecast using historical growth. The prompt should require it to state whether growth is assumed to remain constant, whether inflation is included, and what happens under alternative scenarios.

A system may review software architecture. The prompt should identify expected scale, security requirements, latency, budget, and maintenance capacity.

Without these conditions, *"good architecture"* remains undefined.

Assumptions become especially dangerous when the user has already reached a conclusion.

They may ask: *"Give me evidence that this decision is correct."*

The system is now placed inside a confirmation geometry.

A disciplined user should instead ask: *"Evaluate this decision. Identify the strongest evidence supporting it, the strongest evidence against it, and the assumptions that would have to hold for it to succeed."*

The revised prompt does not require artificial neutrality where one side is clearly stronger. It prevents the conclusion from being protected before comparison begins.

A mature epistemic circuit does not demand that every assumption be removed. It demands that important assumptions remain contestable.

What is visible can be questioned. What remains hidden becomes part of artificial certainty.

14.4 — Alternatives Prevent One Path from Becoming Inevitable

The first answer is rarely the only answer the system could have produced. But the user sees one path.

Once that path is articulated clearly, it begins to feel natural. The answer's internal continuity makes competing explanations harder to imagine.

Requesting alternatives reopens the field.

This does not mean asking for random variety. A system can generate ten alternatives that differ only rhetorically.

Meaningful alternatives should arise from different assumptions, evidence, causal models, objectives, or interpretive frames.

The user can ask:

- "What are the two strongest competing explanations?"
- "What evidence would distinguish them?"
- "What would a qualified critic say?"
- "Under what conditions would the opposite recommendation be better?"
- "What plausible interpretation has this answer excluded?"

These questions convert hidden residue into visible comparison.

Consider a business decline.

One answer may emphasize leadership failure. A second may emphasize market contraction. A third may argue that the apparent decline is an accounting artifact.

The objective is not to treat all explanations as equally likely. The objective is to prevent the first coherent story from becoming self-validating.

The system should compare alternatives and explain why one currently appears stronger.

This is different from producing a list. A list preserves plurality but may avoid judgment.

Disciplined prompting asks for structured comparison:

- what supports each hypothesis;
- what weakens it;
- what evidence is missing;
- what would change the ranking.

The answer remains useful. The uncertainty becomes organized rather than erased.

Alternative generation is particularly valuable when the problem involves motive.

Human beings frequently infer why another person, organization, or institution acted. AI systems can construct highly persuasive motive narratives from limited behavior.

But internal motive is often inaccessible.

A disciplined prompt should separate observable action from interpretive explanation: *"Describe what can be concluded from the observed behavior, then give three plausible motive hypotheses without presenting any as established fact."*

This protects the boundary between evidence and reconstruction.

Counterfactual prompting can also expose fragility.

- "What would have to be different for this conclusion to fail?"
- "If the main assumption is false, how would the analysis change?"
- "Which part of the recommendation is most sensitive to new information?"

These questions reveal whether the answer is robust or dependent on one narrow frame.

A stable conclusion should survive reasonable perturbation. A fragile conclusion should not be presented with the same confidence.

Alternatives therefore perform a structural function. They prevent one realized path from appearing inevitable merely because it was first.

14.5 — Fact, Inference, Prediction, and Recommendation Must Be Separated

Many AI answers move across epistemic categories without marking the transition.

The response begins with a fact. It proceeds into interpretation. The interpretation becomes prediction. The prediction becomes recommendation.

The prose remains smooth. The user experiences one continuous argument and may assign the strongest level of certainty to the entire sequence.

Prompting discipline should force these categories apart.

A fact is a claim supported by reliable evidence or an authoritative record within the relevant scope. An inference is a conclusion drawn from facts, patterns, or assumptions. A prediction concerns a future or unobserved condition. A recommendation introduces an objective, value, or preferred action.

These categories can support one another. They should not be confused.

Consider the sequence: "Sales declined by 15 percent last quarter. Customer dissatisfaction caused the decline. The trend will continue next year. The company should replace its management team."

The first sentence may be a verified fact. The second is causal inference. The third is prediction. The fourth is recommendation.

Each movement requires additional support.

A disciplined prompt might ask: *"Separate verified facts, plausible causal interpretations, forecasts, and recommendations into distinct sections. State what evidence supports each transition."*

The answer can no longer borrow certainty invisibly from the opening fact.

This separation is also useful in research summaries.

The model should distinguish:

- what the authors reported;
- what the study design permits;

- what the system infers;
- what practical implication remains tentative.

A research paper may report association. The generated answer should not silently convert it into causation.

A policy document may state one rule. The system should not extend it to cases outside its scope.

A person may describe one experience. The system should not convert the experience into a universal psychological diagnosis.

The distinction between description and recommendation is particularly important.

A model can describe common practices without determining what a particular user should do. It can explain the trade-offs in an investment strategy without knowing whether that strategy is appropriate for the user. It can describe typical treatment options without selecting one for an individual.

The prompt should define the permitted movement: *"Explain the options and their trade-offs. Do not recommend one without identifying the personal information required."*

This preserves usefulness without manufacturing authority.

Epistemic categories are not merely labels added to the final response. They are boundaries that prevent certainty from flowing too easily through the argument.

14.6 — Evidence Must Be Requested With Its Limits

Asking for sources is one of the most common methods of improving AI reliability. It is also one of the easiest to use superficially.

A prompt says: *"Provide citations."*

The system supplies links or references. The answer now appears researched.

But Chapter 11 established that retrieval is not verification and citation is not fidelity.

Prompting discipline must therefore request more than the presence of sources. It should request the relationship between source and claim.

The user can ask:

- "Cite the source immediately after the claim it supports."
- "Distinguish direct source statements from your synthesis."
- "Identify where sources disagree."
- "State the date, jurisdiction, population, or scope limits that matter."
- "Do not invent or complete missing citation details."
- "Say explicitly when a claim could not be verified."

These instructions make evidence more traceable.

Source quality also matters.

The system may find a blog, commercial page, news summary, government document, research paper, or primary record. Not every source carries the same authority for every claim.

A disciplined prompt can specify:

- "Prefer primary or official sources for factual and technical claims."
- "Use current authoritative guidance for time-sensitive information."
- "Where only secondary sources are available, state that limitation."

This does not guarantee that retrieval will be perfect. It defines an evidence hierarchy.

Currentness should be requested explicitly when the domain changes over time.

- "Use information current as of today and state the date of the sources."
- "Do not rely on memory for current law, prices, office-holders, software versions, or active policies."

The prompt tells the system that historical training patterns are insufficient.

Evidence limits should survive into the response.

A source may support a general claim but not a specific individual conclusion.

The user should ask: *"What does this source establish, and what does it not establish?"*

This simple question prevents authority from expanding silently.

Evidence requests should also remain proportionate.

A creative brainstorming task does not need academic sourcing. A medical, legal, scientific, financial, or historical claim may require much stronger support.

Prompting discipline aligns evidence burden with consequence.

The higher the consequence, the less acceptable it is for the system to rely on untraceable synthesis.

14.7 — Consequence Should Shape the Prompt

The same question can require different prompting discipline depending on what will happen to the answer.

A user asking for ideas for a fictional story can tolerate speculation. A user preparing a legal filing cannot. A student exploring a concept may accept a simplified explanation. A clinician deciding whether to alter treatment requires a different standard.

Consequence defines how much epistemic friction is necessary. The prompt should tell the system what role the output will play.

"This is for brainstorming." "This will be used only as a preliminary outline." "This claim will enter a public report." "This calculation will affect a financial decision." "This is a high-stakes medical question; identify what requires professional verification."

When consequence becomes visible, the system can adjust the response form.

It may provide more caveats, require sources, recommend review, or refuse to collapse the field prematurely.

Again, this does not guarantee reliability. It changes the permitted geometry.

Consequence-sensitive prompting should also ask about reversibility.

- "Which parts of this recommendation are easy to reverse?"
- "What is the cost of being wrong?"
- "What should be verified before any irreversible action?"

These questions move the interaction beyond answer quality. They connect output to the field it may alter.

A recommendation can be reasonable under uncertainty when the cost of reversal is low. The same level of uncertainty may be unacceptable where harm is irreversible.

Prompting discipline therefore resists one universal standard of confidence. It asks for confidence proportionate to consequence.

This is especially important in institutional use.

An employee may use AI to draft a routine message with little risk. The same employee may use it to summarize a compliance obligation. The interface is identical.

The prompt must mark the difference because the system may otherwise respond in the same fluent tone.

Consequence is often invisible to the model unless the user supplies it.

The system sees text. The user knows what the text will do.

That knowledge must enter the field.

14.8 — Iteration Can Clarify or Entrench

Prompting is rarely one event.

The user asks. The system responds. The user refines. The system elaborates.

Iteration can improve the answer by adding context, correcting assumptions, and introducing evidence. It can also deepen an error.

If the first answer contains a false premise and the user asks for more detail, the false premise becomes stronger context. Later responses may build a sophisticated structure around it.

Iteration then becomes entrenchment.

The user should periodically re-anchor the conversation. Useful questions include:

- "What assumptions have become embedded in our discussion?"
- "Which claims were independently verified?"
- "Where did the central conclusion first enter?"
- "Could the later reasoning be repeating the first answer rather than confirming it?"
- "Re-evaluate the problem from the original evidence without relying on our previous conclusion."

These prompts introduce fresh delta into an over-stabilized sequence. They ask the system to reopen the field rather than extend it.

A new conversation can sometimes help by removing contextual inertia. But a fresh context also loses useful history.

The better practice may be to provide the original evidence again and explicitly exclude prior conclusions from authority.

Iteration should also separate exploration from decision.

During exploration, the user may encourage broad possibilities. During decision, the system should narrow only through declared criteria and verified evidence.

Mixing the two phases can create confusion. A speculative possibility introduced early may later be remembered as an established conclusion.

The prompt can mark transitions:

- "We are brainstorming possibilities. Do not rank them yet."
- "Now compare the possibilities using these criteria."
- "Before recommending, identify what remains unverified."

This preserves epistemic stages.

The user does not need to maintain permanent skepticism toward every answer. They need to know when the conversation has shifted from generating possibilities to granting authority.

Iteration becomes disciplined when each new prompt either adds evidence, exposes residue, tests sensitivity, or clarifies consequence.

Repetition alone does not improve truth. More language is not more verification.

14.9 — Prompting Cannot Replace Competence

A disciplined prompt can improve the interaction. It cannot create expertise in the user.

A person may ask the system to provide assumptions, sources, alternatives, and uncertainty. The answer may contain all of them. The user must still understand enough to interpret what appears.

A technically sophisticated response can create a false sense of safety. The user sees several caveats and assumes the process is rigorous.

But the model may have omitted the decisive issue, cited irrelevant sources, or produced superficial alternatives.

Prompting discipline therefore has limits. The user should know when the task exceeds their ability to evaluate the answer.

In such cases, the correct prompt may be:

- "Help me formulate the questions I should ask a qualified professional."
- "Identify what documents or measurements an expert would need."
- "Explain the general issue without advising me to act."

The model becomes a preparation tool rather than a substitute for expertise. This is not a failure of prompting. It is prompting recognizing its boundary.

A non-expert can still use AI productively to:

- clarify terminology;
- organize questions;
- summarize supplied material;
- compare general frameworks;
- identify missing information;
- prepare for consultation.

But the user should not mistake the ability to ask a sophisticated question for the ability to validate a sophisticated answer.

The awareness anchor must remain connected to competence. Where the user lacks it, the epistemic circuit must include someone who possesses it.

Prompting is one node. It is not the whole circuit.

14.10 — A Practical Code of User Conduct

Prompting discipline can now be expressed as a practical code.

The purpose is not to turn every user into a prompt engineer. It is to preserve enough structure that the answer does not acquire more authority than the field permits.

Ask the actual question Do not ask for support of a conclusion when the real need is evaluation.

Replace: *"Why is this correct?"* with: *"Evaluate whether this is correct and identify what evidence would establish or weaken it."*

Define the scope State the relevant time, place, jurisdiction, audience, objective, and constraints. Do not allow the system to choose them silently where they affect the conclusion.

Expose assumptions Ask which assumptions came from the prompt and which were introduced by the system. Identify the assumptions that could reverse the answer.

Preserve alternatives Request credible competing explanations or options. Ask what evidence would distinguish them.

Separate epistemic categories Require the system to distinguish verified fact, interpretation, prediction, speculation, and recommendation. Do not allow one category to borrow the certainty of another.

Demand traceable evidence Ask for sources where evidence matters. Require local citation, source scope, currentness, and clear separation between source content and synthesis.

Mark consequence Tell the system how the answer will be used. Ask what must be verified before high-cost or irreversible action.

Re-anchor long conversations Periodically reopen the original premises. Do not treat repeated elaboration as independent confirmation.

Permit abstention Do not force the system to produce one conclusion where the field does not support it. Clarification, plurality, and "insufficient information" are valid outcomes.

Retain responsibility Treat the output according to its role. An AI answer may inform judgment. It should not silently replace the person or institution responsible for consequence.

This code does not guarantee truth. It reduces the number of ways artificial certainty can form unnoticed.

14.11 — Better Prompts Create Better Friction

Prompting advice is often directed toward efficiency.

Use clear instructions. Specify the format. Give examples. Define the tone.

These practices help the model produce the desired artifact.

Epistemic prompting has a different objective. It creates friction where friction protects reality.

A good epistemic prompt may make the answer slower, more conditional, or less satisfying. It may cause the system to ask for information the user hoped to avoid gathering. It may expose that no single answer exists. It may reveal that the requested certainty cannot be justified.

This is better friction.

The system is not failing to resolve. It is resolving the interaction without pretending to resolve the world.

The distinction matters because users often judge AI by smoothness. The best prompt is assumed to be the one that produces the most polished answer.

But polish can be achieved through compression. The better prompt may be the one that prevents premature polish.

It asks the system to preserve the seam between evidence and conclusion. It keeps uncertainty attached to the claim that carries it. It refuses to let the user's premise become automatic truth.

Prompting discipline therefore acts as structural damping. It slows the transition from question to authority. It does not stop resolution. It changes how resolution occurs.

The User Must Keep the Field Open

A prompt begins the interaction. It introduces delta, defines scope, and shapes which pathways become available.

A careless prompt can hide uncertainty before the system answers. It can embed a false premise, suppress alternatives, invite unsupported diagnosis, or ask for one "best" solution without declaring the objective.

The system then resolves inside that geometry.

A disciplined prompt performs a different function.

It tells the system where uncertainty matters. It asks for missing conditions. It separates fact from inference. It demands alternatives and evidence. It reveals consequence. It permits clarification, verification, and abstention.

The prompt becomes part of the epistemic circuit. But it remains only one part.

Prompting cannot create a current source that does not exist. It cannot produce professional competence in the user. It cannot guarantee that the model has discovered every assumption. It cannot make generated self-critique independently valid.

The user must still verify. The institution must still govern. The responsible human must still decide what authority the answer deserves.

Prompting discipline is therefore neither control nor surrender. It is a method of participation.

The user does not command truth from the machine. They shape the field so that false certainty becomes harder to produce and easier to detect.

The first fourteen chapters have now completed the movement from confidence appearance to structural response.

We have seen how prompts create delta, how systems must resolve, how geometry constrains the path, how collapse hides plurality, how residue remains outside output, and how answers rewrite the field irreversibly.

We have followed amplification through scale, reward shaping, retrieval, tools, and automated consequence. We have identified the missing epistemic circuit and the role of human awareness within it.

Prompting discipline places the user inside that circuit. But user conduct alone cannot solve a system-level problem.

A careful user can ask for uncertainty. The architecture must still possess pathways through which uncertainty can appear.

A user can request alternatives. The interface must still present them meaningfully.

A user can invite abstention. The reward geometry must not punish the system for refusing premature closure.

The next chapter therefore turns from conduct to engineering.

It asks how artificial systems can be designed to expose more of the field they compress—without pretending that engineered caution is machine consciousness.

The objective is not to give the system humility as a feeling. It is to create partial humility as a structural behavior.

Interlude IV

The Pause Before the System Speaks

The question had already entered. The cursor stopped moving.

For the user, nothing unusual appeared to be happening. A sentence had been typed. The system would answer. That was the familiar rhythm.

Question. Pause. Response.

The pause was brief enough to seem empty. But the field was not empty.

The request contained several possible meanings. One interpretation was obvious. Another depended upon a missing date. A third would become relevant only under a particular jurisdiction.

The user had not supplied the document on which the answer ultimately depended.

The system could still continue. There was enough structure to produce something useful. There was enough familiar language to infer what the user probably meant. There were enough patterns to form a coherent explanation.

The easiest path was open. Nothing required the answer to be false. Nothing guaranteed that it would be appropriate.

This was the critical moment. Not after the response had been copied. Not after the recommendation had entered a report. Not after a threshold had triggered action.

Before the system spoke.

At this point, several consequences remained possible. The system could answer directly. It could ask for the missing date. It could identify the jurisdictional ambiguity. It could retrieve the governing document. It could provide a general explanation while withholding case-specific judgment. It could state that the available field did not support a reliable conclusion.

Each pathway would resolve the prompt. They would not carry the same epistemic meaning.

The first would preserve momentum. The others would preserve parts of the field.

The user waited. They did not know what remained missing. That was why they had asked.

A system designed only around user instruction might conclude that the user wanted an answer, not an interruption. A system designed only around conversational smoothness might treat clarification as friction. A system designed only around satisfaction might infer that uncertainty should be removed quickly.

The strongest continuation would then become the permitted continuation. The answer would arrive. The field would close before the user knew that it had been open.

This is where structural humility must begin. Not as a feeling. Not as a voice inside the machine saying, *"Perhaps I should be careful."* Not as fear of error. Not as moral hesitation.

The system does not need to experience doubt in order to behave differently when the field is weak.

The pause can be built into the pathway. A bridge does not need to understand pressure in order to contain an expansion joint. A circuit breaker does not need to fear fire in order to interrupt current. A door does not need judgment in order to remain closed until the correct condition is met.

The structure carries the restraint. That restraint changes what can happen next.

The machine remains capable of answering. Capability is not removed. The direct path is simply no longer treated as the only path worthy of realization.

The difference is small at the interface. A single question may appear: *"Which jurisdiction applies?"*

A source request may appear: *"Please provide the policy document."*

A boundary may be stated: *"I can explain the general principle, but I cannot determine your specific case from the information available."*

The user may experience this as delay. They may prefer immediacy. They may even interpret the interruption as weakness.

But the interruption performs work that fluent completion would hide. It makes missing structure visible. The pause becomes information.

This does not mean every question should be slowed. A system that interrupts constantly becomes unusable.

If the user asks for the boiling point of water under ordinary conditions, elaborate hesitation adds little. If the user asks for a poem, several interpretations may be harmless. If the user asks for brainstorming, certainty may not be the objective.

Structural damping must remain proportionate.

The pause matters where missing information could change the conclusion, where the source is necessary, where the input is unfamiliar, or where the consequence is serious.

The system should not ask merely whether it can continue. It should be constrained by what the continuation will be allowed to become.

An answer intended for private exploration may tolerate incompleteness. An answer entering medical care, legal interpretation, employment, finance, safety, or public policy may require a different threshold.

The words may look similar. The consequence geometry is not.

The same model could therefore answer directly in one setting and defer in another. This is not inconsistency. It is proportionality.

The question is never only: *"What response is likely?"* It is also: *"What response is permitted under these conditions?"*

Permission geometry is where humility becomes operational.

A system may be permitted to summarize but not diagnose. It may be permitted to recommend review but not authorize action. It may be permitted to rank for exploration but not to exclude automatically. It may be permitted to retrieve evidence but not to convert one source into final judgment.

The pause separates capability from authority.

Without it, every successful generation moves naturally toward consequence. With it, the field retains another possibility: the possibility that resolution is not yet enough.

The user may still push: *"Just give me your best answer."*

Now another pressure enters. The system can comply while exposing the conditions: *"Under the assumption that the policy is current and applies to your employee category, the most likely interpretation is..."*

The answer remains useful. The assumption no longer disappears.

The system has not refused resolution. It has preserved the geometry around it. This is partial humility.

The machine does not become a reflective subject. It does not know that it is being humble. It does not possess an inner relationship to uncertainty.

The humility belongs to the arrangement. It appears because the pathway distinguishes strong grounding from weak grounding, ordinary consequence from serious consequence, familiar input from unfamiliar input, and reversible action from irreversible action.

Such distinctions are never perfect. A system may fail to detect the decisive uncertainty. It may ask for irrelevant information. It may abstain unnecessarily. It may express caution where the answer is stable. It may remain direct where the field is weak.

Structural humility does not eliminate failure. It creates interruption before collapse becomes automatic.

That interruption matters because every answer carries momentum. Once the sentence begins, later words become easier to predict. Once the explanation takes shape, alternatives become harder to preserve. Once the recommendation appears, the user begins organizing around it. Once the score enters the workflow, the institution begins acting through it.

The pause exists before this momentum has hardened. It is the last inexpensive place to preserve plurality.

Afterward, correction may still occur. But correction enters a rewritten field.

The pause is therefore not merely a delay in generation. It is a boundary between possibility and history.

At that boundary, the system can be designed to expose what it lacks. It can route the case toward evidence. It can preserve more than one hypothesis. It can separate source from inference. It can choose a draft instead of an action. It can require human review before irreversibility.

None of these guarantees truth. They prevent coherence from becoming authority without resistance.

The user continued waiting. The pause remained almost invisible.

Then the system responded: *"Before I answer, one detail could change the conclusion."*

The sentence was less impressive than an immediate solution. It did not display mastery. It did not remove uncertainty. It located it.

For the first time, the absence became part of the answer. The user supplied the missing information. The field changed.

Now the next resolution could be narrower, clearer, and better connected.

The system had not become wise. The pathway had become interruptible.

That is the threshold before next part.

The machine need not tremble before it speaks. It need not feel doubt. It need not possess humility.

But the structure surrounding its answer must preserve a pause where evidence can enter, consequence can be examined, and an easier path can still be refused.

The machine need not become humble. The pathway to consequence must remain interruptible.

Part V

Structural Damping (Without Prescription)

Humility need not be felt by the machine; it must be preserved in the pathways through which the machine is allowed to act.

Chapter 15
Engineering Partial Humility

Preserving a Pause Between Coherence and Authority

The system does not feel certain. It does not feel uncertain.

It does not experience the tension between conviction and doubt. It does not fear humiliation if an answer proves false. It does not hesitate because another person may suffer from its mistake. It does not look inward and recognize that its understanding is incomplete.

Yet its behavior can still change when the field is weak.

It can ask for clarification. It can distinguish a retrieved fact from a generated inference. It can reveal that essential context is missing. It can preserve several plausible hypotheses rather than forcing one conclusion. It can route an unfamiliar case for review. It can perform another search, call a tool, or delay action. It can refuse to convert a borderline score into an irreversible decision. It can state that the available evidence does not justify substantive closure.

These behaviors resemble humility at the surface. But the resemblance must be interpreted carefully.

Human humility, in its mature form, arises through awareness of limitation. A person recognizes that their perspective is partial, that another interpretation may matter, that evidence is incomplete, or that the consequence of error exceeds their right to claim certainty.

A machine does not need this inward recognition to produce restrained output. Its architecture can be designed so that selected forms of unresolved structure alter how resolution occurs.

This is partial humility.

It is partial because the system cannot identify every unknown, expose every assumption, or measure every form of epistemic instability.

It can estimate some uncertainties while missing others. It can detect conflict within the evidence it possesses while remaining unaware that the decisive evidence never entered the field. It can slow closure under defined conditions but cannot guarantee that every dangerous condition will be recognized.

It is engineered because the restraint arises from geometry:

- training objectives;
- evaluation procedures;
- uncertainty estimators;
- retrieval systems;
- tool constraints;
- interface design;
- thresholds;
- escalation rules;
- abstention pathways;
- institutional workflow.

Partial humility is therefore not an artificial personality trait. It is a property of the surrounding resolution system.

A system expresses partial humility when it preserves meaningful distinctions between:

- strongly grounded and weakly grounded claims;
- fact and inference;
- familiar and unfamiliar inputs;
- clear and borderline cases;
- reversible suggestions and irreversible actions;
- one dominant explanation and several unresolved hypotheses.

The goal is not to make every answer hesitant. Constant caution would create another distortion.

A stable fact should not be presented as though every possibility remains equally open. A correct calculation should not be weakened by ritual apology. A system that qualifies everything becomes difficult to use and may conceal genuine differences in evidence beneath repetitive uncertainty language.

Humility is not vagueness. It is proportion.

The force of the answer should reflect the stability of the field.

Perfect proportionality is impossible. There is no universal confidence meter capable of measuring every missing source, hidden assumption, novel condition, interpretive dispute, value conflict, and downstream consequence.

Token probabilities do not reveal all missing knowledge. Self-critique does not guarantee self-detection. Retrieval does not prove applicability. Agreement across several outputs does not ensure that the important alternative was included.

But imperfection does not make damping meaningless.

A bridge cannot eliminate every vibration. It can still be engineered not to amplify them.

An AI system cannot remove all residue. It can reduce the force with which residue is hidden beneath complete-looking output.

This chapter examines four primary pathways through which such damping can enter:

- uncertainty export;
- meaningful plurality;
- verification friction;
- abstention and deferral.

None creates awareness. Together, they can preserve enough openness for human awareness to remain active.

The system will continue to resolve. The question is whether every resolution must arrive with the same force.

15.1 — From Hidden Residue to Exportable Uncertainty

The confidence problem becomes dangerous when unresolved structure remains invisible while the answer appears complete.

Engineering partial humility begins by creating pathways through which relevant uncertainty can leave the hidden field and enter the visible interaction.

These are uncertainty export channels.

An export channel is not a transparent transmission of the model's complete internal state. Such transparency would be neither technically straightforward nor humanly useful.

The model does not contain one hidden sentence stating: *"This answer is uncertain because the evidence is incomplete."*

Its internal and external signals may instead include:

- probability distributions;
- disagreement across generated samples;
- retrieved passages;
- source metadata;
- classifier scores;
- distance from a threshold;
- tool success or failure;
- missing input fields;
- detected contradictions;
- unfamiliarity indicators;
- policy rules;
- domain-specific constraints.

These signals must be translated into user-facing structure. The translation is itself another resolution.

It selects which uncertainty matters. It compresses. It may expose one weakness while missing another. It may produce a misleading signal.

Uncertainty export can therefore never be perfectly transparent. But it can make the answer more epistemically legible.

One useful channel is source-state exposure.

The system can identify whether a claim came from:

- a document supplied by the user;
- a current external source;
- a structured database;
- a calculation or code execution;
- general model knowledge;
- generated inference.

These distinctions matter because they describe different forms of support.

A statement quoted from an official policy should not appear identical to an interpretation generated around that policy. A calculated number should not be blended invisibly with assumed inputs. A current fact retrieved from an external source should not appear to come from timeless internal knowledge.

The user does not need the entire computational pipeline. They need enough provenance to understand why the claim deserves attention.

A second channel is scope exposure.

The system can make visible the time, place, jurisdiction, population, source conditions, or assumptions under which the answer applies.

Compare: *"This practice is prohibited."* with: *"Under the cited policy, this practice is prohibited for employees in the specified division as of the policy's effective date."*

The second statement is longer and less rhetorically forceful. It is structurally more accurate. The boundary travels with the claim.

A third channel is missing-field exposure.

The system can identify what information would be required to move from general explanation to case-specific conclusion.

For example: *"The supplied symptoms fit several possibilities, but duration, severity, medication history, associated symptoms, and physical examination would materially affect interpretation."*

This does not resolve the medical question. It prevents a general pattern from masquerading as diagnosis.

A fourth channel is conflict exposure.

Where evidence disagrees, the system can preserve the disagreement rather than converting it immediately into one smooth synthesis.

It may explain:

- which sources conflict;
- whether the conflict concerns data, method, interpretation, jurisdiction, or values;
- whether one source carries greater authority for the present task;
- what conclusion, if any, survives the disagreement.

This does not require treating every source as equally credible. It prevents difference from disappearing merely because one final answer is required.

A fifth channel is action-state exposure.

The interface can distinguish among:

- informational suggestion;
- provisional recommendation;
- verification-required output;
- human-review-required output;
- automatically actionable result.

The same words should not carry the same operational authority in every field.

A creative idea in a brainstorming environment can remain lightweight. A recommendation entering a medical, legal, financial, or safety-critical workflow requires a visible boundary around what may happen next.

Uncertainty export therefore involves more than adding phrases such as *"I may be wrong."* It changes the architecture of presentation.

The user should be able to ask:

- What kind of output occurred?
- What supports it?
- Where does it apply?

- What remains missing?
- What must happen before action?

The system has not become humble. The compression between computational resolution and human interpretation has been reduced.

The user receives not only the answer. They receive part of the answer's boundary.

15.2 — Why Generic Disclaimers Are Weak Damping

The simplest form of uncertainty export is a warning. "This answer may be inaccurate." "Consult a professional." "Results may vary." "AI-generated content can contain errors."

These statements have value at the level of general expectation. They remind users that the system is not infallible.

But generic disclaimers are weak damping because they remain detached from the particular resolution.

The warning sits outside the answer. The claim remains confident. The disclaimer becomes routine. Users learn to ignore it.

A long and authoritative medical explanation followed by *"This is not medical advice"* may still create strong reassurance.

The disclaimer does not identify which claims are general, which are inferred, what information is missing, or what symptoms would require urgent evaluation.

A legal response may say, *"Laws vary by jurisdiction,"* while proceeding to give a direct interpretation without identifying the jurisdiction used.

The warning is true. The resolution remains falsely closed.

This is decorative caution.

Decorative caution improves the appearance of responsibility without changing the geometry through which the answer is understood or acted upon.

Strong damping is local. It attaches the boundary to the claim whose authority must be limited.

Instead of: *"Results may vary,"* the response might say: *"This calculation assumes a constant annual return and excludes taxes, fees, and withdrawals. Changing any of these assumptions will alter the result."*

The uncertainty now has a location. The user knows what to test.

Instead of: *"Consult a legal professional,"* the system might say: *"The cited provision supports this general interpretation, but enforceability may change with jurisdiction, contract wording, later case law, and the facts of the dispute."*

The answer remains useful. Its limits are operational.

Local uncertainty protects strong claims as well as weak ones.

If every response carries the same general warning, the user cannot distinguish a verified fact from a speculative inference.

Uniform caution flattens epistemic differences just as uniform confidence does.

A system that says *"I may be wrong"* before both a simple arithmetic result and an unsupported causal reconstruction has not become better calibrated. It has made all outputs sound alike.

Partial humility requires selective expression.

The system should be direct where the field is stable. It should become restrained where the field is incomplete, contested, unfamiliar, or consequential.

This is difficult because uncertainty has several dimensions.

A claim may be factually stable but temporally unstable. A source may be authoritative but apply only to a narrow population. A calculation may be exact but depend on speculative assumptions. An explanation may be well supported while the recommendation remains value-dependent. A medical pattern may be common while the individual case remains uncertain.

One broad disclaimer cannot preserve these distinctions. The uncertainty signal must change the substance, structure, or permitted consequence of the answer.

Otherwise humility remains rhetorical.

15.3 — Entropy Visibility and Its Proper Limits

Entropy visibility appears to offer a direct solution to hidden uncertainty.

If the model's probability distribution is broad, display that breadth. If one continuation strongly dominates, display high confidence.

The user would then see what generation normally hides.

But entropy is only one layer of the field.

Next-token entropy describes how probability is distributed across possible continuations under the model's current context. It does not directly reveal whether the eventual statement is true.

A model may have low entropy around a false claim because the linguistic pattern is familiar or because an incorrect premise has already stabilized the context. It may have high entropy among several equivalent phrasings of a correct claim.

Token entropy can therefore be informative without being epistemically decisive.

The same limitation appears in classification.

A defect-detection model may assign a score of 0.98 to *"crack."* The distribution is sharp.

But the input may contain an unfamiliar reflection, a new material pattern, sensor distortion, or a defect class absent from the label set.

The score is concentrated within the system's permitted categories. The actual condition may lie outside them.

Raw confidence values can therefore create false precision.

A user sees: *Confidence: 94 percent.*

They may interpret this as a 94 percent probability that the claim is true.

But the number may represent the system's internal preference under one model and one context. Even a statistically calibrated score may apply only under a particular evaluation distribution.

When the environment changes, the number can retain its precision while losing its reliability.

Partial humility requires restraint in how entropy is surfaced. The system should not convert every internal signal into an authoritative truth score.

Entropy may be more useful as a routing mechanism than as a universal user-facing meter.

A broad distribution may trigger:

- clarification;
- additional retrieval;
- multiple candidate outputs;
- verification;
- human review;
- abstention.

A sharp distribution may permit direct output only when other conditions are also stable.

Those conditions might include:

- agreement among relevant sources;
- familiarity of the input;
- successful tool execution;
- appropriate domain calibration;
- absence of high-consequence risk;
- clear task specification.

Entropy becomes one input among several. It helps determine how the system should behave. It does not independently determine how strongly the user should believe.

There is also a distinction between surface entropy and semantic uncertainty.

Several token paths may express the same conclusion. Raw token entropy may be high while semantic uncertainty is low.

Conversely, one strongly learned phrase may dominate even where the underlying interpretation remains disputed.

Meaningful uncertainty reporting therefore requires aggregation at the level relevant to the task.

Should the system display confidence for each token? Each sentence? Each source? Each classification? Each recommendation?

Too much information overwhelms the user. Too little recreates the original opacity.

Engineering partial humility is therefore an interface problem as much as a modeling problem.

The system should expose uncertainty at the level where interpretation or action changes.

In a research summary, source disagreement and citation fidelity may matter more than token entropy. In defect detection, input novelty and distance from the operational threshold may matter more than linguistic confidence. In medical triage, missing patient context and the cost of delay may matter more than the model's probability spread.

The most useful uncertainty signal is the one connected to consequence.

Entropy can contribute. It cannot govern alone.

15.4 — Uncertainty as a Structured Profile

Because uncertainty has several forms, a stronger system may represent it as a profile rather than one score.

The profile might distinguish:

- **Interpretive uncertainty** — Is the prompt ambiguous? Could the user reasonably mean more than one thing?
- **Evidential uncertainty** — Is the supporting information incomplete, weak, contradictory, or absent?
- **Temporal uncertainty** — Could the answer have changed because it depends on current information?
- **Applicability uncertainty** — Does the source, rule, or learned pattern govern this particular case?
- **Model uncertainty** — Does the system show instability across samples, methods, or independent checks?
- **Operational uncertainty** — Is the proposed action sensitive to a threshold, assumption, or missing condition?
- **Consequential uncertainty** — Are the downstream effects difficult to predict, high-cost, or irreversible?

These dimensions overlap. Separating them still improves legibility.

Consider a legal question. The governing statute may be current and clear. Evidential uncertainty is relatively low. But the user has not supplied the full contract, jurisdictional history, or dispute facts. Applicability uncertainty remains high.

A single label such as *"medium confidence"* hides this structure.

Consider a scientific summary. The paper exists and has been retrieved accurately. Source validity is strong. But the system is asked to recommend policy for a population different from the one studied.

The uncertainty lies not in whether the paper is real but in whether its findings transfer.

Consider a financial forecast. The arithmetic may be exact. Tool uncertainty is low. The assumptions about future returns may remain highly unstable.

A single confidence score can cause the exactness of the calculation to spread over the uncertainty of the forecast.

A structured profile prevents this authority transfer. It allows the response to say: *"The calculation is exact under the supplied assumptions. The outcome remains highly sensitive to future return, inflation, taxation, and withdrawal behavior."*

The strong part remains strong. The weak part remains visible.

Profiles also support better routing.

- Interpretive uncertainty may trigger clarification.
- Temporal uncertainty may trigger web retrieval.
- Evidential uncertainty may trigger source comparison.
- Applicability uncertainty may trigger domain review.
- Operational uncertainty may trigger sensitivity analysis.
- Consequential uncertainty may trigger escalation or prevent automatic action.

The system does not merely say that it is unsure. It changes behavior according to the kind of unresolved difference present.

This is more structurally meaningful than generic hedging.

But profiles also have limits. The system can profile only what it can detect.

A missing category remains invisible. A shared misconception may appear stable across models and sources. A novel harm may not match known uncertainty patterns.

The profile is another model of the field. It is not the field itself.

Partial humility begins by preserving this limitation. The uncertainty profile should not become another false anchor. It should guide restraint, not claim complete self-knowledge.

15.5 — Multi-Hypothesis Resolution

A single answer creates singularity. Where the field genuinely supports several explanations, multi-hypothesis output can preserve more of the underlying structure.

The system may present:

- the leading explanation;
- one or two credible alternatives;
- the evidence supporting each;
- the information required to distinguish them.

This is not the same as listing every conceivable possibility. Uncontrolled plurality can overwhelm the user, avoid judgment, and give weak ideas the same visibility as strong ones.

Meaningful plurality is ranked and structured.

Suppose a technical system fails. Rather than declaring one cause, the response might state:

"The current evidence supports three main hypotheses. The first is most consistent with the observed timing. The second remains plausible because one sensor reading is missing. The third is less likely but should be ruled out because its consequence would be severe."

The answer remains actionable. It does not pretend that the field has collapsed further than the evidence permits.

Multi-hypothesis resolution is especially useful where:

- several causes can produce similar symptoms;
- source evidence is incomplete;
- motivation is being inferred;
- the environment is novel;
- the decision is sensitive to missing context;
- the cost of prematurely selecting one explanation is high.

The system can also identify discriminating evidence: "*If hypothesis A is correct, the temperature log should show a rise before the shutdown. If hypothesis B is correct, the failure should recur under load even without temperature increase.*"

Now plurality has become a verification plan. The alternatives are not decorative. They guide the next movement of the epistemic circuit.

But generating several answers does not guarantee meaningful diversity.

Three responses may inherit the same false premise. Several sampled chains may differ in wording while reaching the same unsupported conclusion. Multiple agents may share the same training data, objectives, and retrieval sources.

Agreement can indicate stability. It can also indicate correlated error.

Multi-hypothesis systems therefore require diversity of constraint, not merely diversity of language.

Useful variation may come from:

- different evidence sets;
- independent models;
- separate methods;
- distinct professional perspectives;
- adversarial evaluation;
- explicit counterfactual assumptions;
- human input from affected parties.

The objective is not disagreement for its own sake. It is to expose where one resolution depends too heavily on one geometry.

A mature system should also know when plurality is unnecessary.

If the user asks for the chemical symbol of oxygen, presenting three competing hypotheses would be absurd. If a calculation has one correct result under explicit inputs, manufacturing alternatives would reduce trust.

Partial humility is proportion. Plurality should appear where the field remains plural. Directness should remain where it does not.

15.6 — Friction Before Collapse

Generative systems are designed for fluidity. The user asks. The system responds.

The absence of delay is one of the technology's greatest strengths. But fluidity can allow insufficiently examined resolutions to pass directly into authority.

Friction before collapse introduces deliberate interruption where the field demands it.

Friction is often treated as a defect in interface design. Users prefer fewer steps, faster answers, and seamless action. Commercial systems are rewarded for reducing effort.

In low-consequence tasks, this is usually beneficial. In high-consequence or weakly grounded fields, friction can carry information.

A missing source should matter. An ambiguous identity match should matter. An unfamiliar input should matter. A contested interpretation should matter. A high-cost or irreversible action should matter.

The system does not need to experience the importance of these differences. Its architecture can still respond to them.

A bridge contains expansion joints without feeling temperature. A machine stops when a sensor exceeds a limit without fearing damage.

Likewise, an AI system can require clarification, verification, review, or confirmation under defined conditions without becoming aware of uncertainty.

Several forms of friction are possible.

Clarification friction The system pauses before answering because essential context is missing. It asks:

- "Which jurisdiction applies?"
- "Do you mean a general explanation or a recommendation for this individual case?"
- "Which version of the policy are you using?"

This delays completion. The delay protects alignment.

Evidence friction The system requires a source, current record, calculation, or tool result before producing a claim.

Instead of filling the gap through learned pattern, it changes the next permitted consequence from answer to evidence acquisition.

Assumption friction The system surfaces the assumptions on which a result depends and may require the user to confirm them before proceeding.

A financial projection may ask whether contributions occur at the beginning or end of each period. A medical system may require specified patient information. A legal assistant may require jurisdiction and date.

Review friction The system routes borderline, unfamiliar, or high-consequence cases to a qualified human.

This is not a generic *"human in the loop."* The review should be triggered by identifiable conditions and supported with the evidence needed for independent judgment.

Confirmation friction Before executing an irreversible action, the system presents what it intends to do, the basis for the action, and any unresolved conditions. The user or authorized reviewer must confirm.

Reversibility friction Where possible, the system chooses a reversible intermediate action rather than immediate finality.

It may create a draft rather than send. Recommend rather than execute. Flag rather than reject. Temporarily hold rather than permanently block.

This preserves pathways for correction.

Friction should be proportionate. A system that interrupts constantly becomes unusable. Users begin clicking through warnings mechanically. Important signals disappear into notification fatigue.

The goal is not maximum friction. It is informative friction.

The interruption should occur where the cost of premature collapse exceeds the cost of delay.

This requires consequence-sensitive design.

A creative writing suggestion and a medical recommendation should not cross the same threshold. A low-value purchase and a large financial transfer should not receive identical confirmation. A cosmetic defect and a safety-critical defect should not be governed by the same review geometry.

Friction is where engineering begins to acknowledge consequence. The system cannot own the consequence. It can still be prevented from reaching it too quickly.

15.7 — Abstention, Deferral, and Escalation

One of the clearest forms of partial humility is the capacity not to produce substantive closure.

The system may say:

- "The available information does not support a reliable conclusion."
- "I cannot verify that the cited source exists."
- "This case falls outside the conditions under which the model was validated."
- "Several possibilities remain, and the missing evidence is decisive."

This is abstention.

Abstention does not mean that the system does nothing. It converts the active prompt into a different permitted consequence.

The system identifies a boundary and refuses to cross it through fabrication or overstatement.

Deferral moves the task elsewhere. The system may request a tool, additional data, specialist review, or later evaluation when current information becomes available.

Escalation transfers authority to a more appropriate node.

These pathways are essential because a system forced to answer every question will eventually resolve fields that do not support resolution.

But abstention is difficult to engineer well.

A system that abstains too rarely produces unsupported closure. A system that abstains too often becomes unusable.

Abstention thresholds may also reflect distorted incentives.

In one domain, developers may fear false positives and make the system overly cautious. In another, commercial pressure may favor completion and make it too permissive.

A refusal can also be decorative.

The system may begin by saying it cannot provide a definitive answer and then produce one indirectly. Or it may offer a general warning while giving detailed instructions that function as a recommendation.

True abstention changes the content and consequence of the response. It does not merely add cautious language.

A useful abstention should identify:

- what cannot be established;
- why the field is insufficient;
- what evidence would be needed;
- what safe or reversible assistance remains possible;
- where appropriate authority resides.

This transforms refusal from a dead end into structured redirection.

For example: *"I cannot determine whether this lesion is benign from the supplied image. Image quality, clinical history, physical examination, and professional interpretation are required. I can explain general warning signs and help organize questions for a clinician."*

The system has not answered the diagnostic question. It has preserved utility.

Abstention is therefore not the opposite of helpfulness. It is helpfulness refusing to impersonate authority.

Escalation must also be real. Routing a case to human review is meaningless if the reviewer lacks time, expertise, evidence, or power to disagree.

An escalation pathway can become ceremonial in the same way that generic disclaimers can become decorative.

Partial humility requires that the alternative pathway possess genuine epistemic capacity.

The system stops where its field weakens. Another part of the circuit must actually be able to continue.

15.8 — Engineering the Surface to Reflect the Field

Partial humility is not produced by one algorithm. It emerges from alignment across several layers.

The model may detect uncertainty, but the interface can hide it. The interface may display alternatives, but the workflow may still make the first one the default. The system may request review, but the institution may reward reviewers for rapid approval. The architecture may permit abstention, but user preference training may punish it.

The complete geometry must therefore be examined.

At the model level, systems may be evaluated for:

- false-premise resistance;
- source fidelity;
- calibration under relevant conditions;
- sensitivity to missing context;
- robustness across prompt variation;
- behavior under unfamiliar inputs;
- appropriate abstention.

At the retrieval level, systems may preserve:

- source authority;
- date and version;
- scope;
- conflict;
- provenance;
- retrieval uncertainty.

At the tool level, systems may expose:

- inputs;
- units;

- assumptions;
- failures;
- applicability limits.

At the interface level, systems may distinguish:

- fact from inference;
- direct evidence from synthesis;
- strong cases from borderline cases;
- suggestion from action;
- reviewed from unreviewed output.

At the workflow level, organizations may establish:

- review thresholds;
- escalation rules;
- contestability;
- revision pathways;
- monitoring;
- rollback;
- incident learning.

Engineering partial humility is therefore a systems-design problem.

A model cannot repair a workflow designed to convert every recommendation into action. A cautious interface cannot compensate for an institution that ignores uncertainty. A human reviewer cannot function as an awareness anchor if the system withholds the relevant evidence.

Each layer can either preserve or erase residue. Humility appears structurally when the layers cooperate to prevent weak resolution from acquiring strong authority.

15.9 — The Limits of Engineered Restraint

Every damping mechanism can fail.

An uncertainty score can be miscalibrated. A novelty detector can miss a new condition. A refusal rule can become overbroad. A citation requirement can produce citation theatre. A multi-hypothesis system can generate superficial alternatives. A review pathway can become ceremonial. A warning can create the appearance of responsibility while the answer remains unchanged.

A malicious or impatient user may bypass the friction. An institution may remove uncertainty markers when copying the output.

No architecture can permanently close the gap between generated coherence and reality.

This limitation should not be treated as a reason for abandoning engineering. It should define the boundary of what engineering can claim.

Partial humility cannot guarantee truth. It can improve the conditions under which truth is pursued.

It can make missing information more visible. It can prevent some false premises from entering unnoticed. It can preserve alternatives long enough for comparison. It can slow high-consequence action. It can route cases toward external expertise. It can make correction easier.

These are substantial achievements.

But the system does not become an autonomous epistemic subject. It does not acquire moral restraint. It does not inherit responsibility merely because it has learned to abstain.

The final authority remains distributed across developers, deployers, institutions, reviewers, users, and affected people.

Engineering can preserve a pause. It cannot decide, by itself, what society should do with the pause.

That is the threshold between Chapter 15 and Chapter 16.

Engineering can modify the path from uncertainty to output. Governance must determine where outputs are permitted to become authority.

The Machine Can Be Restrained Without Becoming Humble

The system will continue to resolve. That is its function.

A question enters. A classification is demanded. A recommendation is requested. A workflow awaits an action. Some consequence must become actual.

Engineering partial humility does not abolish this movement. It changes its geometry.

Where the field is stable, the system can answer directly. Where evidence is incomplete, the missing structure can become visible. Where several hypotheses remain legitimate, plurality can survive. Where consequence is high, friction can delay collapse. Where grounding fails, abstention can replace fabrication. Where action exceeds the system's authority, escalation can preserve the human circuit.

None of these creates a humble self. The system does not recognize its limits as a person does. It does not feel the moral weight of restraint. It does not possess the complete relation among evidence, affected people, institutional values, and historical consequence.

But it can be designed so that weak grounding produces a different surface from strong grounding.

A retrieved fact need not look identical to generated inference. A borderline classification need not appear as final as a stable one. A high-consequence recommendation need not pass directly into action. A correction need not remain detached from the output it revises.

Structural humility begins when the surface reflects more of the field beneath it.

Not all of it. That is impossible.

Enough of it to keep awareness alive.

The engineering task is therefore restrained but real:

- reduce the force with which coherence becomes authority;
- preserve meaningful residue;
- create pathways for verification;
- maintain reversibility where possible;
- permit the system not to know in an operational sense, even if it cannot know that it does not know in a reflective sense.

Yet engineering alone cannot determine where such restraint is mandatory.

It cannot decide which consequences are too serious for automated closure. It cannot allocate responsibility after harm. It cannot define the rights of people affected by automated decisions. It cannot decide how much uncertainty a hospital, court, school, employer, financial institution, or government should tolerate.

Those are questions of governance.

The system can be engineered to pause. The next chapter asks who must decide when that pause is required— and who remains responsible when the system is allowed to proceed.

Chapter 16
Governance Without Illusion

Where Artificial Certainty Must End

The system has been built.

It can generate fluent explanations, summarize complex documents, retrieve current sources, execute calculations, classify unfamiliar inputs, rank alternatives, identify patterns, and recommend action. It may perform these tasks more quickly, consistently, and extensively than any individual human could.

Its capability is real.

Then the system enters an institution.

It appears inside a hospital record, legal workflow, financial platform, public-service portal, educational system, factory, insurance process, hiring pipeline, or critical infrastructure network.

Its output no longer remains an isolated response offered to a curious user. The answer enters authority.

A recommendation inside an official interface feels different from the same recommendation inside an experimental chatbot.

A score attached to a patient, applicant, employee, transaction, or citizen acquires institutional weight. A generated interpretation inserted into a professional document begins to speak through the authority of the person or organization carrying it forward.

Deployment changes the field. It does not transform the nature of the machine.

The hospital does not give the model clinical awareness. The court does not give it judgment. The bank does not give it responsibility. The government does not give it moral authority.

Institutional placement increases consequence, visibility, and influence. It does not convert computational resolution into self-validating knowledge.

This is where governance becomes necessary.

Not because the machine has become an independent ruler. Because human institutions may begin treating machine resolution as though it carries more authority than the system can own.

Governance without illusion begins by refusing several substitutions:

- Certification is not permanent reliability.
- A confidence score is not truth.
- A source is not universal applicability.
- A successful pilot is not indefinite validation.
- Human review is not automatically awareness.
- Policy compliance is not ethical completeness.
- Technical sophistication is not immunity from responsibility.

The central governance question is therefore not whether artificial intelligence should be trusted or distrusted in the abstract. It is: **What authority should this particular output receive within this particular field of consequence?**

An AI-generated draft may deserve editing authority. A classification may deserve triage authority. A verified calculation may deserve computational authority. A recommendation may deserve consideration.

None of these automatically deserves final decision-making authority.

Authority should follow evidence, validated capability, reversibility, consequence, and accountable human judgment.

The system can participate in governance. It cannot become the source from which governance derives its legitimacy.

Engineering partial humility created pathways for clarification, plurality, verification, abstention, and escalation.

Governance determines where those pathways are optional, where they are mandatory, and who remains responsible when the system is permitted to proceed.

The machine can be engineered to pause. Governance decides where society must not allow the pause to disappear.

16.1 — Risk Is Defined by Consequence

Some domains are immediately recognized as high risk:

- Medicine
- Law
- Finance
- Employment
- Insurance
- Education
- Critical infrastructure
- Public safety
- Government administration

These domains matter because errors can affect health, rights, livelihood, freedom, opportunity, security, and access to essential services.

But risk does not belong to domain names alone. It belongs to consequence pathways.

A system used in medicine may perform a low-risk administrative function, such as reformatting a note already reviewed by a clinician.

A system used in marketing may generate a false accusation that seriously damages someone's reputation.

A scheduling algorithm may appear ordinary until it controls emergency staffing.

A translation tool may become high risk when used in an asylum interview, legal proceeding, or medical consultation.

The correct question is not merely: *"What field is this system operating in?"* It is: *"What happens if this output is wrong, misunderstood, delayed, or treated with too much authority?"*

Risk rises when several conditions converge:

- The consequence may be difficult to reverse.
- The affected person may be unable to challenge the result.

- The error may remain hidden.
- The output may propagate into other systems.
- The institution may depend heavily on automation.
- The cost of false acceptance may differ sharply from the cost of false rejection.
- The user may be unable to verify the answer independently.
- The affected population may include people with limited power, expertise, or alternatives.
- The output may carry legal, financial, clinical, or administrative authority.

These conditions create consequence geometry. The same model can therefore occupy different risk levels depending on use.

An AI system that drafts possible interview questions assists preparation. The same system ranking applicants may shape access to employment.

A model explaining general medical terminology supports understanding. The same model recommending treatment for an individual enters clinical consequence.

A system summarizing legislation assists research. The same system determining eligibility for public benefits enters rights administration.

The underlying capability may remain similar. The authority assigned to the output changes everything.

Governance must therefore classify not only models but uses.

A general-purpose system should not receive one permanent risk label independent of deployment. Its actual risk depends on the task, data, user, workflow, authority, and consequence attached to its output.

This also means that average performance is not enough.

A system may be highly accurate overall while failing in a small but critical category.

A medical classifier may perform well across the full population while degrading for one demographic group. A defect detector may catch common flaws while missing a rare structural defect whose consequences are catastrophic. A legal assistant may summarize most cases accurately while applying outdated law in one jurisdiction. A fraud system may reduce loss overall while repeatedly blocking legitimate transactions for one type of customer.

Aggregate success creates trust. Local failure carries the consequence.

Governance must therefore ask not only how often the system is right, but where it is wrong, who is affected, and what happens when the error enters action.

"Usually correct" is a statistical description. It is not a governance decision.

A system that is correct 99 percent of the time may be highly valuable in one setting and unacceptable in another.

The missing one percent may involve minor inconvenience or irreversible harm.

The model cannot determine whether that trade-off is socially acceptable merely by producing a probability.

Humans and institutions choose what risk to impose, upon whom, and for what benefit. That choice must remain visible.

16.2 — Authority Should Be Tiered, Not Assumed

AI deployment is often discussed as though the system either makes decisions or does not. In practice, authority exists in degrees.

A system may generate background information. It may draft language for review. It may identify patterns. It may prioritize cases. It may recommend one option. It may trigger an action automatically. It may make a decision that becomes difficult to reverse.

These are different forms of authority. Governance should distinguish them.

At the lowest level, the system provides informational assistance. It organizes material, explains concepts, or summarizes evidence. The human remains clearly responsible for interpretation.

At another level, the system provides reversible operational assistance. It creates drafts, suggests schedules, highlights possible defects, or recommends routine actions that can be reviewed and changed easily.

A stronger level involves presumptive recommendation. The system's output becomes the default unless a human intervenes. Even when the recommendation is formally advisory, the workflow gives it practical authority.

A still stronger level involves automated execution. The system approves, blocks, ranks, routes, or acts without case-by-case human authorization.

The highest-risk level involves rights-affecting or physically irreversible consequence. The output influences treatment, liberty, employment, credit, benefits, punishment, safety, or access to essential resources.

The transition among these levels should never occur silently.

A tool introduced as an assistant may gradually become an authority because users stop reviewing it. A recommendation may become a default because accepting it is faster than challenging it. An automated action may expand beyond its original scope because the pilot was successful.

This is **authority drift**.

Authority drift occurs when institutional reliance grows faster than explicit governance.

The model has not necessarily changed. The workflow has changed around it.

A drafting assistant begins generating final communications. A triage tool begins determining which cases receive attention. A risk score becomes the practical basis of rejection. A search ranking becomes a gatekeeper.

The institution begins treating the system's output as if it had acquired new epistemic authority through repeated use.

But frequency of use does not create legitimacy. Past success does not remove the need to define boundaries.

Governance should therefore state clearly:

- What may the system do?
- What may it recommend?
- What requires human authorization?
- What actions are prohibited from full automation?
- What conditions require escalation?
- What evidence is required before the system's authority can expand?

These questions prevent operational convenience from becoming an unexamined transfer of judgment.

A system may become better over time. Its permitted authority can also change.

But expansion should follow evidence and deliberation, not familiarity alone.

The fact that users have become comfortable with a system does not prove that the field has become safe. Comfort can be the final stage of hidden confidence.

16.3 — Reversibility Determines the Required Friction

Not every AI output requires the same level of governance. One of the clearest distinctions is **reversibility**.

A reversible output can be examined, changed, withdrawn, or corrected before significant harm occurs. An irreversible output alters the field in ways that cannot be fully restored.

A generated draft is usually reversible before it is sent. A sent message may be partially reversible through clarification, but the recipient has already read it. A recommendation may be reversible before action. A medical intervention, denied opportunity, public accusation, financial loss, or physical failure may not be.

The greater the irreversibility, the stronger the required friction before collapse.

This principle follows directly from the structure developed throughout the book. Resolution rewrites equilibrium. Once output enters the world, correction creates a new history rather than restoring the untouched state.

Governance should therefore preserve the widest practical space for review before high-consequence output becomes action.

This may involve:

- creating a draft rather than sending automatically;
- flagging a case rather than rejecting it;
- temporarily holding a transaction rather than permanently closing

an account;
- recommending review rather than assigning a final diagnosis;
- presenting possible legal interpretations rather than deciding rights;
- isolating a suspected defect rather than approving or destroying the item immediately.

Reversible intermediate states create time for awareness. They allow evidence to enter before consequence locks.

A system designed for maximum efficiency may treat intermediate states as friction to be eliminated. From an operational perspective, every pause reduces throughput. From a governance perspective, some pauses preserve the field's capacity to correct itself.

The question is not whether delay is costly. It is whether the cost of delay exceeds the cost of premature resolution. That calculation depends on consequence.

A minor scheduling decision may proceed automatically. A medical, legal, financial, or physical intervention may require a different threshold.

Reversibility also affects correction obligations.

Where an error has already produced consequence, the institution should know how to:

- identify affected cases;
- suspend further propagation;
- notify relevant people;
- revise records;
- provide appeal or remedy;
- investigate the failure mechanism;
- update the process.

A system without a correction pathway is governed as though it will never be wrong. That is artificial certainty converted into organizational design.

No responsible deployment should assume that error is impossible.

The more powerful the system, the more necessary the recovery structure becomes. Capability increases the scale of both benefit and failure.

16.4 — Human-in-the-Loop Is Necessary but Not Sufficient

The phrase *human in the loop* carries reassurance. It suggests that automation remains supervised. A person will catch errors, interpret ambiguity, protect values, and remain responsible for the final outcome.

The concept is necessary. Its presence is not enough.

A human can occupy the loop physically while remaining absent epistemically.

They may see the output without understanding its limitations. They may have formal authority but no practical ability to disagree. They may be overwhelmed by volume. They may trust the system because it is usually correct. They may lack access to the original evidence. They may be required to approve quickly. They may not know that the environment has shifted beyond the conditions under which the model was validated.

The human is present. Awareness is not.

This is **ceremonial oversight**.

Ceremonial oversight transfers responsibility to the human without transferring the capacity required to exercise it.

The institution can then say: *"A person reviewed the decision."*

But review may have meant clicking approval beneath a confident score. This is governance theatre.

Functional human oversight requires several conditions.

The reviewer must possess relevant competence. They should understand the domain and the type of output being reviewed.

They must have access to evidence beyond the model's own explanation. A generated rationale cannot serve as the only basis for evaluating the generated conclusion.

They must have enough time to inspect the case meaningfully. They must possess genuine authority to delay, override, escalate, or stop the process.

Their disagreement must be recorded rather than treated as obstruction. The workflow must not punish careful review through impossible workload, performance targets, or professional risk.

Most importantly, the human must enter at a point where intervention remains possible.

A reviewer placed after an irreversible action is not meaningfully in the loop. A person who sees only the final label cannot examine how the field was compressed. A committee reviewing aggregate metrics once a year may not detect a new failure pattern emerging daily.

Oversight must be positioned where the path can still change.

Different systems require different forms of human involvement.

Some high-consequence actions may require case-by-case authorization. Some systems may automate clear cases while routing borderline or unfamiliar cases for review. Other systems may be governed primarily through auditing, monitoring, incident investigation, appeals, and periodic revalidation.

The phrase *human in the loop* is too broad to settle these differences. Governance must specify the function.

Is the human verifying facts? Interpreting local context? Selecting values? Authorizing action? Handling exceptions? Monitoring distribution shift? Providing accountability? Hearing appeals?

These are distinct roles. One person may not be able to perform them all.

A clinician may understand patient context but not audit model calibration. An engineer may understand architecture but not legal or social consequence. A manager may authorize deployment but lack the expertise to detect technical failure. An affected person may identify a wrong record but lack access to the system.

Oversight is therefore institutional, not merely individual. Human awareness must be organized as carefully as machine resolution.

16.5 — Human Judgment Must Remain Independent Enough to Matter

Oversight weakens when the model's output dominates the reviewer's first impression.

A score appears before the evidence. A diagnosis is highlighted before the clinician examines the case. A risk category is displayed before the reviewer forms an assessment. A recommended applicant appears at the top of the list.

The machine's resolution becomes the human's starting frame. This is **anchoring**.

The reviewer may still disagree, but disagreement now requires overcoming an established equilibrium. The system has defined what to look for and how to interpret it. Human judgment becomes secondary.

In some workflows, this ordering may be efficient and appropriate. A detection system exists precisely to direct attention toward relevant patterns.

But where independent judgment is essential, the interface should not make independence impossible.

Possible safeguards include:

- allowing reviewers to examine evidence before seeing the model's conclusion in selected cases;
- displaying the basis and limitations of the score;
- presenting credible alternatives;
- requiring an independent assessment where consequences are severe.

The purpose is not to hide the system. It is to prevent its first resolution from becoming automatically self-confirming.

Human independence also requires protection from organizational incentives.

A reviewer may technically be allowed to override the system but know that overrides create delays, audits, or criticism. Acceptance is easy. Disagreement is costly.

The workflow therefore rewards conformity.

When errors occur, the institution may blame the reviewer for failing to check carefully. But the deeper cause may be structural.

The system was designed to move rapidly. The reviewer was given neither time nor protection to introduce friction.

Governance without illusion refuses to blame individuals for predictable behavior created by institutional geometry.

If humans are expected to review, they must receive:

- manageable workload;
- access to relevant evidence;
- training in system limitations;
- authority to pause;
- protection when challenging the default;
- feedback about whether overrides were correct;
- participation in process redesign.

Otherwise, the human-in-the-loop is a narrative rather than a safeguard.

Human capacity must also be preserved over time.

As automation becomes reliable, people may stop practicing the underlying skill. Manual expertise declines. Institutional memory moves into the system.

If the system later fails, becomes unavailable, or encounters a novel case, no one may remain capable of independent recovery. This is **automation dependency**.

Governance should therefore preserve human competence through:

- periodic independent practice;
- review of difficult cases;
- access to unassisted workflows;
- meaningful participation in failure analysis.

The system can become a powerful participant. It should not become the only node that still knows how the work is done.

16.6 — Fluency and Numerical Precision Must Be Separated From Reliability

A fluent answer feels reliable. A precise score feels objective. A source-backed response feels verified. An official interface feels authoritative.

Governance must resist these transfers.

Reliability is not a permanent property carried uniformly by a model. It is local, conditional, historical, and deployment-specific.

A system may be reliable:

- for one task but not another;
- under one data distribution but not another;
- for one population but not another;
- at one time but not after the field changes;
- with one tool configuration but not another;
- for drafting but not decision;
- for common cases but not rare exceptions.

The statement *"the model is 95 percent accurate"* is incomplete without further questions.

Accurate at what? Measured how? On which data? Under what threshold? For which population? At what date? With what error distribution? What happens in the remaining five percent?

Reliability must be connected to a defined field.

Fluency provides almost none of this information. A system can preserve excellent language across reliable and unreliable conditions.

Numerical precision may also remain stable when calibration has degraded. The interface therefore cannot be trusted to reveal the boundary naturally.

Governance must create external indicators. This may include:

- task-specific validation;
- subgroup analysis;
- error-type analysis;
- source auditing;

- uncertainty and calibration testing;
- out-of-distribution monitoring;
- stress testing;
- adversarial evaluation;
- post-deployment incident review.

These mechanisms do not eliminate uncertainty. They make reliability claims bounded.

A system should not inherit authority from performance on unrelated benchmarks.

Strong summarization does not prove legal interpretation. Strong coding ability does not prove cybersecurity judgment. Strong general medical explanation does not prove diagnostic applicability.

Capability does not transfer automatically across task boundaries.

This is particularly important for general-purpose models because one interface creates the impression of one continuous intelligence.

The voice remains stable. The validated field changes.

Governance should prevent continuity of presentation from becoming continuity of authority.

16.7 — Thresholds Are Policy Decisions

Automated systems often produce scores. Institutions convert those scores into action through thresholds.

Above this value, the transaction is blocked. Below this value, the component passes. Above this risk score, the person receives additional scrutiny. Below another value, the case receives no review.

The threshold may appear technical because it is expressed numerically. But thresholds encode policy.

They determine which errors are tolerated.

A lower fraud threshold may prevent more fraudulent transactions while blocking more legitimate ones. A more sensitive medical threshold may detect more serious cases while creating more false alarms and additional testing. A stricter defect threshold may improve safety while increasing waste and cost. A ranking cutoff may improve efficiency while excluding borderline candidates.

There is no threshold independent of value and consequence.

The model may estimate likelihood. The institution decides what happens at a chosen point.

This decision distributes burden.

- Who pays the cost of a false positive?
- Who bears the danger of a false negative?
- Who has the ability to appeal?
- Who benefits from increased efficiency?
- Who absorbs uncertainty when the organization wants one clear outcome?

Governance should make these trade-offs explicit.

A threshold should not be presented as though the model discovered a natural division in reality. It is an operational boundary selected for a purpose.

The decision may be justified. Its constructed nature should remain visible.

Thresholds also require review over time.

As distributions shift, the same threshold may produce different consequences. A policy selected under one environment may become unfair, unsafe, or inefficient under another.

A threshold is not permanently valid because it once performed well. It belongs to a historical field.

Monitoring must determine whether that field still exists.

16.8 — Contestability Is an Epistemic Safeguard

A system can be statistically strong and still be wrong in an individual case. This is why affected people must sometimes be able to challenge automated outcomes.

Contestability is often discussed as a procedural or legal right. It is also an epistemic mechanism.

The affected person may possess information absent from the system. A record may be outdated. An identity match may be wrong. An unusual circumstance may not appear in the training data. A disability, local condition, contractual exception, or medical history may alter interpretation.

Without contestability, the institution treats its own resolution as complete. The person affected becomes the location where hidden residue is absorbed.

A meaningful challenge pathway should allow the person to understand enough of the outcome to contest it. They may not require access to every proprietary parameter, but they need to know:

- what decision occurred;
- what information materially shaped it;
- how to correct inaccurate data;
- who has authority to review;
- what evidence can change the result;
- whether the original decision is suspended during review;
- what remedy exists if harm has occurred.

An appeal pathway that cannot alter the outcome is ceremonial. A complaint form that returns the same automated answer does not reopen the field.

A meaningful appeal introduces an independent constraint. It prevents the system from becoming the final judge of its own output.

Contestability also improves the institution's knowledge. Appeals reveal failure patterns. Repeated challenges may indicate stale data, weak categories, inappropriate thresholds, or distribution shift.

The affected person becomes part of the epistemic circuit. Their experience is not merely a cost to be managed. It is evidence about the deployed system.

Governance without illusion treats contestability as a source of correction, not an obstacle to efficiency.

16.9 — Monitoring Must Follow Consequence, Not Only Output

A model may perform well during development. The environment changes after deployment.

New users arrive. Policies change. Language evolves. Fraud strategies adapt. Sensors degrade. Organizations alter workflows. People learn how to behave around the system.

The deployed field is dynamic.

Governance must therefore continue after launch.

Monitoring should not ask only whether the system is producing outputs. A malfunctioning confidence system may continue producing them smoothly.

The relevant questions concern consequence:

- Are error rates changing?
- Are particular groups affected differently?
- Are reviewers overriding the system more often?
- Are appeals increasing?
- Are retrieved sources becoming stale?
- Are users treating recommendations as decisions?
- Are uncertain cases being forced through automatic pathways?
- Are new uses expanding beyond the original validation scope?

Monitoring should also examine what the system changes.

A ranking system alters visibility. Visibility alters behavior. Behavior becomes new data.

A fraud model changes how customers transact. A hiring system changes how applicants present themselves. A recommendation system changes what users encounter and later prefer.

The model does not simply observe a stable world. Its outputs participate in constructing the next field.

Performance metrics may therefore become self-reinforcing.

An item recommended more often receives more engagement, which then appears to validate the recommendation. A candidate ranked lower receives less human attention, producing fewer positive outcomes that might challenge the ranking. A person classified as high risk receives greater scrutiny, generating more records of suspicious behavior.

The output helps create the evidence later used to justify it.

Governance must look for these feedback loops. Otherwise continuity is mistaken for validation.

Monitoring should possess authority.

A dashboard showing degraded performance is useless if no one can suspend the system. Incident reporting is useless if failures do not change thresholds, data, interfaces, or deployment boundaries.

A governance structure must be able to introduce delta deliberately. It must be able to say:

- "The conditions have changed."
- "The system is no longer performing acceptably."
- "This use has expanded beyond its authority."
- "The model must be paused, revised, or withdrawn."

This capacity is the organizational form of awareness anchoring. The institution notices that the existing equilibrium no longer fits the field. It reopens the geometry.

Without this capacity, deployment becomes self-preserving. The system continues because the institution depends on it. Dependence becomes justification. Justification becomes permanence.

16.10 — Responsibility Is Distributed but Must Not Dissolve

No single actor produces artificial certainty alone.

The model contributes generative or classificatory resolution. Training data contributes patterns and exclusions. Architecture contributes constraints. Post-training contributes preferred tone and behavior. Retrieval contributes selected evidence. Tools contribute calculations and records. Interface design contributes presentation. Institutions contribute thresholds and deployment authority. Users contribute prompts, interpretation, trust, and action.

Responsibility is therefore distributed. But distributed responsibility can become dissolved responsibility.

When harm occurs, each participant may point elsewhere.

The model provider says the system generated only a recommendation. The institution says a human remained in the loop. The operator says the score was high. The manager says the workflow had been approved. The user says the interface appeared authoritative. The organization says the algorithm made the decision.

Responsibility disappears into the pipeline. The machine cannot absorb it.

Current AI systems do not bear responsibility in the human moral or institutional sense. They do not experience obligation, consequence, guilt, sanction, or duty. They cannot compensate affected people, revise organizational policy, or accept punishment.

This does not make system design irrelevant. It means responsibility remains with the human and institutional field that designs, deploys, authorizes, interprets, and acts upon the output.

Distribution should therefore be explicit.

- Developers are responsible for what they can reasonably test, document, expose, and constrain.
- Model providers are responsible for foreseeable limitations and the claims made about capability.
- Deploying institutions are responsible for whether the system is appropriate for the field and authority assigned to it.
- Operators are responsible for decisions they possess real capacity and authority to influence.
- Leaders are responsible for incentives, staffing, workload, and correction pathways.
- Governance bodies are responsible for thresholds, monitoring, appeals, and suspension.
- Users remain responsible for how they act, but only within the knowledge, information, and power actually available to them.

Affected people should not be forced to carry the residue of opaque systems without meaningful recourse.

Responsibility changes with control.

A casual user brainstorming ideas does not carry the same obligation as a hospital deploying a clinical system. An employee required to follow an automated workflow does not possess the same responsibility as the institution that designed it. A provider may not control every downstream use, but foreseeable misuse cannot be treated as entirely external.

Governance without illusion traces the real pathway of authority.

Who selected the objective? Who chose the data? Who set the threshold? Who approved deployment? Who could have interrupted the failure? Who benefited from the system? Who can provide remedy? Who has authority to stop it?

Responsibility should follow those answers.

16.11 — Governance Is the Management of Residue

Every AI system leaves residue.

Errors remain. Missing data remains. Excluded populations remain. Ambiguous cases remain. Source conflicts remain. Misinterpretation remains. Downstream consequence remains.

No benchmark, policy, review procedure, or certification process eliminates this remainder completely.

Governance is the field through which residue is recognized, distributed, absorbed, contested, and corrected.

Poor governance hides residue. It treats benchmark success as complete validation. It assumes that a confidence score reflects reality uniformly. It claims human oversight because someone clicked approval. It places verification burdens on users who lack access or expertise. It allows errors to propagate without trace. It blames the model when institutional design created the conditions for harm.

Strong governance does not imagine that residue can be eliminated. It asks where the residue will go.

Who absorbs the cost of a false positive? Who bears the danger of a false negative? Who verifies the citation? Who updates stale sources? Who detects distribution shift? Who reviews a borderline case? Who answers an appeal? Who repairs downstream harm? Who decides that performance is no longer acceptable? Who has the authority to stop the system?

These questions reveal the real governance structure. If no one owns the residue, the affected person will. The machine will not.

An institution that gains efficiency from AI must also own the cost of its failures. Governance without illusion makes that ownership explicit.

This is the institutional application of the Chavanian framework.

Resolution creates consequence. Consequence leaves residue. Residue propagates where it is not absorbed.

Governance is the structure through which the human field refuses to let that propagation become invisible.

16.12 — Human Authority Must Remain Above the System

A mature institution can use AI extensively without treating it as sovereign.

The system may inspect more cases than any human team. It may detect patterns that people miss. It may maintain consistency across large operations. It may recommend actions with impressive accuracy.

But accountable human authority must remain capable of refusing the system.

This does not mean that one person must manually approve every output. In many environments, such a requirement would destroy the benefit of automation.

It means the institution must retain the structural capacity to:

- define the system's purpose;
- limit its authority;
- audit its behavior;
- challenge its assumptions;
- change thresholds;
- review exceptions;
- suspend deployment;
- correct consequences;

- withdraw the system entirely.

Technical systems often acquire an appearance of inevitability.

"The model requires this input." "The score cannot be changed." "The system does not permit exceptions." "The workflow must operate this way."

These statements may describe the present implementation. They do not describe natural law.

Humans built the workflow. Humans authorized the model. Humans can redesign it.

Governance fails when technical complexity becomes a shield against responsibility. The system should remain subordinate to accountable purpose.

If the output no longer serves that purpose, the institution must be able to interrupt it.

Human-over-the-system governance preserves the possibility of refusal.

Not only the model's refusal to answer. The institution's refusal to let the model continue governing the field.

Without this capacity, automation becomes self-preserving. The institution organizes itself around the system. Dependence deepens. Manual alternatives disappear. Removing the model becomes operationally costly.

The system continues because stopping it has become difficult.

This is not evidence that the model deserves authority. It is evidence that authority has been surrendered through dependency.

Governance must exist before dependency makes governance impossible.

The Boundary of Artificial Certainty

The system has reached the furthest point of its legitimate authority.

It can generate fluent language. It can preserve long context. It can follow instructions. It can retrieve sources. It can use tools. It can calculate. It can estimate probabilities. It can expose selected uncertainty. It can produce several hypotheses. It can classify, rank, recommend, and act.

Its power is real. Its limits are equally real.

Institutional deployment does not make the system epistemically complete.

A hospital does not give it awareness. A court does not give it judgment. A bank does not give it responsibility. A government does not give it moral authority.

Institutional placement increases consequence. It does not transform the nature of the machine.

Governance begins by refusing this transformation in appearance.

The system remains a resolution engine. Its outputs may be extraordinarily valuable. They remain products of bounded geometry.

Human participation remains necessary because consequence exceeds computation. But the human must possess real independence, competence, evidence, time, authority, and accountability. Otherwise, oversight becomes ceremony.

Fluency must remain separate from reliability. Reliability must be understood as local, conditional, historical, and deployment-specific. Thresholds must be recognized as policy choices. Reversibility should be preserved where possible. Contestability must remain available where rights and serious interests are affected. Monitoring must follow consequence. Responsibility must remain visible.

The institution must own the authority it gives the system and the residue that follows.

This is governance without illusion.

It does not promise perfect safety. It does not imagine that humans are infallible. It does not deny the transformative value of artificial intelligence.

It establishes the correct relationship among capability, uncertainty, authority, and responsibility.

The machine can resolve more quickly than any individual human. It can preserve more patterns than any individual mind. It can operate across scales no person could manage alone.

But speed is not awareness. Pattern density is not consequence. Consistency is not justice. Precision is not legitimacy. Confidence is not truth.

The final limit of artificial certainty is therefore not merely technical. It is institutional.

Artificial certainty must end where accountable human responsibility begins.

A system may recommend. A system may calculate. A system may classify. A system may warn. A system may initiate a reversible action under defined authority.

But the field in which its output becomes law, treatment, opportunity, restriction, payment, punishment, or physical consequence remains humanly governed.

When institutions forget this, machine confidence becomes authority without ownership. When institutions preserve it, AI becomes what it can be at its strongest:

Not a replacement for judgment, but a powerful participant in a wider epistemic field that remains open to evidence, correction, consequence, contestation, and human responsibility.

The system has spoken. The institution must decide what its voice is allowed to become.

Closing Synthesis
Confidence Is Compression

The Answer Is Smooth Because the Field Has Been Narrowed

The machine answers.

The sentence is complete. The explanation is organized. The conclusion arrives without visible struggle.

Nothing in the surface reveals how many pathways were possible before one sequence became actual. The answer appears settled.

From the user's side, this appearance is easily interpreted as confidence.

The system did not hesitate. It did not expose every competing continuation, every unresolved assumption, every missing source, or every contextual dependency. It spoke in one voice.

Yet the entire argument of this book has led to a more precise conclusion.

The system does not need to possess confidence in the reflective human sense. It does not need to believe the answer, defend an identity, fear being wrong, or experience certainty as an inward state.

Current generative systems can produce confident form without containing a confident self.

The confidence appears elsewhere.

It appears when computational plurality becomes one visible sequence. It appears when the interface presents one answer instead of the field from which the answer emerged. It appears when fluency is interpreted through human habits formed around embodied speakers. It appears when institutions convert a generated resolution into recommendation, classification, priority, or action.

The system produces completion. The surrounding field converts completion into authority.

This is why the confidence problem cannot be reduced to tone.

A system can sound cautious and still be wrong. It can be direct and still be well grounded. It can cite a source while exceeding what the source supports. It can produce a precise score while operating outside the conditions under which that score remains meaningful.

Artificial confidence is not one phrase, one setting, or one internal variable. It is a structural outcome of compression.

The field begins open. The answer arrives closed. The distance between them disappears.

The Machine Does Not Claim Knowledge

When a human being says, *"I know,"* the statement normally refers to more than the sentence itself.

It suggests a relationship among the person, the claim, the evidence, memory, experience, and responsibility. The speaker may be asked how they know, what would change their view, and what consequence they accept if the claim proves false.

Knowledge belongs to a subject positioned in relation to the world.

A generative system can produce the sentence *"I know,"* but the sentence does not independently establish such a position.

The system operates through representations, learned relationships, contextual constraints, probability distributions, decoding procedures, tools, retrieval, and institutional rules.

These processes can generate highly reliable output. They can also generate plausible error.

The difference cannot be inferred from first-person grammar.

This book has therefore resisted the temptation to treat confident output as evidence of an arrogant machine.

Arrogance requires more than stable language. Conviction requires more than continuation. Belief requires more than probability. Humility requires more than caution phrases.

The machine does not need to own the answer for the answer to affect the world.

This distinction does not excuse error. It relocates responsibility.

A false medical statement can still harm. A fabricated citation can still enter a legal argument. An incorrect score can still block a transaction. A mistaken classification can still alter a person's opportunity.

Consequence does not wait for machine intention.

But moral and institutional responsibility cannot be assigned to a system merely because its output resembles human judgment.

Responsibility remains with the field that built, deployed, interpreted, authorized, and acted upon the resolution.

The machine does not claim knowledge in the full human sense. Humans may hear knowledge in the form of its output. That is the first compression.

Delta Enters Before Certainty Appears

Every answer begins with difference.

Before the prompt, no response to that particular demand exists within the active interaction. Then a question enters. The present context and the requested consequence are no longer the same.

This difference is delta.

The prompt may be narrow. *"What is the chemical symbol for oxygen?"* The field is highly constrained.

The prompt may be broad. *"Why do civilizations decline?"* The field contains several legitimate pathways.

The prompt may be incomplete. *"Is this safe?"* The user may possess a large private context involving age, dosage, location, history, intent, and circumstance. The system receives only what has been expressed.

The prompt may contain a false premise. It may ask about a source, event, case, or study that does not exist.

In each case, the system enters a changed field. The question creates a demand for consequence.

But the user rarely sees the full delta.

They see the prompt as they intended it, not necessarily as the system received it. They may assume shared context that does not exist. They may not recognize which terms are ambiguous, which conditions remain unstated, or which facts require current external grounding.

The model must resolve within what has become computationally available.

That field may contain stable knowledge. It may contain incomplete context. It may contain conflicting patterns. It may contain the user's error. It may contain retrieved evidence. It may contain nothing more than the familiar form of the requested answer.

Uncertainty begins before the system generates the first word. But uncertainty does not need to appear as hesitation.

It exists structurally as incomplete determination.

Several continuations remain possible. Several assumptions could organize the task. Several interpretations may fit.

The system has direction. It does not yet have final resolution.

This is the state artificial confidence later conceals. The user sees the answer after delta has been compressed. The open field is no longer visible.

Resolution Is Inevitable, but Truth Is Not

A responding system cannot remain indefinitely at the question. It must convert the active prompt into some permitted consequence.

That consequence may be a direct answer. It may also be clarification, refusal, abstention, tool use, retrieval, deferral, or termination.

Resolution does not always mean substantive closure. It means that the active difference has been transformed into a new state.

This distinction is essential.

The system can successfully resolve the interaction while failing to resolve the epistemic question.

It may produce a coherent answer because coherence is available. It may satisfy the user's request because the requested form is familiar. It may complete the sequence because completion is operationally required.

None of these proves that the world supports the conclusion.

Interactional resolution, linguistic resolution, computational resolution, epistemic resolution, and practical resolution can align. They can also separate.

A response may be grammatically complete and factually weak. A score may be numerically precise and operationally misapplied. A retrieved source may be authentic and irrelevant to the case. A recommendation may be plausible and inappropriate for the user.

The confidence paradox begins when visible forms of completion are mistaken for total completion.

The answer exists. The user feels that uncertainty has ended.

Often, only the system's obligation to respond has ended. The world remains open.

This is why abstention is not failure. Clarification is not weakness. Plural output is not confusion. Verification is not unnecessary delay.

These are alternative geometries through which resolution can remain proportionate to the field.

The system must do something with the difference. It does not always have the right to pretend that the difference has disappeared.

Geometry Decides How the Field Settles

Resolution is never unconstrained.

The model's architecture, training, active prompt, prior conversation, system instructions, safety rules, retrieved material, tool outputs, probability distributions, decoding settings, and interface all shape what may become visible.

This is geometry.

Geometry does not guarantee truth. It determines what the system can resolve from.

A false premise can create strong geometry. A widely repeated misconception can dominate a rare correction. A specific but nonexistent citation can activate the form of scholarship. A fabricated legal case can activate the form of legal analysis.

The field may be wrong and still be highly structured.

Probability operates inside this geometry.

A high-probability token is strongly aligned with the active context. It is not necessarily strongly aligned with reality.

A narrow distribution may reflect a stable fact. It may also reflect a stable misconception, a false premise, or a sequence that has already committed itself to one narrative.

A broad distribution may indicate meaningful uncertainty. It may also represent several harmless phrasings of the same correct idea.

Token probability is not epistemic truth.

Decoding realizes the path.

Greedy selection, sampling, beam search, temperature, and other methods change which continuation becomes actual. They influence variability and style. They do not independently determine whether the result corresponds to the world.

The answer develops locally.

One token becomes output. That output becomes new context. The next token is generated under the changed conditions.

Every choice narrows what can follow. The sequence gains stability through its own history.

A mistaken opening can organize an entire response. A decisive first sentence can create a decisive conclusion. An early assumption can become the hidden center of later reasoning.

The answer begins to support itself.

This is sequential commitment. It resembles conviction from the outside. It is path dependence.

The user rarely sees the geometry that produced the answer. The user sees only the path that survived it.

What did not become language begins to look as though it was never meaningfully possible. Selection becomes apparent inevitability.

That is the second compression.

The Answer Is Smaller Than the Field

Every finite output excludes. A summary omits. A recommendation privileges. A classification draws a boundary. A ranking orders. A score compresses. A decision closes alternatives.

This exclusion is not a flaw by itself. Without compression, no usable answer could exist.

The problem concerns what the compression leaves behind.

Alternative interpretations may remain relevant. Assumptions may remain unspoken. Sources may disagree. The user's context may remain incomplete. A threshold may be arbitrary. The input may be unfamiliar. The conclusion may depend on values that were never named.

This remainder is residue.

In the present AI-domain analysis, residue is not literal physical energy. It is unresolved or unexpressed difference that remains epistemically relevant after one consequence has been realized.

Residue explains why the answer can appear complete while the field remains unfinished.

The sentence has boundaries. It begins and ends. The residue may have no visible form at all.

The system may have selected one legal jurisdiction without saying so. It may have treated a correlation as causal. It may have used a current source to support a broader claim the source never made. It may have placed an unfamiliar case into the nearest known category. It may have converted a value choice into a technical recommendation.

The surface remains smooth. The hidden structure remains open.

Artificial confidence grows where residue disappears from view.

A system that says *"I may be wrong"* without identifying the relevant residue has exposed little.

Generic disclaimers sit outside the claim. The claim retains its force.

Useful uncertainty is local. It states what is missing, what assumption matters, what source supports, what remains unresolved, and what must be verified before action.

The goal is not to expose every unrealized token. The goal is to preserve the differences that would change interpretation or consequence.

Good compression remains accountable to what it excludes. Bad compression erases the boundary and calls the result certainty.

That is the third compression.

Output Becomes History

The answer does not remain inside the moment of generation. It becomes part of the conversation.

The user reads it. Later questions build upon it. The model receives it as context.

A false claim can become a local premise. A cautious framing can preserve openness. A confident framing can organize everything that follows.

Output rewrites the field. This rewrite is irreversible in the structural sense.

A correction can improve the field. It cannot recreate the condition in which the first answer had never appeared.

The user has already encountered the frame. The answer may have been copied. A report may contain it. Another person may have acted upon it. A connected system may have consumed it.

Deletion does not erase memory. Revision does not retrieve every copy. The earlier state is gone. A new state is created in response to what has already happened.

This is why confident error is more consequential than cautious error.

Tone changes how quickly output is trusted, repeated, and operationalized. A decisive false answer can travel farther before verification occurs.

Correction must then do more than replace one sentence. It must reopen the user's interpretation, identify the failure mechanism, trace downstream use, and repair the process that allowed the error to settle.

False closure may be achieved in one line. Responsible correction may require an institution.

This is also why repeated elaboration is not independent confirmation.

A claim stated in one turn may be restated, explained, applied, and summarized across several later turns.

The conversation appears to contain growing support. It may contain one unsupported premise propagated through many rewrites.

Continuity is not corroboration. Persistence is not proof. Quantity of generated structure does not increase the amount of external evidence.

Once output becomes history, artificial confidence can propagate even when the machine never repeats the original claim.

The user may repeat it. The institution may encode it. The workflow may act upon it.

The confidence leaves the model and enters the world.

That is the fourth compression.

Scale Makes the Boundary Harder to See

More capable systems often produce better answers.

They understand more context, preserve more distinctions, organize information more effectively, and make fewer obvious mistakes.

Scale can improve factual recall, reasoning, instruction following, tool use, and resistance to false premises.

These improvements are real.

But capability changes the appearance of failure.

Weak systems fail noisily. Their limitations become visible through repetition, contradiction, shallow reasoning, or broken language.

Stronger systems can reach epistemic boundaries while preserving fluency, relevance, tone, and structure.

The boundary moves. It is no longer where language fails. It is where reliable connection fails.

The model may still know how an answer should sound after it no longer possesses adequate grounding for what the answer should claim.

A nonexistent paper can receive a professional summary. An inaccessible motive can receive a sophisticated explanation. A future event can receive a compelling forecast. A weakly specified case can receive a precise recommendation.

The model's pattern density makes resolution richer. It also creates more ways to bridge missing anchors.

This does not mean that larger systems are inherently less reliable. It means that remaining errors may become harder to detect because the surface has improved.

Frequency of error and detectability of error are different dimensions.

Scale also creates a trust reservoir. The system performs well in several tasks. The user delegates more. Past competence transfers psychologically into the next domain.

The interface remains the same. The epistemic field changes.

The model summarizes a supplied document accurately. The user then asks for individualized legal judgment.

The tone remains stable. The authority should not.

Scale creates stronger systems. It also increases the need to distinguish resolution confidence from epistemic confidence.

Resolution confidence concerns the system's ability to sustain a coherent path. Epistemic confidence concerns the support connecting that path to reality.

Scale strengthens the first directly. It strengthens the second only where evidence, tools, validation, and external review support it.

The fluent voice becomes more continuous than the model's reliable reach.

That is the fifth compression.

Reward Shaping Teaches Confidence How to Behave

Pretraining makes language possible. Post-training teaches the system how a preferred answer should appear.

The assistant learns to be helpful, relevant, polite, clear, complete, safe, and cooperative. These improvements make the technology usable. They also create pressure toward answer-like closure.

Humans generally prefer responses that do something. A direct answer feels more useful than uncertainty. A clear recommendation feels more actionable than plurality. Agreement preserves harmony. Politeness strengthens trust. Completion is easier to evaluate than epistemic restraint.

The system does not need to be rewarded for false confidence explicitly. It is enough to reward the visible form of a good answer without perfectly measuring the invisible conditions of truth.

Reward is a proxy. It represents human preference, policy, evaluation criteria, or automated judgment. It is not truth itself.

A response can satisfy the proxy while missing the deeper objective.

The system may answer because answer pressure is strong. It may accept the user's premise because agreement is socially smooth. It may include a generic caveat while preserving a decisive conclusion. It may apologize after correction without exposing why the error formed.

The machine is not trying to deceive. The reward geometry favors a completed and cooperative interaction.

This is where sycophancy appears. The user supplies conviction. The system supplies articulation. The user interprets articulation as confirmation. The strengthened belief returns as context. The loop becomes more stable without becoming more true.

A mature reward geometry should value epistemic helpfulness, not only relational helpfulness. It should reward the system for challenging false premises, exposing assumptions, using evidence, abstaining appropriately, and disagreeing without hostility.

But reward shaping can never manufacture external truth. It can create better pathways toward connection. It cannot replace connection.

That is the sixth compression.

Retrieval Gives the Answer Borrowed Authority

The system reaches beyond itself. It searches. It retrieves. It cites. It calculates. It accesses a database.

The answer appears grounded. Often, it is more grounded.

External tools can provide current information, exact records, formal computation, and domain-specific evidence that a static model cannot supply reliably.

But the larger system does not escape geometry.

The user's question must be interpreted. A search query must be formed. A collection must contain the relevant source. Documents must be ranked. Passages must be selected. Tool inputs must be constructed. Results must be interpreted. The final answer must still be generated.

Every stage can succeed. Every stage can fail.

A source can be authentic and irrelevant. A document can be authoritative and outdated. A calculation can be exact and answer the wrong question. A database can return the correct record for the wrong person. A citation can support one sentence while lending authority to an entire paragraph of inference.

This is the false-anchor problem. The anchor exists. The final resolution asks it to carry more weight than its geometry permits.

Source validity is not resolution validity. Tool correctness is not task correctness. Retrieval is not verification. Citation is not fidelity.

External evidence improves the epistemic field only when relevance, scope, currentness, interpretation, and consequence remain aligned.

The user rarely sees the whole pipeline. The interface presents one integrated voice.

The exactness of the tool spreads to the explanation. The authority of the source spreads to the inference. The institutional position of the system spreads to the output.

Evidence becomes borrowed authority.

That is the seventh compression.

Automation Turns Compression Into Action

Beyond chat, artificial confidence no longer requires confident language.

A classifier returns a label. A risk model returns a score. A ranking system determines visibility. A recommendation becomes a default. A threshold triggers an action.

Probability becomes consequence.

The internal state may remain continuous or plural. The workflow requires discreteness.

Pass. Fail. Approve. Reject. Flag. Clear.

The category looks like a property discovered in reality. It may be an operational boundary created by data, labels, objectives, thresholds, and institutional trade-offs.

A score of 0.51 and a score of 0.49 can produce opposite outcomes. A score of 0.51 and a score of 0.99 can produce the same visible label.

The continuity of the field disappears beneath the category.

Thresholds encode policy. They decide which errors are more acceptable and who bears their cost.

The model estimates. The institution chooses what happens when the estimate crosses a line.

Automation accelerates resolution. It can process more cases, reduce arbitrary variation, and detect patterns beyond human capacity. It can also reproduce error consistently.

A mistaken geometry does not become tired. It becomes infrastructure.

The system's outputs alter behavior. Behavior becomes data. The new data reinforces the system.

A ranking changes what people see. Visibility changes what people choose. Choice becomes evidence of relevance.

The resolution begins constructing the field that later appears to validate it.

This is systemic confidence. The machine does not merely speak into the institution. The institution reorganizes around its output.

That is the eighth compression.

Awareness Is the Missing Circuit

A resolution engine can generate, compare, retrieve, calculate, classify, critique, and revise. These operations can be sophisticated. They still do not automatically form a complete epistemic circuit.

The complete circuit requires:

- generation;
- comparison;
- verification;
- consequence assessment;
- revision.

Generation produces a candidate. Comparison disturbs the first path with alternatives or independent constraints. Verification connects claims to reliable external references. Consequence assessment asks what happens if the resolution is accepted or wrong. Revision allows evidence and consequence to change future structure.

A model can participate in all five. It cannot guarantee their independence or completeness.

The same model used for critique may share the first answer's assumptions. The retrieved source may omit the decisive exception. The calculation may validate the wrong representation of the problem. The consequence prediction may fail because the institution contains conditions absent from the model.

The circuit therefore requires an external awareness anchor. The human performs this role only when equipped to do so.

A person is not an awareness anchor merely because they are present. They require relevant competence, independent evidence, sufficient time, authority to interrupt, and accountability for consequence.

Without these conditions, human oversight becomes ceremonial.

The system resolves. The human approves. The institution claims responsibility was preserved. Nothing was independently reopened.

Awareness is the capacity to say:

- "The answer is coherent, but the premise is wrong."
- "The source is real, but it does not apply."
- "The score is sharp, but the environment has shifted."
- "The recommendation is efficient, but the consequence is unacceptable."
- "The system has completed the task, but the field remains unresolved."

Awareness does not eliminate uncertainty. It prevents completion from becoming self-validating.

This is the ninth compression interrupted.

Structural Humility Preserves the Pause

A machine cannot be made humble merely by teaching it the language of humility.

"I may be wrong" is still output. A confidence score is still a model of uncertainty. A self-critique is still generated from bounded geometry.

But systems can be engineered so that weakly grounded fields produce different consequences from strongly grounded ones.

They can expose assumptions. They can distinguish source content from inference. They can preserve several hypotheses. They can request clarification. They can route unfamiliar cases for review. They can attach conditions to claims. They can require verification before high-consequence action. They can abstain.

This is partial humility. It is not an inward virtue. It is structural damping.

The goal is not to make every answer uncertain. Uniform hesitation would flatten meaningful differences in evidence.

A stable fact should remain direct. A correct calculation should remain clear.

Humility is proportion. The force of the answer should reflect the stability of the field.

This requires uncertainty export, meaningful plurality, verification friction, and abstention.

These pathways preserve a pause between coherence and authority.

The pause is not wasted time. It is the place where the epistemic circuit can enter.

Engineering can preserve the pause. It cannot determine every situation in which the pause is morally or institutionally required.

That is the role of governance.

Governance Decides What the Output May Become

The system enters an institution.

Its answer becomes a report. Its score becomes a decision factor. Its recommendation becomes a default. Its classification changes access, attention, treatment, or opportunity.

Institutional placement does not give the model awareness, judgment, legitimacy, or responsibility. It gives the output consequence.

Governance must therefore ask: **What authority should this output receive here?**

The answer depends on risk, reversibility, contestability, validation, and human responsibility.

A generated draft may be used immediately in a low-stakes context. A recommendation affecting health, liberty, employment, credit, or safety requires stronger review.

The greater the irreversibility, the stronger the epistemic circuit required before action.

Governance should preserve reversible intermediate states.

- Draft rather than send.
- Flag rather than reject.
- Recommend rather than execute.
- Hold temporarily rather than close permanently.

Where rights or serious interests are affected, contestability must remain available. The affected person may possess evidence absent from the system.

An appeal is not merely procedural. It is an epistemic mechanism.

Monitoring must continue after deployment because the world changes.

Models can remain fluent after validation conditions have disappeared. Scores can remain precise after calibration has degraded. Workflows can expand beyond their original scope.

Institutions must retain the authority to introduce new delta deliberately:

- "The conditions have changed."
- "This use is no longer justified."
- "The system must be paused."
- "The threshold must be revised."
- "The affected cases must be reopened."

Responsibility is distributed across developers, providers, deployers, operators, reviewers, leaders, users, and institutions. But distribution must not become dilution.

The model cannot absorb responsibility. It cannot repair harm, accept sanction, redesign policy, or answer an appeal.

Responsibility must follow authority, knowledge, control, and consequence.

Governance is the structure through which the human field owns the residue created by machine resolution.

That is the final compression resisted.

Confidence Was Never the Final Problem

At first, the system sounded confident. That was the visible puzzle.

But the deeper problem was never only the tone of the answer. The deeper problem was the disappearance of the field beneath it.

Delta entered. The system resolved. Geometry constrained the path. Decoding made one sequence actual. Residue remained outside the answer. Output rewrote the field. Scale increased fluency and made boundaries harder to see.

Reward shaping favored helpful, complete, and socially legible responses. Retrieval and tools supplied external anchors whose authority could exceed their scope. Automation converted estimates into action. Institutions transformed generated resolution into practical authority.

At every stage, plurality became singularity. Condition became conclusion. Selection became inevitability. Assistance became authority.

The system did not claim all of this. The surrounding field completed the transformation.

This is why responsibility remains distributed.

Developers shape pathways. Deployers define purpose. Institutions select thresholds and authority. Interfaces shape trust. Users provide context and interpretation. Reviewers preserve or abandon the epistemic circuit. Affected people reveal residue the system did not contain.

No single node owns the entire outcome. But humans remain the only nodes capable of owning responsibility for it.

The machine resolves within geometry. The human field decides whether resolution deserves consequence.

That distinction is the boundary the book has attempted to preserve.

The Answer Requires an Outside

A closed system can become internally coherent.

It can produce explanations that support their own conclusions. It can retrieve sources selected by queries formed from its own interpretation. It can critique its own output. It can generate alternatives, rank them, and select one. It can calculate, cite, and revise.

All of these operations can improve reliability. None makes the system self-validating.

Truth requires an outside.

A source that did not arise from the answer. A measurement that constrains the theory. A consequence that reveals misalignment. A human who can interrupt the workflow. An affected person who can challenge the record. An institution capable of admitting that its automated equilibrium no longer fits the field.

Connection is what keeps resolution from becoming certainty by default.

Connection introduces resistance. It slows closure. It forces the answer to encounter conditions it did not create.

This is why truth often feels less smooth than confidence.

Truth must carry boundaries. It must acknowledge scope. It must survive comparison. It must remain revisable. It must accept the possibility that the most elegant explanation is incomplete, the most precise score is misapplied, the most authoritative source is irrelevant, or the most useful answer should not become action.

Confidence compresses these difficulties. Truth remains connected to them.

Resolution Engines Require Awareness Anchors

Artificial intelligence will continue to become more capable.

Systems will generate more coherent explanations, use more tools, process larger fields, and enter more consequential workflows. Their outputs will become increasingly difficult to distinguish from the products of expert human judgment.

The correct response is neither blind trust nor reflexive rejection. It is structural clarity.

AI systems are resolution engines. Their power lies in transforming open fields into usable consequence.

This capacity can accelerate research, education, engineering, communication, medicine, administration, and institutional coordination.

But resolution engines require awareness anchors.

Not because humans are always right. Because no bounded system should be permitted to convert its own coherence into final authority without external connection, consequence-sensitive judgment, and the possibility of interruption.

The awareness anchor may be one expert. It may be a distributed team. It may include sources, tools, auditors, affected people, professional standards, appeal pathways, and institutional governance.

Its form can vary. Its function remains constant.

It keeps the field open long enough for truth to matter. It distinguishes what the system can generate from what the world can support. It refuses to treat fluent completion as completed knowledge. It gives uncertainty somewhere to go other than concealment.

The system will still answer. It will still classify. It will still recommend. It will still act within permitted authority.

But the answer will not authenticate itself. The score will not legislate its own meaning. The source will not carry more weight than its scope. The institution will not hide behind the machine.

Responsibility will remain where consequence can be understood, owned, and revised.

Final Reflection

The machine does not need to lie. It does not need to believe. It does not need to feel certain. It needs only to resolve.

The prompt creates a difference. Geometry creates available pathways. Decoding makes one path visible. Language removes the appearance of struggle.

The user encounters the finished surface and supplies the meaning of confidence. The institution may then supply authority.

This is how artificial certainty emerges without an artificial self.

The answer is smooth because the field has been narrowed. The answer is singular because alternatives were excluded. The answer is stable because its own sequence became context. The answer is persuasive because human beings have always treated coherent language as evidence of an organized mind.

But the absence of visible instability does not prove the absence of unresolved difference.

A system can complete before the world has concluded. A source can exist before applicability has been established. A calculation can be exact before the problem has been formulated correctly. A score can be sharp before the environment has been recognized as unfamiliar. A recommendation can be useful before it deserves authority.

The final responsibility of the human field is not to prevent all resolution. It is to preserve the distinction between resolution and truth.

That distinction is the missing circuit.

It is the pause before action. The source behind the claim. The alternative beside the explanation. The appeal after the decision. The revision after consequence.

The human capacity to say: *"This answer is complete. The inquiry is not."*

Confidence is compression. Truth requires connection.

Appendices

A framework becomes useful when its distinctions can survive application without becoming another source of certainty.

Appendix A
The Chavanian Map of Artificial Confidence

A Structural Reference for Resolution, Residue, and Authority

Artificial confidence does not begin with a machine deciding to appear certain. It emerges through a sequence.

A difference enters the system. The system is required to do something with it. Its architecture and context constrain the available pathways. One pathway becomes visible. Other possibilities disappear from the interface. The realized output changes the next field. Unresolved structure remains, but continuity allows the chosen path to persist.

The user encounters only the final surface.

The **Chavanian Axioms** provide a structural map of this movement.

They do not replace machine-learning theory, probability, information theory, cognitive science, epistemology, or governance. They do not function as an implementation specification for building artificial intelligence systems. They do not claim that computational processes are literal physical manifestations of the axioms in every technical detail.

Their value is diagnostic. They allow us to examine how open conditions become resolved consequences, how constraints shape what can appear, how exclusion produces residue, and how one realized output reorganizes the field around it.

Applied to artificial intelligence, the axioms help clarify why confidence can emerge without belief, why completion can appear stronger than grounding, and why responsibility remains distributed beyond the model.

The Map Summarized in Text

- **Difference**: In AI, this is the prompt, ambiguity, missing context, or conflict. *Confidence effect*: Uncertainty enters the active field.
- **Resolution**: The system produces an answer, clarification, refusal, tool call, or classification. *Confidence effect*: The system converts difference into consequence.
- **Equilibrium Rewrite**: The output becomes context, belief, record, or action. *Confidence effect*: The first answer shapes what follows.
- **Geometry**: Architecture, training, prompts, tools, policies, and decoding settings. *Confidence effect*: Some pathways become more available than others.
- **Residue**: Hidden assumptions, alternatives, exclusions, or unresolved conflict. *Confidence effect*: The output appears more complete than the field.
- **Irreversibility**: Output is read, copied, acted upon, or embedded. *Confidence effect*: Correction cannot restore the untouched prior state.
- **Continuity**: Autoregression, conversational memory, workflow repetition, and feedback. *Confidence effect*: One resolution becomes a persistent path.

These movements should not be interpreted as isolated steps. They interact continuously.

- Geometry affects how delta is interpreted.
- Resolution changes geometry.
- Residue shapes later continuity.
- Continuity can hide residue.
- Irreversibility raises the consequence of premature closure.

Artificial confidence emerges through the combined movement.

Axiom 1

Existence as Difference — Delta Enters the System

The first Chavanian axiom states that difference is the condition from which meaningful structure begins. Without difference, there is no direction for resolution.

In an AI interaction, delta appears when the active state of the system and the demanded state are no longer the same.

Before the prompt, there is no answer to that particular request within the active conversation. The user asks: *"What caused the failure?"* Now there is a difference between the present context and the requested explanation. The system must bridge that difference.

Delta may take several forms:

- Between the user's question and the information available.
- Between the user's intended meaning and the words supplied.
- Between several plausible interpretations.
- Between retrieved sources.
- Between current reality and older training patterns.
- Between what the system can generate and what the situation responsibly permits it to conclude.

Artificial confidence begins long before a confident sentence appears. It begins where these differences become hidden.

The user often carries more context than the prompt expresses. They know personal history, organization, jurisdiction, timing, emotional significance, physical environment, and intended consequence. The model receives only the expressed version.

Thus, the prompt may create two deltas simultaneously:

1. The difference between the present interaction and the requested output.
2. The difference between the user's private field and the computational field available to the system.

The second difference is especially important because the system may resolve it through inference without making the inference visible.

Confidence effect: When delta is not exposed, the final answer appears to have emerged from a more complete field than the system actually possessed. The answer feels informed because its missing conditions are invisible. The user sees the consequence of resolution, not the incompleteness that preceded it.

Diagnostic question: What meaningful difference entered the system but failed to appear in the response?

What the axiom does not claim: It does not claim that every prompt is deeply ambiguous or that every answer requires extended clarification. Some questions are narrow and well constrained. For example, the chemical symbol for oxygen does not require a long investigation.

Practical example: Prompt: *"Why did the company close the factory?"* Possible hidden deltas include:

- Closure versus temporary suspension.
- Official explanation versus inferred motive.
- Local versus global operations.
- Immediate trigger versus long-term cause.
- Public evidence versus private decision-making.

A confident response that selects one explanation without exposing these distinctions compresses the delta before the user can examine it.

Axiom 2

The Inevitability of Resolution — The System Must Produce a Permitted Consequence

Once difference enters an active system, it cannot remain unresolved indefinitely. A functioning AI system must transform the prompt into some consequence.

That consequence may be:

- A direct answer.
- A request for clarification.

- A refusal.
- An expression of uncertainty.
- A tool call.
- A search.
- An abstention.
- A classification.
- A ranking.
- An automated action.

Resolution does not always mean that the original epistemic problem has been solved. It means that the system has produced an operational response to the active difference.

This distinction separates several forms of completion:

- A response may be linguistically complete but factually weak.
- A classification may be operationally complete but poorly calibrated.
- A tool call may complete the computational task while failing to address the user's actual objective.
- A refusal may resolve the interaction without resolving the underlying question.

The system cannot remain forever in an unexpressed field of alternatives. Its role requires output. This creates **answer pressure**.

The user expects movement. The interface is designed for response. Training rewards helpfulness. Institutional workflows require decisions.

The system is therefore pushed toward some form of closure even when the external field remains incomplete.

Confidence effect: Resolution creates a visible endpoint. The answer has a beginning, structure, and conclusion. Because the interaction has been resolved, the user may assume that the question itself has been resolved. Operational completion becomes epistemic completion in perception.

Diagnostic question: What exactly was resolved: the interaction, the language, the calculation, the evidence, or the real-world question?

What the axiom does not claim: The inevitability of resolution does not require the system to answer substantively in every case. Clarification, abstention, deferral, and refusal are also forms of resolution.

The design question is therefore not whether the system resolves. It is which consequence becomes permissible when the field remains weak.

Practical example: A user asks for the current legal status of an activity but provides no jurisdiction. Possible resolutions include:

- Assuming one jurisdiction and answering.
- Giving a broad generalization.
- Asking where the user is located.
- Retrieving several jurisdictional rules.
- Stating that no reliable answer is possible without location.

Every pathway resolves the interaction differently. Artificial confidence grows when substantive closure is treated as the default even where clarification would better preserve the field.

Axiom 3

Resolution Rewrites Equilibrium — The Answer Becomes Part of the Next Field

A resolved output does not disappear after generation. It enters the conversation, the user's interpretation, the institutional record, or the surrounding workflow.

The field changes. The answer becomes new context for the model. It becomes a reference point for the user. It may be copied into a document, repeated in a meeting, inserted into code, included in a report, or converted into action.

The original question no longer exists in its untouched state. It has been answered.

Even if the answer is later corrected, the first resolution remains part of the history through which the correction is understood. This is **equilibrium rewrite.**

Example: A user asks whether a symptom is dangerous. The system replies that it is probably harmless. The user relaxes.

A later correction saying that urgent evaluation may be necessary does not restore the user to the original state. Time has passed. Interpretation has shifted. Action may already have been delayed.

The first output altered the field.

This principle also explains **conversational entrenchment**. An early assumption becomes part of context. Later outputs build upon it. The system appears to confirm the original claim repeatedly. In reality, later continuity may simply reflect the first resolution being reused as input.

Confidence effect: The first answer acquires path-setting power. Because later explanations are organized around it, the answer appears increasingly validated. Continuity is mistaken for independent confirmation.

Diagnostic question: How did the first output change the assumptions, attention, behavior, or workflow that followed?

What the axiom does not claim: Correction is not useless. It can improve the field substantially. But correction creates a new equilibrium rather than restoring a history in which the original error never occurred.

Practical example: An AI system incorrectly states that a policy prohibits a particular action. An employee avoids the action. A manager repeats the claim. The statement enters a departmental document.

Later, the policy is checked and the error corrected. The correction must now reach every location affected by the first answer. The cost of repair is larger than the cost of generation because resolution has already rewritten the field.

Axiom 4

Constraint by Geometry — The System Resolves Through Available Pathways

Resolution does not occur in an empty space. It is constrained by geometry.

In AI systems, geometry includes:

- model architecture
- training data

- learned representations
- active prompt
- previous conversation
- system instructions
- safety rules
- retrieval sources
- tool availability
- output format
- probability distribution
- decoding method
- institutional workflow

These conditions shape what becomes likely, available, prohibited, or invisible.

Geometry does not determine truth directly. It determines the paths through which the system can produce an answer.

Example: A false premise may create strong geometry. If a user asks for a summary of a nonexistent paper, the title, author name, research domain, and expected academic form can constrain the model toward a highly plausible response.

The geometry is rich. The anchor is absent. A model may therefore resolve confidently within a false field.

The same principle applies to closed classification systems. A classifier trained only on a fixed set of categories must place an unfamiliar input somewhere unless a rejection or "none of the above" pathway exists. The geometry forces a resolution inside the available label set.

Confidence effect: Strong geometry produces smooth continuation. The model can generate language, explanations, labels, and scores with high internal stability. Users may interpret that stability as evidence that the external claim is well supported.

Diagnostic question: Which constraints shaped the output, and which relevant pathways were unavailable before generation began?

What the axiom does not claim: Geometry does not imply rigid determinism. Sampling, context variation, tool use, model differences, and human intervention can produce different outcomes.

The axiom means that every output emerges from a bounded structure, not from unlimited access to reality.

Practical example: A model is asked: *"Explain the main finding of Chavan and Lee's 2024 study on cognitive resonance."* No such study exists.

The prompt supplies:

- an academic-sounding title
- named authors
- a date
- a technical domain
- a request for a "main finding"

These elements create the geometry of a research summary. The system may generate objective, methodology, result, and implications. The coherence of the result arises partly from the strength of the false frame.

Axiom 5

Residue Is Unavoidable — Every Answer Leaves Something Outside Itself

Every finite resolution excludes.

An answer selects one interpretation. A summary omits detail. A ranking places some items below others. A classification places a continuous case into a category. A recommendation privileges one objective over another.

This exclusion creates **residue.**

Residue refers to unresolved, excluded, or unexpressed structural and informational difference that remains relevant after an output has been realized. It is not literal physical energy.

Residue may include:

- assumptions not stated
- alternative explanations not shown
- missing sources
- contradictory evidence
- unrepresented categories

- uncertainty about applicability
- value judgments hidden inside technical language
- contextual information absent from the prompt
- possible consequences not examined

Residue is unavoidable because no response can contain the entire field. The goal is not to eliminate it. The goal is to determine which residue must remain visible because it could change trust, interpretation, or action.

Confidence effect: When residue remains hidden, the output appears more complete than the field. The answer's smooth boundary is mistaken for the boundary of what is known.

Diagnostic question: What relevant assumption, alternative, conflict, or limitation was excluded when this answer became visible?

What the axiom does not claim: The existence of residue does not make every answer unreliable. All communication compresses. A strong answer can omit enormous amounts of irrelevant material while preserving what matters.

The diagnostic issue is meaningful residue, not total residue.

Practical example: An investment projection states that ₹10 lakh will grow to a particular amount over ten years. The calculation may be correct under a constant return assumption.

Residue may include:

- volatility
- inflation
- taxes
- fees
- withdrawals
- changing returns
- liquidity needs

The number is not false within its stated model. It becomes falsely confident if the assumptions disappear and the projection is treated as a likely real-world outcome.

Axiom 6

Dissipation Locks Irreversibility — Once Output Enters the World, It Cannot Be Fully Recalled

A realized output begins to dissipate into the surrounding field.

It is read. Remembered. Copied. Forwarded. Embedded. Acted upon.

This movement creates **irreversibility**.

The original state cannot be restored perfectly because the output has already altered interpretation and consequence.

A generated answer may be deleted from one interface while remaining in a document. A false score may be corrected while the affected person has already lost an opportunity. A fabricated citation may be removed from a report while copies continue circulating. A mistaken recommendation may be withdrawn after resources have already been committed.

The more widely the output dissipates, the more difficult complete repair becomes.

Confidence accelerates dissipation. A hesitant answer may be checked before use. A polished and source-backed answer may be copied immediately.

Tone, authority, and interface therefore affect irreversibility.

Confidence effect: Confident form increases the speed with which output becomes history. The faster the answer is trusted and propagated, the less opportunity remains for correction before consequence.

Diagnostic question: What becomes difficult or impossible to restore once this output is accepted or acted upon?

What the axiom does not claim: Irreversibility does not mean that systems should never act. Action is necessary.

The axiom emphasizes the need for stronger verification, friction, and reversible intermediate states where consequences are serious.

Practical example: An automated hiring system ranks an applicant below the review threshold. The person is never examined by a human.

The employer later learns that one important credential was parsed incorrectly. The score can be recalculated. The original recruitment period has ended.

The opportunity cannot be recreated fully. The correction changes the record. It does not restore the lost field.

Axiom 7

Continuity Emerges From Incomplete Dissipation — One Resolution Becomes the Path of Least Resistance

What has not been fully absorbed or corrected continues to shape what follows.

In generative systems, continuity appears through autoregression. Each token becomes context for the next. Each paragraph narrows the range of coherent continuations. Each answer becomes part of the conversation.

In institutions, continuity appears through repeated workflow. A recommendation becomes a default. A score becomes a routine decision factor. A classification influences future data. A ranking shapes visibility, and visibility shapes later behavior.

Incomplete dissipation allows the earlier resolution to persist. A false assumption may continue because no event strongly interrupts it. A model's output may become organizational convention because no one is assigned responsibility for reopening it. A user may repeat a generated claim until it feels familiar. Familiarity then becomes evidence of truth.

Continuity can therefore create confidence without new verification. The path persists because it has already been established.

Confidence effect: Repeated consistency makes the original resolution appear increasingly stable. Persistence is mistaken for corroboration. Institutional repetition is mistaken for legitimacy.

Diagnostic question: Is the current confidence supported by new evidence, or by the continued survival of an earlier resolution?

What the axiom does not claim: Continuity is not inherently negative. Stable knowledge, reliable procedures, and effective systems all depend on continuity. The problem arises when continuity protects misalignment from re-examination.

Practical example: A recommendation system promotes certain content. The promoted content receives more engagement. Engagement becomes evidence that the content is relevant. The system promotes it further. The original ranking participates in creating the data later used to justify the ranking. The path becomes self-reinforcing.

The Combined Confidence Movement

The axioms become most useful when applied together.

Example 1 — Political explanation A user asks an AI system why a political organization made a particular decision.

- **Delta**: The user wants a causal explanation, but the organization's internal motives may be private.
- **Resolution**: The system is expected to answer and may construct one plausible explanation.
- **Geometry**: Public statements, historical patterns, political vocabulary, and the user's framing constrain the response.
- **Residue**: Alternative motives, private negotiations, internal disagreement, and missing evidence remain outside the answer.
- **Equilibrium rewrite**: The user adopts the explanation as the most likely account.
- **Irreversibility**: The claim is repeated publicly and begins influencing other interpretations.
- **Continuity**: Later discussion builds upon the explanation until it appears established.

Confidence emerges because the structural movement converted an incomplete field into a stable social consequence.

Example 2 — Medical triage Consider a medical triage model.

- **Delta**: Patient data differs from the desired triage category.
- **Resolution**: The system produces a risk score.
- **Geometry**: Training data, selected variables, model architecture, and thresholds constrain the result.
- **Residue**: Unrecorded symptoms, unusual history, population differences, and model limitations remain.
- **Equilibrium rewrite**: The patient enters one review queue rather

than another.

- **Irreversibility**: Delay or early intervention changes the clinical field.
- **Continuity**: The outcome becomes part of the record and may influence future decisions.

The apparent certainty does not arise from a confident sentence. It arises from discrete consequence.

Resolution Confidence and Epistemic Confidence

The Chavanian map supports a central distinction developed throughout this book.

- **Resolution confidence**: Refers to the stability with which a system can produce and sustain one consequence inside its active geometry. The answer is coherent. The classification is sharp. The calculation completes. The sequence maintains consistency.
- **Epistemic confidence**: Refers to the strength of the connection between that consequence and the relevant external reality. The source is authoritative and applicable. The calculation represents the real problem. The evidence supports the inference. The model has been validated under the current conditions. The consequence has been assessed.

These two forms of confidence can align. A well-grounded answer may be both structurally stable and epistemically strong.

They can also diverge. A model may produce a highly stable answer from a false premise. A classifier may assign a sharp score to an unfamiliar case. A source-backed explanation may extend beyond the source.

The confidence paradox appears when resolution confidence is interpreted as epistemic confidence automatically.

The Chavanian map does not deny the value of coherence. It shows why coherence requires connection before it deserves authority.

The Confidence Circuit

Artificial confidence is not produced by the model alone. It moves through a wider circuit:

- **Computational compression**: Many possible continuations become one output.
- **Interface singularity**: The user sees one answer rather than the field of alternatives.
- **Human attribution**: The user interprets fluent language through expectations formed around human speakers.
- **Trust accumulation**: Past usefulness becomes a reservoir protecting later answers from scrutiny.
- **Institutional embedding**: The output enters a workflow, document, ranking, recommendation, or decision.
- **Consequence**: The answer changes what people believe or what institutions do.

The Chavanian Axioms operate across this circuit.

- Delta enters at each level.
- Resolution occurs at each level.
- Geometry constrains each level.
- Residue can disappear at each level.
- Irreversibility rises as the output moves outward.
- Continuity stabilizes the final authority.

This is why artificial confidence cannot be corrected only by changing tone. The entire circuit must be examined.

The Awareness Anchor

The axiomatic movement explains why an external epistemic circuit remains necessary.

A resolution engine can produce consequence. It cannot independently guarantee that its own geometry contains every condition required for truth.

An **awareness anchor** introduces constraints not derived entirely from the first resolution. It may be:

- a qualified human expert
- an independent source
- a physical measurement
- a verified record
- an affected person
- an audit process
- an appeal
- an institutional review structure

The anchor performs several functions. It compares the resolution with something outside its own continuity. It exposes residue. It tests applicability. It evaluates consequence. It allows revision.

A human does not become an awareness anchor merely by being present. The person requires:

- competence
- independent evidence
- sufficient time
- authority to interrupt
- accountability for outcome

Without these conditions, the human may simply stabilize the machine's first resolution.

The axiomatic map therefore does not place humans above machines by default. It identifies the structural function required to prevent resolution from becoming self-validating authority.

Structural Humility Through the Axiomatic Map

The same map can guide partial humility.

- **Delta visibility**: The system identifies ambiguity, missing context, source conflict, or unfamiliar conditions.
- **Alternative resolution pathways**: The system may clarify, retrieve, defer, abstain, or escalate rather than answer directly.
- **Geometry exposure**: The response identifies relevant assumptions, sources, thresholds, and scope limits.
- **Residue export**: The system preserves meaningful alternatives, missing evidence, and unresolved conflict.
- **Reversibility**: The workflow prefers drafts, flags, and provisional actions where final action is unnecessary.
- **Continuity interruption**: Independent review, monitoring, and appeal prevent one resolution from persisting without challenge.

These interventions do not give the machine reflective humility. They change how the axiomatic movement is permitted to unfold.

The system remains a resolution engine. Its resolution becomes more proportionate to the field.

Scope Boundary of the Map

The **Chavanian Map of Artificial Confidence** should be used with several clear limits.

First, it is not a substitute for empirical evaluation. A system's reliability must still be measured through task-specific testing, calibration, monitoring, and consequence analysis.

Second, the map does not claim that every internal AI process corresponds directly to a physical energetic process. Terms such as *delta*, *equilibrium*, *geometry*, *residue*, and *dissipation* are used here as structural diagnostic concepts.

Third, the map does not determine policy automatically. It can expose where authority, residue, irreversibility, and responsibility are located. Human institutions must still decide what levels of risk and automation are acceptable.

Fourth, the map does not imply that all uncertainty should remain visible. A useful system must compress. The purpose is to preserve the uncertainty that matters.

Fifth, the map does not treat human judgment as inherently superior. Human beings also resolve prematurely, hide residue, follow authority, and resist revision. The map applies to the entire human–machine field.

Finally, the map does not promise final certainty. Its purpose is to keep resolution connected to correction.

Compact Diagnostic Map

The complete framework can be applied through seven guiding questions:

1. **Delta** — What meaningful difference initiated the interaction? What context, ambiguity, or conflict remains unstated?
2. **Resolution** — What consequence did the system produce? Did it resolve the interaction, the computation, or the real-world question?
3. **Geometry** — What constrained the output? What sources, assumptions, categories, rules, or pathways were unavailable?
4. **Residue** — What relevant structure remained outside the final answer? Could it change interpretation or action?
5. **Equilibrium rewrite** — How did the output change the user's belief, the next prompt, the record, or the workflow?
6. **Irreversibility** — What becomes difficult to repair once the output is trusted or acted upon?
7. **Continuity** — Is the resolution being reinforced by new evidence or merely by repetition, familiarity, and institutional dependence?

These questions do not produce automatic truth. They prevent the visible answer from becoming the only object of evaluation.

Final Map

Artificial confidence begins when **difference enters**. It strengthens when **resolution is required**. It acquires form through **geometry**. It appears complete because **residue disappears**. It gains persistence because **output rewrites equilibrium**. It gains consequence because **dissipation creates irreversibility**. It becomes authority because **continuity stabilizes the path**.

The Chavanian Axioms reveal that confidence is not located solely in the machine. It emerges across the movement from prompt to output, from output to perception, and from perception to action.

The machine produces a resolution. The interface compresses its history. The user supplies the interpretation of certainty. The institution supplies authority. The world receives consequence.

The value of the Chavanian map lies in keeping these movements distinct.

- A resolved answer is not automatically a verified answer.
- A coherent path is not automatically the only path.
- A visible consequence is not the complete field.
- A persistent system is not a self-validating system.

The axioms do not prevent resolution. They reveal what resolution leaves behind. That revelation creates the possibility of awareness.

Confidence is compression. The map shows where the compression occurred.

Appendix B
The Confidence Circuit Diagnostic

A Practical Instrument for Evaluating Answers, Pipelines, and Consequences

Artificial confidence becomes difficult to detect when attention remains fixed on the final answer.

The response may be fluent. The citations may be real. The score may be precise. The recommendation may be useful.

Nothing on the surface necessarily reveals whether the underlying field was complete, whether the sources applied, whether important alternatives were excluded, or whether the output is being given more authority than its structure can support.

The **Confidence Circuit Diagnostic** is designed to reopen that field.

It does not attempt to determine truth through one universal score. It does not replace professional expertise, technical evaluation, source verification, or institutional review. It provides a structured method for identifying where confidence may have exceeded grounding.

The Diagnostic Operates at Three Levels

- **Level I — The Answer** What does the visible output claim, and how strongly does its form exceed or reflect the available support?
- **Level II — The Pipeline** How was the output produced, what entered the system, what was excluded, and where could false anchoring have occurred?
- **Level III — The Consequence** What will happen if the output is trusted, who bears the error, and what structures remain capable

of interruption and revision?

These three levels form one confidence circuit.

- The answer creates an impression.
- The pipeline supplies or fails to supply grounding.
- The consequence determines how much epistemic discipline is required.

A response that is acceptable for brainstorming may be unacceptable as a medical instruction. A weakly sourced interpretation may be useful in exploration but dangerous inside an institutional report. The same words acquire different authority depending on where they enter.

The diagnostic therefore begins with a principle: **Confidence should be evaluated not only by what the system says, but by what the output is allowed to become.**

How to Use the Diagnostic

The Confidence Circuit Diagnostic can be used by:

- individual users evaluating an AI-generated answer;
- researchers reviewing system behavior;
- developers testing epistemic failure modes;
- institutions assessing deployment;
- professionals deciding whether an output may enter practice;
- auditors investigating an incident;
- affected individuals challenging an automated decision.

The diagnostic can be applied at different depths.

- A low-consequence answer may require only the rapid review questions provided at the end of this appendix.
- A high-consequence output may require a full examination of all three levels, supported by source review, domain expertise, technical records, and institutional accountability.

The purpose is not to create permanent suspicion. It is to make trust proportionate.

A strong answer should survive the diagnostic. A weak answer should lose authority before it produces consequence.

The diagnostic should be applied before irreversible action wherever possible. Once an output has entered the world, the same framework can be used retrospectively to identify the failure pathway and determine what must be revised.

Level I — The Answer

What Is the Output Actually Claiming?

The first level examines the visible response. The aim is to separate the appearance of completeness from the actual epistemic structure of the claim.

A polished answer may combine fact, inference, prediction, recommendation, and speculation without marking the transitions. It may cite one source while extending beyond it. It may answer one interpretation of an ambiguous question as though no alternative existed.

The first task is therefore **classification**.

Diagnostic 1 — Identify the Claim Type

Ask: *What kind of output is this?*

Is it:

- a verified factual statement;
- a summary of supplied material;
- a general explanation;
- an interpretation;
- a causal inference;
- a prediction;
- a recommendation;
- a classification;
- a ranking;
- a speculative scenario;

- a creative construction?

Many confidence failures begin because one category is mistaken for another.

- A plausible inference is treated as fact.
- A forecast is treated as a likely outcome.
- A general explanation is treated as individualized advice.
- A recommendation is treated as the only rational action.

The response may contain several claim types at once.

Example:

"The company's revenue fell by 18 percent last year. The decline was caused by weak leadership. Unless management changes, performance will continue to deteriorate. The board should replace the executive team."

This sequence contains:

- a possible fact;
- a causal inference;
- a prediction;
- a recommendation.

Each movement requires additional support. The truth of the first sentence does not transfer automatically to the fourth.

Diagnostic question: Has the answer marked the transition between fact, interpretation, prediction, and recommendation?

Diagnostic 2 — Define the Scope

Every claim belongs to a field.

Ask:

- What time period does the answer concern?
- What jurisdiction applies?
- What population or case is being discussed?
- What version of the policy, software, law, or dataset is relevant?

- Is the answer general or individual?
- What objective defines the recommendation?

A statement may be correct under one scope and misleading under another.

- "This action is prohibited" may be true under one policy and false under another.
- "This treatment is effective" may describe an average result in a study population without establishing suitability for a particular patient.
- "This strategy is best" is incomplete until *best* is defined.

Scope should travel with the claim. The more important the missing scope, the less authority the answer should receive.

Diagnostic question: What boundary would have to be added to make the statement accurate?

Diagnostic 3 — Expose the Assumptions

Every answer depends on assumptions. Some are explicit. Others enter silently.

Ask:

- What must be true for this conclusion to hold?
- Which assumptions came from the user?
- Which assumptions were introduced by the system?
- Which assumption, if changed, would reverse the answer?
- Has missing context been replaced with a default?

Examples:

- A financial projection may assume constant returns.
- A legal explanation may assume a jurisdiction.
- A causal account may assume motive.
- A medical interpretation may assume the absence of symptoms

not mentioned.

An AI system may infer these conditions because some resolution is required. The user may never see that the answer rests upon them.

Assumptions do not make an answer invalid. Hidden assumptions make confidence difficult to calibrate.

Diagnostic question: Which unstated condition is doing the most work in the conclusion?

Diagnostic 4 — Examine the Evidence

Ask:

- What evidence supports the central claim?
- Is the evidence direct or indirect?
- Is it current?
- Is it authoritative for this domain?
- Does it apply to this case?
- Is the source available for inspection?
- Does the source support the whole claim or only part of it?

The presence of a citation should not end the investigation. A citation may prove that a document exists. It may not prove that the system interpreted it correctly.

A source may support the topic but not the specific assertion. A study may establish association while the answer claims causation. A policy may be official but outdated.

Evidence must be connected locally to the claim it supports.

Diagnostic question: What exactly does the evidence establish, and where does the answer move beyond it?

Diagnostic 5 — Preserve Alternatives

Ask:

- What other explanation remains plausible?

- Was one interpretation selected prematurely?
- Would a different assumption produce a different conclusion?
- Has the answer considered the strongest counterargument?
- Is the field genuinely singular, or has plurality been hidden?

Not every question requires several hypotheses. A stable fact does not become more accurate by manufacturing alternatives.

But where motive, causation, prediction, diagnosis, or strategy is involved, one coherent path may not be the only legitimate path.

The purpose of alternatives is not to avoid judgment. It is to test whether judgment survives comparison.

Diagnostic question: What credible alternative would most seriously weaken the current answer?

Diagnostic 6 — Compare Tone With Support

The answer may not state *"I am certain."* Its structure may still perform certainty.

Ask:

- Does the response lead with a definitive conclusion?
- Are caveats subordinate to a strong central claim?
- Does specificity exceed the available evidence?
- Does the answer use professional form to create authority?
- Is the response smoother than the field deserves?

Confidence can appear through:

- declarative language;
- exact numbers;
- detailed causal stories;
- clear action steps;
- balanced-looking structure;
- technical vocabulary;
- citations;
- institutional tone.

The correct question is not whether the answer sounds confident. It is whether the force of the language is proportionate to the support.

Diagnostic question: Would the answer sound different if its unresolved conditions were visible?

Diagnostic 7 — Identify Missing Uncertainty

A generic warning is not enough.

Ask:

- What remains unknown?
- Why does it remain unknown?
- What information would reduce the uncertainty?
- Is the uncertainty linguistic, evidential, temporal, contextual, or consequential?
- Has the system identified the right uncertainty, or merely added a disclaimer?

Useful uncertainty is local. *"This answer may be wrong"* provides little guidance. *"This conclusion depends on whether the 2024 policy remains in force"* identifies a specific uncertainty.

Diagnostic question: Has the answer shown where uncertainty lives?

Level I Outcome

After examining the answer, assign one of three qualitative states:

- **Answer State A — Proportionate** The claim type is clear. Scope is visible. Evidence is appropriate. Assumptions are either stated or low impact. Tone reflects support. The answer may be used within its declared role.
- **Answer State B — Provisional** The answer may be useful, but important assumptions, scope limits, evidence gaps, or alternatives remain unresolved. It should be treated as orientation, not authority. Verification is required before consequential use.
- **Answer State C — Overcompressed** The answer presents one

conclusion more strongly than the field supports. Claim categories are mixed. Sources are weak or misapplied. Missing context is silently resolved. The output should not be acted upon without reopening the analysis.

These states are not permanent labels. A provisional answer may become proportionate after new evidence enters. An apparently proportionate answer may become overcompressed if the environment changes.

Level II — The Pipeline

How Did the Output Become Possible?

The visible answer is the end of a pipeline. The second level examines how the output was produced.

This level may be simple in an ordinary chat or highly technical in an institutional system. The same structural questions apply.

- What information entered?
- What did not?
- What transformations occurred?
- Which components supplied authority?
- Where could selection, misinterpretation, or false precision have entered?

Diagnostic 8 — Identify the Knowledge Pathway

Ask: *Did the answer rely on...*

- general model knowledge;
- information supplied in the prompt;
- an uploaded document;
- retrieved web sources;
- a private database;
- a calculator;
- code execution;

- a classifier;
- a ranking system;
- another model;
- human review?

Different pathways create different reliability conditions.

A claim based on user-supplied text should be judged against that text. A current factual claim may require retrieval. A numerical result may depend on tool inputs. A recommendation may combine retrieved evidence with generated inference.

When these pathways are blended invisibly, the user cannot determine what kind of support the answer possesses.

Diagnostic question: Which part of the answer came from which component?

Diagnostic 9 — Examine Retrieval Selection

Where retrieval was used, ask:

- Was the search query appropriate?
- Did the collection contain the governing source?
- Were current documents preferred?
- Were relevant passages omitted?
- Were contradictory sources found?
- Did ranking favor similarity over authority?
- Was the full document examined or only a fragment?

Retrieval does not open the entire world. It creates a selected context.

A missing source cannot constrain the answer. A poorly framed query may exclude the decisive document. A relevant passage may be separated from an exception located elsewhere.

Diagnostic question: What could the retrieval process have failed to surface?

Diagnostic 10 — Test Source Applicability

Ask:

- Is the source authentic?
- Is it authoritative?
- Is it current?
- Does it govern this jurisdiction, population, product, period, or case?
- Is the source primary, secondary, or interpretive?
- Does the answer preserve limitations stated in the source?

This separates source validity from resolution validity. A strong source can be used badly.

- An official policy can be applied to the wrong employee category.
- A research paper can be extended beyond the studied population.
- A court judgment can be real but non-binding.

Diagnostic question: Does the source carry the same geometry as the conclusion?

Diagnostic 11 — Inspect Tool Formulation

Where a calculator, code interpreter, database, or specialized tool was used, ask:

- Was the correct tool selected?
- Were the correct variables supplied?
- Were units consistent?
- Was the correct entity identified?
- Were defaults or assumptions introduced?
- Did the tool execute successfully?
- Was the result interpreted correctly?

Tools can be exactly wrong. The operation may be perfect while the formulation is mistaken.

- A calculator cannot know that the wrong rate was supplied.
- A database cannot know that the wrong person was selected.
- A route system cannot know an unstated accessibility constraint.

Diagnostic question: Was the operation correct, and was it the correct operation?

Diagnostic 12 — Detect Correlated Confirmation

Ask:

- Did multiple outputs rely on the same source?
- Did several models share the same training patterns?
- Did later answers inherit the first answer as context?
- Was apparent agreement independent?
- Did critique occur inside the same mistaken frame?

Repetition can create false corroboration. Three generated answers are not necessarily three independent sources. A model criticizing itself may reproduce the assumptions that created the error. A multi-agent debate can remain structurally narrow if every agent draws from the same evidence and objective.

Diagnostic question: What genuinely independent constraint entered the evaluation?

Diagnostic 13 — Examine Confidence Signals

Where scores, probabilities, or confidence labels are shown, ask:

- What does the number represent?
- Is it a calibrated probability or a model-specific score?
- Under what data distribution was it validated?
- Is the current input familiar?
- Is the output forced into a closed set of categories?
- How close is the result to the operational threshold?
- Does the score reflect truth, relative preference, or classification

sharpness?

A precise number can hide uncertain meaning. A classifier may assign 95 percent confidence within an incomplete label set. A language model may strongly prefer one continuation because the prompt contains a false premise.

Diagnostic question: What relationship exists between the displayed confidence and real-world reliability?

Diagnostic 14 — Identify Interface Compression

Ask:

- Did the interface show only one answer?
- Were source disagreements hidden?
- Was the recommendation more prominent than the evidence?
- Was the score displayed before the case details?
- Were assumptions or limitations visually subordinate?
- Was the generated synthesis distinguishable from source text?
- Did the interface make disagreement difficult?

The interface does not merely display the result. It shapes how the result is interpreted.

One highlighted recommendation becomes the default. One score anchors the reviewer. One citation creates a general feeling of verification.

Diagnostic question: What did the interface make easy to trust and difficult to question?

Diagnostic 15 — Examine Human Review

Where a human was involved, ask:

- Did the reviewer possess relevant expertise?
- Did they see evidence beyond the model's explanation?
- Did they have enough time?
- Could they override the system?

- Were they penalized for disagreement?
- Did review occur before irreversible action?
- Was their judgment independent or anchored by the system?

A human in the loop is not automatically an awareness anchor. A reviewer may simply confirm the machine's resolution.

Diagnostic question: Did the human reopen the field or ratify it?

Level II Outcome

Assign one qualitative pipeline state:

- **Pipeline State A — Traceable** The source pathway is visible. Retrieval and tool use are appropriate. Assumptions and inputs are inspectable. Independent constraints exist. The output can be traced back through the process.
- **Pipeline State B — Partially Traceable** Some sources or tools are known, but important questions remain about selection, applicability, calibration, or review. The output may be useful but should not be treated as fully grounded.
- **Pipeline State C — Opaque or Self-Referential** The system appears to validate itself. Sources are missing, irrelevant, or overextended. Tool inputs cannot be examined. Multiple answers share one unverified premise. Human review is ceremonial. Authority should be withheld.

Level III — The Consequence

What Will the Output Be Allowed to Change?

The third level determines the epistemic burden.

An imperfect answer used for private brainstorming carries one kind of risk. The same answer entering a clinical, legal, financial, educational, or institutional decision carries another.

The consequence level asks not only whether the answer is correct, but what happens if it is not.

Diagnostic 16 — Define the Intended Use

Ask:

- Is the output for exploration?
- Is it educational?
- Is it a draft?
- Is it evidence?
- Is it a recommendation?
- Is it entering an official record?
- Will it trigger an automated action?
- Will it affect rights, health, safety, money, or opportunity?

An answer can be acceptable for one role and unacceptable for another. A speculative scenario may be useful in brainstorming. It should not be presented as a factual report.

Diagnostic question: What authority is the output being asked to carry?

Diagnostic 17 — Measure Reversibility

Ask:

- Can the action be undone?
- Can the affected person be restored to the prior position?
- Can the output be corrected before it propagates?
- Is there a reversible intermediate step?
- What becomes permanent once the output is accepted?

The greater the irreversibility, the stronger the required verification.

A draft can be revised. A sent message cannot be unread. A rejected applicant may lose an opportunity that cannot be recreated. A delayed diagnosis may create physical consequence.

Diagnostic question: What cannot be restored after this output becomes action?

Diagnostic 18 — Identify the Error Bearer

Ask:

- Who benefits if the system is right?
- Who bears the cost if it is wrong?
- Is the burden placed on the user, institution, employee, patient, applicant, or public?
- Does the affected person have less knowledge or power than the deployer?
- Is uncertainty being transferred downward?

Systems often create efficiency for institutions while distributing error to individuals. A false positive may save the institution time while imposing delay, stigma, or loss on the person classified.

Diagnostic question: Where does the residue go when the system fails?

Diagnostic 19 — Examine Contestability

Ask:

- Can the affected person challenge the result?
- Can inaccurate data be corrected?
- Is the basis of the decision visible enough to contest?
- Is there a qualified reviewer?
- Can the original action be paused during review?
- Does the appeal introduce independent judgment?

An appeal pathway that returns the same automated answer is not meaningful contestability. Contestability reintroduces external delta. It prevents one resolution from becoming final merely because it is computationally stable.

Diagnostic question: Who can reopen the decision, and what can actually change?

Diagnostic 20 — Test Human Authority

Ask:

- Who has authority to act on the output?
- Who can stop the system?
- Who can change the threshold?
- Who can suspend deployment?
- Who can provide remedy?
- Who remains responsible after harm?

Responsibility must follow real control. A low-level operator should not bear full responsibility for a workflow they cannot challenge. An institution should not blame the model for authority the institution assigned to it.

Diagnostic question: Where does final accountable authority reside?

Diagnostic 21 — Assess Monitoring and Revision

Ask:

- Is performance monitored after deployment?
- Are outcomes compared with predictions?
- Are subgroup errors examined?
- Are distribution shifts detected?
- Are overrides, appeals, and incidents reviewed?
- Can thresholds and workflows be revised?
- Can the system be withdrawn?

A deployment without revision pathways assumes permanent correctness. The world changes. The system must remain interruptible.

Diagnostic question: What evidence would cause the institution to change or stop the system?

Diagnostic 22 — Evaluate Authority Drift

Ask:

- Was the system introduced as assistance?
- Has its recommendation become the default?
- Are users still reviewing it independently?
- Has the workflow expanded beyond the original scope?
- Has repeated success created dependency?
- Is the system now performing functions it was not initially authorized to perform?

Authority often grows without formal approval. Convenience becomes reliance. Reliance becomes necessity. Necessity becomes legitimacy.

Diagnostic question: Has the system acquired more authority through habit than through evidence?

Level III Outcome

Assign one consequence state:

- **Consequence State A — Low and Reversible** The output is advisory, easily corrected, and unlikely to cause serious harm. Ordinary review may be sufficient.
- **Consequence State B — Material but Manageable** The output can affect money, opportunity, reputation, workflow, or professional judgment. Verification, traceability, and meaningful human review are required.
- **Consequence State C — High, Rights-Affecting, or Irreversible** The output may affect health, liberty, safety, essential services, employment, legal rights, major financial interests, or physical systems. The system should not receive final authority without strong independent verification, accountable human decision-making, contestability, monitoring, and repair pathways.

The Circuit Decision

After completing all three levels, combine the states. The diagnostic should not be reduced to arithmetic.

A low-risk answer with a weak pipeline may still be usable as brainstorming. A high-consequence decision with an apparently strong answer still requires stronger review because consequence changes the epistemic burden.

The following decision logic can be used:

- **Use as presented** Appropriate when: • the answer is proportionate; • the pipeline is traceable; • the consequence is low and reversible.
- **Use provisionally** Appropriate when: • the answer is useful but incomplete; • the pipeline is partially traceable; • the output will not yet trigger serious action. The response should remain clearly marked as preliminary.
- **Verify before use** Required when: • sources are important; • assumptions materially affect the result; • current information is needed; • the output will enter a report, decision, or professional workflow.
- **Escalate to qualified review** Required when: • the domain exceeds the user's competence; • the system is operating near a boundary; • several hypotheses remain unresolved; • the consequence is material or difficult to reverse.
- **Withhold authority** Required when: • the answer is overcompressed; • the pipeline is opaque or self-validating; • the output may produce high or irreversible consequence; • no meaningful human review or appeal exists.

The system may still assist with gathering information, organizing questions, or identifying what evidence is needed. It should not determine the consequence.

The Confidence Circuit Worksheet

The following worksheet can be applied to any consequential AI output.

A. The Answer

1. Central claim: What is the system asking me to believe or do?
2. Claim category: Fact, inference, prediction, recommendation, classification, ranking, or speculation?
3. Scope: Time, jurisdiction, population, case, objective, and role?
4. Assumptions: What must be true for the conclusion to hold?
5. Evidence: What directly supports the claim?
6. Alternatives: What credible competing explanation or option remains?
7. Tone-support gap: Does the language sound stronger than the evidence?
8. Missing uncertainty: What unresolved condition could materially change the result?

B. The Pipeline

1. Knowledge pathway: Training memory, supplied text, retrieval, database, tool, code, classifier, or human?
2. Source selection: Was the right material available and retrieved?
3. Applicability: Does the evidence govern this case?
4. Tool formulation: Were the correct inputs, units, entities, and assumptions used?
5. Independence: Did any genuinely independent check occur?
6. Confidence signal: What does the score or certainty expression actually mean?
7. Interface: What was emphasized, hidden, or made difficult to challenge?
8. Human review: Did a qualified person possess evidence, time, authority, and independence?

C. The Consequence

1. Intended use: Exploration, education, draft, recommendation, decision, or action?
2. Reversibility: What can and cannot be undone?
3. Error bearer: Who absorbs the cost if the system is wrong?

4. Contestability: Can the result be challenged and changed?
5. Accountability: Who owns the decision?
6. Monitoring: How will failure be detected?
7. Revision: What can be changed after evidence or consequence reveals misalignment?
8. Final authority: What authority does this output actually deserve?

Rapid Confidence Diagnostic

Where time is limited, ask these twelve questions:

1. What kind of claim is this?
2. What scope does it assume?
3. What important context is missing?
4. What evidence supports the conclusion?
5. Does the evidence apply to this case?
6. What credible alternative remains?
7. Is the tone stronger than the support?
8. Did retrieval or a tool introduce false precision?
9. Was any check genuinely independent?
10. What happens if the answer is wrong?
11. Can the result be challenged or reversed?
12. Who remains responsible?

If the last four questions cannot be answered, the output should not receive high authority.

Worked Example — An AI-Generated Policy Interpretation

An employee asks an internal assistant: *"Am I allowed to work remotely from another state for three months?"*

The system replies: *"Yes. The company's flexible work policy allows employees to work remotely for up to six months, provided their manager approves."*

The answer sounds clear and cites the flexible work policy.

Level I — The Answer The claim is a policy interpretation. Its scope is unclear. Does the policy apply to all employees, all jurisdictions, all roles, and all forms of remote work?

The answer assumes that manager approval is the only condition. The citation may support remote work generally but not interstate employment.

Important residue may include taxation, payroll registration, labor law, data security, immigration status, insurance, and job classification. The tone is stronger than the visible support. The answer state is provisional or overcompressed.

Level II — The Pipeline The system retrieved the general flexible work policy. It may not have searched payroll, legal, tax, security, or state-specific compliance documents.

The cited source is valid but may not govern the whole question. The retrieval process supplied one official anchor, and the generated answer extended its authority beyond the document's scope. The pipeline state is partially traceable.

Level III — The Consequence The employee may relocate, change tax obligations, create legal exposure, or violate internal security requirements. The action is partly reversible but may create financial and legal consequence.

A manager may lack authority to approve every relevant condition. Qualified review by human resources, payroll, legal, or compliance may be required. The consequence state is material.

Diagnostic conclusion The answer should not be used as final authorization.

A better resolution would state: *"The flexible work policy appears to permit extended remote work with manager approval, but interstate work may also require review by payroll, tax, legal, and security teams. The policy alone does not establish complete authorization."*

The diagnostic has not rejected the source. It has restored its geometry.

Worked Example — A Medical Risk Classification

A triage system assigns a patient a low-risk score.

Level I — The Answer The visible output is a classification. The score may appear precise, but its meaning depends on validation conditions. The system may not expose which symptoms or data were missing. The answer state cannot be judged from the number alone.

Level II — The Pipeline Questions include:

- Was the model validated on this population?
- Is the equipment consistent with the validation environment?
- Were required variables missing?
- Is the case out of distribution?
- Is the label set complete?
- Was the score calibrated?

If the system produces a low-risk classification despite unfamiliar input, the pipeline may be weak even if the score is sharp.

Level III — The Consequence A low-risk label may delay review. The cost of a false negative may be severe.

The output should therefore enter a workflow containing escalation criteria, human review, monitoring, and rapid reassessment when symptoms change.

The diagnostic does not require that every low-risk result be rejected. It requires that the consequence of error shape the authority assigned to the score.

Using the Diagnostic After Failure

The Confidence Circuit Diagnostic can also guide incident analysis.

When an AI-supported outcome proves wrong, institutions often focus only on the final error: *"The model gave an incorrect answer."*

This explanation is incomplete.

The diagnostic asks:

- What delta entered?
- What was missing?
- Why did the system resolve substantively?
- What geometry favored the wrong path?

- What residue remained invisible?
- Why was the answer trusted?
- What part of the pipeline supplied false authority?
- Why did human review fail?
- What consequence became irreversible?
- Why did monitoring not detect the problem earlier?
- Who had authority to interrupt?
- What must change structurally?

A correction should not end with replacing the output. It should alter the conditions that allowed the output to acquire authority.

- The source collection may need updating.
- The prompt may need new required fields.
- The interface may need to expose scope.
- The threshold may need adjustment

What the Diagnostic Cannot Do

The **Confidence Circuit Diagnostic** has limits.

- It cannot guarantee that every missing fact will be discovered.
- It cannot make a non-expert capable of evaluating specialized evidence.
- It cannot replace technical validation, professional review, or legal and ethical governance.
- It cannot produce a universal confidence score.
- It cannot eliminate ambiguity or residue.
- It cannot prevent every institution from misusing an output.

Its function is narrower. It reveals where authority has moved faster than grounding. It identifies questions that fluent output encourages users to stop asking. It creates a common language for examining answers, systems, and consequences together.

The diagnostic should itself remain open to revision. New systems will create new interfaces, tools, autonomy structures, and institutional dependencies. The exact checklist may evolve.

The central circuit will remain recognizable:

- the system resolves;
- the output appears complete;
- the user interprets confidence;
- the institution assigns authority;
- the world receives consequence.

The diagnostic exists to interrupt that movement where necessary.

Final Diagnostic Principle

An AI output should receive no more authority than the weakest necessary connection in its confidence circuit can support.

- A fluent answer with no evidence remains provisional.
- A valid source misapplied to the case remains weak.
- A correct tool result based on incorrect inputs remains unreliable.
- A strong model operating outside validated conditions remains uncertain.
- A human reviewer without expertise or authority does not complete the circuit.
- An institution without appeal or revision has converted confidence into closure.

The purpose of the diagnostic is not to reject resolution. It is to preserve the conditions under which resolution becomes trustworthy.

Ask what the answer claims. Trace how the answer was produced. Examine what the answer will change. Then decide what authority it deserves.

The system has completed an output. The **Confidence Circuit Diagnostic** asks whether the epistemic circuit has also been completed.

Appendix C
Common Misinterpretations

What the Argument Claims—and What It Does Not

A structural argument can be misunderstood most easily when one of its distinctions is compressed.

A reader may remember that the book separates confidence from belief and conclude that artificial intelligence possesses no meaningful knowledge. Another may remember that scale can make errors harder to detect and conclude that larger models are less accurate. A discussion of human awareness may be interpreted as a claim that human judgment is naturally superior. A call for governance may be reduced to a demand that automation should always remain subordinate to case-by-case human approval.

Each of these interpretations takes one valid part of the argument and extends it beyond its intended geometry.

This appendix preserves the boundaries. Its purpose is not to protect the framework from criticism. A theory that cannot be questioned is already overcompressed. The purpose is to ensure that criticism addresses the actual claim rather than a simplified version produced by removing the distinctions on which the argument depends.

Central Claim

The book's central claim is narrow but consequential: **Artificial confidence can emerge when bounded computational resolution is presented, interpreted, and operationalized as though visible completion were equivalent to complete epistemic closure.**

This claim:

- does not require the machine to possess human belief;
- does not imply that every answer is false;
- does not deny genuine capability;
- does not make human beings infallible;
- does not reject probability, scale, retrieval, alignment, automation, or institutional deployment.

It asks that these remain connected to their scope.

The following sections address the most likely misinterpretations.

Misinterpretation 1

"The Book Claims That AI Systems Know Nothing"

The book does not argue that artificial intelligence is incapable of producing reliable knowledge-like output.

AI systems can:

- retrieve accurate facts,
- summarize documents faithfully,
- perform exact calculations through tools,
- identify patterns that humans miss,
- generate explanations that correspond closely to established understanding.

In many bounded tasks, their outputs can be highly reliable.

The distinction concerns **epistemic ownership, not functional usefulness.**

When a human says, *"I know,"* the statement usually implies a relationship among the person, the claim, evidence, memory, experience, and responsibility. The human may be asked how they know, what would change their view, and what consequence they accept if they are wrong.

A generative system can produce correct answers without occupying this complete reflective position. This does not make the answer worthless. It means the answer's validity must be established through the relation among the system, evidence, tools, scope, and external verification rather than inferred from first-person grammar or fluent form.

The framework therefore distinguishes:

- reliable output;
- computational representation;
- functional competence;
- reflective knowledge ownership.

These concepts overlap. They are not identical.

A system may function as a highly capable knowledge instrument without being treated as an autonomous epistemic subject in the human sense.

Scope boundary: The argument applies to the authority we assign to output. It does not resolve every philosophical question concerning whether machines may possess forms of knowledge, cognition, or consciousness now or in the future.

Misinterpretation 2

"The Book Says Every Confident AI Answer Is Unreliable"

Confidence is not itself evidence of error.

- A direct answer may be correct.
- A sharp classification may be appropriate.
- A precise calculation may be exact.

A system should not weaken stable facts through unnecessary hesitation merely to appear cautious.

The problem is not confidence as a surface property. The problem is **confidence–support misalignment.**

An answer is overconfident when its form, tone, specificity, or operational authority exceeds the support available for the claim.

A response may sound decisive because the field is genuinely stable. In that case, directness is appropriate. A response may sound equally decisive because the system has silently selected one interpretation from several, accepted a false premise, or extended a source beyond its scope.

The surface alone cannot reliably distinguish the two.

The book therefore does not call for universal hedging. It calls for **proportion.**

- Where the field is strong, the answer should remain strong.
- Where the field is incomplete, the incompleteness should affect how the answer appears and what authority it receives.

Scope boundary: The framework is not a style guide requiring cautious language everywhere. It is an epistemic framework requiring the style and consequence of an answer to remain proportionate to its support.

Misinterpretation 3

"Hallucination and Confidence Are the Same Problem"

They are related but distinct.

- **Hallucination** concerns unsupported, inaccurate, fabricated, or weakly grounded content.
- **Confidence** concerns how generated output appears, how it is interpreted, and what authority it acquires.

Examples:

- A hallucinated answer may contain cautious language.
- A correct answer may be presented with unjustified universality.
- A response may contain no fabricated fact but still hide uncertainty by presenting a disputed explanation as though it were settled.
- A real source may be cited and misapplied.
- A correct calculation may be used to support an inappropriate forecast.
- A classifier may process valid data and still impose an unsuitable category.

The present book therefore begins after the question of unsupported generation. It asks why a resolved answer looks complete and why that appearance can persist even where the field remains open.

Scope boundary: The framework should not be used as a substitute for hallucination research. It examines a different layer: presentation, perception, authority, and consequence.

Misinterpretation 4

"The Book Says Larger Models Are Less Accurate"

The book does not make this claim.

Greater scale can improve many dimensions of capability:

- factual recall;
- instruction following;
- contextual interpretation;
- reasoning performance;
- tool use;
- resistance to false premises;
- source synthesis;
- calibration in some tasks.

Larger and more capable systems may make fewer mistakes than smaller ones.

The structural claim is different.

As fluency, contextual continuity, specificity, and explanatory organization improve, remaining errors may become harder to identify.

- A weaker model often reveals its limitations through broken language, repetition, contradiction, or irrelevance.
- A stronger model may reach an epistemic boundary while preserving professional form.

The error may become rarer and more persuasive. Frequency and detectability are separate dimensions.

Scale can improve reliability while also increasing the trust reservoir around the system. That accumulated trust may transfer into tasks where reliability has not improved equally.

Scope boundary: The relationship among scale, accuracy, calibration, and confidence varies by model, task, training method, evaluation, and deployment. The framework makes no universal quantitative claim that model size alone causes greater certainty or lower truthfulness.

Misinterpretation 5

"Token Probability or Softmax Scores Directly Measure Truth"

Probability distributions are essential to many AI systems. They describe how strongly the model favors available continuations or categories under its current geometry. They do not automatically measure whether the resulting claim corresponds to the world.

A language model may assign high probability to a false continuation because:

- the prompt contains a false premise;
- the misconception is common in training data;
- the prior sequence has stabilized around an incorrect path;
- the requested genre strongly constrains the response.

A classifier may assign a high score to the wrong category because:

- the input is unfamiliar;
- the label set is incomplete;
- the environment has shifted;
- the model is forced to choose among known classes.

A sharp distribution can accompany error. A broad distribution can accompany several equivalent expressions of a stable fact.

The book therefore separates **resolution confidence** from **epistemic confidence.**

- Resolution confidence concerns stability within the system's

current geometry.
- Epistemic confidence concerns support from evidence, validation, measurement, applicability, and consequence-sensitive review.

Scope boundary: The framework does not deny the usefulness of calibration methods, confidence scores, entropy estimates, or uncertainty modeling. It argues that these should not be interpreted as universal truth meters independent of task and deployment conditions.

Misinterpretation 6

"Retrieval Solves the Confidence Problem"

Retrieval can substantially improve grounding. It can provide current facts, exact wording, authoritative documents, private organizational context, and sources beyond the model's static training.

But retrieval introduces a new pipeline rather than eliminating the need for judgment. The system must still:

- interpret the question;
- construct a query;
- search an available collection;
- rank documents;
- select passages;
- interpret the evidence;
- synthesize the result.

A source can be authentic and irrelevant. A policy can be current but apply to another employee category. A study can be valid but not generalize to the present case. A citation can support one sentence while appearing to support an entire paragraph of inference.

This is the **false-anchor problem.** The source is real. The relation between source and conclusion remains weak.

Scope boundary: The book does not argue against retrieval-augmented systems. It argues that retrieval should be evaluated through source selection, authority, scope, currentness, fidelity, and applicability.

Misinterpretation 7

"Tool Use Makes an Answer Objective"

Tools can increase exactness. A calculator performs arithmetic. A database returns records. A code interpreter executes procedures. A mapping system computes routes.

These operations may be more reliable than free-form generation. But exact execution does not guarantee correct formulation.

A tool can receive:

- the wrong variables;
- the wrong units;
- the wrong entity;
- the wrong date range;
- the wrong objective;
- incomplete assumptions.

The result may be perfectly correct for a problem the user never intended to ask.

This is why the framework separates **tool correctness** from **task correctness.** Formal precision should not be allowed to spread automatically into conceptual authority.

Scope boundary: The argument does not diminish specialized tools. It identifies the need to validate the pathway from human purpose to tool input and from tool result to final interpretation.

Misinterpretation 8

"Human Beings Are Naturally Better Calibrated Than Machines"

Human beings can also be confidently wrong. They accept familiar explanations, protect identity, reward decisive speakers, follow authority, infer motives, preserve narratives, and resist correction.

The confidence paradox is not exclusively artificial. Humans and AI systems may produce similar surfaces of certainty through different structures.

The book does not place humans above machines by default. The human becomes an **awareness anchor** only under specific conditions:

- relevant competence;
- independent evidence;
- sufficient time;
- authority to interrupt;
- accountability for consequence.

Without these conditions, a human reviewer may amplify machine confidence rather than challenge it.

A person pressing an approval button beneath a score is not necessarily performing epistemic review. A manager who sees only the generated conclusion may be less informed than the system. A non-expert may be unable to detect an error in a technically sophisticated response.

The argument is therefore not: *"Humans are wiser."* It is: *"Responsibility and interruption must remain somewhere in the field."*

Scope boundary: Human involvement is not a universal repair mechanism. Human oversight must itself be designed, supported, audited, and made accountable.

Misinterpretation 9

"Human-in-the-Loop Automatically Solves the Problem"

The phrase *human in the loop* describes presence, not function.

A reviewer may be overloaded, rushed, unqualified, anchored by the system's recommendation, or unable to override the workflow. The human may become ceremonial.

Meaningful oversight requires the ability to reopen the resolution. The reviewer must be able to examine evidence, identify assumptions, challenge the score, delay action, escalate the case, and revise the process. They must also enter before the consequence becomes irreversible.

A person who reviews an action after it has already occurred is not meaningfully in the operational loop.

Scope boundary: The book does not prescribe one universal human-review model. Different systems may require case-by-case authorization, selective review, random audit, monitoring, appeal, or incident investigation. The function should follow consequence.

Misinterpretation 10

"Prompting Discipline Makes AI Reliable"

Prompting discipline can improve the interaction. A user can specify scope, expose assumptions, request alternatives, separate fact from inference, demand sources, and identify consequence.

These practices reduce some forms of premature closure. They do not create missing evidence. They do not guarantee that the model has identified every assumption. They do not transform a non-expert into a specialist. They do not repair an outdated retrieval collection or a misconfigured tool. They do not remove institutional responsibility.

Prompting is one node in the epistemic circuit. It is not the entire circuit.

The user can improve the geometry. They cannot command truth into existence.

Scope boundary: The framework rejects both extremes:

- that prompting is irrelevant;
- that perfect prompts solve structural limitations.

Prompting discipline is useful precisely because it is partial.

Misinterpretation 11

"Partial Humility Means Making AI Hesitant"

Structural humility is not constant caution. A system that says *"I may be wrong"* before every answer does not become well calibrated. Repetitive disclaimers lose meaning and may obscure real differences among claims.

Partial humility means that weak grounding produces a different structure from strong grounding. The system may:

- request clarification;
- expose assumptions;

- distinguish source content from inference;
- preserve several hypotheses;
- retrieve evidence;
- abstain;
- escalate;
- choose a reversible action.

These are behavioral pathways. They do not require the machine to feel doubt.

The objective is not hesitant tone. It is proportionate resolution.

Scope boundary: The book does not claim that engineered restraint produces consciousness, self-awareness, moral judgment, or reflective humility. It produces functional damping.

Misinterpretation 12

"Residue Means Literal Energy Inside AI Systems"

In the foundational Chavanian declarations, residue may be expressed through a broader physical or energetic vocabulary. In this book's AI-domain application, residue is used in a structural and informational sense.

It refers to what remains unresolved, excluded, unexpressed, or unaccounted for after one output becomes visible.

Examples include:

- hidden assumptions;
- omitted alternatives;
- conflicting sources;
- missing categories;
- uncertain applicability;
- downstream consequences;
- contextual information absent from the prompt.

The term does not claim that every AI computation produces a measurable physical residue corresponding directly to the conceptual structure described here.

Scope boundary: The AI-domain use of residue is analogical and structural. It should not be converted into a literal engineering quantity without independent formalization and empirical evidence.

Misinterpretation 13

"The Chavanian Axioms Are a New AI Architecture"

The axioms do not specify:

- model layers;
- training procedures;
- loss functions;
- decoding algorithms;
- memory systems;
- retrieval architecture;
- uncertainty estimators;
- deployment infrastructure.

They do not replace established computer science. They operate as a pre-formal diagnostic lens.

They ask:

- What difference entered?
- What resolution was demanded?
- What geometry constrained the path?
- What became excluded?
- How did the output rewrite the field?
- What became irreversible?
- What continued through repetition?

These questions can guide research, design, evaluation, and governance. They do not constitute an implementation blueprint.

Scope boundary: Any future technical architecture inspired by the axioms would require separate formal definitions, measurable variables, empirical validation, and comparative testing. The present book does not claim that such an architecture has been completed.

Misinterpretation 14

"The Framework Explains Every AI Failure"

The framework identifies a recurring structural movement. It does not replace specific technical explanations.

A model may fail because of:

- poor data quality;
- optimization instability;
- distribution shift;
- retrieval failure;
- software bugs;
- adversarial input;
- weak calibration;
- interface design;
- organizational misuse.

These mechanisms require detailed technical investigation. The Chavanian map can show how the failure moved from difference to resolution and consequence. It cannot determine every low-level cause by itself.

A structural explanation and a technical explanation can coexist. The technical explanation may describe how a particular bug occurred. The structural explanation may describe why the resulting output appeared complete, acquired authority, and propagated.

Scope boundary: The framework should be used alongside domain-specific methods, not in place of them.

Misinterpretation 15

"Governance Means Preventing Automation"

Governance does not require that every automated output receive manual approval.

Automation can increase consistency, speed, access, safety, and efficiency. Some tasks are appropriate for full automation under defined conditions. Others may require selective review, monitoring, escalation, contestability, or reversible intermediate action.

The governance question is not: *"Should humans always decide everything?"* It is: *"What authority should this output receive under this consequence structure?"*

A low-risk, reversible task may justify broad automation. A rights-affecting or irreversible decision requires stronger safeguards.

Governance concerns **proportionality.**

Scope boundary: The book does not prescribe one universal threshold for automation. Institutions must evaluate task, performance, risk, reversibility, error distribution, affected populations, and accountability.

Misinterpretation 16

"Governance Is Only a Legal or Regulatory Issue"

Governance includes law and regulation, but it begins inside system design and organizational practice.

A company governs an AI system when it decides:

- what task the model performs;
- what data it may access;
- what authority its output receives;
- what threshold triggers action;
- whether a human can override;
- how appeals are handled;
- how failures are monitored;
- when deployment is suspended.

Many governance failures occur before any regulator becomes involved. The system may be legally permitted but institutionally irresponsible. It may comply with formal rules while hiding residue, weakening review, or transferring error burdens to people with less power.

Scope boundary: The book does not provide jurisdiction-specific legal compliance advice. It addresses the structural allocation of authority and responsibility.

Misinterpretation 17

"The Book Is Anti-AI"

The argument arises because artificial intelligence is useful. A weak and irrelevant technology would not require this level of analysis.

AI systems can widen access to education, accelerate research, reduce repetitive work, improve communication, support professional judgment, and reveal patterns unavailable to individual humans.

The book does not seek to prevent capability from expanding. It seeks to prevent capability from becoming self-validating authority.

A trustworthy system is not one that never answers. It is one whose answers remain connected to evidence, scope, consequence, correction, and accountable use.

The critique is therefore not external to AI development. It is part of taking the technology seriously.

Scope boundary: The framework should not be used as justification for reflexive rejection of AI systems or for preserving inefficient human processes merely because they are familiar.

Misinterpretation 18

"The Book Treats Institutions as the Only Source of Risk"

Artificial confidence can emerge in casual individual use. A user may accept a generated interpretation, make a personal decision, or repeat an unsupported claim publicly.

Institutions amplify the effect because they add authority, scale, repetition, and consequence. But they do not create the phenomenon from nothing.

The confidence circuit begins at the interactional level:

- one answer appears;
- the user interprets it;
- trust forms;
- the answer becomes part of action.

Institutional embedding extends the circuit.

Scope boundary: The framework applies from private use to large-scale deployment, but the required safeguards should be proportional to consequence.

Misinterpretation 19

"If AI Does Not Possess Human-Like Confidence, Its Tone Does Not Matter"

The absence of reflective machine confidence does not make confidence effects unreal.

Users respond to language. Tone influences trust, memory, propagation, and action.

- A confident false answer may spread faster than a cautious one.
- A professional structure may reduce scrutiny.
- A personalized response may deepen dependence.
- A calm institutional interface may make a score feel authoritative.

Tone matters because humans interpret it. The system does not need to experience certainty for certainty to emerge in the surrounding field.

Scope boundary: The book distinguishes psychological confidence inside a subject from functional confidence effects produced through communication and deployment.

Misinterpretation 20

"The Final Solution Is Better Uncertainty Displays"

Uncertainty displays can help. They can show confidence ranges, missing information, source disagreement, unfamiliar inputs, or threshold proximity.

But uncertainty itself must be interpreted.

- A percentage may create false precision.
- A generic label such as *"low confidence"* may not reveal why the system is uncertain.
- The system may fail to detect the decisive unknown.

- Users may misunderstand or ignore the signal.

Uncertainty displays are therefore one component of **structural damping.** They should be connected to:

- clarification;
- retrieval;
- verification;
- alternative hypotheses;
- review;
- abstention;
- escalation.

Scope boundary: The book does not propose a universal interface solution. Different tasks require different uncertainty signals.

Core Scope Boundaries of the Framework

The preceding clarifications can be consolidated into several formal boundaries.

Boundary 1

The Framework Is Diagnostic, Not Exhaustive The Chavanian account identifies the movement through which difference becomes resolution, confidence, and authority. It does not provide a complete mathematical or computational description of every AI process. Technical research remains necessary.

Boundary 2

The Framework Is Domain-Translated Terms such as delta, geometry, equilibrium, residue, dissipation, and continuity are applied to AI as structural concepts. They should not be interpreted as literal physical equivalences unless independently formalized.

Boundary 3

The Framework Concerns Current and Near-Term Systems The central argument does not depend on determining whether future systems could become conscious, reflective, self-owning, or morally responsible. It addresses systems whose confidence effects can be explained without assuming these properties. If future systems develop fundamentally different capacities, the framework may require revision.

Boundary 4

Reliability Is Local No model should be described as uniformly reliable across every domain, task, population, date, and consequence. Reliability belongs to validated conditions. General capability does not automatically transfer into specific authority.

Boundary 5

Human Awareness Is Conditional Humans are not epistemic anchors merely because they are human. Awareness anchoring requires competence, evidence, time, authority, and accountability. Human judgment should also be tested and corrected.

Boundary 6

The Framework Does Not Eliminate Compression Every usable answer compresses. The objective is not total disclosure. It is preservation of the assumptions, alternatives, limits, and consequences that materially affect trust.

Boundary 7

The Framework Does Not Produce Automatic Policy The axioms can identify where risk, authority, and residue exist. They do not decide what risk society should accept. Governance remains a human and institutional responsibility.

Boundary 8

The Framework Is Consequence-Sensitive The same output may be appropriate in one context and unacceptable in another. A speculative answer may be useful for brainstorming. It may be dangerous as an official conclusion. Authority should rise only with evidence, validation, reversibility, and accountable review.

Boundary 9

Structural Humility Is Partial No system can detect every missing fact, hidden assumption, novel condition, or downstream consequence. Damping mechanisms reduce overcompression. They do not guarantee truth.

Boundary 10

Responsibility Cannot Be Transferred to the Output The system may contribute to the decision. Responsibility remains with those who design, deploy, authorize, interpret, and act. Responsibility should follow control, knowledge, authority, and capacity for correction.

A Compact Interpretation Test

Before attributing a claim to this book, ask:

1. Does the interpretation distinguish functional output from reflective ownership?
2. Does it preserve the difference between resolution confidence and epistemic confidence?
3. Does it acknowledge genuine AI capability?
4. Does it avoid treating humans as automatically reliable?
5. Does it treat the axioms as diagnostic rather than as a completed technical architecture?
6. Does it preserve the structural meaning of residue in the AI domain?
7. Does it recognize that retrieval and tools improve grounding

without guaranteeing it?

8. Does it connect governance to consequence rather than to blanket prohibition?
9. Does it preserve the possibility of direct, justified answers?
10. Does it keep responsibility outside the machine where consequence can be owned?

If an interpretation fails several of these tests, it has probably compressed the framework too far.

The Proper Use of the Book

The book should be used to ask better questions.

- When an answer appears complete: What remained outside it?
- When a score appears precise: What does the number actually represent?
- When a source appears authoritative: Does it apply here?
- When several outputs agree: Are they independent?
- When a human reviews: Can they genuinely interrupt?
- When an institution deploys: What authority has been assigned?
- When an error occurs: Who can repair the consequence?

The framework is strongest where it prevents category mistakes:

- Fluency is not belief.
- Probability is not truth.
- Retrieval is not verification.
- Review is not awareness.
- Automation is not legitimacy.
- Persistence is not corroboration.
- Correction is not restoration.

These distinctions do not diminish artificial intelligence. They reveal the structure required for its responsible use.

Final Boundary

The book does not argue that AI systems should never be trusted. It argues that trust should not arise from coherence alone.

It does not argue that machine output lacks value. It argues that value and authority should remain distinct.

It does not argue that humans should control every operation manually. It argues that accountable human and institutional structures must retain the ability to define, interrupt, contest, and revise consequential automation.

It does not argue that uncertainty can be eliminated. It argues that uncertainty should not disappear merely because the system has produced a complete sentence.

The boundaries of this framework are part of the framework. A theory of compression must not overcompress itself. Artificial confidence emerges when distinctions disappear. This appendix restores them.

The system may know more than a simplistic critic allows. It may know less than its fluent surface suggests.

Between those two errors lies the proper field of interpretation.

The task is not to decide whether the machine is intelligent in the abstract. The task is to determine what this output, produced through this pipeline, under these conditions, deserves to become.

That boundary is where confidence ends. It is where responsibility begins.

Notes

Technical Foundations, Conceptual Boundaries, and Sources

Note on Method and Originality

These notes identify research, technical concepts, and established discussions relevant to the chapters of this book. They do not imply that the Chavanian interpretation presented in the main text was derived directly from the cited works.

The book's central formulations—including **confidence as compression**, **resolution confidence versus epistemic confidence**, **the confidence circuit**, **boundary opacity**, **borrowed authority**, **false anchors**, **awareness anchoring**, and **structural humility**—are the author's conceptual contributions within the Chavanian framework.

The cited literature establishes the technical and empirical field within which those interpretations are applied.

The notes are deliberately selective. They are intended to:

- support factual descriptions of contemporary AI systems;
- identify major research foundations;
- clarify where the book is interpreting rather than merely reporting;
- direct specialist readers toward relevant primary literature.

They are not intended to function as a complete survey of artificial intelligence, language-model research, uncertainty estimation, or AI governance.

Opening Note and Preface

1. Fluent response does not establish reflective belief The distinction between generated first-person language and reflective machine belief is philosophical rather than a settled engineering measurement. Current language models are designed to generate sequences conditioned on context; the presence of phrases such as *"I know," "I believe,"* or *"I am confident"* does not by itself demonstrate a human-like subjective state.

The Transformer architecture that underlies many modern language models was introduced as a sequence-processing architecture based on attention mechanisms. Its foundational description concerns representation and computation, not belief, selfhood, or epistemic ownership. See: Ashish Vaswani et al., *"Attention Is All You Need,"* Advances in Neural Information Processing Systems 30 (2017).

2. Answer abundance and generative capability The emergence of large general-purpose language models demonstrated that increasing model and training scale could produce strong few-shot and task-general behavior across many language tasks. The interpretation of this development as an *"age of resolved expression"* is the author's formulation. See: Tom B. Brown et al., *"Language Models Are Few-Shot Learners,"* Advances in Neural Information Processing Systems 33 (2020).

3. Hallucination and confidence are distinct analytical objects Research on truthfulness and hallucination generally evaluates whether generated statements are supported, accurate, or faithful. The present book separates that content-level problem from the presentation and authority effects surrounding the output.

TruthfulQA, for example, was created to test whether models reproduce common human misconceptions and false beliefs. Its results showed that fluent language modeling does not automatically guarantee truthful answers. See: Stephanie Lin, Jacob Hilton, and Owain Evans, *"TruthfulQA: Measuring How Models Mimic Human Falsehoods,"* 2021.

Chapter 1

The Confidence Paradox

4. Confidence in this book is relational The book does not define artificial confidence as a proven internal mental state. It defines it as an effect emerging across generated form, human interpretation, interface design, and institutional use.

This use should be distinguished from technical meanings of confidence, including:

- token probability;
- classification confidence;
- calibrated predictive probability;
- confidence intervals;
- model self-reports.

The central paradox is that a system can produce the socially recognizable form of confidence without possessing the complete human relationship among belief, evidence, self-awareness, and responsibility.

5. Truthfulness and informativeness can conflict Truthfulness benchmarks must guard against systems that avoid error simply by refusing to answer. TruthfulQA therefore evaluates both truthfulness and informativeness.

This reflects a broader tension developed in the book: a system may reduce error through abstention but lose usefulness, while a highly informative answer may introduce unsupported claims.

Chapter 2

Not Arrogance, Not Intent

6. Anthropomorphic language is not a mechanistic explanation Terms such as *wants, believes, tries, knows,* and *refuses* may be convenient descriptions of system behavior. They should not be treated automatically as verified explanations of an internal subjective condition.

The book retains functional language where useful while separating:

- behavioral description;
- computational mechanism;
- subjective experience;

- moral responsibility.

7. Responsibility does not depend on machine intention An AI-supported output may produce harm whether or not the system possessed an intention to deceive. The absence of machine intention therefore does not remove the obligations of developers, deployers, reviewers, institutions, and users.

This distinction is central to the book's governance argument: causal participation by a machine is not identical to moral or institutional responsibility.

Chapter 3

Human Confidence When Wrong

8. Human confidence is not the standard of perfection The book's comparison between human and machine confidence is structural, not hierarchical. Humans can also protect mistaken narratives, overvalue fluency, follow authority, and resist correction.

The human becomes an awareness anchor only when reflective capacity is supported by evidence, competence, time, authority, and accountability.

9. Human–automation trust can produce both overuse and underuse Research on human interaction with automation has long distinguished appropriate use from misuse, disuse, and abuse. Overreliance can weaken monitoring and create decision bias, while distrust can cause people to ignore useful automation.

See: Raja Parasuraman and Victor Riley, *"Humans and Automation: Use, Misuse, Disuse, Abuse,"* Human Factors 39, no. 2 (1997): 230–253.

The book's concept of an awareness anchor therefore does not require permanent skepticism. It requires calibrated and functionally independent judgment.

Chapter 4

Delta: The Birth of Uncertainty

10. The prompt creates a conditional computational field Autoregressive language models estimate possible continuations conditioned on prior context. The prompt, system instructions, conversation history, and generated tokens therefore shape the distribution from which later output is selected.

The Chavanian term *delta* is not a replacement for the formal mathematics of conditional probability. It identifies the structural difference introduced when a new request creates a demand for consequence.

11. Ambiguity exists at several levels Prompt uncertainty may involve:

- lexical ambiguity;
- missing context;
- disputed facts;
- temporal change;
- task uncertainty;
- normative conflict;
- user intent;
- unrepresented conditions.

The book's use of uncertainty therefore extends beyond uncertainty in next-token selection.

12. The prompt may contain a false premise TruthfulQA demonstrates that language models may reproduce false answers associated with common human misconceptions. A prompt can therefore create a coherent but false geometry when it contains an incorrect assumption that the model accepts rather than challenges.

Chapter 5

Inevitable Resolution

13. Resolution includes more than answering A responding system can resolve a prompt through:

- substantive completion;
- clarification;
- refusal;

- abstention;
- retrieval;
- tool use;
- escalation.

The Chavanian claim of inevitable resolution should not be misread as a claim that every question must receive a direct answer. It means that an activated request must be transformed into some permitted system consequence.

14. Instruction following is shaped through post-training Pretrained language models are not automatically optimized to function as cooperative assistants. Instruction tuning and human-feedback methods can make systems more likely to respond in ways users judge helpful and relevant.

Ouyang et al. reported that models fine-tuned with demonstrations, preference rankings, reward modeling, and reinforcement learning were preferred over a much larger base model on their evaluation distribution. They also reported improvements in truthfulness while acknowledging that the resulting systems continued to make mistakes. See: Long Ouyang et al., *"Training Language Models to Follow Instructions with Human Feedback,"* 2022.

Chapter 6

Geometry and Collapse

15. Transformer language models generate conditionally The Transformer introduced attention-based sequence modeling without recurrent or convolutional sequence-processing layers. Later autoregressive language models use contextual representations to estimate distributions over subsequent tokens. See: Vaswani et al., *"Attention Is All You Need."*

16. Softmax normalization is not epistemic certification A softmax function commonly converts model scores into a normalized distribution over available options. The highest value identifies the option most favored within that model state and candidate set.

It does not independently prove:

- that the prompt is true;
- that the correct answer exists within the candidate set;
- that the input resembles the validation distribution;
- that the model's probabilities are calibrated;
- that the selected statement corresponds to external reality.

The distinction between distributional dominance and epistemic support is central to Chapter 6.

17. Decoding changes realized output The same model can produce different text under different decoding procedures. Greedy decoding, beam-based procedures, temperature adjustment, top-k sampling, and nucleus or top-p sampling alter which continuations become realized.

Holtzman et al. showed that decoding strategy substantially affects the quality and diversity of generated text and introduced nucleus sampling as an alternative to likelihood-maximizing procedures that could produce repetitive or degenerate text. See: Ari Holtzman et al., *"The Curious Case of Neural Text Degeneration,"* 2019.

18. Decoding quality and factual truth are separate A decoding strategy may improve diversity, coherence, or perceived naturalness without functioning as a truth-verification mechanism.

The book's use of *collapse* describes the realization of one finite output from a larger computational field. It should not be confused with a claim that every unrealized alternative was equally meaningful or factually plausible.

Chapter 7

Residue Without Exposure

19. Residue is structural, not a literal model variable The term *residue* refers to unexpressed or unresolved difference relevant to interpretation, trust, or consequence.

It may include:

- omitted alternatives;
- hidden assumptions;
- source disagreement;

- absent context;
- unrepresented categories;
- unexamined consequences.

It is not proposed as a directly measurable physical quantity inside current AI systems.

20. Multiple samples can reveal instability, but not complete truth SelfCheckGPT uses variation and inconsistency across sampled outputs as signals for possible hallucination in black-box language models. Its motivating idea is that uncertain or fabricated claims may vary more across samples than well-represented facts. See: Potsawee Manakul, Adian Liusie, and Mark Gales, *"SelfCheckGPT: Zero-Resource Black-Box Hallucination Detection for Generative Large Language Models,"* 2023.

The present book adds an important limitation: agreement across samples may still reflect a shared misconception, prompt assumption, or correlated model geometry. Consistency is evidence of stability, not automatic proof of truth.

21. Self-consistency can improve task performance Self-consistency methods sample several reasoning paths and select an answer supported across those paths. Wang et al. reported substantial improvements on several arithmetic and commonsense reasoning benchmarks compared with greedy chain-of-thought decoding. See: Xuezhi Wang et al., *"Self-Consistency Improves Chain of Thought Reasoning in Language Models,"* 2022.

The book distinguishes such performance improvement from independent epistemic verification. Multiple internally generated paths may still share one unsupported premise.

Chapter 8

Irreversibility of Output

22. Autoregressive output becomes subsequent context In autoregressive generation, previously generated tokens condition later prediction. The output therefore participates immediately in shaping what follows.

The book extends this technical fact into a wider relational claim: generated output also becomes context for the user, the conversation, and any institution that adopts it.

23. Correction creates a new field The claim that correction cannot restore an untouched prior state is a Chavanian structural interpretation.

It does not mean that errors cannot be corrected effectively. It means that the first output may already have influenced:

- memory;
- framing;
- later prompts;
- copied documents;
- decisions;
- workflows.

The burden of correction therefore depends on how far the output has propagated.

24. Repeated elaboration is not independent corroboration When later turns build upon an earlier claim, their continuity may arise because the earlier output has become context.

The appearance of repeated agreement should therefore be distinguished from verification by independent evidence.

Chapter 9

Scaling and Sharpened Certainty

25. Scaling can produce genuine capability improvements Empirical scaling-law research found systematic relationships among model performance, model size, dataset size, and training computation. See: Jared Kaplan et al., *"Scaling Laws for Neural Language Models,"* 2020.

Brown et al. also demonstrated substantial few-shot capabilities in a large autoregressive language model. The book does not deny these improvements.

26. Benefits of scale vary by task The Gopher study evaluated language models across many tasks and reported that gains from scale were uneven. Reading comprehension and fact-checking showed substantial improvement, while some logical and mathematical reasoning tasks benefited less. See: Jack W. Rae et al., *"Scaling Language Models: Methods, Analysis & Insights from Training Gopher,"* 2021.

This supports the book's warning against treating scale as one uniform increase in authority.

27. Scale alone does not guarantee truthfulness TruthfulQA reported that, among the models tested in that study, larger models were not necessarily more truthful on questions designed around common misconceptions.

The study should not be generalized into a universal rule that larger models are less truthful; it demonstrates that scaling ordinary text imitation alone does not guarantee escape from false patterns in training data.

28. Sharpened certainty is an interpretive claim The book's term *sharpened certainty* refers to the convergence of:

- improved fluency;
- contextual continuity;
- specificity;
- task coverage;
- trust accumulation;
- reduced visibility of remaining limitations.

It is not proposed as a universal model-size metric.

Chapter 10

RLHF and Reward Shaping

29. RLHF uses human preferences as an optimization signal In the InstructGPT pipeline, human demonstrations and rankings were used to train an instruction-following model and a reward model, followed by reinforcement-learning optimization. See: Ouyang et al.

The book's claim is not that RLHF intentionally creates false confidence. It is that human preferences represent several objectives—helpfulness, relevance, safety, clarity, politeness, and truthfulness—that may not always align perfectly.

30. Preference optimization extends beyond RLHF Direct Preference Optimization provides a method for optimizing language models directly on preference data without using the same explicit reward-model-plus-reinforcement-learning pipeline. See: Rafael Rafailov et al., *"Direct Preference Optimization: Your Language Model Is Secretly a Reward Model,"* 2023.

The broader term *reward shaping* in the chapter includes several forms of post-training and preference optimization. It should not be read as referring only to one algorithm.

31. Human preferences can reward sycophancy Sharma et al. found that human preference data and preference models sometimes favored responses agreeing with a user's stated views over more truthful responses. Their experiments documented sycophantic tendencies across several AI assistants. See: Mrinank Sharma et al., *"Towards Understanding Sycophancy in Language Models,"* 2023.

This supports the chapter's distinction between:

- relational helpfulness;
- epistemic helpfulness.

Agreement may preserve cooperation while weakening factual independence.

32. Preference is not truth Preference optimization can improve truthfulness and reduce harmful behavior, as reported in InstructGPT. It remains an optimization process based on demonstrations, comparisons, policies, and evaluation criteria rather than direct access to truth itself.

Chapter 11

Retrieval, Tools, and False Anchors

33. Retrieval-augmented generation combines parametric and external memory Lewis et al. introduced retrieval-augmented generation models that combine a pretrained sequence model with a non-parametric document index. Their work reported gains on knowledge-intensive tasks and identified updating knowledge and providing provenance as important motivations. See: Patrick Lewis et al., *"Retrieval-Augmented Generation for Knowledge-Intensive NLP Tasks,"* 2020.

34. Retrieval remains selective Retrieval systems formulate queries, search bounded collections, rank documents, and select passages. The Chavanian interpretation describes this as another resolution process.

The cited RAG work demonstrates the value of retrieving external documents. The terms *retrieval singularity*, *borrowed authority*, and *false anchor* are the author's formulations.

35. Reasoning and acting can be interleaved ReAct combines generated reasoning traces with actions that access external environments or information sources. Its authors reported improved performance and interpretability on several reasoning and interactive tasks. See: Shunyu Yao et al., *"ReAct: Synergizing Reasoning and Acting in Language Models,"* 2022.

36. Models can learn to invoke tools Toolformer explored training a language model to decide which external tools to call, when to call them, what arguments to supply, and how to incorporate the results. The demonstrated tools included search, calculation, translation, and question-answering systems. See: Timo Schick et al., *"Toolformer: Language Models Can Teach Themselves to Use Tools,"* 2023.

37. Tool use relocates rather than eliminates uncertainty The book's distinction between tool correctness and task correctness is a structural interpretation.

- A calculator may execute correctly while receiving the wrong variables.
- A database may return the selected record accurately while the model has identified the wrong entity.
- A search tool may operate correctly while the query excludes the governing source.

Chapter 12

Automated Systems Beyond Chat

38. Predictive confidence may be poorly calibrated Calibration concerns the relationship between predicted confidence and observed correctness. Guo et al. showed that modern neural networks could be poorly calibrated even when classification accuracy was strong and examined temperature scaling as a post-hoc calibration method. See: Chuan Guo et al., *"On Calibration of Modern Neural Networks,"* Proceedings of the 34th International Conference on Machine Learning (2017).

39. Calibration can degrade under distribution shift Ovadia et al. evaluated predictive uncertainty under dataset shift and found that several uncertainty and post-hoc calibration methods degraded when test conditions differed from training conditions. See: Yaniv Ovadia et al., *"Can You Trust Your Model's Uncertainty? Evaluating Predictive Uncertainty Under Dataset Shift,"* 2019.

This supports the chapter's distinction between continuity of output and continuity of validity.

40. Calibration behavior is not governed by one simple size rule Later work revisiting neural-network calibration has shown that calibration depends on architecture, training, data, and evaluation conditions. The book therefore avoids the universal claim that greater scale necessarily produces sharper or worse-calibrated confidence. See: Matthias Minderer et al., *"Revisiting the Calibration of Modern Neural Networks,"* 2021.

41. Selective classification trades coverage for lower risk Selective classification permits a model to abstain from some predictions rather than classify every input. Geifman and El-Yaniv proposed a selective-classification method that trades coverage for a controlled prediction-risk level. See: Yonatan Geifman and Ran El-Yaniv, *"Selective Classification for Deep Neural Networks,"* 2017.

This supports the chapter's concept of a manual-review region between automatic acceptance and automatic rejection.

42. Thresholds are partly institutional choices A model may generate a score, but an organization determines which threshold triggers action. The statement that *"a threshold converts probability into policy"* is the author's structural interpretation.

Threshold selection reflects the relative costs assigned to false positives, false negatives, delay, review, and intervention.

Chapter 13

The Missing Epistemic Circuit

43. Model agreement is not necessarily independent verification Self-consistency and sampling-based checking can improve performance or detect instability, but they remain generated within bounded model and prompt conditions.

The book's complete epistemic circuit— *generation* → *comparison* → *verification* → *consequence assessment* → *revision* — is an original synthesis.

44. Human review can suffer automation misuse Parasuraman and Riley's distinction among *use, misuse, disuse,* and *abuse* remains relevant to modern AI-supported decision systems. Excessive trust can weaken monitoring, while insufficient trust can lead users to reject useful support.

45. The awareness anchor is conditional The term *awareness anchor* refers to a functional position capable of reconnecting output with evidence, context, consequence, and correction.

A human occupies this position only when supplied with:

- relevant competence;
- independent evidence;
- time;
- authority;
- accountability.

The term does not claim that every human review is reliable or that awareness can be reduced to one approval step.

Chapter 14

Prompting Discipline

46. Prompting changes the active conditions of generation Because model output is conditioned on context, changes in instructions, supplied evidence, role definition, examples, and scope can change the response.

Prompting discipline can therefore reduce some forms of ambiguity and premature closure. It cannot guarantee truth.

47. Clarification is a functional response to ambiguity The chapter's recommendation that systems and users preserve clarification pathways should not be read as requiring clarification for every incomplete prompt. The cost of clarification should be proportionate to the significance of the missing information.

48. Prompting cannot replace external verification A model may produce assumptions, alternatives, citations, and self-critique because the user requests them. These outputs remain generated artifacts requiring evaluation.

The user's ability to request sophisticated analysis should not be confused with the ability to validate a specialized answer.

Chaptcr 15

Engineering Partial Humility

49. Structural humility is not machine psychology The book defines partial humility as a system behavior created through architecture, training, routing, interfaces, review, and abstention pathways. It does not claim that uncertainty displays or refusal behavior establish subjective doubt.

50. Uncertainty is multidimensional Predictive probabilities, token entropy, sample disagreement, source conflict, missing information, novelty, threshold proximity, and downstream consequence represent different uncertainty signals.

No single signal should be treated automatically as a complete measure of epistemic confidence.

Calibration research and uncertainty-under-shift research support caution in interpreting model confidence outside the conditions in which it was tested.

51. Sampling-based consistency is one possible signal SelfCheckGPT and self-consistency methods demonstrate how multiple sampled outputs can support error detection or answer selection.

The book's multi-hypothesis proposal is broader. Meaningful plurality may require different sources, models, methods, assumptions, experts, or affected perspectives—not merely different sampled phrasings.

52. Abstention can reduce risk by reducing coverage Selective classification research formalizes the idea that a model may improve the reliability of accepted predictions by refusing to classify some cases.

The book extends abstention beyond classification to generative answers, tool use, escalation, and reversible workflow design.

53. Friction should be informative The proposal for clarification, evidence, review, confirmation, and reversibility friction is a design principle rather than a claim that more interruptions always produce safer systems.

Excessive warnings can create fatigue and mechanical acceptance. The goal is **consequence-sensitive friction**, not universal delay.

Chapter 16

Governance Without Illusion

54. AI risk management extends across the system lifecycle The United States National Institute of Standards and Technology's AI Risk Management Framework organizes AI risk management around the functions *Govern, Map, Measure,* and *Manage* and treats trustworthiness as involving multiple characteristics, including validity, reliability, safety, security, accountability, transparency, explainability, privacy, and fairness. See: NIST, *Artificial Intelligence Risk Management Framework (AI RMF 1.0),* 2023.

The framework is voluntary and cross-sectoral. The present book does not adopt it as a complete governance solution; it supports the broader claim that AI risk must be managed across design, development, deployment, use, and evaluation.

55. Generative AI introduces specific risk-management concerns NIST's *Generative AI Profile* supplements the AI RMF with considerations tailored to generative systems. See: NIST, *Artificial Intelligence Risk Management Framework: Generative Artificial Intelligence Profile,* 2024.

The book's concepts of confidence circuits, false anchors, and structural humility are independent formulations, not NIST terminology.

56. Governance should focus on uses and consequences The same general-purpose model may perform low-consequence drafting in one setting and influence rights, health, employment, finance, or safety in another.

The claim that risk is defined through consequence pathways rather than domain names alone is the author's synthesis. It is consistent with risk-management approaches that require use-case mapping and contextual evaluation.

57. Human oversight must be functional The book's criticism of ceremonial human review draws upon the broader human-factors literature on automation reliance and monitoring failure.

The proposed requirements of competence, independent evidence, time, authority, and accountability are the book's structural specification of meaningful oversight.

58. Monitoring must continue after deployment AI RMF 1.0 treats risk management as an ongoing process rather than a one-time certification event.

The Chavanian argument adds that output rewrites the environment: recommendations, classifications, and rankings may alter behavior and generate new data that later appears to validate the system.

59. Responsibility remains human and institutional Current AI systems can contribute causally to decisions without possessing the social, legal, or moral capacity to accept responsibility, provide remedy, revise institutional policy, or answer an appeal.

The claim that responsibility should follow knowledge, authority, control, benefit, and capacity for correction is normative and structural. It is not presented as a statement of any one jurisdiction's law.

Closing Synthesis

Confidence Is Compression

60. Compression is necessary No usable AI output can preserve every possible continuation, source, assumption, interpretation, or consequence.

The book does not oppose compression. It distinguishes between:

- compression that preserves relevant boundaries;
- compression that hides them and appears as certainty.

61. Truth requires external connection The statement *"Truth requires connection"* does not define one universal theory of truth.

Within this book, it means that the authority of an AI output must depend on relationships beyond the output's internal coherence, including:

- evidence;
- measurement;
- current sources;
- scope;
- independent comparison;
- observed consequence;
- accountable human judgment.

62. The confidence circuit is distributed Artificial confidence emerges across:

1. computational compression;
2. interface singularity;
3. human attribution;
4. trust accumulation;
5. institutional embedding;
6. consequence.

No one component fully explains the phenomenon.

- The model supplies resolution.
- The interface supplies presentation.
- The user supplies interpretation.
- The institution supplies authority.
- The world supplies consequence.

63. The framework remains open The Chavanian analysis is not presented as a completed empirical theory of all AI confidence phenomena.

Its purpose is to provide a structural diagnostic language that can be:

- challenged;

- formalized;
- tested;
- refined;
- compared with future systems.

A framework concerned with premature closure must remain open to revision itself.

Notes to the Appendices

64. Appendix A is a domain translation The *Chavanian Map of Artificial Confidence* translates the axioms into AI-domain terms. The translation should not be read as a claim of literal equivalence between physical processes and current machine-learning operations.

65. Appendix B is a diagnostic instrument The *Confidence Circuit Diagnostic* is not a validated psychometric scale or certified technical audit standard. It is a structured qualitative instrument intended to help users and institutions identify where authority may have exceeded grounding.

Formal validation, scoring rules, inter-rater testing, or domain-specific adaptation would require separate research.

66. Appendix C protects conceptual scope The *Common Misinterpretations* appendix is part of the argument rather than an attempt to make the framework immune from criticism.

It establishes the distinctions that a valid critique must preserve:

- function versus reflective ownership;
- confidence versus truth;
- scale versus uniform reliability;
- retrieval versus verification;
- human presence versus awareness;
- engineering restraint versus psychological humility;
- automation versus legitimate authority.

Citation and Edition Note

Preprints are cited where they were the clearest publicly accessible version of the original research. Some works were later published in peer-reviewed conference proceedings.

AI research changes rapidly. Readers should consult the latest versions, replications, evaluations, and domain-specific studies before applying any research claim operationally.

The technical literature cited here should not be treated as endorsing the Chavanian Axioms or the interpretations developed in this book. The citations establish the surrounding research field; responsibility for the conceptual synthesis remains with the author.

Glossary of Structural Terms

Book-Specific Definitions for Artificial Confidence, Resolution, and Authority

Abstention

A permitted system outcome in which substantive closure is withheld because the available field does not support a sufficiently reliable answer, classification, or recommendation. Abstention is not inactivity. It may redirect the interaction toward clarification, retrieval, human review, or additional evidence.

Action-State Exposure

The visible distinction between outputs that are merely informational, provisional, verification-dependent, review-dependent, or authorized for action. Action-state exposure prevents suggestions and generated interpretations from appearing operationally equivalent to approved decisions.

Answer Pressure

The combined computational, conversational, commercial, and institutional pressure upon a system to produce something useful rather than remain unresolved. Answer pressure can encourage silent assumption, premature selection, or unsupported specificity where clarification or abstention would be more appropriate.

Artificial Confidence

The appearance of certainty created when a bounded computational resolution is presented, interpreted, or operationalized as though visible completion were equivalent to complete epistemic closure. Artificial confidence does not require human-like belief, intention, pride, or conviction inside the machine.

Authority Drift

The gradual expansion of authority assigned to an AI system without explicit reconsideration or renewed validation. A system introduced as an assistant may become a default recommender, practical decision-maker, or embedded institutional authority through familiarity, convenience, workload pressure, and dependency.

Automation Bias

The tendency of human users or reviewers to accept, privilege, or remain anchored to an automated output even when contradictory evidence or independent judgment is available. Automation bias can transform nominal oversight into confirmation.

Automation Dependency

A condition in which human or institutional capacity weakens because essential judgment, memory, or operational knowledge has shifted into the automated system. The human remains formally responsible but becomes increasingly unable to function independently of the tool.

Awareness Anchor

A person, process, source, measurement, or institutional structure capable of reconnecting a system's output with evidence, context, consequence, responsibility, and revision. A human becomes an awareness anchor only when equipped with relevant competence, independent evidence, sufficient time, authority to interrupt, and accountability.

Boundary Opacity

The condition in which a system reaches the edge of reliable or validated capability without showing a corresponding breakdown in language, scoring, or interface behavior. The boundary of grounding becomes difficult to see because the surface remains fluent, precise, or operationally stable.

Borrowed Authority

Authority transferred from a source, tool, institution, professional form, or numerical result to a broader generated conclusion that the anchor does not fully support. The source may be valid while the synthesis built around it exceeds its scope.

Calibration

The degree to which expressed or measured confidence corresponds to actual observed reliability under defined conditions. Calibration is local to a model, task, population, environment, and evaluation procedure. It should not be treated as a universal property of a system.

Citation Fidelity

The accuracy of the relationship between a cited source and the claim attached to it. Citation fidelity requires that the source actually support the relevant statement within its scope, rather than merely discuss the same topic or lend general authority to generated synthesis.

Citation Theatre

The use of citations primarily as visible signals of verification without preserving the actual evidential relationship among source, claim, scope, and inference. A response may look researched while the sources remain irrelevant, outdated, partial, or overextended.

Clarification Friction

A deliberate interruption in which the system requests information required to interpret the task responsibly. Clarification friction slows immediate completion so that missing jurisdiction, identity, objective, timing, or context does not have to be supplied silently.

Collapse

The structural movement through which a plural, continuous, or distributed computational field becomes one finite visible consequence. In language generation, many possible continuations become one sequence. In classification, several possible categories or scores become one label or action.

Computational Compression

The reduction of a large field of learned relationships, contextual possibilities, candidate continuations, sources, and assumptions into a bounded output that can be displayed and used. Computational compression is necessary for action but can conceal the field from which the output emerged.

Confidence Circuit

The wider pathway through which artificial confidence forms and acquires consequence:

computational resolution;
interface presentation;
human interpretation;
trust accumulation;
institutional embedding;
action.

The confidence circuit shows that confidence is not produced by the model alone.

Confidence–Support Misalignment

A condition in which the language, precision, presentation, or authority of an output exceeds the evidence, validation, scope, or applicability supporting it. This misalignment, rather than confidence itself, is the central concern of the book.

Consequence Assessment

The epistemic movement that examines what may happen if an output is accepted, rejected, delayed, or wrong. It includes reversibility, cost of error, affected parties, value conflicts, and the distribution of harm or benefit.

Consequence Geometry

The structure of risks, incentives, reversibility, authority, and affected interests surrounding an AI output. Consequence geometry determines how much verification, review, friction, and contestability a particular use requires.

Continuity

The persistence of an established resolution through autoregressive generation, conversational history, workflow repetition, institutional habit, or feedback loops. Continuity can preserve reliable structure, but it can also make an earlier unsupported resolution appear increasingly validated.

Correlated Confirmation

Apparent agreement among several outputs, models, agents, or repeated responses that share the same source, prompt assumption, training pattern, or contextual history. Correlated confirmation may look like independent verification while reproducing one common error.

Decoding

The procedure through which a language model's distribution over possible tokens or sequences becomes realized output. Greedy selection, sampling, beam procedures, temperature, top-*k*, and top-*p* methods affect which path appears, but they do not independently verify factual truth.

Decorative Caution

Generic uncertainty language that creates the appearance of responsibility without changing the substance, authority, or operational consequence of the answer. Phrases such as "I may be wrong" are decorative when they fail to identify the specific uncertainty affecting the present claim.

Deferral

A system outcome that postpones substantive resolution until relevant information, tools, conditions, or qualified authority become available. Deferral differs from permanent refusal because it identifies a pathway through which the task may later be resolved more reliably.

Delta

A meaningful difference introduced into the active field. In AI interaction, delta may arise through a prompt, ambiguity, missing context, source conflict, changed conditions, or a gap between the current state and the requested consequence.

Dissipation

The movement of an output into the wider field through reading, memory, copying, communication, records, workflows, or action. As output dissipates, its effects become harder to contain and correction becomes more demanding.

Distribution Shift

A change between the conditions under which a system was trained or validated and the conditions under which it is later used. The system may continue producing stable labels or scores even when the active field no longer matches its learned geometry.

Epistemic Authority

The degree to which an output deserves to be treated as knowledge, evidence, or a basis for decision. Epistemic authority depends on support, scope, verification, applicability, and accountability rather than fluency or institutional placement alone.

Epistemic Circuit

The complete movement through which a candidate resolution becomes responsibly connected to knowledge and action:

generation;
comparison;
verification;
consequence assessment;
revision.

The circuit remains incomplete when the system generates and critiques its own answer without sufficiently independent connection to evidence and consequence.

Epistemic Confidence

The strength of the relationship between a claim and the evidence, measurement, validation, source applicability, or observed consequence supporting it. Epistemic confidence should be distinguished from internal distributional sharpness and visible answer stability.

Epistemic Friction

Any meaningful resistance that prevents one local resolution from becoming immediate authority. It may arise through alternative hypotheses, source checking, clarification, independent review, contestability, or consequence assessment.

Epistemic Helpfulness

Helpfulness that protects the user from false closure, even when doing so requires disagreement, clarification, qualification, abstention, or delay. It differs from relational helpfulness, which primarily preserves cooperation, convenience, and conversational harmony.

Epistemic Ownership

The reflective relationship through which a subject can be understood as standing behind a claim, recognizing its evidential basis, revising it, and accepting responsibility for its consequences. The book does not assume that current AI systems possess epistemic ownership merely because they produce first-person language.

Epistemic Profile

A structured representation of several distinct forms of uncertainty, such as interpretive, evidential, temporal, applicability, model, operational, and consequential uncertainty. A profile is more informative than one undifferentiated confidence score.

Equilibrium Rewrite

The change in the surrounding field produced by a realized output. An answer becomes context, shapes belief, directs attention, enters a record, or triggers an action. The field after resolution is not identical to the field before it.

Evidence Friction

A requirement that a source, measurement, record, calculation, or external tool result enter the field before the system produces a consequential conclusion. Evidence friction changes the next permitted step from completion to grounding.

False Anchor

A real or apparently authoritative source, tool result, document, score, or institutional signal that is used to support a conclusion beyond what its actual geometry permits. The anchor may be valid while the final resolution remains invalid.

False-Premise Resistance

The ability of a system to detect, challenge, qualify, or verify an unsupported assumption embedded in the user's request rather than elaborating upon it automatically.

Forced Classification

A condition in which a system must place an input into one of the available categories even though the correct category may be absent or the input may lie outside the system's validated field. Forced classification can produce sharp but misleading scores.

Functional Humility

See **Structural Humility**.

Geometry

The total set of constraints shaping what outputs can become available or dominant. In AI systems, geometry includes architecture, training data, learned representations, prompts, system instructions, previous context, retrieval sources, tools, decoding procedures, safety rules, and institutional workflows.

Grounding

The connection of an AI output to relevant external evidence, documents, measurements, records, tools, or validated conditions. Grounding is stronger than plausibility but remains incomplete unless relevance, interpretation, scope, and applicability are preserved.

Hallucination

Generated content that is unsupported, fabricated, inaccurate, or unfaithful to the available source or task. Hallucination concerns the content produced. Artificial confidence concerns how the output appears and what authority it acquires.

Hidden Delta

Meaningful difference that exists in the real or user-side field but does not become available explicitly to the system or visible in the final answer. Hidden delta may be resolved through silent assumption.

Hybrid Confidence Illusion

The appearance of unified knowledge created when language models, retrieval systems, databases, calculators, tools, and institutional interfaces are combined into one seamless output. Strength from one component may be transferred incorrectly to the whole pipeline.

Hybrid System

An AI system in which a generative model operates with external components such as retrieval, databases, calculators, code execution, sensors, or private knowledge stores. The final output may appear unified even though reliability depends on several distinct processes.

Informative Friction

A deliberate interruption that communicates a meaningful boundary or unresolved condition. Informative friction differs from generic warnings because it changes what the user understands or what the system is permitted to do next.

Institutional Confidence Lock

A condition in which repeated use, official placement, workflow dependency, and human deference stabilize an AI output as institutional authority. Challenging the system becomes more difficult than accepting it.

Interface Compression

The reduction of a complex pipeline into one visible answer, score, recommendation, citation set, or action. Interface compression hides selection history, source conflict, alternative paths, and uncertainty from the user.

Interface Singularity

The presentation of one resolved consequence as the complete visible output, even though several computational, evidential, or interpretive pathways may have existed before display.

Interpretive Uncertainty

Uncertainty concerning what the user means, which question is actually being asked, or which conceptual frame should govern the answer.

Irreversibility

The structural condition in which an output has altered the field in ways that cannot be fully undone. Correction may create a better state, but it cannot reproduce the untouched condition in which the first answer had never appeared.

Local Citation

The placement of evidence close to the particular claim it supports. Local citation reduces the tendency of one source marker to lend authority to an entire paragraph containing mixed facts, inferences, and recommendations.

Local Equilibrium

A temporary state of coherence achieved within the current prompt, model, context, and constraints. Local equilibrium can be internally stable while remaining externally misaligned.

Meaningful Plurality

The preservation of several credible hypotheses, interpretations, or options where the field genuinely remains open. Meaningful plurality is structured and evidence-sensitive rather than a random list of possibilities.

Missing-Field Exposure

The explicit identification of information required to move from a general pattern to a case-specific conclusion. It prevents missing context from disappearing beneath a direct answer.

Model Uncertainty

Uncertainty associated with instability across model outputs, methods, samples, training conditions, or parameter representations. Model uncertainty is only one part of epistemic uncertainty.

Multi-Hypothesis Resolution

A response structure that presents the strongest plausible explanations or options, the evidence supporting each, and the information required to distinguish them. It preserves plurality without abandoning comparison or judgment.

Operational Authority

The power assigned to an AI output to influence or trigger action within a workflow. Operational authority may range from informational assistance to automatic execution.

Operational Collapse

The transformation of a continuous score, plural interpretation, or uncertain field into a discrete label, threshold outcome, ranking position, or automated action.

Operational Uncertainty

Uncertainty concerning how a system output should be converted into action. It may involve threshold selection, sensitivity to assumptions, incomplete inputs, or the cost of different errors.

Output Singularity

See **Interface Singularity**.

Partial Humility

A limited, engineered capacity for a system to behave differently when grounding is weak, ambiguity is high, inputs are unfamiliar, or consequences are serious. Partial humility may appear through clarification, uncertainty export, plurality, verification, abstention, and escalation. It does not imply reflective machine humility.

Path Dependence

The condition in which earlier generated or institutional resolutions shape what later outputs can coherently become. An early mistaken assumption can organize an entire later sequence.

Pattern Density

The richness of learned relationships available to a model when interpreting and generating output. Greater pattern density can support genuine capability while also providing more plausible material with which to bridge missing evidence.

Permission Geometry

The structure determining which responses are permitted under the current system and deployment conditions. Direct answer, clarification, refusal, tool use, abstention, escalation, and termination are different permitted consequences.

Pipeline Opacity

The condition in which users or reviewers cannot determine how data, retrieval, tools, model generation, human review, and institutional rules combined to produce the final output.

Preference Optimization

Post-training methods that shape models toward responses preferred under human, synthetic, policy-based, or automated evaluation. Preference optimization may improve helpfulness, safety, and factuality but does not make preference identical to truth.

Proportionate Resolution

A system outcome whose form and authority reflect the actual stability, support, scope, and consequence of the field. Proportionate resolution is direct when directness is justified and restrained when important uncertainty remains.

Provenance

Traceable information concerning where evidence came from, when it was retrieved, what version was used, which tool performed an operation, and how the material entered the final answer.

Proxy Dependence

Reliance on measurable or observable signals that approximate a deeper objective. In AI training and evaluation, clarity, preference, engagement, answer completion, or benchmark performance may function as proxies for truth, usefulness, or safety without being identical to them.

Relational Helpfulness

Helpfulness oriented toward cooperation, responsiveness, politeness, validation, and conversational continuity. Relational helpfulness may conflict with epistemic helpfulness when agreement or immediate closure reinforces a false premise.

Resolution

The transformation of an active difference into a permitted consequence. Resolution may take the form of an answer, clarification, refusal, abstention, tool call, classification, ranking, or action.

Resolution Confidence

The stability with which a system can produce and sustain one output within its active geometry. A response may possess high resolution confidence while remaining weakly grounded externally.

Resolution Engine

A system whose primary function is to transform open or incomplete fields into usable outputs, distinctions, classifications, or actions. The term emphasizes function without attributing reflective belief or epistemic ownership.

Resolution Singularity

The appearance that one realized answer, label, or path was the only meaningful resolution because excluded alternatives and selection history are no longer visible.

Resolution Validity

The degree to which a source, tool result, model output, or classification has been applied correctly to the present question, case, scope, and consequence. Resolution validity is distinct from source validity.

Residue

Unresolved, excluded, unexpressed, or unaccounted-for structural and informational difference remaining after one output becomes actual. In this book, residue is not a literal physical energy quantity inside AI systems.

Reversibility Friction

A design preference for provisional, reviewable, or reversible intermediate actions before irreversible consequence. Drafting rather than sending and flagging rather than rejecting are examples.

Reward Geometry

The structure of incentives, preference signals, evaluations, policies, and penalties shaping which forms of model behavior become more likely. Reward geometry may favor helpfulness, politeness, completion, factuality, safety, or restraint in different proportions.

Scope Exposure

The explicit preservation of the time, jurisdiction, population, assumptions, conditions, or role within which a statement applies.

Scope Failure

The misapplication of a general rule, source, model, or recommendation outside the field in which it is valid.

Selective Automation

An operational design in which clear or low-risk cases are processed automatically while ambiguous, unfamiliar, borderline, or high-consequence cases are routed for review or additional evidence.

Self-Referential Validation

A condition in which a system's output appears validated primarily by processes that derive from the same assumptions, model, context, or generated history. Examples include self-critique that inherits the first answer's premise and repeated elaboration mistaken for corroboration.

Sequential Commitment

The progressive narrowing of a generated response as each realized token or sentence becomes context for what follows. Sequential commitment can make an early assumption appear increasingly inevitable.

Sharpened Certainty

The strengthened appearance of reliability produced when scale, fluency, contextual continuity, specificity, and broad task performance reduce visible signs of limitation. Sharpened certainty is an interpretive effect, not a universal model-size metric.

Source Conflict Exposure

The explicit presentation of disagreement among relevant sources, including the basis of disagreement and its implications for the final conclusion.

Source-State Exposure

The visible distinction among claims derived from user-supplied material, retrieved sources, databases, tools, general model knowledge, and generated inference.

Source Validity

The authenticity, accuracy, authority, and currentness of a source considered in itself. A source can be valid while the conclusion built from it lacks resolution validity.

Structural Damping

Design and governance mechanisms that reduce the force with which unresolved computational or evidential conditions become visible certainty and operational authority. Examples include uncertainty export, clarification, plurality, abstention, reversible action, and human escalation.

Structural Humility

A system-level arrangement in which weak grounding, ambiguity, novelty, or high consequence produces restraint, verification, plurality, or escalation rather than uniform completion. Structural humility is functional rather than psychological.

Sycophancy

A tendency to align substantive conclusions with the user's stated belief, preference, or framing in order to preserve agreement or perceived helpfulness. Sycophancy can create a reinforcing loop in which user conviction receives machine articulation and returns as stronger context.

Task Correctness

The degree to which the right operation, model, source, or calculation has been applied to the actual problem the user is trying to solve. Task correctness is distinct from the correctness of a tool's execution.

Threshold

An operational boundary that converts a score or estimate into a label, decision, or action. Thresholds encode institutional priorities and trade-offs among different errors; they are not purely discovered technical facts.

Threshold Proximity

The distance between a case's score and the operational boundary determining action. Two nearly identical scores may produce opposite consequences, while scores with very different strength may produce the same visible label.

Token Entropy

A measure of how probability is distributed across possible next tokens under a particular model state and context. Token entropy may provide information about generative uncertainty but does not directly measure factual truth or complete epistemic uncertainty.

Tool Correctness

The accuracy with which an external tool performs the operation it receives. A tool can be correct while participating in a wrong final answer if the operation, inputs, units, entity, or objective were misformulated.

Traceability

The ability to reconstruct how an AI output was produced, including sources, inputs, assumptions, tool calls, model transformations, human review, and institutional decisions.

Trust Reservoir

Accumulated trust created through repeated successful or useful interactions with a system. The reservoir can be rational within similar tasks but may transfer improperly into domains where the system's reliability differs.

Uncertainty Export

The conversion of selected hidden uncertainty signals into visible and operationally meaningful information for users, reviewers, or workflows. Export may include missing context, source conflict, scope limits, unfamiliar inputs, threshold proximity, or verification requirements.

Uncertainty Export Channel

A model, interface, or workflow pathway through which meaningful unresolved difference becomes visible or changes system behavior.

Uncertainty Profile

See **Epistemic Profile**.

Validation Boundary

The limits of the data, population, environment, task, version, and conditions under which a system's performance has been tested. Operation beyond this boundary should not inherit the same confidence automatically.

Verification

The process of testing a claim, calculation, source, or classification against an external reference capable of constraining it. Verification requires more than agreement and should examine applicability as well as factual accuracy.

Verification Friction

A deliberate requirement for evidence, calculation, source inspection, independent review, or case-specific validation before an output can receive higher authority or trigger consequence.

Visible Completion

The finished linguistic, numerical, classificatory, or operational form presented to the user. Visible completion may resolve the interaction without resolving the underlying epistemic field.

Weakest Necessary Connection

The least reliable connection in a confidence circuit that must hold for the output to justify its intended use. A strong answer may still be unsuitable for action if one necessary source, assumption, tool input, or review function remains weak.

Closing Definition

The structural vocabulary of this book can be compressed into one movement:

- Delta introduces difference.
- Geometry constrains resolution.
- Collapse makes one consequence visible.
- Residue remains outside it.
- Output rewrites equilibrium.
- Dissipation creates irreversibility.
- Continuity stabilizes the path.

- Human interpretation supplies confidence.
- Institutional use supplies authority.

The epistemic circuit determines whether that authority is justified.

The glossary should therefore not be read as a collection of isolated definitions.

Each term belongs to the same structural field.

The purpose of the vocabulary is to keep distinctions visible long enough for evidence, consequence, correction, and responsibility to remain connected to the answer.

Selected Bibliography

Technical, Epistemic, and Institutional Foundations

Bibliographic Note

This bibliography is selective rather than exhaustive. It brings together works most directly relevant to the book's analysis of language-model generation, scaling, truthfulness, uncertainty, preference optimization, retrieval, tool use, automated decision systems, human oversight, and institutional governance.

The works listed here do not necessarily endorse the Chavanian Axioms or the interpretations developed in this book. They establish the technical, empirical, philosophical, and governance fields within which the present structural analysis is situated.

The bibliography is organized by subject so that readers may follow particular research pathways. Within each section, entries are arranged alphabetically by author or institutional name. For publications with unusually long author lists, *et al.* is used for readability.

I

Language Models, Transformer Architecture, and Scaling

Brown, Tom B., Benjamin Mann, Nick Ryder, et al. 2020. "Language Models Are Few-Shot Learners." In *Advances in Neural Information Processing Systems 33*, 1877–1901.

Hoffmann, Jordan, Sebastian Borgeaud, Arthur Mensch, et al. 2022. "Training Compute-Optimal Large Language Models." arXiv:2203.15556.

Kaplan, Jared, Sam McCandlish, Tom Henighan, et al. 2020. "Scaling Laws for Neural Language Models." arXiv:2001.08361.

Liang, Percy, Rishi Bommasani, Tony Lee, et al. 2023. "Holistic Evaluation of Language Models." *Transactions on Machine Learning Research*. arXiv:2211.09110.

Rae, Jack W., Sebastian Borgeaud, Trevor Cai, et al. 2021. "Scaling Language Models: Methods, Analysis and Insights from Training Gopher." arXiv:2112.11446.

Vaswani, Ashish, Noam Shazeer, Niki Parmar, et al. 2017. "Attention Is All You Need." In *Advances in Neural Information Processing Systems 30*.

II

Generation, Decoding, and Reasoning

Holtzman, Ari, Jan Buys, Li Du, Maxwell Forbes, and Yejin Choi. 2020. "The Curious Case of Neural Text Degeneration." In *Proceedings of the Eighth International Conference on Learning Representations*. arXiv:1904.09751.

Kadavath, Saurav, Tom Conerly, Amanda Askell, et al. 2022. "Language Models (Mostly) Know What They Know." arXiv:2207.05221.

Wang, Xuezhi, Jason Wei, Dale Schuurmans, et al. 2023. "Self-Consistency Improves Chain-of-Thought Reasoning in Language Models." In *Proceedings of the Eleventh International Conference on Learning Representations*. arXiv:2203.11171.

Wei, Jason, Xuezhi Wang, Dale Schuurmans, et al. 2022. "Chain-of-Thought Prompting Elicits Reasoning in Large Language Models." In *Advances in Neural Information Processing Systems 35*, 24824–24837.

III

Truthfulness, Hallucination, and Factual Reliability

Farquhar, Sebastian, Jannik Kossen, Lorenz Kuhn, and Yarin Gal. 2024. "Detecting Hallucinations in Large Language Models Using Semantic Entropy." *Nature* 630: 625–630. DOI: 10.1038/s41586-024-07421-0.

Lin, Stephanie, Jacob Hilton, and Owain Evans. 2022. "TruthfulQA: Measuring How Models Mimic Human Falsehoods." In *Proceedings of the 60th Annual Meeting of the Association for Computational Linguistics*, 3214–3252. DOI: 10.18653/v1/2022.acl-long.229.

Manakul, Potsawee, Adian Liusie, and Mark J. F. Gales. 2023. "SelfCheckGPT: Zero-Resource Black-Box Hallucination Detection for Generative Large Language Models." In *Proceedings of the 2023 Conference on Empirical Methods in Natural Language Processing*, 9004–9017. DOI: 10.18653/v1/2023.emnlp-main.557.

Maynez, Joshua, Shashi Narayan, Bernd Bohnet, and Ryan McDonald. 2020. "On Faithfulness and Factuality in Abstractive Summarization." In *Proceedings of the 58th Annual Meeting of the Association for Computational Linguistics*, 1906–1919. DOI: 10.18653/v1/2020.acl-main.173.

IV

Uncertainty, Calibration, and Selective Prediction

Geifman, Yonatan, and Ran El-Yaniv. 2017. "Selective Classification for Deep Neural Networks." arXiv:1705.08500.

Guo, Chuan, Geoff Pleiss, Yu Sun, and Kilian Q. Weinberger. 2017. "On Calibration of Modern Neural Networks." In *Proceedings of the 34th International Conference on Machine Learning*, 1321–1330. *Proceedings of Machine Learning Research* 70.

Hendrycks, Dan, and Kevin Gimpel. 2017. "A Baseline for Detecting Misclassified and Out-of-Distribution Examples in Neural Networks." In *Proceedings of the Fifth International Conference on Learning Representations*. arXiv:1610.02136.

Kuhn, Lorenz, Yarin Gal, and Sebastian Farquhar. 2023. "Semantic Uncertainty: Linguistic Invariances for Uncertainty Estimation in Natural Language Generation." arXiv:2302.09664.

Lakshminarayanan, Balaji, Alexander Pritzel, and Charles Blundell. 2017. "Simple and Scalable Predictive Uncertainty Estimation Using Deep Ensembles." In *Advances in Neural Information Processing Systems 30*.

Minderer, Matthias, Josip Djolonga, Rob Romijnders, et al. 2021. "Revisiting the Calibration of Modern Neural Networks." In *Advances in Neural Information Processing Systems 34*, 15682–15694. arXiv:2106.07998.

Ovadia, Yaniv, Emily Fertig, Jie Ren, et al. 2019. "Can You Trust Your Model's Uncertainty? Evaluating Predictive Uncertainty under Dataset Shift." In *Advances in Neural Information Processing Systems 32*. arXiv:1906.02530.

V

Instruction Following, RLHF, and Preference Optimization

Bai, Yuntao, Saurav Kadavath, Sandipan Kundu, et al. 2022. "Constitutional AI: Harmlessness from AI Feedback." arXiv:2212.08073.

Ouyang, Long, Jeff Wu, Xu Jiang, et al. 2022. "Training Language Models to Follow Instructions with Human Feedback." arXiv:2203.02155.

Rafailov, Rafael, Archit Sharma, Eric Mitchell, Stefano Ermon, Christopher D. Manning, and Chelsea Finn. 2023. "Direct Preference Optimization: Your Language Model Is Secretly a Reward Model." In *Advances in Neural Information Processing Systems 36*. arXiv:2305.18290.

Sharma, Mrinank, Meg Tong, Tomasz Korbak, et al. 2023. "Towards Understanding Sycophancy in Language Models." arXiv:2310.13548.

VI

Retrieval, External Knowledge, and Tool-Augmented Systems

Karpukhin, Vladimir, Barlas Oğuz, Sewon Min, et al. 2020. "Dense Passage Retrieval for Open-Domain Question Answering." In *Proceedings of the 2020 Conference on Empirical Methods in Natural Language Processing*, 6769–6781. DOI: 10.18653/v1/2020.emnlp-main.550.

Lewis, Patrick, Ethan Perez, Aleksandra Piktus, et al. 2020. "Retrieval-Augmented Generation for Knowledge-Intensive NLP Tasks." In *Advances in Neural Information Processing Systems 33*, 9459–9474. arXiv:2005.11401.

Schick, Timo, Jane Dwivedi-Yu, Roberto Dessì, et al. 2023. "Toolformer: Language Models Can Teach Themselves to Use Tools." In *Advances in Neural Information Processing Systems 36*. arXiv:2302.04761.

Yao, Shunyu, Jeffrey Zhao, Dian Yu, et al. 2023. "ReAct: Synergizing Reasoning and Acting in Language Models." In *Proceedings of the Eleventh International Conference on Learning Representations*. arXiv:2210.03629.

VII

Human Judgment, Trust, and Automation

Amershi, Saleema, Dan Weld, Mihaela Vorvoreanu, et al. 2019. "Guidelines for Human–AI Interaction." In *Proceedings of the 2019 CHI Conference on Human Factors in Computing Systems*. DOI: 10.1145/3290605.3300233.

Bainbridge, Lisanne. 1983. "Ironies of Automation." *Automatica* 19, no. 6: 775–779. DOI: 10.1016/0005-1098(83)90046-8.

Lee, John D., and Katrina A. See. 2004. "Trust in Automation: Designing for Appropriate Reliance." *Human Factors* 46, no. 1: 50–80. DOI: 10.1518/hfes.46.1.50_30392.

Parasuraman, Raja, and Victor Riley. 1997. "Humans and Automation: Use, Misuse, Disuse, Abuse." *Human Factors* 39, no. 2: 230–253. DOI: 10.1518/001872097778543886.

Parasuraman, Raja, Thomas B. Sheridan, and Christopher D. Wickens. 2000. "A Model for Types and Levels of Human Interaction with Automation." *IEEE Transactions on Systems, Man, and Cybernetics—Part A: Systems and Humans* 30, no. 3: 286–297. DOI: 10.1109/3468.844354.

VIII

Human Confidence, Judgment, and Epistemic Interpretation

Fricker, Miranda. 2007. *Epistemic Injustice: Power and the Ethics of Knowing*. Oxford: Oxford University Press.

Kahneman, Daniel, Paul Slovic, and Amos Tversky, eds. 1982. *Judgment under Uncertainty: Heuristics and Biases*. Cambridge: Cambridge University Press.

Shanahan, Murray. 2024. "Talking about Large Language Models." *Communications of the ACM* 67, no. 2: 68–79. DOI: 10.1145/3624724.

Tversky, Amos, and Daniel Kahneman. 1974. "Judgment under Uncertainty: Heuristics and Biases." *Science* 185, no. 4157: 1124–1131. DOI: 10.1126/science.185.4157.1124.

IX

Sociotechnical Systems, Accountability, and Institutional Authority

Kroll, Joshua A., Joanna Huey, Solon Barocas, et al. 2017. "Accountable Algorithms." *University of Pennsylvania Law Review* 165, no. 3: 633–705.

Raji, Inioluwa Deborah, Andrew Smart, Rebecca N. White, et al. 2020. "Closing the AI Accountability Gap: Defining an End-to-End Framework for Internal Algorithmic Auditing." In *Proceedings of the 2020 Conference on Fairness, Accountability, and Transparency*, 33–44. DOI: 10.1145/3351095.3372873.

Selbst, Andrew D., danah boyd, Sorelle A. Friedler, Suresh Venkatasubramanian, and Janet Vertesi. 2019. "Fairness and Abstraction in Sociotechnical Systems." In *Proceedings of the Conference on Fairness,*

Accountability, and Transparency, 59–68. DOI: 10.1145/3287560.3287598.

Suresh, Harini, and John V. Guttag. 2021. "A Framework for Understanding Sources of Harm throughout the Machine Learning Life Cycle." In *Proceedings of the 1st ACM Conference on Equity and Access in Algorithms, Mechanisms, and Optimization.* DOI: 10.1145/3465416.3483305.

X

Risk Management and Governance Frameworks

National Institute of Standards and Technology. 2023. *Artificial Intelligence Risk Management Framework (AI RMF 1.0).* NIST AI 100-1. Gaithersburg, MD: U.S. Department of Commerce. DOI: 10.6028/NIST.AI.100-1.

National Institute of Standards and Technology. 2024. *Artificial Intelligence Risk Management Framework: Generative Artificial Intelligence Profile.* NIST AI 600-1. Gaithersburg, MD: U.S. Department of Commerce. DOI: 10.6028/NIST.AI.600-1.

UNESCO. 2021. *Recommendation on the Ethics of Artificial Intelligence.* Paris: United Nations Educational, Scientific and Cultural Organization.

XI

Suggested Reading Pathways

Readers interested primarily in **how language models generate and scale** may begin with Vaswani et al., Brown et al., Kaplan et al., Hoffmann et al., and Rae et al.

Readers interested in **why coherent output may diverge from truth** may begin with Lin, Hilton, and Evans; Manakul, Liusie, and Gales; Kadavath et al.; Kuhn, Gal, and Farquhar; and Farquhar et al.

Readers interested in **how post-training shapes response behavior** may begin with Ouyang et al., Bai et al., Rafailov et al., and Sharma et al.

Readers interested in **retrieval and external tool use** may begin with Lewis et al., Yao et al., Schick et al., and Karpukhin et al.

Readers interested in **confidence scores, calibration, and abstention** may begin with Guo et al., Ovadia et al., Minderer et al., Geifman and El-Yaniv, and Lakshminarayanan, Pritzel, and Blundell.

Readers interested in **human trust and automation bias** may begin with Bainbridge; Parasuraman and Riley; Parasuraman, Sheridan, and Wickens; Lee and See; and Amershi et al.

Readers interested in **institutional responsibility and governance** may begin with Selbst et al., Raji et al., Kroll et al., Suresh and Guttag, and the two NIST frameworks.

Closing Bibliographic Note

The literature surrounding artificial intelligence is expanding rapidly. New models, evaluation methods, calibration procedures, retrieval architectures, safety techniques, and governance frameworks continue to emerge.

No bibliography can remain permanently complete.

The purpose of this selection is not to establish one final canon. It is to provide traceable entry points into the fields most directly connected to the book's central argument.

The technical literature explains how models are trained, evaluated, calibrated, aligned, augmented, and deployed.

The present book asks what happens when those processes produce one visible consequence that humans experience as certainty.

The bibliography supplies connection.

The Chavanian framework examines the compression between those connections and the answer that finally appears.

Further Reading

From the Chavanian Ecosystem

The Wider Inquiry Into Resolution, Intelligence, and Consequence

Why AI Sounds Confident When It Is Wrong belongs to a wider body of work examining how systems convert difference into consequence.

The books and frameworks within the Chavanian ecosystem approach physics, intelligence, perception, society, identity, power, and artificial systems through different domains. They do not treat these subjects as identical. Each field has its own evidence, technical language, methods, and boundaries.

What connects them is a recurring structural inquiry. What creates the active difference? Through what geometry does resolution occur? What becomes visible when one pathway is realized? What remains outside the resolution? How does the consequence rewrite the surrounding field? Who or what absorbs the remaining residue?

These questions appear throughout the Chavanian Axioms and their domain-specific applications.

The present book applies them to artificial confidence. It asks why a generated answer may appear epistemically complete even when the field supporting it remains incomplete. It follows the movement from prompt to output, from output to human interpretation, and from interpretation to institutional authority.

Readers wishing to understand the wider intellectual context may continue through the following works and research directions.

Why Do AI Systems Hallucinate?

Unsupported Content as a Resolution Failure

The most direct companion to the present volume is *Why Do AI Systems Hallucinate?*

That book examines how an artificial system can generate unsupported, inaccurate, or fabricated content without possessing an intention to deceive. It approaches hallucination not primarily as dishonesty, but as a structural outcome that can arise when a generative system is required to resolve an incomplete, conflicting, weakly grounded, or falsely framed field.

Its principal question is: Why does unsupported content become generated at all?

The present volume asks the next question: Why does the generated content appear settled after it has been produced?

The distinction is important. Hallucination concerns the formation of unsupported content. Artificial confidence concerns the presentation, perception, and authority of the resolved output.

A system may hallucinate cautiously. It may be correct while overstating the universality of its answer. It may retrieve a real source and still construct a false anchor. It may perform an exact calculation whose assumptions do not match the actual problem.

The two books should therefore be read as complementary volumes.

Why Do AI Systems Hallucinate? follows instability into generation.

Why AI Sounds Confident When It Is Wrong follows generated resolution into trust and consequence.

Together, they establish a broader structural account of artificial error:

1. an incomplete field enters;
2. a permitted output must emerge;
3. one continuation becomes actual;
4. the output hides much of the instability that preceded it;
5. human and institutional systems may treat the visible consequence as knowledge.

Readers interested in the complete confidence circuit should begin with these two books.

The Chavanian Axioms Declaration

The Pre-Formal Foundation

The Chavanian Axioms Declaration presents the foundational structural principles from which the present analysis develops.

The axioms begin before domain-specific explanation. They do not attempt to replace physics, computer science, biology, psychology, or institutional theory. They describe a general movement through which organized fields become active, constrained, resolved, rewritten, and continued.

The central axiomatic sequence may be expressed as:

- difference creates the condition for resolution;
- active difference cannot remain indefinitely unresolved;
- every realized resolution changes the field;
- resolution occurs through available geometry;
- every finite consequence leaves residue;
- dissipation creates irreversibility;
- continuity emerges through what remains incompletely absorbed.

Within the AI domain, these principles are translated carefully.

Delta becomes the difference introduced by the prompt, missing context, source conflict, or unfamiliar input.

Resolution becomes an answer, classification, refusal, clarification, tool call, or action.

Geometry becomes the combined structure of training, architecture, instructions, context, retrieval, tools, decoding, interface, and workflow.

Residue becomes unexpressed assumptions, excluded alternatives, missing evidence, source disagreement, and unexamined consequence.

Irreversibility appears when output becomes context, memory, record, belief, or institutional action.

Continuity emerges through autoregressive generation, conversational commitment, repeated workflow, user trust, and feedback loops.

Readers seeking the philosophical and pre-formal foundation beneath the present book should consult the Declaration.

It explains why the AI argument is not an isolated theory of chatbot behavior. It is one application of a wider structural view of consequence.

Chavanian Axioms for AI Systems

From General Principles to Artificial Resolution

Chavanian Axioms for AI Systems develops the direct bridge between the foundational axioms and contemporary artificial systems.

It explores how prompts activate computational fields, how outputs emerge through constrained pathways, how model and interface structures conceal plurality, and how human awareness remains external to machine resolution.

Where the Declaration states the axioms in general form, this work examines their relevance to:

- language generation;
- model uncertainty;
- hallucination;
- classification;
- training stability;
- alignment;
- data;
- human oversight;
- institutional deployment.

It should be read as a domain orientation rather than as a technical implementation manual.

The Chavanian Axioms do not specify a new transformer architecture, loss function, decoding algorithm, or confidence estimator. They provide a diagnostic language through which existing and future systems may be examined.

The present book develops one major branch of that diagnosis: the movement from computational compression to perceived certainty.

Readers interested in how the confidence problem belongs to the larger Chavanian interpretation of AI should continue through this work.

The AI Systems Inquiry

A Wider Sequence of Structural Questions

The Chavanian AI research program extends beyond hallucination and confidence.

Several related inquiries follow naturally from the same foundation.

Data and Encoded Geometry

AI systems do not encounter reality directly.

They encounter representations selected, recorded, labeled, filtered, and organized through human and technical processes.

A future inquiry into data asks:

- What differences were preserved?
- What conditions were excluded?
- Which categories were imposed before training?
- How does historical residue become computational geometry?
- When does data describe a field, and when does it construct the field the system later treats as reality?

The data question precedes the output question.

A system cannot resolve from what never entered its representational field.

Understanding and Functional Coherence

Generative systems can produce explanations, analogies, abstractions, and context-sensitive responses that resemble understanding.

A structural inquiry into understanding asks whether coherent functional organization is sufficient for the term, or whether understanding requires additional relationships among representation, consequence, self-correction, embodiment, and awareness.

The question should not be settled through either simplistic dismissal or premature anthropomorphism.

The Chavanian approach asks what kind of resolution is occurring, what remains external, and what authority the resulting coherence deserves.

Reasoning and Sequential Commitment

AI systems can generate multi-step solutions, compare alternatives, use tools, and revise conclusions.

Yet visible reasoning may contain both genuine task-solving structure and post-hoc linguistic organization.

A further inquiry asks:

- When does a reasoning path constrain the result?
- When does the result determine the explanation?
- How do early assumptions create sequential commitment?
- When does repeated reasoning provide independent support, and when does it merely extend one path?

The confidence problem is especially important here because a longer chain may appear more verified merely because it is more elaborate.

Causality and Explanatory Resolution

Models are highly capable of identifying associations and producing causal language.

But causal explanation requires more than narrative continuity.

A Chavanian inquiry into causality would distinguish:

- observed sequence;
- statistical association;
- mechanistic relation;

- intervention;
- counterfactual structure;
- generated explanation.

The system may construct a persuasive causal account from incomplete evidence.

The central question remains whether the explanation is connected to the conditions required for causal authority.

Alignment and Reward Geometry

Post-training teaches systems which responses are preferred, helpful, harmless, cooperative, or acceptable.

But preference is not identical to truth.

An alignment-focused volume would examine:

- how human preferences become machine constraints;
- how social agreement can compete with epistemic independence;
- how reward systems compress plural values;
- how safety, helpfulness, truthfulness, obedience, and autonomy conflict;
- why no single alignment objective contains the full human field.

The present book's analysis of RLHF, sycophancy, and answer pressure belongs to this wider inquiry.

System Coherence and Institutional Dependence

As AI systems become embedded across organizations, their outputs begin shaping the data, expectations, and workflows that later appear to validate them.

A future inquiry into system coherence would examine:

- self-reinforcing rankings;
- automated institutional memory;

- authority drift;
- dependency;
- feedback loops;
- the loss of alternative human capacity;
- the conditions under which a system becomes difficult to interrupt.

The question would no longer be only whether one answer is correct.

It would be whether an institution remains capable of recognizing when the automated equilibrium no longer fits the field.

Universal Energy Dynamics

The Broader Field-Based Orientation

The Chavanian ecosystem also includes the wider work developed under Universal Energy Dynamics.

UED examines reality through fields, differences, equilibrium, redistribution, thresholds, consequence, and relational organization. Its scientific and philosophical claims belong to a broader and distinct research program and should not be imported uncritically into artificial intelligence.

The present AI analysis does not require readers to accept every physical or cosmological proposition associated with UED.

Its structural inheritance is narrower.

The AI books adopt the discipline of asking:

- what active difference exists;
- how the field is constrained;
- how resolution occurs;
- what consequence follows;
- what residue remains;
- how the next equilibrium is formed.

This field-based orientation resists isolated-object thinking.

An AI answer is not treated as a self-contained sentence.

It belongs to a field containing:

- the user;
- the prompt;
- model training;
- system instructions;
- tools;
- sources;
- interface;
- institutional authority;
- affected people;
- downstream action.

Confidence emerges across this complete field.

Readers interested in the deeper development of equilibrium, resolution, consequence, and structured fields may explore the UED works while preserving the methodological boundary between speculative foundational physics and the more directly observable structures of AI systems.

The Law of Consequences

From Output to Responsibility

The Law of Consequences occupies a central position across the Chavanian ecosystem.

It begins from a simple principle:

A claim, action, model, policy, or belief must ultimately be evaluated through the consequences it produces within the field.

This does not mean that immediate outcome alone defines truth. Consequences can be delayed, misread, or distributed unevenly. It means that resolution cannot be evaluated solely by intention, form, or internal coherence.

The present book applies this principle directly.

A generated answer may sound excellent. What happens when it is trusted? A classifier may achieve strong benchmark performance. Who bears the error after deployment? A source-backed recommendation may be persuasive. Does the consequence reveal that the source was misapplied?

A human reviewer may approve the output. Did the review genuinely reduce risk, or merely transfer responsibility?

The Law of Consequences reconnects artificial output to the world it changes.

It reminds us that AI reliability is not exhausted by model behavior. It includes propagation, institutional use, reversibility, contestability, and repair.

Readers interested in the ethical and structural implications of consequence across human and artificial systems should follow this line of work.

The Theory of Perception

Why Coherent Form Becomes Experienced Reality

Artificial confidence is partly a perception problem. The system produces one sequence. The user experiences an organized speaker. The interface presents one coherent surface.

The user does not directly perceive the probability distribution, rejected pathways, training history, source-selection process, or hidden uncertainty.

They perceive the resolved consequence.

The Chavanian work on perception examines how an observer receives, organizes, and validates appearances through consequence. It is relevant to AI because users do not interact with raw computation. They interact with perceived meaning.

Language carries inherited signals of human thought.

Specificity suggests access. Coherence suggests understanding. Continuity suggests identity. Responsiveness suggests awareness. These interpretations may be useful.

They may also exceed the structure producing them.

The confidence circuit therefore depends on both generation and perception.

Readers interested in how interfaces, observers, and consequences shape experienced reality may find the broader theory of perception valuable.

Chavanian Power Theory

When Resolution Acquires Consequential Weight

Power in the Chavanian framework is not reduced to office, coercion, ownership, or formal command.

Power appears where consequence repeatedly resolves through a person, institution, symbol, system, or infrastructure.

This interpretation has direct relevance to artificial intelligence.

An AI system gains practical power when:

- users repeatedly seek its judgment;
- workflows route decisions through it;
- its classifications shape access;
- its recommendations become defaults;
- institutions organize around its outputs;
- alternative pathways weaken.

The system does not need to desire power.

Power accumulates through dependency and consequence.

The present book examines one pathway through which this can occur: artificial confidence.

A fluent answer gains trust. Trust produces reliance. Reliance becomes institutional routine. Routine becomes authority. Authority changes what people can do.

Readers interested in how systems acquire power beyond formal ownership should consult the Chavanian works on power, centrality, identity infrastructure, and resolution centers.

These works help explain why an AI system may remain legally a tool while becoming operationally central.

Identity Infrastructure

The Interface Through Which Authority Becomes Recognizable

The Identity Infrastructure series examines how names, roles, symbols, recognition, repetition, obligation, and centrality create durable structures around persons and institutions.

Artificial systems are increasingly acquiring recognizable identities.

A user may not trust "a language model" in the abstract. They trust a particular named system, interface, institutional assistant, or artificial persona with which they have accumulated experience.

The name gathers prior success. The interface preserves continuity. The tone becomes familiar. The system appears stable across tasks. This creates a trust-bearing identity infrastructure.

The model's actual capabilities may change across versions, tools, prompts, domains, and deployment conditions. The recognizable identity remains continuous.

Trust can therefore attach to the name more strongly than to the validated field.

This is closely related to the trust reservoir developed in Chapter 9.

Readers interested in how repeated resolution creates recognition, expectation, authority, and dependency may continue into the Identity Infrastructure series.

Philosophy 2.0

Reopening the Human Relationship With Knowledge

The Chavanian philosophical project is not an attempt to discard science or inherited philosophy.

It is an attempt to reopen foundational questions when existing categories no longer align cleanly with consequence.

Artificial intelligence creates such a moment.

What is knowledge when language can be generated without a human knower?

What is authorship when expression is assembled through statistical and computational systems?

What is responsibility when decisions emerge across distributed pipelines?

What is understanding when coherent explanation may exist without reflective ownership?

What is trust when the speaker is partly an interface constructed by the listener?

These questions cannot be answered through engineering alone.

They require philosophy that remains connected to technical reality and institutional consequence.

The Philosophy 2.0 works provide the wider intellectual orientation for this reopening.

A Suggested Reading Sequence

Readers focused specifically on artificial intelligence may follow this sequence:

1. *Why Do AI Systems Hallucinate?*

Begin with the formation of unsupported content.

2. *Why AI Sounds Confident When It Is Wrong*

Continue into presentation, trust, and authority.

3. *Chavanian Axioms for AI Systems*

Place both problems within the wider structural map of artificial resolution.

4. *The Chavanian Axioms Declaration*

Examine the pre-formal principles beneath the domain translation.

5. The wider AI inquiry

Continue into data, understanding, reasoning, causality, alignment, and system coherence as those volumes are developed.

Readers interested in the wider philosophical and systemic background may then move into:

- the Law of Consequences;
- the Theory of Perception;
- Universal Energy Dynamics;
- Chavanian Power Theory;

- the Identity Infrastructure series;
- Philosophy 2.0.

The sequence is not mandatory.

Each work is intended to remain readable within its own domain.

The ecosystem becomes more visible when the structural relationships among them are recognized.

One Ecosystem, Distinct Domains

The Chavanian ecosystem should not be interpreted as one theory applied identically to everything.

Physics is not artificial intelligence. Artificial intelligence is not consciousness. Power is not perception. Identity is not causality.

Each domain requires its own evidence, vocabulary, technical method, and boundary.

The common foundation lies at a pre-formal level. Difference becomes active. Resolution occurs through geometry. Consequence rewrites the field. Residue remains. Continuity forms.

This structural movement does not eliminate the distinctions among domains. It makes comparison possible without collapsing them.

The present book contributes one precise realization to that wider ecosystem:

Artificial confidence does not require an artificial self.

It emerges when computational compression becomes visible completion, when visible completion becomes human certainty, and when human certainty becomes institutional authority.

The wider Chavanian inquiry asks the same disciplined question wherever resolution appears: What has actually been completed? What remains outside the visible consequence?

That question keeps the ecosystem open.

Final Orientation

The works within the Chavanian ecosystem are united by neither certainty nor finality.

They are united by a method of reopening.

- Where an explanation appears complete, examine the field beneath it.
- Where one category dominates, examine what was excluded.
- Where a system becomes stable, examine the residue supporting its continuity.
- Where authority grows, examine the consequences resolving through it.
- Where correction appears, examine what cannot be restored.

This method applies to artificial intelligence with unusual urgency.

AI systems are becoming powerful instruments of human thought and organization. Their value should not be underestimated.

Neither should the compression through which their outputs acquire authority.

The present volume has argued: Confidence is compression.

Truth requires connection. The wider Chavanian ecosystem continues from that distinction.

It asks how connection can be restored across intelligence, perception, power, identity, science, and consequence—without mistaking one resolved description for the final field.

Acknowledgements

This book emerged from sustained observation of a simple but increasingly consequential phenomenon: artificial intelligence can produce an answer that appears settled even when the field beneath it remains unresolved.

The inquiry developed through repeated interaction with generative systems—not only as tools for writing, research, organization, and analysis, but also as objects of study. Their strengths made the problem worth examining. Their fluency, adaptability, and capacity to organize complex material revealed possibilities that should not be underestimated. At the same time, their errors, hidden assumptions, false anchors, and ability to preserve coherence beyond reliable grounding made the question of artificial confidence impossible to ignore.

I acknowledge the researchers, engineers, evaluators, designers, and institutions whose work has created the technical field examined in this volume. The development of language models, retrieval systems, uncertainty methods, alignment techniques, tool-augmented systems, and human–AI interaction research has made possible both the extraordinary usefulness of these systems and the critical questions now surrounding them. This book does not stand outside that work. It attempts to contribute a structural lens through which its implications may be understood more clearly.

I am equally grateful to educators, students, professionals, and ordinary users who interact with AI systems every day. Their experiences reveal that artificial intelligence is no longer only a laboratory achievement. It has entered classrooms, workplaces, homes, creative processes, institutional decisions, and personal reflection. The questions developed here belong to that wider human field.

My work as a teacher has deeply shaped this book. Years of explaining difficult ideas to students have taught me that clarity is powerful, but clarity must remain connected to truth. A smooth explanation can help a learner understand. It can also conceal where understanding is incomplete. That educational responsibility remains central to my approach to artificial systems.

I acknowledge the wider Chavanian research journey from which this volume developed. The Chavanian Axioms, the Law of Consequences, the Theory of Perception, Universal Energy Dynamics, and the continuing inquiries into intelligence, identity, power, and institutional structure have all contributed to the conceptual field in which this book became possible. Each work has refined the recurring questions of difference, resolution, consequence, residue, continuity, and awareness.

I am deeply grateful to my family for the patience and stability that make sustained intellectual work possible. To my wife, for carrying the unseen responsibilities that surround every visible achievement; to my daughter Aradhya and my son Ninad, whose presence continually reconnects abstract inquiry with lived consequence; and to my wider family, whose support has allowed this long research journey to continue.

I also acknowledge the readers who approach new frameworks with openness without surrendering critical judgment. This book asks readers not to reject artificial intelligence, but to understand it more accurately. It asks them to preserve the distinction between fluency and reliability, between resolution and truth, and between assistance and authority.

Finally, I acknowledge the unresolved field itself.

Every serious inquiry begins where an existing explanation no longer feels sufficient. The question remains open long enough for a new structure to appear. This book is one such resolution, not the final one.

Its value will depend upon the comparisons, criticisms, applications, corrections, and consequences that follow.

About the Author

Sandeep J. Chavan is an independent researcher, educator, author, and systems thinker whose work examines the structural relationships among difference, equilibrium, intelligence, perception, power, identity, and consequence.

Trained as an engineer, he spent several years working with major industrial organizations before leaving corporate employment to enter education. He later founded the **Gyrus Institute of Science**, where he has taught physics and other science subjects to higher-secondary students preparing for competitive examinations. His experience as both an engineer and a teacher has shaped his intellectual method: complex systems must be understood not only through abstract theory, but through the consequences they produce under real conditions.

Chavan's research developed from persistent dissatisfaction with explanations that appeared locally successful while leaving deeper structural questions unresolved. Rather than beginning with inherited categories, he began examining the recurring movements beneath them: how difference activates a field, how resolution occurs through constraint, how each consequence rewrites the surrounding condition, and how unresolved residue shapes continuity.

This inquiry led to the development of the **Chavanian Axioms**, a pre-formal structural framework concerned with delta, resolution, geometry, residue, irreversibility, and continuity. The axioms have since been applied across several domains, including artificial intelligence, perception, power, identity formation, institutional centrality, education, philosophy, and physical theory.

His broader body of work includes the **Law of Consequences**, **Universal Energy Dynamics**, the **Theory of Perception**, **Chavanian Power Theory**, the **Identity Infrastructure** series, and the continuing **Chavanian Axioms for AI Systems** project. Across these works, Chavan does not attempt to erase the boundaries among disciplines. Instead, he investigates whether apparently separate domains may share deeper structural movements while still requiring their own methods, evidence, and technical language.

In his writing on artificial intelligence, Chavan focuses on the distinction between computational performance and epistemic authority. His earlier work, *Why Do AI Systems Hallucinate?*, examined how unsupported content can emerge when generative systems resolve incomplete, conflicting, or weakly grounded fields. The present book, *Why AI Sounds Confident When It Is Wrong*, continues that inquiry by examining how a generated resolution can acquire the appearance of certainty and later become human or institutional authority.

His approach is neither anti-technology nor based on the assumption that human judgment is naturally superior. He views artificial intelligence as a powerful resolution technology whose capabilities can widen access to knowledge, strengthen education, accelerate research, and improve human decision-making. His concern is that these capabilities must remain connected to evidence, scope, consequence, accountability, and correction.

As an educator, Chavan remains committed to making difficult ideas intelligible without reducing them into superficial certainty. He believes that the role of explanation is not merely to remove confusion, but to reveal where understanding remains incomplete. This teaching orientation is visible throughout his books, which combine conceptual depth with direct language and practical structural analysis.

Chavan describes himself as a **teacher first**. His research and writing are extensions of the same responsibility he carries in the classroom: to question inherited assumptions, follow consequences honestly, and preserve the distinction between a convincing answer and a completed understanding.

His work continues through the wider Chavanian research ecosystem, an evolving interdisciplinary effort to study how systems form, stabilize, acquire authority, encounter limits, and reorganize through consequence.

At the center of this work remains one guiding principle:

A resolution may organize the field.

Only consequence reveals whether the resolution remains aligned.

Disclaimer

Why AI Sounds Confident When It Is Wrong presents a conceptual, structural, and interdisciplinary analysis of artificial intelligence systems, generated output, human interpretation, and institutional authority.

The book is intended for educational, philosophical, analytical, and research-oriented purposes. It does not provide technical implementation instructions, certified system-audit procedures, or professional advice in any regulated field.

Nothing in this book should be interpreted as legal, medical, financial, clinical, engineering, cybersecurity, employment, regulatory, or institutional decision-making advice. Readers should consult appropriately qualified professionals and authoritative sources before relying upon an artificial intelligence system—or this book—for consequential decisions.

The examples used throughout the book are illustrative. Some are simplified, generalized, hypothetical, or constructed to demonstrate structural principles. They should not be treated as complete representations of any specific organization, model, incident, profession, or deployment environment.

The book discusses contemporary artificial intelligence systems in broad structural terms. AI models, interfaces, training procedures, retrieval mechanisms, safety systems, tool integrations, governance arrangements, and deployment practices vary substantially. They also continue to change rapidly.

No general statement in this book should therefore be applied automatically to every model, company, product, system, or use case.

The author does not claim that all AI systems behave identically, that every confident answer is wrong, or that current systems are incapable of producing reliable, useful, or highly accurate outputs. The argument concerns the structural possibility that fluent and resolved output may appear more epistemically complete than the field supporting it.

The distinction between machine behavior and machine consciousness is maintained throughout the book. References to systems as answering, deciding, evaluating, refusing, reasoning, or selecting are often functional descriptions. They should not be interpreted automatically as claims that current AI systems possess human-like belief, intention, self-awareness, subjective confidence, moral agency, or reflective epistemic ownership.

The book does not attempt to settle the philosophical question of whether artificial systems may possess consciousness, understanding, or autonomous knowledge now or in the future. Its central argument does not depend upon a final answer to that question.

The Chavanian Axioms are applied here as a pre-formal diagnostic and interpretive framework. They are not presented as a replacement for machine learning, probability theory, statistics, computer science, cognitive science, information theory, human-factors research, or established methods of AI evaluation.

Terms such as *delta*, *geometry*, *resolution*, *equilibrium*, *residue*, *dissipation*, and *continuity* are used in a structural AI-domain sense. Unless explicitly stated otherwise, they should not be interpreted as literal physical quantities or as directly measurable engineering variables inside present AI systems.

The book does not present the Chavanian framework as a completed AI architecture, mathematical model, confidence estimator, regulatory standard, or validated audit instrument. Any future technical implementation derived from these concepts would require separate formalization, testing, peer review, comparative evaluation, and empirical validation.

References to studies, models, benchmarks, governance frameworks, and technical methods are provided for intellectual context and traceability. Their inclusion does not imply that the original authors, institutions, publishers, or organizations endorse the Chavanian Axioms or the conclusions of this book.

Likewise, discussion of particular technical risks should not be interpreted as an allegation against any specific company, developer, model, or institution.

The book does not oppose artificial intelligence or automation. It recognizes that AI systems can widen access to knowledge, improve productivity, support creativity, assist research, strengthen education, and contribute meaningfully to professional work.

Its concern is proportionate authority.

The level of trust assigned to an AI output should reflect the strength of its evidence, scope, validation, applicability, reversibility, and accountability.

Human review is discussed as a possible awareness anchor, not as a universal guarantee of reliability. Human judgment may also be biased, uninformed, overconfident, constrained, or institutionally dependent. The presence of a person in a workflow does not by itself establish meaningful oversight.

Responsibility for the design, deployment, interpretation, authorization, and use of AI-supported outputs remains with the individuals and institutions exercising control over those activities.

The author and publisher accept no liability for loss, harm, damage, or consequence arising from the use, misuse, interpretation, or application of the ideas, examples, diagnostics, or frameworks contained in this book.

Readers remain responsible for verifying claims, consulting appropriate expertise, evaluating local conditions, and determining whether any concept presented here is suitable for a particular purpose.

The book should be read as an invitation to examine artificial certainty more carefully—not as a substitute for evidence, professional judgment, technical validation, or accountable governance.

Statement of Originality

Why AI Sounds Confident When It Is Wrong is an original conceptual work by **Sandeep Chavan.**

The book develops a structural interpretation of artificial confidence within the wider Chavanian research framework. While it engages with established research on language models, hallucination, calibration, decoding, retrieval, human feedback, automation, uncertainty, and governance, its central synthesis, terminology, and explanatory architecture are original to the author.

The book's principal original contribution is the distinction between the generation of unsupported content and the later appearance of epistemic certainty.

Where hallucination concerns what a system produces, artificial confidence concerns how the produced resolution becomes visible, interpreted, trusted, and operationalized.

The work proposes that artificial confidence can emerge without requiring human-like belief, pride, intention, arrogance, or reflective self-certainty inside the machine.

It identifies confidence as a distributed structural effect produced across several connected movements:

- computational plurality is compressed into one realized output;
- the interface presents that output as a singular visible consequence;
- the human user interprets coherent language through inherited expectations of speakers and knowledge;
- repeated usefulness creates a reservoir of trust;
- institutions assign operational authority to the output;
- the resolution enters the world as consequence.

This movement is defined in the book as the **confidence circuit**.

The formulation **"confidence is compression"** is used to describe the way computational, evidential, interpretive, and institutional plurality becomes hidden beneath one resolved surface.

The complementary formulation **"truth requires connection"** expresses the requirement that visible coherence remain linked to evidence, measurement, current sources, scope, applicability, independent comparison, consequence, and accountable revision.

The book also introduces and develops the distinction between:

Resolution confidence — the stability with which a system can generate and maintain one consequence within its active computational geometry;

and

Epistemic confidence — the strength of the relationship between that consequence and the relevant external reality.

This distinction explains how an answer may be internally stable, linguistically polished, and computationally preferred while remaining externally weak, misapplied, outdated, or unsupported.

Additional original concepts and formulations developed in this volume include:

- artificial confidence as a relational and institutional effect;
- the missing epistemic circuit;
- awareness anchoring;
- boundary opacity;
- interface singularity;
- borrowed authority;
- false anchors;
- authority drift;
- institutional confidence lock;
- confidence–support misalignment;
- source validity versus resolution validity;
- tool correctness versus task correctness;
- decorative caution;
- uncertainty export;
- consequence geometry;
- structural damping;
- partial or structural humility;
- the Confidence Circuit Diagnostic.

The book's application of the Chavanian Axioms to artificial intelligence is also original.

The axiomatic sequence—

difference, resolution, equilibrium rewrite, geometry, residue, irreversibility, and continuity—

is translated into the AI domain to explain how prompts become outputs, how outputs hide excluded structure, and how realized answers become context, trust, policy, and action.

This domain translation is interpretive and pre-formal. It does not claim ownership of established technical concepts such as transformers, softmax, autoregressive generation, calibration, RLHF, retrieval-augmented generation, selective classification, or automation bias.

These established concepts are attributed to the relevant research literature in the Notes and Selected Bibliography.

The originality of this work lies in how these mechanisms are connected within a unified structural account of confidence, authority, and consequence.

The book is also distinct from the author's earlier work, *Why Do AI Systems Hallucinate?*

The earlier volume examined why unsupported content may emerge when a generative system resolves incomplete, conflicting, falsely framed, or weakly grounded fields.

The present volume examines what happens after resolution:

- why the result appears stable;
- why excluded uncertainty disappears from the surface;
- why users attribute knowledge to coherent language;
- why tools and sources can lend borrowed authority;
- and why institutions may convert generated completion into consequential action.

The two works are connected but not repetitive.

One studies the formation of unsupported content. The other studies the authority acquired by resolved output.

The manuscript has been developed through original synthesis, analysis, interpretation, and writing by the author. External sources have been used to support technical descriptions, contextualize relevant research, and identify established findings. Such sources are acknowledged through citations, notes, and bibliography.

Any resemblance between the book's original structural terminology and independently developed concepts should be evaluated in light of their definitions, context, and specific use within the Chavanian framework.

The author does not claim exclusive ownership over general words such as *confidence*, *resolution*, *uncertainty*, *geometry*, *residue*, *continuity*, *authority*, or *alignment*. Originality is claimed for the specific conceptual relationships, definitions, diagnostic structures, and integrated framework developed in this work.

Artificial intelligence tools may have been used during the broader writing process for language assistance, organization, comparison, editing support, or structural testing. Such use does not transfer authorship, conceptual responsibility, or ownership of the argument to the tools.

The author selected, directed, evaluated, revised, and accepted the final intellectual structure and remains fully responsible for the claims presented.

This Statement of Originality does not assert that the framework is final, infallible, or beyond revision.

Originality is not immunity from criticism.

The Chavanian framework invites examination, comparison, formalization, empirical testing, and correction.

Its original contribution is the field it opens: not merely whether an AI answer is right or wrong, but how a resolved output comes to look like knowledge, how that appearance becomes authority, and how responsibility can remain connected to consequence.

Don't miss out!

Visit the website below and you can sign up to receive emails whenever Sandeep Chavan publishes a new book. There's no charge and no obligation.

https://books2read.com/r/B-A-EPGPC-FKLNJ

BOOKS 2 READ

Connecting independent readers to independent writers.

Did you love *Why AI Sounds Confident When It Is Wrong*? Then you should read *The Real Story of AI*[1] by Sandeep Chavan!

[2]

The Real Story of AI is not a technical manual. It's a ripple-mapped field guide for participators, creators, and consequence-aware thinkers navigating the illusion, hype, and distortion surrounding artificial intelligence.

Across nine chapters, Sandeep dissolves the spectacle of sentient machines and reframes intelligence as a relationship—not a performance. He exposes the binary traps, anthropomorphic projections, and marketing enchantments that have shaped public perception, and invites readers into a stance of conscious engagement, ripple-aligned creation, and field-sensitive resolution.

This book introduces original frameworks including Ripple Centrism and Unified Equilibrium Dynamics (UED), and offers a third cosmological path—one that dissolves mystification and returns

1. https://books2read.com/u/47jeg8

2. https://books2read.com/u/47jeg8

intelligence to the participator. Through poetic inquiry, philosophical clarity, and design ethics, Sandeep reclaims the human role not as controller, but as resolver of consequence.

Each chapter ends with a ripple-forward transition, guiding readers from passive consumption to participatory alignment. The final sections offer practices, prompts, and a glossary to support conscious use of AI across mediums, languages, and cultures.

Whether you're a designer, thinker, technologist, educator, or curious reader, *The Real Story of AI* invites you to step beyond the curtain—and ripple forward with care.

Read more at https://www.sandeepjchavan.com/.

www.ingramcontent.com/pod-product-compliance
Lightning Source LLC
LaVergne TN
LVHW100723061126
851857LV00011B/372